UPON THE FIELDS OF BATTLE

Conflicting Worlds

New Dimensions of the American Civil War

T. MICHAEL PARRISH, *Series Editor*

UPON THE FIELDS OF BATTLE

Essays on the Military History of America's Civil War

Edited by **ANDREW S. BLEDSOE**
and **ANDREW F. LANG**

Foreword by **GARY W. GALLAGHER**

Louisiana State University Press
Baton Rouge

Published by Louisiana State University Press
Copyright © 2018 by Louisiana State University Press
All rights reserved
Manufactured in the United States of America
FIRST PRINTING

DESIGNER: *Mandy McDonald Scallan*
TYPEFACE: *Whitman*
PRINTER AND BINDER: *Sheridan Books, Inc.*

Cataloging-in-Publication Data are available from the
Library of Congress.

ISBN 978-0-8071-6977-3 (cloth: alk. paper) — ISBN 978-
0-8071-7029-8 (pdf) — ISBN 978-0-8071-7030-4 (epub)

For
JOHN B. BOLES
and
IRA D. GRUBER

CONTENTS

III. THE SOLDIERS' WAR

FOREWORD

The Civil War was preeminently a military event. It played out on a vast strategic landscape, involved millions of men in uniform and many more millions of civilians behind the lines, shaped nonmilitary elements of society in the United States and the Confederacy, and created memory traditions that resonate after more than 150 years. No one better understood the centrality of arms than Abraham Lincoln. On March 4, 1865, he delivered his Second Inaugural Address to listeners who had gathered at the Capitol after drenching rains earlier in the day. Both the president and his audience understood that victory over the Confederacy almost certainly lay just ahead. Six hundred thousand Union soldiers had died or suffered wounds during the war, and Lincoln left no doubt about the role those men had played. "The progress of our arms, upon which all else chiefly depends," he remarked, "is as well known to the public as to myself, and it is, I trust, reasonably satisfactory and encouraging to all." The audience fully grasped that the president's "all else" included the conflict's two surpassing outcomes—restoration of the Union and emancipation.

Walt Whitman similarly described the reach of military events. He termed the war "that many-threaded drama with its sudden and strange surprises, its confounding of prophesies, its moments of despair, the dread of foreign interference, the interminable campaigns, the bloody battles, the mighty and cumbrous and green armies, the drafts and bounties . . . with, over the whole land the last three years of the struggle, an unending, universal mourning-wail of women, parents, orphans." Whitman's passage catalogs conventional military operations, expansion of governmental power to keep ranks filled, ties between the home and battle fronts, and scale of loss as parts of the sprawling whole that brought creation of a system of national cemeteries, establishment of Memorial Day (originally Decoration Day), and, eventually, massive outlays for veterans and their families.

The war highlighted continuities with previous and subsequent American history. For example, the concept of the citizen-soldier, imbedded in the nation's culture from the eighteenth century onward, lay at the heart of efforts to build great armies in the United States and the Confederacy. Union occupation of Southern cities and territory raised issues that had flared during Britain's military presence in the colonies after the Seven Years' War (1756–63), arose again during U.S. control of Monterrey and Mexico City during the Mexican-American War (1846–48), and would provoke bitter debate and violence during Reconstruction. Guerrilla activity on the margins reached levels of intensity and depravity reminiscent of action in the Revolution's southern theater in 1778–81 and, to a lesser degree, in parts of Mexico during Zachary Taylor's and Winfield Scott's operations. Conflicts with Indians in Minnesota, Arizona and New Mexico, and Colorado mirrored episodes extending from "feed fights" of the colonial era through the Second Seminole War (1835–42) to Wounded Knee (1890), and the Navajo's "Long Walk" recalled the "removal" of the "Five Civilized Tribes" from the Old Southwest to what is now Oklahoma. As in all American wars, federal military policy, failed campaigns, and escalating casualties fueled debates about the proper role of dissent in a free society. Perhaps most obviously, the Civil War produced commanders who took their place among earlier celebrated figures—on the winning side, Ulysses S. Grant, William Tecumseh Sherman, and Philip H. Sheridan joined George Washington and Nathanael Greene, Andrew Jackson and Jacob Brown, and Taylor and Scott. Somewhat incongruously, Robert E. Lee and Thomas J. "Stonewall" Jackson, whose labors might have scuttled the republic, eventually achieved iconic status throughout much of the restored nation.

Much of the continuing fascination with the Civil War stems from the ways in which it departed from earlier examples and patterns. The scale dwarfed all other American wars. A hackneyed yet still effective way to make this point is to compare casualties during the Gettysburg Campaign, which approached 60,000 Americans between mid-June and mid-July 1863, and the smaller number of battlefield losses during the Revolutionary War, the War of 1812, and the war with Mexico combined. In terms of direct effect on the largest percentage of the population, even the two world wars of the twentieth century far fall short. Military operations, as well as the intrusive presence of armies during winter encampments, wreaked havoc on economic infrastructure, agricultural patterns, and both the built and natural environments. Moreover, though British armies and naval forces temporarily disrupted slaveholding social structures during the Revolution and the War of 1812, Union military success ensured destruction of the entire institution of slavery. The voracious military demands of the Civil War also brought unprecedented expansion of federal authority, including national conscription and income taxes in both the United States and the Confederacy.

The essays in *Upon the Fields of Battle* underscore the importance and complexity of the Civil War's military history. They reflect a field that has undergone a sea change over the past twenty years, yielding a body of work that engages old questions and topics from new perspectives, opens fresh avenues of scholarly investigation, and, somewhat akin to Emerson's oversoul, seems capable of almost infinite expansion. The contributors, whose interests and specialties fall along a wide spectrum, collectively afford readers a sense of the war as Whitman's "many-threaded drama."

Gary W. Gallagher
Charlottesville, Virginia

ACKNOWLEDGMENTS

We conceived of this book late one night after a long day at the 2015 annual meeting of the Society for Military History. We are grateful to Earl Hess, Gary Gallagher, and Mike Parrish, who all endorsed the project from its earliest stages. Special thanks go to Mike and to Rand Dotson at LSU Press for shepherding the book through the various stages of publication. Kevin Brock, an expert and conscientious copy editor, transformed the manuscript into a first-rate piece. Essay collections are ultimately measured by the worth of their contributors, and we consider ourselves immensely fortunate to feature a superb lineup of historians. We thank each author individually for offering their research, communicating freely and openly, and serving as a wonderful colleague. Each contributor to this collection testifies to the enduring proficiency and collegiality of the historical profession. Finally, we thank our wives—Trish Bledsoe and Anne Lang—who supply ceaseless encouragement, penetrating editorial eyes, and thoughtful criticism. Our collective work is a tribute to their unflagging support.

This book is dedicated to John B. Boles and Ira D. Gruber, both of whom acted as our mentors at Rice University. We consider ourselves eternally grateful for their incisive instruction, careful critiques, reflective minds, and everlasting encouragement. This troubled world is a much better place with John's and Ira's profound influence. We hope that this collection demonstrates a small measure of our gratitude.

I

CONSIDERATIONS

MILITARY HISTORY AND THE AMERICAN CIVIL WAR

Andrew S. Bledsoe and Andrew F. Lang

S EVERAL WEEKS BEFORE he forced the capitulation of Atlanta, an event that would safeguard the reelection of Pres. Abraham Lincoln and pave the road for a grand march through Georgia and the Carolinas, Maj. Gen. William Tecumseh Sherman corresponded with an old friend from Kentucky about the conditions of the American Civil War. Remembering that the rule of law and the people's sacred will had long governed domestic affairs, Sherman remarked that "our hitherto political and private differences were settled by debate, or vote, or decree of a court." Yet the slaveholding South had "dared us to war" to resolve the irreconcilable entanglement between the champions of liberty and the guardians of slavery. "We are still willing to return to that system"—the democratic-republican arrangement that conceived an American Union that defied the world's tyrannical monarchies—"but our adversaries say no, and appeal to war." In a turn of phrase that perhaps only Sherman could have concocted, he proclaimed that "war is the remedy our enemies have chosen," adding, "I say let us give them all they want; not a word of argument, not a sign of let up, no cave in till we are whipped or they are." The impossible American dispute would be settled by soldiers in the ranks who marched upon the fields of battle, and peace would dawn only "when one or the other party gives in, [and] we will be the better friends."[1]

Sherman, like myriad Americans of his time, clearly understood the importance of military affairs in charting the course of history. Nothing less than the future of the republic depended upon the success or failure of armed conflict. When he declared that "war is the remedy," Sherman voiced a consensual faith that free societies acquiesced to military solutions when politics miscarried and peaceful alternatives failed to reconcile incompatible differences. Contrary to postwar mythmaking, Sherman did not conceive of war in unlimited

3

terms, nor did he see it as a senseless, interminable exercise that wrought needless destruction on society. War was not an arbitrary vacuum that consumed its participants in unrestrained violence, yielding worthless results and pointless armistices. Nineteenth-century Americans instead gave profound meaning to their civil war, ascribing cultural and societal values to the purposes of armed conflict, its particular conduct, its notable limitations, and its remarkable devastation. They agreed that formal armies, clashing on the field of battle and contesting the national will, dictated the desired outcomes of war. They accordingly saw war as a terrible but necessary harbinger of peace, no matter how tenuous or unsatisfactory—especially to modern observers. It was indeed the remedy for a discordant people who looked to their military institutions to settle political disputes upon the fields of battle, to bring societal change on the home front, and to resolve forever the meaning of Union.[2]

Americans of that era likely would not be surprised at the dramatic outpouring of scholarship produced on the Civil War ever since the guns fell silent in 1865. The field appears stronger than ever, emboldened by an annual publication of books and essays that address previously neglected aspects of the conflict, employ innovative methodologies and frameworks, and reveal new answers to old questions. Recent literature has successfully collapsed artificial barriers between home front and battlefield, explained the complicated processes of emancipation, questioned the meaning of freedom in a white republic, cataloged the multifaceted civilian experience, humanized the soldiers in the ranks, and navigated the tortured avenues of historical memory.[3]

Yet the profession is seemingly embroiled in an internecine conflict in which the fate, future, and definition of Civil War history are at stake. This debate hinges on a simple yet challenging question: are academic historians losing the conflict's military narrative that Sherman found so central to societal evolution? A pair of state-of-the-field essays published in 2014 seem to think so. "Academic historians who study the Civil War have in recent decades retreated further and further from investigating what the generation that experienced the conflict would have considered mainline military topics," Gary W. Gallagher and Kathryn Shively Meier write in their piece published in the *Journal of the Civil War Era*. This volume attempts to rectify the disparities between military and other histories of the Civil War, bringing a necessary balance to the field. Much of this imbalance, we believe, stems from honest, though fundamental, misapprehensions about what military histories of the

Civil War are, what they are not, and the potential that practitioners of Civil War military histories seek to realize. Critics of "traditional" or "conventional" military history are often caught up in a dismissive paradox, viewing studies of tactics, strategy, biography, campaigns, logistics, and technology as "too geared toward a popular audience and yet too technical and complex." We believe that this misperception has led to needless lacunae in Civil War studies that risk tribalizing historians, whose work otherwise suggests a collective enrichment of the field. Our view is that the "military history" of the Civil War should grow—and has grown—beyond its more traditional and old-fashioned boundaries to encompass the martial, cultural, social, political, and applied dimensions of military service and institutions. After all, the Civil War generation thought precisely in these collective terms—and so should we.[4]

Campaigns, battles, and biography formed the backbone of traditional Civil War military history, even appearing before the conclusion of the conflict itself. The intervening decades have seen a glut of such "drum-and-trumpet" histories and chronological narratives, often bounded by the battlefield and tightly focused on commanders, strategies, and tactics. In the mid-twentieth century, Bell I. Wiley brought the experiences of the "common soldier" of the Civil War into the public consciousness, inspiring social historians to take a fresh look at the armies from the bottom up. Perhaps even more influential to the generations of Civil War historians who followed Wiley, John Keegan's sensitive examination of the "face of battle" inspired them to dig deep into and employ traditional methodologies of military history, informing new ways of thinking about the experience of war.[5]

Important methodological changes brought to the historical profession occasioned the rise of the "new" military history—though that now-dated term has itself fallen somewhat out of favor—linking the armed forces and the field of battle, both defined broadly, to wider societal conditions and cultural values. In truth, there is now very little that is "new" about the new military history of the Civil War. In a 1991 article, Joseph T. Glatthaar observed the trend toward a new approach to the military history of the war, describing it as an effort "to link military history, whether in wartime or peacetime, to broader themes in society. Thus, studies of the new military history relate directly to larger historical issues and trends, and this has enabled military historians to gain a legitimacy in the historical profession and also to attract the interest of scholars who would never consider themselves military historians."[6]

While many recent historians may not explicitly claim the mantle of "military history" as their own, pioneering works during the previous two decades nevertheless operate within a vibrant and diverse sphere of military study. These profound endeavors have necessarily complicated the new military history's emphasis on culture and society. Scholars have explored soldiers' motivations and lived experiences, the multiplicity of reasons for and implications of victory and defeat, the role of armies in the processes of emancipation and Reconstruction, an increasing understanding of the importance of ethnicity and gender, and the essential role of women and people of color in the course and conduct of the war. The military aspects of the Civil War era continue to be scrutinized through considerations of class concerns, religious and intellectual history, and the complex interplay and blurring of boundaries between home front and battlefield. Authors still push the envelope of traditional military history by evaluating the makeup and movement of armies and navies, leadership, command, contingency, tactics and technology, asymmetrical and irregular warfare, counterinsurgency, logistics, desertion and disloyalty, the process of professionalization, and the seemingly confusing transition from war to peace, mobilization to demobilization. Historians also link the military aspect of the war to its contested memory and meaning, to participants' sensibility and ways of knowing, to material culture, and to the relationships between armies and the natural environment. Explorations of Civil War trauma and stress, the "dark turn," and the rejection of triumphalist, reconciliatory, heroic, and tragic narratives all provide more subtle understandings of the war's violence and destruction as well as its larger meanings and lasting influence.[7]

This stunning litany alone demonstrates the energetic variety of Civil War military histories. We thus encourage our colleagues to don the uniform of a military historian, recognizing that their work fits neatly within an expanding field not subject to marginalization, but one that diversifies intellectual strategies and tactics. The structure of this collection thus reflects the evolution of professional Civil War military historiography, pushing the boundaries of the current state of the field through innovative methodologies and fresh questions. Understanding where war took place, who waged that war, the reasons for which societies practiced and explained war, and the implications of war itself underscore the explanatory power of military history in general and this volume in particular.

To that end, this volume underscores several interpretative themes, establishing that military history is no longer engaged solely as a limited approach to a bygone era, one defined only by the movement of armies, the analysis of tactics, and the debate about strategies. Nor is it marginalized by the "war and society" school, which aims to broaden the limited parameters of traditional military history's apparent shortcomings. Instead, we submit that traditional military history and war-and-society studies should not function as disparate, irreconcilable schools unto themselves but ought to be united in a common purpose. Traditional military history now relies on the methods of war-and-society studies just as much as the latter rely on the methods of the former. This is one of the most notable attributes about our field's maturity. We thus encourage that the military narratives of the Civil War avoid the unnecessary competition between the narrow drum-and-trumpet histories and the more theoretical war-and-society approaches that sometimes minimize or circumvent military considerations. The field has seasoned well enough to integrate both methodologies, yielding a richer understanding of an immensely complicated past.[8]

And yet each essayist in this volume is guided by an unbending premise that informs their historical awareness, one not to be discarded or ignored by future scholars seeking to probe the era's broad military dimensions. We must remember, as our authors implicitly establish, the guiding principle of military history, which "investigates warfare and the relationship between military institutions and the societies from which they sprang." Indeed, "a foundational assumption underlying military history is that the scholar brings to bear knowledge of the makeup and history of the armed forces and works from the military out." The study of war should not be embroiled in a stubborn contest between traditionalists and culturalists. Societal values and cultural assumptions give meaning to war; establish when, how, and by what means conflicts are fought; inform tactical and strategic decisions; influence the ethos, composition, and purpose of military institutions; and explain the transitions from war to peace to memorialization. Military history comprises diverse interpretative elements. Thus it should always link the practitioners of war to their cultural and societal contexts, each of which informs martial behavior, the disposition of military institutions, and the means and motivation for waging armed conflict. Only then can we appreciate the guiding rationales undergirding humankind's most destructive tendencies.[9]

A cultural analysis of military history, however, as our contributors recognize, must never overlook the power of contingency. While historical actors all pattern their martial behavior, create military institutions, and practice war within limited cultural realms, armed conflict is inherently unpredictable, shaped indelibly by what Carl von Clausewitz called "the fog of war." Military history reminds us that contingency is a potent concept that should inform our thinking and serve as a corrective to myopic presentism, teleological determinism, or the conceit of perfect retrospection. Battles and campaigns, perhaps more than any other historical arena, illustrate the power of contingency to shape human events. Historians must resist the temptation to see the Civil War's outcome as predetermined or else risk falling into a trap of elevating Union victory to an a priori assumption. The pernicious ideology of the Lost Cause of the Confederacy is predicated upon just such a willful disregard of historical contingency. Certainly at the war's outset the United States possessed material and manpower advantages over the slaveholding republic and continued to do so throughout the conflict, imparting certain important benefits to the Union war effort. Causation in history is immensely complex, and identifying the chain of events that dictate historical outcomes is often an exercise in subjectivity. But to surrender to the notion that the principal outcomes of the war—preservation of the Union and emancipation—were foreordained ignores the fact that the ultimate issue of victory or defeat hung in the balance and could only be adjudicated, even if imperfectly, by battlefield outcomes. A failure to account for contingency also dismisses the interconnectedness and unpredictability of actions. We see military history, particularly an acceptance and understanding of historical contingency intrinsic to war, as an antidote to the kind of thinking that fueled the Lost Cause for a century and a half or more and that continues to cloud modern understandings of the Civil War and its consequences.[10]

Finally, we believe that a thoughtful assessment of command and control must lie at the heart of an analysis of war. The fine-grained sensibility of the historian is particularly well suited to frame analyses of leadership, culture, shared experience, and the personal relationships of the actors. Since Russell Weigley's influential 1973 effort to define the American approach to war, scholars of the Civil War have attempted to pinpoint what, if anything, distinguishes that conflict from others. Weigley argues for an American adherence to a strategy of attrition, then an evolution to annihilation. As the United

States grew in size and power, military minds pursued the destruction of enemies rather than simple attrition.[11] This volume interrogates the controversial
assumption of a distinctly American way of war. If history is a human story,
then the military history of the Civil War must be understood as a narrative of
connection, interaction, and agency among people.

Some locate the Civil War within the continuum of total warfare, citing the
employment of modern weaponry, massive mobilization, strategies of attrition, blurred lines of violence, and a lack of restraint as evidence of a new kind
of fighting, a prophecy of the carnage of future conflicts. Wayne Wei-siang
Hsieh necessarily challenges this perspective, which he argues portrays the
Civil War as "a crucial way station in a new era of industrial violence that in-
exorably leads to Hiroshima, the Holocaust, and a doomed present," an interpretation that has "seriously distorted" the historiography of the war.[12] Recent
efforts to refine Weigley's thesis cast doubt on both the Civil War's exceptional
nature and excessive destructiveness, urging historians to place the conflict
within its proper transnational context. Military historians question the concept of annihilation as an American strategy, pointing to the improvisation,
peace-building efforts, counterinsurgency operations, and pursuit of coalitions
in the nation's war-making history. Indeed, aversions to casualties, attributes
of professionalism, emphases on aggressiveness, and confidence in technolog-
ical superiority underscore the most salient characteristics of American wars,
including the Civil War.[13] Definitions of how U.S. conflicts are decided remain
elusive, but historians should continue to evaluate—as the contributors in this
volume demonstrate—the connections between Civil War military operations
and important social transformations, including emancipation, national policy, democracy, the home front, nationalism, gender and cultural changes, and
other topics.

The bulk of this volume showcases new ways to think about the essential
binary of any armed conflict—the fields of battle and the soldiers in the ranks.
Part II challenges a conception of battlefields in which faceless armies sought
limited ends by way of limited means in distant arenas of combat. As the
essays here demonstrate, battlefields included soldiers and civilians; hosted
powerful armies unlike any before seen on the North American continent;
complicated the uses and abuses of language; and were shaped irrevocably by
natural forces that stunted humankind's feeble control. Expanding the traditional conceptions of the battlefield, Kenneth W. Noe, Jennifer M. Murray,

Andrew S. Bledsoe, John J. Hennessy, and Brian D. McKnight encourage historians to reconceptualize the interpretive limits of the locales of battle because contemporaries themselves viewed the domains of war in broad terms. Shaped by human decision and subject to human indecision, battlefields—as idyllic landscapes, surreptitious neighborhoods, populous cities, and even sites of extraordinary political disputes that linked the armies to their societies and governments—gave profound meaning to the imagined *place* of war.

In particular, Noe, Murray, and Bledsoe offer fresh ways to interpret military campaigns. Each of these authors takes seriously the proposition that army commanders were influenced intimately by both internal and external stimuli, which affected battles and campaigns as much as the generals' abilities, temperaments, and personalities. Noe's essay employs the methodologies of environmental history, meteorological science, and soil appraisals to evaluate George B. McClellan's performance during his ill-fated Peninsula Campaign, focusing on how weather patterns played a crucial role in directing and employing massive armies. Revising McClellan's traditionally stained tactical and strategic reputations, Noe explains that an El Niño weather pattern affecting the Virginia Peninsula during the spring of 1862 influenced military planning and deployments in unimaginable ways. He reveals the power of environmental forces in shaping, directing, and altering McClellan's allegedly timid will. Unseasonably heavy rains contributed to the Army of the Potomac's halting movements up the Peninsula and reinforced the Union commander's seemingly indecisive strategies. Sieges could not be conducted adequately in rivers of mud, new roads had to be built and rebuilt, and soldiers were transformed into sopping-wet laborers whose efforts sometimes proved absolutely futile. Noe's essay is a sobering reminder that wars are conducted outdoors, where military practitioners, no matter how brilliant or questionable their strategic visions may be, are subject to powerful natural forces beyond man's simple design.[14]

Reevaluating another famed Union general—George Gordon Meade—Murray's essay acknowledges how professionalization and politics fragmented the Army of the Potomac's command structure, influencing how Meade approached and directed his councils of war in the tortuous wake of the decisive Union victory at Gettysburg in July 1863. Challenging conventional wisdom, largely established by President Lincoln, who castigated Meade for not hastily pursuing Robert E. Lee's Army of Northern Virginia, Murray argues that decisive battlefield victories during the Civil War rarely culminated in the permanent destruction of enemy armies. She necessarily demonstrates how a postbattle pursuit was among the most difficult military operations undertaken by any commander during the war, especially given the limitations of mid-nineteenth-century military culture and the contested definitions of "victory." Carefully reappraising how we think about the relationships between the home front and battlefield—Unionists and Confederates both looked to their armies' successes and failures as barometers of the respective national causes—Murray suggests the importance of balancing civilian and political expectations of military campaigns alongside the actual purposes and boundaries of the campaigns themselves.

Bledsoe evaluates the complicated intersection of human fallibility with the inexactitudes of battlefield-orders language in Civil War command relationships, using examples from the Chickamauga Campaign to illustrate the power of wartime historical contingency. Much like the unpredictable influence of weather or the unanticipated limitations of mobility following a massive battle, the control and deployment of language shaped campaigns. Reading battle orders as a confirmation of human imperfection, especially when governed by the interminable stresses of combat, Bledsoe explains that battles advanced according to the flawed ways in which orders were written and received. He uses Braxton Bragg's performance at McLemore's Cove, Georgia, the site of disastrous Confederate operations at the beginning of the Chickamauga Campaign, to contextualize traditional explanations for the Army of Tennessee's performance. Although influenced by a toxic officer corps and Bragg's exhausting maladroitness, the power of words, orders, and language shaped, in mere moments, the entire course of that campaign (as with others). Lessons can and should be drawn from Civil War battles, but Bledsoe reminds us that, far from inevitable or uniform, those campaigns were shaped by the precision—or imprecision—of the men who penned the orders.

Departing from the macro level, Hennessy explores how the bombardment of Fredericksburg, Virginia, reshaped the formality of war—at least to that point in 1862—into one that engaged civilians and focused on the destruction of property, both of which affected military campaign policy. Drawing on the rich literature of civilian-military relations, he explores the meaning of enemy combatants, a problematic identification that frustrated formal armies waging an increasingly expansive war. Citing the implications of practicing war within urban centers, Hennessy raises important questions about the Civil War's deteriorating but persistent restraint coupled with simultaneous and ironic efforts to limit the destruction wrought on civilians and property.[15]

In moving beyond traditional narratives of guerrilla warfare, McKnight also challenges historians to rethink existing conceptions of battlefields and combatants. For him, guerrilla warfare was not designed exclusively to occasion or shape particular military ends. Instead, irregular conflicts often sought social change as a violent byproduct of war. Largely due to the influence of presentism, McKnight suggests that we often see regime change or nation building as processes that are presumably sanctioned by the will of a democratic people. Yet on a much more intimate and devastating level, the guerrilla warfare that bedeviled the Appalachian borderlands evolved into a sort of social compact between adversaries who invited and resisted irregular warfare to stabilize and regulate communities. Opponents wielded the imagined threat and tangible force of guerrillas to maintain a level of internal security that had been shattered by the chaos of civil war. McKnight's essay underscores the importance of thinking not only about how large fields of battle determined the fate of nations but also how the blurred lines of irregular conflict indelibly shaped small communities attempting to survive a seemingly endless conflagration.[16]

Part III considers the common soldiers of the Civil War. Building from the model undertaken so well by previous historians, essays by Andrew F. Lang, Kevin M. Levin, Keith Altavilla, Brian Matthew Jordan, and Robert L. Glaze place Billy Yank and Johnny Reb within the broader societies and cultures from which they came. In particular, each highlights the unanticipated challenges of serving in democratic armies that privileged the political power of common soldiers while also exposing the troubling limits to those democratic prerogatives. The authors also investigate the powerful human dimensions of war, linking the horror and transformative consequences of the battlefield to their lingering influences at home, their commanding presence in national politics, their sometimes irreconcilable effects on an uncertain future, and their celebratory influences in popular memory. Soldiers not only fought the Civil War but also, as free citizens, *explained* the war, *rationalized* the war, and *lived* the war long after permanently stacking their muskets.

Lang's essay treats the contentious topic of "American exceptionalism" as a historical concept, arguing that common Union soldiers took seriously the idea of the United States as the "last best hope" to a world consumed by tyranny, oligarchy, and aristocracy. Yet the experiences of wartime military occupation, in which Union soldiers regulated Confederates and implemented the processes of emancipation, unmasked seemingly dangerous threats to American "civilization." Underscoring the power of military contingency in occasioning social transformation—in this case Union armies subduing white resistance and shaping emancipation—Lang shows how Union soldiers expressed deep concern about the rapid societal changes occurring at the point of a bayonet. These soldiers asked whether a preserved United States, which would occur only through military victory, could incorporate white and black southerners whom the troops considered unfit for the progress of American modernity.[17]

Shifting focus to the Confederate perspective, Levin suggests that soldiers in the Army of Northern Virginia became resigned to the violence of military executions, believing in the necessity of martial order in the quest for national independence. He poignantly underscores how Civil War soldiers thought of themselves first as citizens who fiercely guarded their rights as individuals. And yet adherence to decorum, uniformity, and discipline mandated consent from young volunteers who, in their civilian lives, normally shunned such militaristic doctrines. Executions thus functioned as vivid and blunt examples of regulating men's otherwise fierce independence. Locating soldiers' reactions to executions at the intersection of abject horror and justified necessity, Levin's evaluation underscores the stunning commitment made by white southern men in Lee's famed army to establish a slaveholding republic. Despite martial violence and the flouting of social norms, a functioning military culture, Levin explains, was crucial to realize the southern national destiny.[18]

The twin themes of American exceptionalism and national fortune frame Altavilla's inspection of Union soldiers who, in the presidential election of 1864, supported George B. McClellan's Democratic candidacy. His analysis reveals the ways in which some troops translated into political action their conceptions about the conduct and purpose of the Union war effort when supporting McClellan's presidential bid against Lincoln. The election, both unprecedented in the context of civil war and consistent in its various political appeals, featured the Democratic Party assailing what it declared a failed war waged by the Republicans. The inability to extinguish the rebellion, the unconscionable stripping of constitutional rights, and the revolutionary implications of emancipation all transformed what was supposed to be a limited conflict for Union into the fanatical design of radical Republicans. Altavilla uncovers the unique dimensions of an army of democracy at war, engaging the perspective of the 20 percent of Union soldiers who voted for McClellan. Using a wartime presidential election as a useful platform, Altavilla springboards into the broader political issues raised by the Civil War itself: the question of loyalty, the price of Union, and the consequences of biracial freedom.[19]

Taken together, Lang's, Levin's, and Altavilla's essays move away from traditional questions of why soldiers fought to focus instead on how volunteers' citizenship and their place in the broader body politic manifested functioning cultures in Union and Confederate armies, influencing an unwavering, if not always consistent, commitment to the respective national cause. Although also approaching the common soldier's war, Jordan departs from these interpretive strains and engages the controversial framework known as the "dark side" of Civil War studies. Endorsing the revealing power of regimental histories and, on a broader level, the explanatory depth of microhistory, Jordan explores the intimate confines of one regiment, the 107th Ohio Volunteers, and their bloody endeavors on the first day at Gettysburg. Rather than extrapolating from the Civil War's horrendously massive casualty figures, he looks at the heartrending ways in which individual casualties tied soldiers to their home fronts, later shaping a somber peace for the living. Summoned by the more than 50 percent casualties endured by the 107th Ohio at Gettysburg, Jordan sees—through regimental histories, pension applications, and monument dedications—the terrible, shocking, and unimaginable human cost of war on its most personal level. While recognizing the interpretive limits of individual experiences, and thus hesitant to draw broad conclusions about the varied ways that soldiers transitioned into postwar veterans, Jordan's analysis nonetheless contributes to a provocative conversation on the place of tragedy in our narratives.[20]

The final essay in this collection, Glaze's treatment of white southern memory of Albert Sidney Johnston, challenges the presumed Virginia-centered focus of previous scholarship on Confederate recollections of the war. Arguing that Confederate memory, much like the Confederate experience itself, was conditioned by regional variations, Glaze suggests that the military contingencies of the western theater, and indeed the wartime fate of that region in general, played a crucial role in constructing postwar memory.

Emphasizing that command of the war's military history is vital in framing any interpretation of postwar memory, Glaze proposes that a full understanding of Johnston's historical memory goes a long way in coming to terms with the colorful ways that white southerners constructed the Lost Cause. Integrating a cultural analysis (Johnston's masculine and courageous image) with military scrutiny (the ways that Johnston commanded at Shiloh), Glaze uncovers the ease with which former Confederates assimilated the general within their pantheon of heroes. The "what-might-have-been" conditions of Shiloh itself and Johnston's untimely death helped construct his postbellum mystique. Confederate memory thus equated Johnston with all of the virtues that had died with the slaveholding republic and that the postwar years attempted to rebuild: nobility, courage, masculinity, and selflessness.[21]

Earl Hess, in the essay to follow, sets the volume's tone by recommending ways to re-situate the field toward a more diverse, yet traditional, military history. He encourages scholars to consider military history both in its insular practice and in its collective reach to the broader profession. Addressing the field from a macro perspective, Hess suggests numerous paths to approach military topics in fresh temporal, international, and professional ways, some of which are reflected in the essays herein. Reviving his call to reintegrate traditional military history in its rightful professional place, Hess carefully explains that writing such studies for their own sake possesses some promise for a field in need of redefinition. His own widely respected works on the rifled musket, field fortifications, and infantry tactics offer ideal ways by which to blaze new trails. Encouraging connections between military ideas and practices and their broader social and cultural contexts, as well as plotting future research agendas, Hess gives historians a valuable road map with which to consider the many unforeseen directions of a new Civil War military history.[22]

This collection operates with one foot firmly planted in older, more traditional methodologies and lines of thinking, while also accounting for and expanding new kinds of knowledge within the larger field of Civil War military history. We do not strive to dismantle the fine, crucial body of work that traditional military historians and "war and society" scholars have assembled. To ensure that Civil War history reaches its diverse potential, distinguished by the period's sundry conditions and experiences, we believe that future studies must achieve a balanced understanding of the military aspects of the conflict. Moreover, we do not intend for this to be the final word on the subject. Instead, the following essays offer insight into the various ways historians might approach future military history topics. By offering fresh areas of inquiry and demonstrating the field's potential to provide us with valuable insights, this collection seeks to realign military studies on the American Civil War with other scholarly avenues of inquiry.

NOTES

1. William Tecumseh Sherman to James Guthrie, Aug. 14, 1864, in U.S. War Department, *The War of the Rebellion: A Compilation of the Official Records of the Union and Confederate Armies,* 70 vols. in 128 pts. (Washington: GPO, 1880–1901), ser. 1, 39(2):247–49 (quotes, 248).

2. On these themes, see Charles Royster, *The Destructive War: William Tecumseh Sherman, Stonewall Jackson, and the Americans* (New York: Knopf, 1991); Gary W. Gallagher, *The Confederate War* (Cambridge, MA: Harvard University Press, 1997); Mark E. Neely Jr., *The Civil War and the Limits of Destruction* (Cambridge: Harvard University Press, 2006); Wayne Wei-siang Hsieh, *West Pointers and the Civil War: The Old Army in War and Peace* (Chapel Hill: University of North Carolina Press, 2009); Gary W. Gallagher, *The Union War* (Cambridge, MA: Harvard University Press, 2011); Wayne E. Lee, *Barbarians and Brothers: Anglo-American Warfare, 1500–1865* (New York: Oxford University Press, 2011), 1–11, 232–45; D. H. Dilbeck, *A More Civil War: How the Union Waged a Just War* (Chapel Hill: University of North Carolina Press, 2016).

3. For a comprehensive historiographical treatment on the current state of Civil War historiography, see the many essays in Aaron Sheehan-Dean, ed., *A Companion to the U.S. Civil War,* 2 vols. (Malden, MA: John Wiley and Sons, 2014).

4. Gary W. Gallagher and Kathryn Shively Meier, "Coming to Terms with Civil War Military History," *Journal of the Civil War Era* 4 (Dec. 2014): 487–508 (quotes, 490, 487); Earl J. Hess, "Where Do We Stand? A Critical Assessment of Civil War Studies in the Sesquicentennial Era," *Civil War History* 60 (Dec. 2014): 371–403. These diverse approaches are explored and advocated in John Shy, "The Cultural Approach to the History of War," *Journal of Military History* 57 (Oct. 1993): 13–26; John A. Lynn, "The Embattled Future of Academic Military History," *Journal of Military History* 61 (Oct. 1997): 777–89; Wayne E. Lee, "Mind and Matter—Cultural Analysis in American Military History," *Journal of American History* 93 (Mar. 2007): 1116–42; and Robert M. Citino, "Military Histories Old and New: A Reintroduction," *American Historical Review* 112 (Oct. 2007): 1070–90.

5. Bell I. Wiley, *The Life of Johnny Reb: The Common Soldier of the Confederacy* (Indianapolis: Bobbs-Merrill, 1943); *The Life of Billy Yank: The Common Soldier of the Union* (Baton Rouge: Louisiana State University Press, 1952); John Keegan, *The Face of Battle: The Face of Battle: A Study of Agincourt, Waterloo, and The Somme* (New York: Viking, 1976).

6. Joseph T. Glatthaar, "The 'New' Civil War History: An Overview," *Pennsylvania Magazine of History & Biography* 116 (July 1991): 340.

7. This rich literature is too vast to recount here. For a comprehensive historiographical treatment, see the essays in Sheehan-Dean, *Companion to the U.S. Civil War.*

8. See Maris A. Vinovskis, "Have Social Historians Lost the Civil War? Some Preliminary Demographic Speculations," *Journal of American History* 76 (June 1989): 34–58. Vinovskis's field-changing essay encourages scholars to seek out the *effects* of war upon society, rather than focusing narrowly on traditional military history.

9. Gallagher and Meier, "Coming to Terms with Civil War Military History," 490–91. Our understanding of cultural military history derive from Lee, "Mind and Matter," 1116–42; Shy, "Cultural Approach to the History of War," 13–26; Lynn, "Embattled Future of Academic Military History," 777–89; and Citino, "Military Histories Old and New," 1070–90.

10. Military contingency forms the backbone of James M. McPherson, *Battle Cry of Freedom: The Civil War Era* (New York: Oxford University Press, 1988), 857–58; and Gallagher, *Union War*, 88–92. For views that complicate contingency, preferring instead "deep contingency," see Jason Phillips, *Diehard Rebels: The Confederate Culture of Invincibility* (Athens: University of Georgia Press, 2007), 126–27, 145–46; and Edward L. Ayers, *What Caused the Civil War? Reflections on the South and Southern History* (New York: W. W. Norton, 2005), 134–35, 141–43.

11. Russell F. Weigley, *The American Way of War: A History of United States Military Strategy and Policy* (Bloomington: Indiana University Press, 1977), xxii.

12. Wayne Wei-siang Hsieh, "Total War and the American Civil War Reconsidered: The End of an Outdated 'Master Narrative,'" *Journal of the Civil War Era* 1, no. 3 (Sept. 2011): 394–95.

13. Brian M. Linn, *The Echo of Battle: The Army's Way of War* (Cambridge, MA: Harvard University Press, 2007), 3; Colin S. Gray, "Irregular Enemies and the Essence of Strategy: Can the American Way of War Adapt?" (Carlisle, PA: Strategic Studies Institute, U.S. Army War College, 2006), 30; Antulio J. Echevarria II, "An American Way of War or Way of Battle?" (Carlisle, PA: Strategic Studies Institute, U.S. Army War College, 2004).

14. Noe's essay contributes to a growing body of literature that engages the relationship between the environment and military events. See, for example, Lisa M. Brady, *War upon the Land: Military Strategy and the Transformation of Southern Landscapes during the American Civil War* (Athens: University of Georgia Press, 2012); Megan Kate Nelson, *Ruin Nation: Destruction and the American Civil War* (Athens: University of Georgia Press, 2012); Kathryn Shively Meier, *Nature's Civil War: Common Soldiers and the Environment in 1862 Virginia* (Chapel Hill: University of North Carolina Press, 2013); and Matthew M. Stith, *Extreme Civil War: Guerrilla Warfare, Environment, and Race on the Trans-Mississippi Frontier* (Baton Rouge: Louisiana State University Press, 2016). For conventional accounts of McClellan's campaign performances, see Stephen W. Sears, *To the Gates of Richmond: The Peninsula Campaign* (New York: Ticknor and Fields, 1992), 18–20, 22–23, 28–35, 67–68, 90–98, 103–6, 111–13, 351–54; and Mark Grimsley, *The Hard Hand of War: Union Military Policy toward Southern Civilians, 1861–1865* (New York: Cambridge University Press, 1995), 67–74.

15. For an excellent treatment of military history that integrates social, political, and cultural contexts, see George C. Rable, *Fredericksburg! Fredericksburg!* (Chapel Hill: University of North Carolina Press, 2002). The policy, social, cultural, and military implications of civilian-military

relations are best explored in Stephen V. Ash, *When the Yankees Came: Conflict and Chaos in the Occupied South, 1861–1865* (Chapel Hill: University of North Carolina Press, 1995); Grimsley, *Hard Hand of War;* and William A. Blair, *With Malice toward Some: Treason and Loyalty in the Civil War Era* (Chapel Hill: University of North Carolina Press, 2014). See also Judkin Browning, *Shifting Loyalties: The Union Occupation of Eastern North Carolina* (Chapel Hill: University of North Carolina Press, 2011); Joseph W. Danielson, *War's Desolating Scourge: The Union's Occupation of North Alabama* (Lawrence: University Press of Kansas, 2012); Timothy W. Smith, *Corinth 1862: Siege, Battle, Occupation* (Lawrence: University Press of Kansas, 2012); Chester G. Hearn, *When the Devil Came Down to Dixie: Ben Butler in New Orleans* (Baton Rouge: Louisiana State University Press, 1997); Michael D. Pierson, *Mutiny at Fort Jackson: The Untold Story of the Fall of New Orleans* (Chapel Hill: University of North Carolina Press, 2008); Jacqueline Campbell, *When Sherman Marched North from the Sea: Resistance on the Confederate Home Front* (Chapel Hill: University of North Carolina Press, 2003); Lisa Tendrich Frank, *The Civilian War: Confederate Women and Union Soldiers during Sherman's March* (Baton Rouge: Louisiana State University Press, 2015); Gregory P. Downs, *After Appomattox: Military Occupation and the Ends of War* (Cambridge, MA: Harvard University Press, 2015); and Andrew F. Lang, *In the Wake of War: Military Occupation, Emancipation, and Civil War America* (Baton Rouge: Louisiana State University Press, 2017).

16. Two comprehensive treatments of guerrilla warfare during the Civil War are Daniel E. Sutherland, *A Savage Conflict: The Decisive Role of Guerrillas in the American Civil War* (Chapel Hill: University of North Carolina Press, 2009); and Brian D. McKnight and Barton A. Myers, eds., *The Guerrilla Hunters: Irregular Conflicts during the Civil War* (Baton Rouge: Louisiana State University Press, 2017).

17. A vast literature exists on the common soldier of the Civil War. For a comprehensive historiographical evaluation, see Lorien Foote, "Soldiers," in Sheehan-Dean, *Companion to the U.S. Civil War,* 1:114–31. On the centrality of American exceptionalism to the loyal citizenry of the Union, see Gallagher, *Union War.* For an interpretation of Civil War soldiers as representative of the nineteenth-century democratic tradition, see Andrew S. Bledsoe, *Citizen-Officers: The Union and Confederate Volunteer Junior Officer Corps in the American Civil War* (Baton Rouge: Louisiana State University Press, 2015).

18. The most recent and comprehensive account of the Army of Northern Virginia is Joseph T. Glatthaar, *General Lee's Army: From Victory to Collapse* (New York: Free Press, 2008).

19. The political sensibilities of Civil War soldiers are addressed in Joseph Allan Frank, *With Ballot and Bayonet: The Political Socialization of American Civil War Soldiers* (Athens: University of Georgia Press, 1998).

20. For examples of microhistory serving as broadly interpretive military history, see Barton A. Myers, *Executing Daniel Bright: Race, Loyalty, and Guerrilla Violence in a Coastal Carolina Community, 1861–1865* (Baton Rouge: Louisiana State University Press, 2009); and Lesley J. Gordon, *A Broken Regiment: The 16th Connecticut's Civil War* (Baton Rouge: Louisiana State University Press, 2014). For a historiographical evaluation of the "dark turn" literature, see Yael A. Sternhell, "The Antiwar Turn in Civil War Scholarship," *Journal of the Civil War Era* 3 (June 2013): 239–56. For a rejoinder against the theme of "tragedy," see Gallagher and Meier, "Coming to Terms with Civil War Military History," 491–92; and Peter S. Carmichael, "Relevance, Resonance, and His-

toriography: Interpreting the Lives and Experiences of Civil War Soldiers," *Civil War History* 62 (June 2016): 182–84.

21. On the vast literature of Civil War memory, see Caroline E. Janney, "Memory," in Sheehan-Dean, *Companion to the U.S. Civil War*, 2:1139–54.

22. A sampling of Hess's work includes *The Union Soldier in Battle: Enduring the Ordeal of Combat* (Lawrence: University Press of Kansas, 1997); *Banners to the Breeze: The Kentucky Campaign, Corinth, and Stones River* (Lincoln: University of Nebraska Press, 2000); *Pickett's Charge: The Last Attack at Gettysburg* (Chapel Hill: University of North Carolina Press, 2001); *Lee's Tar Heels: The Pettigrew-Kirkland-MacRae Brigade* (Chapel Hill: University of North Carolina Press, 2002); *Field Armies and Fortifications in the Civil War: The Eastern Campaigns, 1861–1864* (Chapel Hill: University of North Carolina Press, 2005); *Trench Warfare under Grant and Lee: Field Fortifications in the Overland Campaign* (Chapel Hill: University of North Carolina Press, 2007); *The Rifled Musket in Civil War Combat* (Lawrence: University Press of Kansas, 2008); *In the Trenches at Petersburg: Field Fortifications and Confederate Defeat* (Chapel Hill: University of North Carolina Press, 2009); *Into the Crater: The Mine Attack at Petersburg* (Columbia: University of South Carolina Press, 2012); *The Knoxville Campaign: Burnside and Longstreet in East Tennessee* (Knoxville: University of Tennessee Press, 2012); *The Civil War in the West: Victory and Defeat from the Appalachians to the Mississippi* (Chapel Hill: University of North Carolina Press, 2012); *Kennesaw Mountain: Sherman, Johnston, and the Atlanta Campaign* (Chapel Hill: University of North Carolina Press, 2013); *The Battle of Ezra Church and the Struggle for Atlanta* (Chapel Hill: University of North Carolina Press, 2015); and *Civil War Infantry Tactics: Training, Combat, and Small-Unit Effectiveness* (Baton Rouge: Louisiana State University Press, 2015).

REVITALIZING TRADITIONAL MILITARY HISTORY IN
THE CURRENT AGE OF CIVIL WAR STUDIES

Earl J. Hess

I N 1996 MARK GRIMSLEY posted an entry on his internet blog entitled "Why Military History Sucks." The basic message was that, while valuable in its own right, the subfield had fallen far behind the times in terms of new perspectives, methods, and conclusions in contrast with advances in social and cultural perspectives on the Civil War. Grimsley identified a kind of academic Social Darwinism, implying that military historians had no one to blame but themselves for failing to keep step with developments in their field. Their marginalization resulted from that failure.[1]

Frank J. Wetta addressed a related topic when wondering if battle and campaign studies, the heart and soul of Civil War military historiography, had any relevance to the field in 2007. "Doing Civil War battle history, then, is nothing new; but doing it well is another matter. Considering the vast literature on Civil War battles, is it still worth doing? Has the topic been exhausted? Are there too many accounts, even good ones, of that familiar regiment's charge through the wheat field, too many drums, too many bugles? What makes for good battle history? Is battle history still relevant in the Age of Race, Class, and Gender?"[2]

Indeed, these points by Grimsley and Wetta offer important opportunities for discussion, and there are many more as well. Instead of ignoring, denigrating, or worrying about the role of traditional military history in Civil War studies, we need to discuss its future with care, understanding, and hope. I would further argue that we not only need to think of ways the subfield can modernize to accommodate advances in other subfields of Civil War studies but also need to recognize that it is an old, hallowed, and still important part of the field in its own right. There are in fact many kinds of military history, not just one, and all of them have important perspectives on every facet of the Civil War, not just on the battlefield or the campaign trail or within the ranks of the armies. The fact that we argue so much about its role in our field is an implication that we recognize its importance. As a community of scholars, we have not yet come to grips with defining what that importance is, how it shapes the field, or what we can expect of it in the future.

DEFINITIONS

According to the *Oxford English Dictionary*, the word "military," used as an adjective, means "relating to or characteristic of soldiers or armed forces."[3] Those armed forces are by their very nature separated from civilian society, although drawn from it and usually returning to it. The social and cultural turn that hit Civil War studies with a wallop by the 1990s had a strong tendency to draw attention mostly to civilian society at war rather than applying social or cultural perspectives to the armed forces. That development had both good and bad consequences, but one result was to lead to a redefinition of military history as any study that looked at society during wartime, even if it paid no attention to soldiers or sailors.

One cannot complain too much about this development, for it produced highly relevant studies of Civil War–era society and culture. But it had the unfortunate effect of drawing away most academic attention from old-fashioned military history, the traditional approach of studying battles, strategy, supply, generalship, and a host of other subjects.

To some extent this social and cultural turn has inspired a few Civil War historians to look at ways it can be applied to soldiers and sailors, but they remain in the minority.[4] These scholars have pursued a line of research historians of the 1980s called the "new military history," a term that has fallen out of favor since then. Phrases such as "war and society" have supplanted new military history because the social and cultural turn produced only limited interest in studying armed forces. Therefore anyone who essays a social or cultural study of armies in the current era of Civil War studies has to accept that the term "military history" might never be used to define their work.

My purpose here is to focus attention on the aspect of military history that is in danger of being forgotten by the academy: traditional studies of how armed forces worked in the field. It is a line of research that largely pursues the history of tactics, weapons, organization and operations, logistics, and many other vital topics. Traditional military historians of the Civil War were more numerous among college and university professors in the 1960s and for some twenty years beyond that time than they became by the 1990s. Today relatively few historians in academia turn their hand to traditional military studies. One rarely sees an article on the subject in either *Civil War History* or the *Journal of the Civil War Era*. While a handful of academic presses enthusiastically publish traditional Civil War history, most others do not.[5]

In the responses to a survey I sent to Civil War historians in 2013, which contained several questions relevant to the state of military history in our field, everything pointed to the increasing marginalization of military history in general and traditional military history in particular. One question asked respondents to list what percentage of their work fell into three categories— traditional military history (tactics, strategy, generalship), new military history (social studies of soldiers and the armies), and war studies (social and cultural history of civilian society during the Civil War years). Concentrating work in war studies has increased four times in the past thirty years, while concentrating in traditional military history has declined to almost nothing, and concentrating in new military history has been cut in half. These trends will likely continue into the immediate future.[6]

But one must set all this within the proper context. Traditional military history is certainly on a steep decline in academia in general, not just in Civil War studies. In fact, academic jobs specifically defined as Civil War positions of any kind are on the decline as well.[7] There will always be a popular market for Civil War history, but it is shrinking, and if academia continues to marginalize traditional military history, readers will find fewer good studies produced by trained historians. There have always been Civil War military histories written by nonacademic authors, but their quality has ranged from those that are as good as any scholarly work down to those that misinform the reader and distort the subject.

The significance of traditional military history within Civil War studies will never be adequately served if left entirely in the hands of nonacademic writers. The field needs traditional military history, and the people who can do it well are those with academic and historiographic training.

WEAKNESSES

Any evaluation of traditional military history in the Civil War field has to start with an honest appraisal of its weaknesses, and there are several. One of the chief causes is the large popular market for combat studies. Traditional military historians write for at least three potential audiences: their peers in the academic world, a small class of nonacademic readers who are serious-minded students of the war, and a much larger class of nonacademic readers who have only a casual interest in the conflict. The best kind of works reach the first two classes, while the lesser quality products tend to be more popular among the third class. In general, nonacademic readers tend to expect colorful narrative, to desire an emphasis on action and personalities, and to have little interest in new interpretations or linking Civil War studies with general trends in Western military history, which of course are important for academics. The more serious-minded nonacademic reader is far more open to new ideas and the larger context of military operations, but the more casual reader rarely seems to be so.[8]

Traditional military historians of the Civil War have tended to write for the lower common denominator rather than for the higher. When asked if audience expectations negatively influenced the quality of this military history, a few survey respondents were uncertain, but many others agreed that it does create a problem. They cited repetition in coverage (how many books do we really need about a particular battle, no matter how popular the topic?) and too much narrative at the expense of asking hard questions that challenge preconceived notions.

Survey respondents also mused on another effect the popular market has on Civil War military historiography. The ready market for books has attracted a large number of nonacademic writers who have produced works of poor quality. In the minds of many scholars, this has branded Civil War military history as tainted, diluted, and unacademic. "It has been hurt by the distaste academic historians feel for discussions that might be seen as promoting war, or casting war in a favorable light," Allen Carl Guelzo wrote in his survey response, "and by 'buffs' who seem to take an almost pornographic delight in scenes of carnage, as though war was a kind of professional sport."

"Many authors and presses stereotype readers as 'buffs,' and editors expect authors to conform to those preconceptions by providing books that will sell without serious challenges to traditional approaches," Kenneth Noe wrote in his survey response. "My experience is that we sell many of the enthusiasts short, but there's still no doubt that [a] book about a battle will outsell a work of War Studies—and I say that as someone who has written both. There is an audience for comfortable, familiar history with a lot of maps, but it discourages breaking out of the mold."[9]

It should be easy enough to deal with this problem as long as historians are aware of it and consciously target their audience. In my own work in traditional military history, I have tried very hard to write for both an academic audience and the more serious-minded Civil War reader in the "real world." Quality of research, writing style, and analysis should be the objectives; there is both an academic and a nonacademic audience for good scholarship on a Civil War topic. Sales will never be as high among the academic and more serious-minded readership compared to the third and larger class of casual nonacademic readers, but the audience is more appreciative.[10]

QUESTIONING PAST RESEARCH

Writing toward audience expectations can happen even when historians aim at an academic audience. We are heavily trained to pay attention to historiography, to set our own work within the context of what has been done before by scholars in our field. Sometimes I think we are too heavily trained in this way and are not encouraged enough to strike out on our own path. It is astonishing how readily academic historians fall into line behind a salient interpretation or a line of research set by prominent predecessors as if it is inappropriate to reevaluate their work.

A good example of how academic historians tend to cluster behind a single interpretation lies in the role of the rifle musket in Civil War military operations. Its introduction before the war offered the possibility of infantry fire delivered at ranges of up to 500 yards instead of the smoothbore's more limited range of about 100 yards. Contemporaries predicted a revolution in infantry combat, with greater power for the defensive side and a reduction of the effectiveness of field artillery and cavalry when those arms engaged infantry. Those men did not later study the actual use of the new weapon on

Civil War battlefields and continued to assume that the conflict was bloody and seemingly stalemated because of the rifle musket's use. Generations of historians afterward assumed the same thing.

This rifle thesis dominated Civil War military history for many decades. It portrayed the conflict as exceptional in the context of Western military history, with the new weapon having a revolutionary effect on land operations because the rifle produced far more casualties than was possible with the outdated smoothbore musket. Every characteristic of the Civil War seemed to be shaped by the use of this weapon, introducing a strong element of modern warfare into our internecine conflict.[11]

Several historians, including Paddy Griffith, Mark Grimsley, and Brent Nosworthy, began to question this thesis in the 1980s and 1990s by looking at the actual distances of typical infantry combat during the Civil War. Their findings indicated that despite the 500-yard range of the rifle musket, most of the actual fighting took place at much shorter distances, roughly consistent with the 100-yard range of the smoothbore musket. Griffith's work, published in 1989, became a target of criticism and was largely rejected by the scholarly community. Grimsley's and Nosworthy's works appeared later (2001 and 2003 respectively) and were received more openly. My reevaluation of all aspects of this topic was published in 2008. That study not only looked at the range of infantry fighting but also compared loss ratios in rifle battles of the Civil War with those in smoothbore battles of the previous century. This approach was well received by a newer generation of historians willing to revise or reject the old rifle thesis.[12]

The result of this reevaluation by Griffith, Grimsley, Nosworthy, and myself has been to free Civil War scholarship from the tight constraints of the rifle thesis. Union and Confederate commanders and their men certainly wanted to be armed with the latest rifle, but they did not want to use it at long range. For many reasons officers and men preferred to wait until the enemy was very close, and the evidence is overwhelming that they were right to do so. It was difficult to even see a man 500 yards away on the cluttered battlefields of the Civil War and even more difficult to adjust the crude sights on the rifle musket to have a hope of hitting someone at that distance. Almost everyone wisely preferred to wait until the enemy was so near that there would be a greater chance of hitting him at close range. Moreover, smoothbore battles of the eighteenth century were just as bloody as those of the Civil War; in fact many were far more costly. While 30 percent of Lee's men became casualties at Gettysburg, 47 percent of the British troops at Bunker Hill were shot down by American smoothbore muskets.[13]

The new interpretation opens many doors to reevaluate infantry tactics, the role of artillery and cavalry in military operations, and the soldiers' experience of battle. It also has important implications for larger issues than those that concern tactics. Viewing the rifle musket as having little effect on changing the nature of combat allows us to see the Civil War as largely a product of the past rather than a harbinger of the future in war making. It also demonstrates that the Civil War was not so exceptional within the course of Western military history but instead a minor segment of that long and complex lineage. The rifle musket was a comparatively unusual weapon. Introduced in the national armies of Europe and North America only in the 1850s, it was rapidly superseded by a far more modern weapon during the Franco-Prussian War of 1870–71. It already was outdated only five years after Appomattox and had little influence on the shaping of military history.[14]

Ironically, it was not necessary to uncover a new set of primary sources to offer evidence that a new interpretation of the rifle musket was necessary. *The War of the Rebellion,* popularly known as the *Official Records,* provided ample evidence to document the short range of infantry fighting, as did many personal accounts by soldiers.[15] Historians had assumed the rifle thesis was right and tended to seek the evidence that supported it. Griffith, an English military historian who has produced fine studies of the Viking way of war, Napoleonic fighting, and the British army on the western front of World War I, was not immersed in Civil War historiography and therefore not constrained by the assumptions of the rifle thesis when he essayed his first and only study of Civil War combat. It literally took a new generation of historians to be open to his suggestions and follow through with them.

UTILIZING AVAILABLE PRIMARY MATERIAL

As the rifle-musket case illustrates, it is important to cast our research nets far, wide, and deep. Civil War military historians are blessed with an abundance of primary material, most of it already published and easily accessible. The 128 thick books that constitute the *Official Records* are crammed with important material on virtually every aspect of the war's military history, and they also have enormous material importance to the study of civilian society during wartime. Any social and cultural historian would find their time and effort well spent in perusing relevant volumes of this important government compilation of reports, dispatches, and telegrams produced by both armies during the conflict. Its exclusion from the bibliographies of many pertinent social and cultural studies is a source of regret. The *Official Records* is the foundation of our military understanding of the conflict and a vitally important source for a Civil War historian of any stripe. Searching for selected topics on the CD-ROM version of the *Official Records* is not a substitute for scanning literally every page of this compilation with the naked eye, as I did a few years ago to gather material for several research projects. That long process proved to be a revelation, giving me more respect for the content and value of the *Records* than I had ever had before.[16]

And it is not just the *Official Records* that offer scholars an immense amount of primary material. The effect of the internet on making other sources of such material available to Civil War military historians is earthshaking. The topic is too large to fully discuss here, but it ranges from altering the way unpublished letters, diaries, and memoirs are made accessible by the staff of archival institutions, to the placing of out-of-print regimental histories on websites such as www.books.google.com in electronic format, to the Library of Congress website making available the pages of an important veterans' newspaper called the *National Tribune* for easy access. Literally millions of pages of service records and other microfilmed documents held by the National Archives have been made available to anyone who pays a modest yearly subscription fee to the website www.fold3.com. There is far less opportunity now for historians to make excuses about not being able to access a wide variety and depth of primary-source material. With this ready accessibility of documentation, the standard has been raised in terms of how impressive a bibliography and footnote can be to the discerning reader, but many historians are not keeping pace.

SEEKING NEW PERSPECTIVES

Traditional Civil War military history has a heritage of its own. It has been a feature of the academic literature since the 1960s and, although on the wane in recent decades, continues to be practiced by at least a handful of scholars. Making traditional military history relevant to the current era involves first admitting its significance, then figuring out ways to improve it so it can continue to enlighten us well into the future. As demonstrated above with the rifle-musket argument, traditional military history is not a narrowly focused sector of Civil War studies. It has implications that stretch out into the international perspective, inform longitudinal studies over time, and shape cultural definitions relating to the very nature of the Civil War as a historical phenomenon.

Traditional Civil War military historians need to stretch themselves out of comfortable niches imposed by their large popular audiences. They need to not only write more thoroughly researched battle books and campaign studies that offer new interpretations of their subject but also seek the larger implications of their effort well beyond the battlefield and develop fundamentally new views of their subject when justified. They need to become true military historians rather than mere chroniclers of Civil War battles, a point Mark Grimsley has made on several occasions.[17] The potential certainly exists and, if exploited, would vitalize traditional military history within the current culture of Civil War studies significantly.

There seems to be more readiness to incorporate military history into the fold of academic Civil War studies if it involves a distinctly social or cultural twist. This is not surprising considering the current climate of opinion in the field, but it seems that only a relative minority of Civil War scholars actually do such work. It is an area that I defined as new military history for the purposes of crafting the survey and conducting research for "Where Do We Stand?" and that proved to have surprisingly little representation in the literature compared to studies of civilian society at war. In dissertation topics, articles in academic journals, and even in books published by university presses, the new-military-history category ranked pretty low. For example, of 146 Civil War books published by the University of North Carolina Press from 1940 to 2013, only 7.5 percent fall into this category, while 49.3 percent are in war studies and 43.1 percent in traditional military history. Additionally, the percentage of work reported by survey respondents indicates that focus on new military history has been cut in half over the past thirty years (from 40 percent to 22.2 percent), while work in war studies has increased from 20 percent to 77.8 percent.[18]

In order to vitalize the old category of new military history, it will be necessary to redefine how military history is conceptualized so that it becomes more recognizable as an aspect of the war-and-society approach. Barton A. Myers has argued in favor of such a redefinition. As important as this process will be in the near future, it hardly affects traditional military history. Redefining new military history should not leave the traditional approach out in the cold, for this study of tactics, strategy, weapons, and generalship still remains vital to any full understanding of warfare.[19]

But it is possible to modernize traditional military history in an effort to create a more cozy relationship with the war-and-society approach. It can be done in smaller ways as well as larger ones. Every battle, for example, had important connections with the home front of both belligerents during the Civil War, reflecting and affecting society and culture in various ways. While authoring half a dozen battle books, I have always included a discussion of the engagement's effect on American culture. The Battle of Pea Ridge, for example, inspired Herman Melville to write a poem about this well-known engagement in Arkansas, and it also inspired twentieth-century filmmakers and novelists to produce original work. There is a battlefield-preservation story and a memory story behind every Civil War engagement, and traditional military historians ought to tell those stories as part of their drum-and-bugles narrative of the engagement rather than leaving it as a separate study to be done by someone who has little training or experience in military history.[20]

Integration of different but related approaches to the subject, blended within a single study, would weaken the somewhat artificial boundaries that exist between categories within the larger subfield of Civil War military history. A book on the Atlanta Campaign, for example, that contained essays on tactics, troop morale, the political consequences of the operation for Lincoln's reelection bid, and the links between civilian morale, newspaper reporting, and Confederate hopes of survival would be a fascinating way to illustrate how interrelated traditional military history truly is with everything else in Civil War studies. Such a project could be constructed by a single scholar who is adept in all areas or collaborated on by several historians.[21]

Traditional military scholarship on the Civil War also needs more analysis of numbers. This can be done in light ways that do not demand huge databases of statistics or knowledge of number-crunching methods. Simple use of statistics was an invaluable aid in *The Rifle Musket in Civil War Combat* because so much of the older rifle thesis rested on assumptions about the range of fire, the rate of fire, and the losses inflicted by that weapon. All of these issues cried out for actual data rather than assumptions, and it became a process of finding the numbers, using a calculator to determine totals and percentages, and presenting the results in tables. Those numbers accomplished more in pointing out the fallacy of assuming the rifle musket revolutionized warfare than my own qualitative analysis could have done. While academic historians quickly accepted these findings as valid, nonacademic audiences often were resistant. When I speak to Civil War round tables on this issue, audience members usually suspend their belief in the new interpretation until seeing a table demonstrating that the percentage of battlefield loss in smoothbore combat of the eighteenth century equaled or exceeded the percentage of loss in Civil War rifle battles. At that point my argument is always accepted by the audience.[22]

In short, numbers, especially simple ones that do not demand much understanding of statistical analysis, have power in driving home new interpretations. While traditional military historians rarely use them, scholars working in the new-military-history category have used statistics very effectively to illuminate the life of Civil War soldiers. Joseph T. Glatthaar has employed sophisticated statistical analysis is his study of the men who served in the Army of Northern Virginia to produce interesting and important results. Such methods perhaps lend themselves less well to traditional military history, but it is well worth any scholar's time and effort to see if that assumption is true.[23]

It would also be heartening to see traditional military historians branch out and write in a more comparatively global way. They tend to see the American Civil War as an exceptional experience in the world. By ignoring developments in Western military history and our conflict's place in those developments, Civil War historians give the impression that their war was set apart from global trends. Nothing could be further from the truth. The connections between the war of 1861–65 and European and Asian conflicts of the mid-nineteenth century need to be explored. The facile tendency to see campaigns such as Petersburg and Atlanta as foreshadowing trench warfare in World War I is an example of false connections, for there really is no basis of comparison here. An international perspective must be based on significant research outside the Civil War literature. It needs deep analysis rather than simply connecting the dots in a superficial game of comparison.[24]

In my work on the rifle musket and on Civil War infantry tactics, understanding the European and North American heritage of both topics aided enormously in setting them within their appropriate context. In the latter case I tried to understand the history of linear tactical formations and maneu- vers from their origin in the late 1600s through the Civil War and on to the development of modern fire-team tactics after World War II. The result not only helped in understanding and evaluating the effectiveness of infantry tac- tics (especially small-unit tactics) but also was an exhilarating experience that taught me more about the subject than I could have guessed. Exploring the international perspective was a liberating, intellectually gratifying process.[25]

Just as the international perspective can be liberating, looking at Civil War history from a multidisciplinary perspective yields insights not found within our own methodology. For the past twenty years or so, historical archaeologists have been digging Civil War battlefields, campsites, civilian homes, and cem- eteries. They have produced an impressive body of books and papers on their findings. The results of surveys and excavations of battlefields can especially benefit traditional military historians; in some cases the archaeologist is the key to locating exactly where an engagement took place. Despite the flood of documents produced during the Civil War, it is ironic that there still exist a handful of significant battles whose exact location is uncertain. Historical archaeologists can, in other words, enlighten us on some questions that the paper trail fails to answer. Their work on civilian sites and encampments can also inform the social and cultural historian as well as those scholars inter- ested in the life of the common soldier.[26]

EXAMINING THE FUTURE

The academic study of Civil War military history is a comparatively recent phenomenon, only about fifty years old. The beginning dates to the 1960s, when a generation of traditional military historians appeared in academia. The popular reading market soared as a result of the war's centennial and increased to a peak by the 1990s before slowly declining. The number of aca- demic historians who work in traditional military history has declined sharply since then in the face of surging interest in the social and cultural history of the Civil War.[27]

Where will we end up in another fifty years? Traditional military history will survive within the halls of academia even if graduate training and the trends in our field do not encourage it. There will always be a handful of younger scholars who elect to become traditional military historians after doing their dissertations in some other topic and after they obtain tenure. The genre will not thrive under such conditions, but at least it will survive. In contrast, if traditional military history was left mostly in the hands of un- trained amateur historians, there would be little hope for its survival. While the better nonacademic military historians can do work that is on the same level as academic historians as far as research and description is concerned, none of them have demonstrated the capability of taking the genre into new areas such as comparative international history or cross-disciplinary work. It takes an academic historian to realize the scholarly potential inherent in the field.

What will become of the audience for traditional military history during the next half century? There is no doubt that it is on the decline, but exactly how far that will go is anyone's guess. The centennial of the 1960s played a key role in creating a large audience for Civil War books outside the academic world and also marked the beginning of an academic corps of historians who write as well as read traditional military history. But the passing of this generation will surely affect the size of the Civil War reading public for decades to come.

Coinciding with the rise of readership spurred by the centennial, Civil War round tables (which had started in the 1950s) became a major national movement. But we should not assume that these organizations represent all or even the major part of Civil War readership. In fact most books on the topic are purchased by people who do not belong to round tables. Moreover, round-table membership is dominated by older white men; one rarely sees an audience member younger than fifty years old at such meetings. There is no doubt that some members of the younger generations are interested in Civil War military history, but they engage in ways other than round-table meetings; I receive emails from high school students interested in the war. We should not judge the state of the nonacademic reading audience by what is happening to the round tables. They are a distinctly older person's venue, and it is quite possible that young Civil War enthusiasts will want to join them as they advance through middle age.[28]

PLOTTING A RESEARCH AGENDA

We can assume that traditional military history will survive in some form in Civil War academia, but will there be topics to discuss during the next fifty years? The answer to that question is a resounding yes. It is one of the myths that everything has already been said about the military history of our war. As demonstrated earlier, there is expansive opportunity to reevaluate old ideas, explore new areas, and craft innovative approaches to the subject that link it with developments in social and cultural studies. Rather than being a dried-up old genre, traditional military history is as potentially vibrant as any other approach to understanding the complexities of the Civil War. The problem has always been in the way we tend to approach it, not in the subject itself. We need a new awareness of what traditional military history is and what it can be in order to vitalize the genre.

Because of the wide reading public for Civil War military studies, historians have strongly tended to concentrate on writing books that deal with the staple of popular interest in warfare—strategy, tactics, and generalship. We have many books about battles and virtually no studies of a wide range of topics fundamental to understanding the military history of our conflict. To a greater or lesser degree, the same can be said of historians who study other wars as well. Currently the readership for World War II military history is bigger than the Civil War audience ever was and with predictable results—an overemphasis on battles, campaigns, weapons, and generalship in Second World War historiography.[29]

But it is interesting that wars that have drawn far less popular interest— such as the Mexican-American War, the War of 1812, or the Spanish-American War—typically do not suffer such effects. Writing mostly for other scholars and for a small group of nonacademic readers, historians of less popular wars are more willing to address topics that popular readers find less exciting.[30]

Civil War historians are in an enviable position—we still have a substantial popular readership and a wide range of interesting and important topics yet unstudied. We should not underestimate the educated nonacademic reader's willingness to learn new ideas or explore new areas of research. With the shrinking of the Civil War audience, such people may become the core of what is left of the readership fifty years from now.

There are many important aspects of Civil War military history that have been ignored or only scantily explored. For example, armies cannot operate without a variety of support services. Included in this category are the activities of the many bureaus in Washington, D.C., and in Richmond that guided and supported army operations as well as naval activities. We need histories of how the quartermaster, commissary, ordnance, signal, engineer, justice, adjutant general, and many other departments operated, all the way from the national capitals down to the individual regiments in the field.

Both governments relied mostly on private enterprise to make and transport the bulk of what they needed. Few other research topics so well illustrate the close cooperation between the governmental and private sphere in American life as mobilizing and supporting a large military force. A deep study of this topic would include the process of contracting government business to private companies and individuals. It would discuss how agencies dealt with civilian fraud, disciplined suppliers, and exercised quality control over military products made by contractors. The result would provide a clear view of how the army and navy systems interacted with civilians in positive as well as negative ways, both North and South, and reflect on motivation by civilian suppliers—did they work for the cause or mostly for their own profit?

Whatever their motivation, civilians became part of the war effort in very intimate ways when they engaged with the supply mechanisms used by both governments. Studies of this interaction would blur distinctions about what constitutes military history and social history. They would also temper the general idea that Civil War armies callously took what they wanted from helpless citizens who happened to live in their path. These large military formations could not survive by foraging off the countryside alone. They needed heavy shipments of food for men and fodder for horses from their own governments if they hoped to survive for long. Moreover, they were completely dependent on the channels of supply and logistics for weapons and ammunition, which were impossible to take from the countryside. Understanding where all that material came from, who made it, and how it was purchased and distributed involves far more than just an arcane study of military administration but charts the many ways that the military system extended its tentacles into the civilian community of an entire nation.

In short, administrative history is a topic that bridges the divide between traditional military history and the war-and-society emphasis. We should remind ourselves that the military system was topped by civilian administrators, including the president, secretary of war, and the heads of other bureaus in Washington and Richmond. It is true that the army and navy were social organizations with their own special purposes, ethos, and cultures. But they also were intimately connected to the civilian society that gave rise to them. Many topics of inquiry, such as administrative history, have yet to be explored as a way of gaining insight into the interconnectedness of the military and civilian spheres.[31]

In addition to researching the operation of government bureaus, it is important to study how support officers and troops worked in the field. Army mobility depended on the ability of quartermaster and commissary officers to move material and collect food for men and fodder for animals. Officers in the field often had to improvise when shortfalls in transportation and supply took place. Again, this topic has important implications for a variety of interests inherent in the war-and-society paradigm because both Union and Confederate armies foraged from the countryside, imposing devastating consequences on civilian society.

Historians of the classical and medieval periods have produced far more studies of logistics than Civil War historians have, even though thousands of documents concerning the subject are readily available in the *Official Records*. In comparison, our colleagues who study these other wars are compelled to tease out small bits of information from a variety of sources that are difficult to locate. They often have done so by using innovative and even cross-disciplinary methods that go far beyond any methodology traditional Civil War historians have yet to employ.[32]

Leadership studies have grown in popularity both within academia and outside it. Traditional military historians and popular readers alike have loved studies of generalship, even if many of those books tend to be superficial, colorful narratives of personalities rather than serious studies of leadership principles. Despite the many books already published about Ulysses S. Grant, Robert E. Lee, and their subordinates, we need far more work on leadership in the Civil War based on concepts developed outside our field, especially within the modern military training system. The focus also should be lowered until our sights are firmly on leadership among corps, division, brigade, regimental, and company officers, who were as important as Grant and Lee in determining how well field armies worked during the Civil War.[33]

Joint operations (the close cooperation of army and navy units) underlay the success of dozens of Civil War campaigns. The Federal government literally could not have opened the Mississippi River to northern commerce or captured ports along the Atlantic and Gulf Coasts without the combined efforts of the two services. Yet we have only two studies of combined operations during the conflict, both of them pointing the way without constituting a full or definitive study of this complicated topic.[34]

It is difficult to understand why academic historians have tended to shy away from discussing the role of artillery and cavalry in the Civil War. Virtually all books and articles on these topics have been penned by nonacademic historians, with widely varying results. One of the few discussions in a scholarly book is contained in Grady McWhiney and Perry Jamieson's *Attack and Die*, but that discussion is tightly focused on how the rifle musket affected those two arms.[35] In fact there is no general history of field artillery in the Civil War written by anyone, in or out of the academy, and the only general studies of cavalry have been produced by nonacademic writers and contain little analysis or evaluation of its effectiveness.[36]

The technical aspects of weapons of all kinds, from small arms to artillery, have been left entirely in the hands of amateur historians. Many of them know this subject very well, but there is a real difference between being able to identify a Schenkl shell and knowing how well it was employed by artillerymen and whether it proved effective on the battlefield. The technical literature on Civil War ordnance is just that—studies about the small details of production and design. That is an important part of understanding the conflict, but the lines of research need to go beyond it as well, and only academically trained historians can make larger conclusions in this area. Knowing how weapons actually were used is more important than knowing their technical capabilities if one wants to understand the influence of a gun on shaping military operations during the Civil War.[37]

In fact military historians have paid far too little attention to the entire topic of military effectiveness in the war. It is not enough to detail the movements of units on the battlefield—one ought to evaluate why and how they achieved their tactical goals on a given day of battle or why they failed to do so. Discussions such as this ought to permeate every battle and campaign book; they would immeasurably add to the value of the study. Standalone books that evaluate unit effectiveness on the army, corps, division, brigade, regiment, and company levels would be breaths of fresh air in a genre that tends to be stultifying in its lack of new ideas. This topic lends itself very well to comparison with other American wars and European conflicts, promoting a healthy global context within which to contemplate the Civil War experience.[38]

How the Federal army conducted occupation duties during the Civil War is another area much in need of study. It has little of the "glamor" associated with combat and personalities but a great deal to do with a fundamental role played by thousands of citizen-soldiers. Occupation involved connection with the life of local communities, rehabilitation of local political life under the old flag, civilian morale, and area business activities. The Union army attempted to do much along these lines before the end of the conflict. How far it succeeded and what effect occupation duties had on the troops are vital topics of discussion.[39]

A subject closely allied to occupation duties is the role of the Federal army as an agent of humanitarian relief. Union officers took on a good deal of responsibility for feeding thousands of civilians across occupied Confederate territory, and the army became the main relief agency for newly freed slaves. Union forces not only fed refugee blacks, placing them in special contraband camps and putting them to work on abandoned plantations, but also enrolled more than 180,000 eligible black men into military service. The army's role in changing the lives of black southerners was far greater than its influence on changing the lives of white Americans. A mechanism fundamentally designed for destruction also served a constructive purpose; historians have not yet dealt with that dichotomy in Civil War military history. The topic is also an important link between traditional military studies and the social history of the war.

Another area ignored by traditional military historians is guerrilla conflict. A surge of interest in the subject during the past few years has been taking place mostly within the ranks of social and cultural historians rather than military historians. Understanding the irregular warrior is to a large degree the purview of the social historian since that combatant was not part of a regularly organized military unit. But occupation forces also were participants in guerrilla warfare, and traditional military historians have an important role to play in studying how these troops succeeded in containing the irregular threat.[40]

We also would do well to recognize that armies were but one element in a complicated artificial and natural environment with which they interacted in countless ways. What happens when 100,000 armed men move through the countryside? What is the effect on the built environment as well as the natural environment? Armies heavily polluted everything they encountered, depositing human and animal waste on the ground and in streams, draining springs of usable water, and cutting down thousands of trees for fuel, fortifications, and winter quarters. Battles destroyed forests and littered the ground with animal carcasses. Soldiers left behind dirty camps and threw away thousands of items of clothing and other government-issued material. One could track the path of a marching column by the debris it left along the roadside, the carcasses of mules that died along the line of march, and the houses and fences burned along the way.[41]

Closely allied with the environmentalist approach is the emerging field of animal history. This is based on the idea of interpreting human history through the perspective of the animals people have used: in the context of the Civil War, artillery horses, cavalry horses, and mules. These animal populations had lives of their own that intersected with human needs; they suffered devastating diseases while in military service, endured battle (and suffered terribly for their exposure to enemy fire), and fulfilled important human needs with barely a nod from historians thus far.[42] We should also pay attention to the wild animals that soldiers interfered with, killed, and ate. In some ways wild animals fulfilled an important need also, and in other ways they were simply impinged on needlessly by bored young men with guns, for instance those who wantonly shot alligators simply because they happened to see them in a Louisiana swamp.

It may well be that the oldest approach in Civil War studies, traditional military history, has the most potential for future work. If so, it will be because academic historians will finally realize how narrow the stream of military history research has become and seek to widen it. There is every reason to hope that the coming fifty years of inquiry into the military history of the Civil War could be far more brilliant than the past half century.

NOTES

1. Mark Grimsley, "Why Military History Sucks," www.warhistorian.org/why_military_history_sucks.php, accessed Jan. 23, 2015.

2. Frank J. Wetta, ed., "Battle Histories: Reflections on Civil War Military Studies," *Civil War History* 53, no. 3 (Sept. 2007): 231.

3. *Oxford English Dictionary*, www.oxforddictionaries.com, accessed Oct. 27, 2014.

4. Good examples of important studies on soldiering in the Civil War include Lorien Foote, *The Gentlemen and the Roughs: Manhood, Honor, and Violence in the Union Army* (New York: New York University Press, 2010); Joseph T. Glatthaar, *Soldiering in the Army of Northern Virginia: A*

Statistical Portrait of the Troops Who Served under Robert E. Lee (Chapel Hill: University of North Carolina Press, 2011); and Michael D. Pierson, *Mutiny at Fort Jackson: The Untold Story of the Fall of New Orleans* (Chapel Hill: University of North Carolina Press, 2008).

5. For more discussion of these points, see Earl J. Hess, "Where Do We Stand? A Critical Assessment of Civil War Studies in the Sesquicentennial Era," *Civil War History* 60, no. 4 (Dec. 2014): 371–403.

6. Hess, "Where Do We Stand?," 373–74.

7. Aaron Sheehan-Dean, "The Nineteenth-Century U.S. History Job Market, 2000–2009," *Journal of the Civil War Era* 1, no. 1 (Mar. 2011): 135, 138.

8. For a further discussion of the audiences for Civil War military history, see Hess "Where Do We Stand?," 384–86, 388.

9. "Not only does most military history written for the popular market lack perceptive insights, new material or judicious reflection; there is often also a style of writing that is novelistic, if not partisan." Jeremy Black, *Rethinking Military History* (New York: Routledge, 2004), 28. For further discussion of how audience expectations can affect the quality of academic military history see Joseph T. Glatthaar, "Battlefield Tactics," in *Writing the Civil War: The Quest to Understand,* ed. James M. McPherson and William J. Cooper Jr. (Columbia: University of South Carolina Press, 1998), 78–79.

10. See for example Earl J. Hess, *Kennesaw Mountain: Sherman, Johnston, and the Atlanta Campaign* (Chapel Hill: University of North Carolina Press, 2013), and Hess, *The Battle of Ezra Church and the Struggle for Atlanta* (Chapel Hill: University of North Carolina Press, 2015).

11. For the older rifle interpretation, see Grady McWhiney and Perry D. Jamieson, *Attack and Die: Civil War Military Tactics and the Southern Heritage* (Tuscaloosa: University of Alabama Press, 1982).

12. For the new rifle interpretation, see Paddy Griffith, *Battle Tactics of the Civil War* (New Haven, CT: Yale University Press, 1989); Mark Grimsley, "Surviving Military Revolution: The U.S. Civil War," in *The Dynamics of Military Revolution, 1300–2050,* ed. Macgregor Knox and Williamson Murray (Cambridge, UK: Cambridge University Press, 2001), 74–91; Brent Nosworthy, *The Bloody Crucible of Courage: Fighting Methods and Combat Experience of the Civil War* (New York: Carroll & Graf, 2003); and Earl J. Hess, *The Rifle Musket in Civil War Combat: Reality and Myth* (Lawrence: University Press of Kansas, 2008).

13. Hess, *Rifle Musket,* 199, 202.

14. Ibid., 217–27; Hess, *Civil War Infantry Tactics: Training, Combat, and Small-Unit Effectiveness* (Baton Rouge: Louisiana State University Press, 2015), 202–38.

15. U.S. War Department, *The War of the Rebellion: A Compilation of the Official Records of the Union and Confederate Armies,* 70 vols. in 128 pts. (Washington, D.C.: Government Printing Office, 1880–1901).

16. My survey of the *Official Records* took place in preparation for writing *The Civil War in the West: Victory and Defeat from the Appalachians to the Mississippi,* (Chapel Hill: University of North Carolina Press, 2012). Two other compilations of Civil War documents are nearly as important as the *Official Records* of the armies. They are the *Official Records of the Union and Confederate Navies in the War of the Rebellion,* 30 vols. (Washington, D.C.: Government Printing Office, 1894–1922);

and the *Supplement to the Official Records of the Union and Confederate Armies,* 100 vols. (Wilmington, NC: Broadfoot, 1995–99).

17. Grimsley, "Why Military History Sucks." For thoughts about improving research and analysis in traditional historiography of European battles and campaigns, see Black, *Rethinking Military History,* 30–32.

18. Hess, "Where Do We Stand?," 374, 377–79.

19. Barton A. Myers, "The Future of Civil War Era Studies: Military History," in "Forum: The Future of Civil War Studies," online supplement to *Journal of the Civil War Era* 2, no. 1 (Mar. 2012), accessed Oct. 26, 2014.

20. William L. Shea and Earl J. Hess, *Pea Ridge: Civil War Campaign in the West* (Chapel Hill: University of North Carolina Press, 1992), 319–30; Hess, *Pickett's Charge—The Last Attack at Gettysburg* (Chapel Hill: University of North Carolina Press, 2001), 352–84; Hess, *Into the Crater: The Mine Attack at Petersburg* (Columbia: University of South Carolina Press, 2010), 239–46; Hess, *The Knoxville Campaign: Burnside and Longstreet in East Tennessee,* (Knoxville: University of Tennessee Press, 2012), 269–93; Hess, *Kennesaw Mountain,* 235–61; Hess, *Battle of Ezra Church,* 205–7.

21. Albert Castel, *Decision in the West: The Atlanta Campaign of 1864* (Lawrence: University Press of Kansas, 1992) is the standard history of the campaign. It fulfills the most important requirement, providing a good understanding of the grand tactics and high-level leadership on both sides, but there are many more aspects important to understanding this campaign that historians have not yet addressed.

22. Hess, *Rifle Musket,* 99–102, 107–13, 128, 133–34, 150–51, 154–55, 159–60, 180–81, 199–200, 202. For another example of using simple statistics in traditional military history, see Hess, *Civil War Infantry Tactics,* 163–65.

23. Glatthaar, *Soldiering in the Army of Northern Virginia.*

24. Justin S. Solonick's *Engineering Victory: The Union Siege of Vicksburg* (Carbondale: Southern Illinois University Press, 2015), in comparing Federal siege operations with European theory, broadens our perspective on Civil War military procedure. For a convincing exploration of the Mexican-American War as a precedent for the Civil War, see Wayne Wei-siang Hsieh, *West Pointers and the Civil War: The Old Army in War and Peace* (Chapel Hill: University of North Carolina Press, 2009), 34–53.

25. Hess, *Rifle Musket,* 9–34, 217–227; Hess, *Civil War Infantry Tactics,* 1–33, 202–38.

26. There is yet no survey of the historical archaeological literature pertaining to Civil War sites, but one can start with important book-length collections of essays such as Clarence R. Geier Jr. and Susan E. Winter, eds., *Look to the Earth: Historical Archaeology and the American Civil War* (Knoxville: University of Tennessee Press, 1994); and Clarence R. Geier, David G. Orr, and Matthew B. Reeves, eds., *Huts and History: The Historical Archaeology of Military Encampment during the American Civil War* (Gainesville: University Press of Florida, 2006).

27. Hess, "Where Do We Stand?," 380, 400–401; Joseph T. Glatthaar, "The 'New' Civil War History: An Overview," *Pennsylvania Magazine of History & Biography* 115, no. 3 (July 1991): 369.

28. For a proposed agenda aimed at improving the health of military history in Civil War studies, see Hess, "Where Do We Stand?," 401–3.

29. One can get a good idea of where Second World War military historiography is heading

by examining the publication list of the University Press of Kansas, the best academic publisher in this field.

30. Historians have written comparatively few battle and campaign studies for these three conflicts; examples include Donald E. Graves, *Where Right and Glory Lead! The Battle of Lundy's Lane, 1814* (Toronto: Robin Brass Studio, 1999), and Timothy D. Johnson, *A Gallant Little Army: The Mexico City Campaign* (Lawrence: University Press of Kansas, 2007).

31. Among the few studies that deal with the administrative history of the Civil War is Mark R. Wilson's *The Business of Civil War: Military Mobilization and the State, 1861–1865* (Baltimore: Johns Hopkins University Press, 2006), which focuses mostly on state action rather than the workings of the entire military system.

32. For two good examples (out of many) representing the sophisticated coverage of logistics and supply in conflicts other than the Civil War, see Paul Erdkamp, *Hunger and the Sword: Warfare and Food Supply in Roman Republican Wars (264–30 B.C.)* (Amsterdam: J. C. Gieben, 1998); and Yuval Noah Harari, "Strategy and Supply in Fourteenth-Century Western European Invasion Campaigns," *Journal of Military History* 64, no. 2 (Apr. 2000): 297–333.

33. Andrew S. Bledsoe's contribution to this collection and his *Citizen-Officers: The Union and Confederate Volunteer Junior Officer Corps in the American Civil War* (Baton Rouge: Louisiana State University Press, 2015) address issues concerning leadership and effectiveness, as does Jennifer M. Murray's essay in this volume.

34. For combined operations, see Rowena Reed, *Combined Operations in the Civil War* (Annapolis, MD: Naval Institute Press, 1978); and Craig L. Symonds, ed., *Union Combined Operations in the Civil War* (New York: Fordham University Press, 2010).

35. McWhiney and Jamieson, *Attack and Die*, 112–39.

36. Stephen Z. Starr, *The Union Cavalry in the Civil War,* 3 vols. (Baton Rouge: Louisiana State University Press, 1979–85).

37. For example, see James C. Hazlett, Edwin Olmstead, and M. Hume Parks, *Field Artillery Weapons of the Civil War*, rev. ed. (Urbana: University of Illinois Press, 2004).

38. I include a discussion of small-unit effectiveness in *Civil War Infantry Tactics*.

39. Judkin Browning's *Shifting Loyalties: The Union Occupation of Eastern North Carolina* (Chapel Hill: University of North Carolina Press, 2011) has a chapter on the effect of occupation duty on the lives of Federal soldiers. Andrew F. Lang's essay in this volume and his study *In the Wake of War: Military Occupation, Emancipation, and Civil War America* (Baton Rouge: Louisiana State University Press, 2017) address the effects of occupation duty on soldiers.

40. Robert Russell Mackey's *The Uncivil War: Irregular Warfare in the Upper South, 1861–1865* (Norman: University of Oklahoma Press, 2004) is the only military study of antiguerrilla operations by the Federal army. Joseph M. Beilein Jr. includes a discussion of guerrilla strategy and tactics in *Bushwhackers: Guerrilla Warfare, Manhood, and the Household in Civil War Missouri* (Kent, Ohio: Kent State University Press, 2016). Brian D. McKnight's contribution to this volume illustrates a good example of how important the social-history approach is to understanding guerrilla conflict.

41. Lisa Brady's *War upon the Land: Military Strategy and the Transformation of Southern Landscapes during the American Civil War* (Athens: University of Georgia Press, 2012) is a good

introduction to the complicated topic of environmentalism and war. Kenneth Noe's essay in this volume illustrates one way in which the environment affected military operations, while John Hennessy's essay discusses a case study of how armies destroyed the built environment.

42. Ann N. Green includes a chapter on horses during the Civil War in *Horses at Work: Harnessing Power in Industrial America* (Cambridge, MA: Harvard University Press, 2008), while Emmett M. Essin offers a brief discussion of mules during the Civil War in *Shavetails and Bell Sharps: The History of the U.S. Army Mule* (Lincoln: University of Nebraska Press, 1997).

II

THE CONTESTED BATTLEFIELD

"I AM COMPLETELY CHECKED BY THE WEATHER"

George B. McClellan, Weather, and the Peninsula Campaign

Kenneth W. Noe

W HEN FUTURE GENERATIONS look back on the Civil War's sesqui-centennial, the defining factor may seem to be that it occurred at the dawn of a digital age. For every scholar who expressed concerned about an apparent lack of popular interest vis-à-vis the centennial of the 1960s, there were dozens of Facebook postings, YouTube videos, blog entries, and live-tweeted reenactments. Future Civil War historians of the bicentennial might well ask, however, whether all of that new media advanced fresh approaches or simply regurgitated accepted wisdom. The coverage of Maj. Gen. George B. McClellan raises a red flag in this regard. Nuanced and often revisionist recent works such as Ethan Rafuse's 2005 biography, Donald Stoker's favorable reassessment of McClellan's strategic vision, and Glenn David Brasher's evaluation of slavery and the Peninsula Campaign seemingly did little to stem the popular tide of McClellan bashing. The general's digital presence during the sesqui-centennial more typically involved popular cut-and-pasted web articles such as "Commanders in Chaos: The 5 Worst Generals in U.S. History," in which the author concluded, "had Lincoln retained McClellan in command of the Union armies, many former Americans might still be whistling 'Dixie.'"[1] Not to be outdone, another author ranked McClellan seventh among the "Top 10 Worst Military Leaders in History," just between Robert Nivelle and Saddam Hussein.[2] On the popular webzine *Slate*, John Swansburg entitled his article on McClellan, "The Civil War's Most Chicken General."[3] In making these arguments, modern e-authors simply added hyperbole and repeated the judgments of previous generations of print historians who repeatedly damned McClellan as slow, timid, and petulant.[4]

Not surprisingly, the Peninsula Campaign figures prominently in the timidity/petulance trope. Popular authors can draw upon significant historians who paint a picture of an overly elaborate operational plan and a grand turning movement through the Chesapeake Bay that Abraham Lincoln wisely disdained. McClellan's lack of aggressiveness against outnumbered Confederates, whose inflated numbers "Little Mac" foolishly accepted, further undermined the march to Richmond. At Yorktown, according to James M. McPherson, his "only action was to inch forward with his siege while [Confederate general Joseph] Johnston brought 40,000 more men to the peninsula." At least the historians acknowledge another factor. Once Johnston retreated, McPherson continues, "further Union pursuit bogged down in heavy rains that turned the roads into a morass. The rains persisted for nearly a month, during which there was much sickness, much corduroying . . . of bottomless roads, much building of bridges over swollen creeks, and much cursing—but little fighting." McClellan's muddy men crawled to the outskirts of Richmond, where Robert E. Lee took command after Johnston was wounded and broke the Union commander's will to fight in a week of hard combat. McClellan was "a beaten general" whose only response was to blame the White House.[5]

This chapter seeks to move beyond the hoary "good general–worst general" straightjacket in order to better assess the factor that scholarly critics admit contributed to McClellan's defeat—the weather. Usually described as "rainy" or "bad," precipitation on the Peninsula during the campaign in fact was unusually torrential that spring, and it played more of a role in delaying the army than McClellan's personality. The causes of that heavy and persistent rain remain elusive, but over the last few years, many meteorologists with a historical bent have speculated that El Niño–Southern Oscillation (ENSO) might have been involved at some level. Hundreds of miles off the western coast of South America, subsurface waters sometimes heat up or cool down a few degrees for reasons that still defy easy explanation. Ocean currents and winds churn those waters to the surface, where contact with eastward-blowing trade winds occurs. Growing stronger, west winds transport the warmer or cooler air toward land. Warmer temperatures bring the El Niño phenomenon, while cooler air leads to the opposite La Niña effect. Both involve dramatically shifting weather patterns worldwide. Scientists first hypothesized the existence of ENSO in the late 1870s as an explanation for the devastating monsoon of 1876 in India. They could only begin to prove its existence in the late 1960s, however. Meteorologists more recently have read backward into the records from the later decades of the nineteenth century in order to identify ENSO's earlier handiwork. Lacking full data from modern tools, any conclusions remain tentative and debatable. Meteorologists have considered both El Niño and La Niña, while other recent work leans toward the North Atlantic Oscillation as a more critical factor in the early 1860s, perhaps in conjunction with a mild El Niño. Whatever the final verdict, the Peninsula Campaign ultimately serves as a useful example of how considerations of climate, weather, and soil can help better explain the experience and conduct of the Civil War, as opposed to "good/bad general."[6]

Unusual and intense weather dramatically influenced the Civil War everywhere during its first winter. In Virginia December was remarkably warm, but the new year brought heavy rain and acres of mud to the Potomac. All across the embattled Confederacy that following spring, farmers delayed planting, hoping their fields would dry out. Heavy rains and flooding powerfully shaped campaigns at places such as Fort Donelson and Shiloh in Tennessee.[7]

Those same torrential rains undermined McClellan's hopes from the start. As the general's struggle with Lincoln over how to best approach Richmond reached its climax in early March 1862, Confederate commander Joseph E. Johnston retreated from Manassas in rain and mud. McClellan briefly pushed after him despite the raw weather. Arriving at Johnston's abandoned camps on March 11, just a day behind the Confederates, McClellan and his subordinates immediately (and reasonably) deemed the muddy roads too wretched for further pursuit and halted.[8] In a cabinet meeting that day, the administration's boiling dissatisfaction with the general in chief came to an ugly head as they discussed Johnston's escape and McClellan's refusal to pursue. Secretary of War Edwin Stanton particularly hammered McClellan's generalship, and Lincoln announced that he was relieving him of everything except command of the Army of the Potomac. To be sure, Little Mac had given his superiors much to criticize that winter, but the angry reaction to Johnston's escape draws attention to a problem he would face throughout the Peninsula Campaign and indeed all through his tenure as commander of the army. Time after time and in every theater, Lincoln and Stanton showed little appreciation for the effects of weather on troop movements and logistics. Nor did their understanding of such matters deepen appreciably as the war dragged on. In that respect they might well be regarded as the war's first armchair generals, expecting commanders in the field to will their men through any and all conditions. As events would prove, it was a no-win situation for McClellan.[9]

McClellan first learned of his demotion from general in chief from a newspaper. Insulted, he began having second thoughts about his larger plan. Johnston's retreat across the Rappahannock meant that he still would be between McClellan and Richmond if the Union army landed at Urbanna, the planned disembarkation point. Then there was the Confederate ironclad CSS *Virginia*, popularly known as the *Merrimack*, stymied by the USS *Monitor* but still dangerously lurking at the mouth of the James River.[10] Unwilling to discard months of work and persuasion or to give in to the White House either, McClellan improvised. The turning movement would go forward, but it would shift farther south to the protection of Fortress Monroe, still in Union hands at the tip of the Virginia Peninsula, formed by the York and the James Rivers. He would advance on Richmond from there generally along the banks of the York; the navy would have to deal with the Confederate ironclad, which denied the James River to McClellan. Lincoln approved the change in plans the next day, March 13, as an afternoon drizzle fell on the capital. McClellan immediately began preparations to move most of the Army of the Potomac to the Peninsula. Boats assembled at Alexandria to begin transporting the men and their equipment.[11]

From Manassas and Centreville, the Union troops retraced their muddy steps north to the Potomac. Over an inch-and-a-half of rain fell during the night of March 14 and throughout the next day. A thunderstorm that came up the following night brought wind and nearly another inch of precipitation. The rain, swollen creeks, and ever-present mud made marching and sleeping unpleasant, especially as many regiments were without tents. During the stormy night of the fifteenth, some soldiers simply stood in the rain rather than lay in the mud. Others tried to construct shelter from surrounding trees, but the effort left them soaked nonetheless.[12] At Washington's Chain Bridge, the 10th Massachusetts "lay . . . in the rain until night, . . . drenched to the skin." It was "such a rain as you never saw, it seemed as if the windows of heaven were open, and it actually poured down, and the water in some places was knee deep in the road besides fording creeks where it was waist deep."[13]

On March 17, with many of the regiments still on the road, the first of McClellan's troops boarded transports for the two-day voyage to Fortress Monroe, a process that continued into the first week of April. Close to four hundred vessels of every shape and size eventually delivered over 121,000 fighting men to the Peninsula. In Alexandria the weather during those weeks was fickle for queued-up soldiers, and their descriptions of dry weather or rainy skies and even occasional snow varied with the timing of the correspondent's arrival. Weather on the Peninsula, however, generally seemed much better than what the army left behind, with mostly fair skies and highs around fifty. Soldiers who had endured the winter in the Washington defenses enjoyed the apparent coming of spring on the Peninsula and looked forward to relief at last from bad conditions.[14]

McClellan was less satisfied. In the Shenandoah Maj. Gen. Thomas J. "Stonewall" Jackson's Valley Campaign threw Federal planning into disarray. On April 4, with McClellan just out of the city, Lincoln stopped Maj. Gen. Irvin McDowell's 30,000-man corps from marching south, instead holding it back to protect Washington. He then detached from McClellan's chain of command McDowell's corps as well as Maj. Gen. Nathaniel Banks's army in the Valley. McClellan would end up on the Peninsula with 40,000 fewer troops than planned.[15]

On the Peninsula itself, weather conditions grew ominous as the Union commander packed to join his men. On March 26 Maj. Gen. John Wool at Fortress Monroe reported deep mud that precluded troop movements. During the afternoon of March 29, a "pelting rain" began that evolved into "torrents" as it continued through the night and into the next morning. At the fort the resident army weather observer recorded three-quarters of an inch of rain. Camped in a plowed field, soldier Charles Brewster of the 10th Massachusetts lamented the great quantities of red mud it produced. These were clay-laden ultisols, unfamiliar in most of the Union but dominant over the face of the Confederacy. When wet, ultisols produce sticky mud the likes of which most Federals had never seen. Unlike northern soils, southern ultisols also fail to produce a more solid layer beneath the surface topsoil, causing wagons, artillery trains, and unfortunate horses to sink deeply into "bottomless" terrain. And this effect was even worse on the Peninsula. Nearly all of the Confederacy's ultisols belong to the udult suborder. Along the relatively flat Virginia coast, however, the suborder aquult dominates. Sandy aquults are found in wet areas near sea level where the water table is near the surface. They are even wetter soils than udults and thus are even more prone to producing "bottomless" mud. Any great quantities of rain quickly turned aquult ultisol roads and fields into quagmires while simultaneously flooding the Peninsula's many streams into so many swamps. Worse, those morasses teemed with mosquitoes carrying malaria. To paraphrase historian Kathryn Shively Meier, weather and climate, coupled with other environmental factors, was primed to become a third combatant on the Peninsula.[16]

On the night of April 2, McClellan arrived at last, and the grand army made its last preparations for marching. That same evening "a tremendous Thunder shower" struck the camps. Undeterred, on April 4, with temperatures in the fifties, 55,000 Federal soldiers took up the march to Richmond and victory on two parallel roads. The columns' initial objective was Yorktown, located on the northern side of the Peninsula. From there as well as fortified forward positions, Confederate major general John Magruder had warded off forces advancing from Fortress Monroe all winter with only about 13,000 men. Stymied by Johnston's works at Manassas and Centreville, McClellan did not intend a repeat performance. His plan for Yorktown was to quickly swing around Magruder's right flank and get in the enemy's rear. While the southern column nearer the James warded off any movement from Richmond, the other would force Yorktown's works and reduce them.[17] The weather mitigated against speed from the very start, however. Rain already had left the roads in poor shape for the first day on the march, and almost immediately the Federal advance literally began to bog down. "The roads were narrow and muddy," Col. Regis De Trobriand of the 55th New York observed, "and the two columns stretched along almost interminably."[18] While the morning itself was "beautiful," according to Brewster, in the afternoon it again began to "rain like guns." The next day was worse. "Many awful mud holes" filled the road, with "the consistency of thick molasses on a hard floor, and awful slippery."[19]

McClellan seemed to be everywhere those two days despite the rain and mud.[20] But the general worried about how the weather had slowed his advance, writing, "the roads are infamous & I have had great difficulty in moving." Still, by the rainy evening of April 6, Union cavalry had reached Yorktown. There the horsemen first caught sight of the Warwick Line, stretching across the wet gray horizon behind a rising Warwick River and marshy ground. Reality revealed the Union maps to be faulty, not showing the actual course of the Warwick, which in truth ran directly across McClellan's line of march. Behind the dirty river, an unwilling army of impressed slave laborers had constructed fourteen miles of engineered works across the Peninsula from river to river.

Imposing river batteries as well as the *Virginia* on the James anchored its flanks and kept the Federal navy from landing men behind it.[21] In effect, as historian Richard Miller pithily describes it, McClellan faced a fortified "isthmus."[22] Intelligence collected on the fly after the general abandoned Urbanna as an objective had told him nothing about the Warwick Line's existence.

Sunday, April 6, broke clear and even lovely aside from yet another brief storm that kept the roads soft and deep. Fair conditions and light winds allowed Thaddeus Lowe to go aloft in his hot-air balloon to get a better look at the Confederate works. On the ground, however, the mud remained deep. "We have no baggage tonight," the commanding general wrote his wife, "our wagons being detained by the bad roads."[23] But by then he had bigger problems than a change of clothes. Unexpectedly facing Magruder's works and fooled yet again by the amateur actor's stagecraft—sights and sounds designed to inflate his numbers in Federal minds—McClellan stopped. After reconnoitering, he decided that assaulting such works would be madness and instead decided to bring up his heavy artillery and lay siege to Yorktown. Historian Stephen Sears, often a critic of McClellan, asserted that this was the safe decision. But that evening came another seeming thunderclap. The general had counted on having McDowell's corps at hand to participate in the siege and assault, but now he learned of Lincoln's decision to keep those troops at Washington.[24]

The real necessities of siege operations, coupled with the continuing rainy weather, rather than timidity now stalled operations. McClellan's men used the next ten days simply preparing for siege warfare. As historian Earl Hess points out, among other things this involved improving or building roads. The big siege guns necessitated relatively flat roads, which in turn meant hand grading. Toiling largely at night, sometimes under sniper fire, Union infantry began working axes, picks, and shovels on April 17 to build batteries. At the same time, Magruder's Confederates labored to strengthen and extend their works, which in fact were far less complete than McClellan believed. In part that meant constructing dams that could flood the Warwick River to a width of fifty feet while rendering any existing fords useless. Richmond had sent reinforcements as well. Arriving on April 14 ahead of his rapidly shifting army, Johnston inspected the works and nonetheless judged them inadequate for a long siege.[25]

All of this labor-intensive work would have been hard enough in normal conditions, but it took place in rainy weather that produced acres of mud.

"The weather has varied between rain and sunshine," a Federal soldier wrote from a steamer in the Chesapeake, "in the proportion of about two hours of sunshine to twenty two of rain."[26] While that was an exaggeration, everyone recognized that it was atypically rainy. At Fortress Monroe the official observer recorded seven days of precipitation back in April 1861, totaling 5.5 inches. In contrast it rained fourteen out of thirty days a year later, although the monthly total actually was lower, 4.3 inches. But it was the frequency of the rain, not its total volume, that made for mud and hard digging. April 1862 was notably cooler as well, with an average high of fifty-five degrees (as opposed to sixty degrees) and a daily mean temperature of fifty-two degrees (as opposed to fifty-seven degrees). Afternoon high temperatures rose into the sixties on April 14 and on into the seventies on the seventeenth, but then a cooling trend beginning on twentieth reduced highs into the fifties (and twice into the upper forties) for the rest of the month. That left wet men feeling cold. And it was stormy. On April 7, just as the work began, a major coastal storm over the bay blew up around noon with such intensity that transports off Fortress Monroe were unable to unload troops. Conditions were no better once the men could step foot on land. Lt. Col. Harry Purviance complained on April 9 that his 85th Pennsylvania could not get to the front due to the roads. It rained each day from April 7 to April 10, always after noon, with close to two inches falling on the tenth alone.[27]

Up the Peninsula, the storm brought muddy misery to soldiers in the field, few of whom relished manual labor under any conditions. Inside the Warwick Line, soaked Confederates, increasingly augmented by Johnston's equally wet arriving army, tried to stay warm and dry in the trenches while knee deep in water. Few had tents, most sleeping beneath "little houses made of blankets."[28] Maj. Gen. Daniel Harvey Hill compared their trials to those that "our Revolutionary sires" suffered at Valley Forge.[29] Lt. Oliver Wendell Holmes Jr. of the 20th Massachusetts complained that the mud at his regiment's camp was knee deep and his men were soaked. "No tents," he continued, "no trunks—no nothing—it has rained like the devil last night all day and tonight and you may guess what the mud is in clayey soil where it was a real annoyance before. Marching will have to be slow, for the roads have constantly to be made or mended for artillery."[30] Some men fended well enough. Six companies of Oliver Norton's 83rd Pennsylvania spent April 26 working on approaches to the Warwick defenses "all day in the rain. . . . It was a very disagreeable day and we came back soaked through, cold and hungry, but a merry a lot of fellows as you ever saw."[31] Others were less jovial. "Rain and mud have outgeneraled the Army of the Potomac the last week," Purviance complained. "The forces about Yorktown have lain inactive, waiting for re-inforecements, especially artillery, which swamp, and morass, swollen into turgid lakes and inland seas, refused to pass."[32]

The muddy, heavy, physically exhausting work took until the end of the month, in part due to what McClellan's chief of artillery called "the peculiarities of the soil and by the continuance of heavy rains during the greater part of the operations."[33] Finally, on April 30—the fourth rainy day out of five—the first siege battery opened up on the Warwick Line. McClellan had designated May 5 for the beginning of the general bombardment, followed two days later by an infantry assault. The Confederates returned fire, but their inferior weapons were no match. That barrage, combined with his concerns about the fortifications and Yankee reinforcements, was enough to convince Johnston that the time had come to beat a quick retreat to Richmond before McClellan overwhelmed his fortifications. May opened cloudy but warmer, with a high of sixty degrees. Seemingly the rain had passed. Johnston wanted to evacuate the very next day, but concerns about his supply train delayed his start for twenty-four hours. On the warm, still fair night of May 3, Confederate artillerymen opened up with everything they had in order to cover the infantry's retreat, then afterward fled, leaving almost eighty mud-locked smoothbore guns in their works. The next morning observers in the balloon reported the enemy works abandoned. Surprised but delighted, McClellan telegraphed Washington, announcing his triumph. His soldiers were less enthused; their month of labor and exposure seemingly had only allowed the Rebels to run to another redoubt.[34]

Retreating from Yorktown, the Confederates marched all day on May 4 along two roads that intersected just east of the old colonial capital of Williamsburg. There they found a wet, reddish wasteland and heavy roads that slowed their columns to a crawl. Maj. Charles Wainwright later described the ground around Williamsburg as "underlain by a bed of shell marl which again lies in a subsoil of heavy clay; the soil above the marl is a very light sand, and in places not over a foot or two thick." He continued, "the immense rains we have had all this spring, sinking directly through the sand and finding no outlet from the mark, have converted it into the consistency of soft mortar; so that when a heavy substance once breaks through the top soil, there is nothing to stop its sinking until it reaches the hard clay."[35] Confederates agreed. "The highways . . . were saturated by the spring rains," Maj. Gen. James Longstreet would later remember, "cut into deep ruts by the haul of heavy trains, and puddled by the tramp of infantry and cavalry. The wood and fallow lands were bogs, with occasional quicksands adding severest labor to the usual toils of battle."[36] As the 8th Virginia's Pvt. Randolph Shotwell happily observed, Confederate feet and wheels left the churned roads in even worse shape for the Federal divisions leading the pursuit, full of "ruts, holes, and muck."[37]

Shotwell was right. Pvt. Edwin Y. Brown of the 1st Massachusetts described the "wretched roads" as "soft and ouzy . . . , cut up and rendered almost impassable by the passage of the enemy's artillery and trains." The day itself had been lovely at first, but clouds began to gather late in the afternoon. Before dark it began to drizzle. After midnight hard showers began, chilling wet men. Rainfall stretched through the darkness and into the new day.[38] By the morning of May 5, Johnston feared that his train would bog down entirely on the one narrow road west, leaving it ripe for capture. Accordingly, he sent Longstreet and about a fourth of the entire command to hold off the Yankees while the rest of the army dragged the wagons to safety through the deepening mud. With the train moving so slowly, Longstreet decided to stop and fight. As Stephen Sears points out, Magruder already had partially constructed a fallback line at Williamsburg, running four miles between two creeks and anchored by a large earthen redoubt that he typically had named for himself. Lacking enough men to use the entire line, Longstreet concentrated on defending Fort Magruder.

At about 7:00 A.M., with the sky overcast and gloomy with thick gray clouds, Brig. Gen. Joseph Hooker's mud-covered men moved against a stiff west wind toward the fort. The rain picked up again, falling so hard that Union gunners could not properly situate their guns or even sight them effectively. Already soaked, the infantry slogged across sodden fields and picked their way through wet abatis. Hooker expected support from his right in the form of Brig. Gen. Edwin Vose "Bull" Sumner's column on the other road from Yorktown, led by Brig. Gen. William F. "Baldy" Smith's brigade, but that division had stopped a mile back. When assistance did not arrive, Hooker wrote a note to Sumner, who sent back nothing more than the countersigned envelope— Hooker later asked for the note back since the rain later destroyed the envelope. Sensing the shift in momentum, Longstreet launched a counterattack that shoved the Federals backward. Some ran for the rear. Brig. Gen. Samuel Heintzelman ordered some drummers to beat a cheerful roll, but their drums were too soaked to make noise. Reinforcements moving up the road sank to their knees. Only a Confederate shortage of cartridges—the ammunition wagons were stuck in the rear, up to their axles in mud—and the midafternoon arrival of Brig. Gen. Philip Kearney's muddy brigade prevented a rout. Together, Hooker and Kearney drove the Confederates back into the abatis as the rain again intensified. Roughly at the same time, the artillery of Brig. Gen. Winfield Scott Hancock's brigade opened up on the Confederate left after a roundabout, two-mile scamper through the dripping woods. Longstreet sent Brig. Gen. Jubal Early's reserve brigade to deal with this new threat. Early attacked clumsily, his men slipping and falling in the muck, which allowed Hancock to counterattack with bayonets, take prisoners, and ultimately hold his position on the flank.[39]

The Battle of Williamsburg ended in stalemate, murky darkness, and continuing drizzle and rain. During the night, having accomplished his main job of protecting the army and its train, Longstreet withdrew. But this was not easy, as both his artillery and wagons were axle-deep in mud. Men tugged at them with ropes, but in the end they had to abandon five more guns and many vehicles and horses; some animals on both sides drowned or died of their futile exertions to escape.[40] The roads themselves were "cut into deep mud by the trains," Longstreet later wrote, "and the sideways [too] by troops far out on either side, making puddles ankle-deep in all directions, so that the march was slow and trying."[41] Shotwell similarly described the night march as horrendous: "roads literally knee-deep in soft mud and slush—and with artillery, wagons, ambulances and footmen all jumbled together in the narrow roads. . . . The clay and sand of the roads was now worked into a liquid mortar," he continued, "which overspread the entire surface, hiding the deep holes cut by heavy gunwheels, until man or beast discovered them by stumbling therein."[42]

May 6 broke fair before the clouds again darkened and brought more rain in the afternoon. D. H. Hill, who commanded the Confederate rear guard that day, described two armies on the brink of collapse as they reeled to the west. "The roads were in truly horrible condition," he wrote. "Horses with difficulty could wade through the mud and slush, and to footmen the task seemed almost impossible. . . . Six miles from Williamsburg we encountered a swamp of the most formidable character [w]here many wagons and ambulances were found abandoned and had to be destroyed by the rear guard. The Yankee pursuit, rendered very cautious by the battle of the day before, ceased altogether at this point."[43] Back at Williamsburg, after a night of "indescribable misery and horror," the Federal army could do little more. Having slept in the mud without fires, the soldiers were rain-soaked, cold, sometimes sick, and hungry. In the wet woods and sodden fields, wounded men and animals continued to moan in pain.[44] Most of the survivors rested; McClellan did not mount a serious pursuit until evening, before then harassing the Confederates with some token cavalry and fire from navy gunboats, which Longstreet termed "hardly annoying."[45] The Union commander blamed the "infamous" state of the roads and the renewed rain for his inactivity. "No signs of stopping," he wrote his wife, "roads awful."[46]

Conditions in the Federal rear indeed were staggeringly bad. Mud covered men from head to foot and sucked up batteries and ammunition wagons. "The roads, and the fields by this time were worked up into mud," Brewster wrote, "knee deep and it would start my long boots partly off, at every step." His 10th Massachusetts then moved to the front "through such horrible mud, that you cannot by any possible means get any idea of it." He also noted a number of abandoned enemy wagons, "many of them stuck in the mud up to the bottoms of them and of dead mules and horses there is no end, and the stench is horrible."[47]

Finally the weather cleared. The next week was fairer and warm, with high temperatures rising into the seventies and even reaching eighty degrees on May 11. Both armies used the break in the weather and the drying roads to make faster headway toward Richmond, even though the heat made for hard and dusty marching. That was especially true for the withdrawing Confederates, whose teams were so worn down that many men carried their belongings on their backs to save the horses and mules. Not surprisingly, the Rebels left a trail of abandoned equipment and effects in their wake. As for the roads, the degree of damage that McClellan's army especially faced behind Johnston was severe. Mud that had been knee deep dried into powder. Some Federals blamed their commander's lack of will for their failure to catch Johnston's army, but the general himself cited the poor state of the roads and a lack of good maps.

The labor at Yorktown and the rigors of Williamsburg also added greatly to the sick detail. McClellan's acerbic medical director, Dr. Charles Tripler, did little to hide his disgust with the state of affairs after the battle. The men had marched to Williamsburg in a "drenching rain" and "with nothing in their haversacks. They had no shelter from the rain, and nothing to eat. The roads were shocking." Not surprisingly, "when the columns were again put into motion a large number of men were thrown on my hands—some of them sick, most of them tired and exhausted. They came straggling in from the rear of the army, without reports, nurses, or subsistence." Overwhelmed by numbers, Tripler, with help from the U.S. Sanitary Commission, sent shiploads of sick men back to Washington and housed the rest in hospitals in Williamsburg.[48]

From the York River Brig. Gen. William B. Franklin's division *had* landed and moved up the Peninsula to West Point but failed to interdict the retreating gray columns. At Norfolk, pressed by the navy and with President Lincoln on hand, the Confederates blew up the *Virginia* and made for Suffolk on a hot, dusty road. By May 13, a hot day with plenty of sun, McClellan had pushed forward to Cumberland Landing on the Pamunkey River, a tributary of the York. There the army halted. Rain returned on the evening of May 14 and continued off and on through the next two days, leaving the roads once again miry and difficult. After this latest weather system passed and the roads again dried, the army returned to the march, aiming for the rain-swollen Chickahominy River, flowing east of Richmond and southeast to the James. Johnston had crossed the Chickahominy on May 16 after learning that the James was open to the enemy. His army now only seven miles from the capital, Johnston hoped to lure McClellan away from the protection of his gunboats and then strike at an opportune moment, assuming that one arose. The Union commander, however, was in no hurry to provide an opening. He planned to meet McDowell's corps, which according to reports finally was on the way overland via Fredericksburg, before attacking the Confederates.[49]

McClellan's cavalry first saw the Chickahominy on a rainy May 20. As the rest of the army slowly closed up and sometimes skirmished with the enemy, McClellan waited for his missing corps. On May 24, however, he learned that it was not coming after all; Lincoln had decided to send McDowell into the Shenandoah Valley. Making matters worse, after several hot days the rain returned. Afternoon thunderstorms hit Union camps on May 22. Then starting with drizzle on the following afternoon, rain fell on four of the next five days, bringing a total of nearly five inches of precipitation. Once again soldiers encountered mud in abundance.[50] On May 24 Wainwright described "a steady, hard rain all day, turning the whole country into a sea of mud and rendering the roads almost impassable." The next day brought "another heavy rain; and a very cold one too. . . . The water comes down most tropically, in sheets instead of detached drops as it does farther north."[51]

During this period, McClellan wrote constantly about rain and the poor state of the roads to explain his slow pace. As May drew to a close, he put his men to work constructing bridges across the Chickahominy. He planned to carefully push his army across the morass and bring his artillery within range of Richmond, but weather and an erroneous report of Confederate activity to the north altered those intentions. On May 26 misty rain and light showers began to fall. The next morning brought torrential rain, two inches falling at Fortress Monroe that day alone, by far the heaviest total of the month so far. Advancing in the mud and through flooded, snake-infested streams and a steady morning downpour heavy enough to snuff out cooking fires, elements of Brig. Gen. Fitz John Porter's new corps slogged fourteen slow miles before overwhelming an isolated Confederate brigade at Hanover Court House, north of Richmond. Tactically a complete victory, the battle's real effect was another story. As historian Stephen Sears maintains, the action delayed the completion of McClellan's advance across the Chickahominy. As a result, Maj. Gen. Erasmus Keyes's sickly IV Corps became isolated west of the rising river near Seven Pines, about a mile southeast of the Fair Oaks station on the railroad from Richmond to West Point. Heintzelman's III Corps was set to follow, but the troops moved slowly through the muck. Sensing an opportunity, Johnston decided to strike the Federals at last. After scouting the front, the Confederate commander issued orders to attack on May 31, using three parallel roads that led to the river. Farthest to the south, Longstreet would open the battle, then the attack would roll to the north.[52]

By then the Peninsula rains had returned with renewed force. May 30 began with a morning fog that receded with rising temperatures to reveal "lowering clouds from horizon to horizon, with scarcely a rift throughout the day."[53] That afternoon at about 4:30 P.M., as IV Corps skirmishers advanced under an artillery barrage, the looming thunderstorm first broke with such force that it halted the advance and left the men scurrying back through an ankle-deep flash flood to their camps.[54] It roared on throughout the night, torrential rains easily penetrating tents while lightning lit the sky; one man in the 44th New York actually died from a lighting strike. High water flooded

Federal camps; a member of Baldy Smith's staff described picket posts knee deep in water. More crucially the fearsome storm raised water levels in the Chickahominy and other waterways so rapidly that the onrushing muddy torrent began to wash away the Federal bridges, leaving only two intact at dawn. According to Col. Wesley Brainerd, who actually tried to erect another bridge during the storm, floodwaters up to a foot in depth extended for a half mile beyond the river's channel. Watching the water rise near his own camps, Johnston deduced that the Chickahominy had to be out of its banks. Brig. Gen. William Pendleton, commanding Confederate artillery, assured him that it would take twenty-four hours for high waters to fall back, thus trapping any Federal forces on the west side of the river. McClellan's army was effectively cut in two, and the trapped, isolated corps could receive little help from the other side.[55]

The next morning, foggy at sunup and sixty-eight degrees at 7:00 A.M., found the area around the river still inundated. Edgar Newcomb of the 19th Massachusetts measured 30 inches of floodwater at his regimental campsite, while Lt. Col. Joseph Kirkland of the 102nd Pennsylvania remembered up to two feet of water on his front. At the other end of the Peninsula, the weather observer at Fortress Monroe recorded 2.25 inches of rain, about a third of the month's entire total. "The unfinished rifle pits in front were filled," Luther Dickey of the 85th Pennsylvania wrote, "and every depression in the roads and elsewhere had become tiny lakes."[56] The sky remained cloudy, and from time to time it drizzled.[57] For the Confederates preparing to march, the view was no better. "The storms had flooded the flat lands," Longstreet remembered, "and the waters as they fell seemed weary of the battle of the elements, and inclined to have a good rest on the soft bed of sand which let them gently down to the substratum of clay."[58] Events of the morning quickly proved that the storm had been less of a boon to the attackers than Johnston had expected. Soldiers on both sides were exhausted from lack of sleep, including one Confederate division commander, Maj. Gen. Benjamin Huger, who slept late and got his men moving even later. The roads were boggy with enough red clay to impede rolling artillery and marching men. Flooded roads caused halts. The surrounding countryside, in some cases knee deep with water (or hip deep on swampier expanses), delayed the attackers as much as Johnston's vague and confusing orders, which soon had some of his columns—including Longstreet's—marching at cross-purposes on the wrong roads. At one point Longstreet halted his men to build a bridge over a fordable creek. In all, it took until the steamy early afternoon (seventy-six degrees at 2:00 P.M.) for the first Confederates to untangle their lines and commence the attack, encountering felled trees and partially built earthworks surrounded by natural moats as they struck. Piecemeal assaults initially succeeded but ultimately failed to dislodge the Federals at Seven Pines. About a mile north at Fair Oaks, in what essentially became a separate battle, Bull Sumner used a still-surviving (but ready to collapse) bridge to cross a division and turn back the Confederate attack there. Again, swollen streams and deep mud impeded both armies, especially their artillery, some of which never even made it to the field. Because of the effects of the storm plus the confusion at headquarters, Johnston never got half of his intended attacking force into action, and he himself fell late in the afternoon, wounded by a bullet and shrapnel.[59]

"Sunday morning, June 1st, dawned as cheerless and chilly as one can imagine," Private Shotwell wrote, "but after a while the sun came out from a bank of clouds, and the occasional bursts of sunshine alternating with dripping showers, added to the ghostliness of the numerous corpses lying about as we moved toward the forest."[60] The Confederate command situation was equally murky. Johnston's second in command, Maj. Gen. Gustavus Smith, had floundered through overnight before launching a renewed attack in the morning. This too failed and was over by noon. Two hours later a worried President Davis ordered Smith to turn over command of the army to Gen. Robert E. Lee.[61] The new commander's first action was to pull the army back toward Richmond. The Federals followed gingerly, with McClellan again citing weather and ground conditions as the chief delaying factors. "I only wait for the river to fall," he confidently wrote Stanton on June 2, "to cross with the rest of the force & make a general attack." Later that day he assured his wife, "the Chickahominy is now falling & I hope we can complete the bridges tomorrow. I can do nothing until that is accomplished." The Peninsula's fierce spring was not done with him, however. That night clouds rolled in. Late on June 4 it rained hard again, continuing through most of the night, followed by four days of rain beginning on the seventh. At Fortress Monroe two inches fell in total, bringing new flooding. The days were hot too, with highs generally in the eighties until plunging into the sixties on June 9. The new rainy spell played havoc with the Federal advance. "Terrible rain storm during the night & morning—not yet cleared off," McClellan wrote Lincoln on June 4. "Chickahominy flooded, bridges in bad condition."[62] Three days later he wrote Stanton that "the Chickahominy River has risen so far as to flood the entire bottoms to the depth of three & four feet. . . . The whole face of the country is a perfect bog entirely impassable for artillery or even cavalry except directly in the narrow roads which renders any general movement either of this or the rebel army utterly out of the question at present until we have more favorable weather."[63]

On the morning of June 10, McClellan wrote his wife again, "it is raining hard & has been for several hours!" Hoping to somehow find God's will expressed in the constant rain, he added, "it is quite certain that there has not been for years & years such a season—it does not come by chance." The rain still prohibited movement, he went on, for "the Chickahominy is so swollen & the valley so covered with water that I cannot establish safe communication over it—then again the ground is so muddy that we cannot use our artillery—the guns sink up to their axle trees." He sounded a similar note to Stanton, admitting: "I am completely checked by the weather. The roads and fields are literally impassable for Artillery, almost so for Infantry. The Chickahominy is in a dreadful state—we have another rain storm on our hands." This was only a delay, however, he assured the secretary. "I shall attack as soon as the weather & ground permit, but there will be a delay—the extent of which no one can foresee, for the season is altogether abnormal."[64]

While historians have either ignored the weather at this stage or else characterized McClellan's assertions as making excuses, many of his men supported his conclusions. One assured his reader, "we can make no advance till return of fine weather."[65] For others, still without shelter as their tents lay in the rear in mud-bound wagons, morale reached a low ebb. What rose in them was a growing conviction that the Southern environment was malevolent. Writing home on June 5, Private Brewster listed his return address, "in the mud near Richmond," and continued, "we are lying in the mud and it rains incessantly and not rains as you have in the north, but torrents, such as you never saw. . . . I am daub with mud from head to foot, my clothes are wet and have been for three days and night[s]."[66] Another Federal narrated a scene "where Jupiter Pluvius seemed to be the only reigning sovereign."[67]

June 11 dawned fair, with temperatures in the sixties. The next day found McClellan hopeful that the rain finally was behind him. "I think we will have good weather now," he wrote home, "it *seems* to have changed for the better." In fact it would rain four more times in June, though lightly enough except for what McClellan called "a terrible storm" on the twenty-fourth. Steamy heat now became the main weather story. On June 13 the high at Fortress Monroe reached eighty-five degrees. Although temperatures fell back into the seventies from June 16 through June 23, heat and humidity characterized the rest of the month.[68] McClellan planned to use the better weather to reconstruct bridges lost to "flood & fire" before moving forward, but he warned Stanton that it would take a good month to complete the work. Informed that McDowell's forces would be sent to him after all, the general advised Stanton to send them by water, for the roads were still in terrible shape. He reiterated the bad state of the roads on June 15, when an afternoon rain set back his plans. "This will retard our operations somewhat," he warned Stanton, "as a little rain causes the ground in this section to become soft and boggy rendering it impossible to move Artillery except directly in the travelled roads. . . . it is absolutely necessary that we should have some few days of dry weather to make the ground firm enough to sustain our horses & guns."[69]

Desperate to save his capital, Lee had neither the time nor the patience to hope for dry weather. As Davis's advisor, he had opposed Johnston's steady withdrawal to Richmond. Now that he commanded the army, Lee was determined to retreat no more. He presented a plan on June 5 that in broad outline involved using some of his men to cover Richmond while leading the rest on a counteroffensive. Holding the capital with only part of the army meant constructing new lines of earthworks east of the city. Working in the same heat, mud, and dust that discouraged their foe, the Confederates griped constantly about how the "King of Spades" made them work (literally) like slaves. Finally, after midnight on June 12—and after the first day following the rainy spell—Brig. Gen. J. E. B. Stuart led his cavalry north from the city in order to gather intelligence about Porter's corps and the Federal right flank. Stuart and his men in the end would ride completely around the Federal army, returning with valuable information. McClellan's right beyond the Chickahominy was in the air, open to attack, and did not extend far enough north to block Confederate reinforcements. Even better, the York River Railroad—the spine of McClellan's supply line—also was vulnerable to attack. As Stephen Sears notes, a successful strike would not only turn McClellan's flank but sever his communications as well. Now all Lee needed were the proper reinforcements to overwhelm Porter. He thus called upon Stonewall Jackson, who for the last month had defied both the enemy and torrential rain in the Shenandoah.

A season of heat and storms continued during the Seven Days' Battles as

Lee stopped McClellan and saved the Confederate capital. Two years would pass before a Federal army returned to the scene with, as some officers noted in 1864, more favorable weather conditions than McClellan ever enjoyed. The observations were prescient. Frequent rain and ultisol mud bedeviled McClellan in 1862 to a degree that cannot be dismissed. Acknowledging Little Mac's very real personality flaws or the cancerous politics of his army's commanders does not negate the fact that the soggy spring of 1862 would have been the worst season of the war for any general trying to move a massive army up the Peninsula. From Samuel Curtis's campaign in Arkansas and Missouri to Ulysses S. Grant's actions on the Cumberland and Tennessee Rivers, unusually heavy late winter and spring precipitation shaped campaigns to a degree official Washington never grasped nor forgave. So did the blistering summer drought that followed, an event that also cannot be ignored when reviewing Gen. Braxton Bragg's Kentucky campaign or Grant's operations in northern Mississippi.[70]

Yet with rare recent exceptions, historians have been reluctant to examine the relationship between the Civil War and its physical environment. Most discussions of weather narrowly relate to one battle or campaign without connections to others. Robert K. Krick's *Civil War Weather in Virginia* remains the only book in the field solely devoted to the subject. While a vital reference source, even it is ultimately narrowly focused.[71] The task will not be easy or familiar. Integrating environmental history into the sectional conflict demands interdisciplinary and intradisciplinary conversations with meteorologists, soil engineers, and other scientists as well as with other historians. Yet the effort will be worthwhile if it helps us better understand what really happened on those bloody—and often muddy—hallowed grounds. The mud-soaked men of the Army of the Potomac, slogging through the domain of Jupiter Pluvius toward the heat and thunderstorms of the Seven Days, understood that reality all too well.

NOTES

1. Michael Peck, "Commanders in Chaos: The 5 Worst Generals in U.S. History," Nov. 8, 2014, *The National Interest*, http://nationalinterest.org/feature/commanders-chaos-the-5-worst-generals-us-history-11630, accessed Dec. 10, 2015.

2. Jeff Danelek, "Top 10 Worst Military Leaders in History," Feb. 15, 2011, *TopTenz*, http://www.toptenz.net/top-10-worst-military-leaders-in-history.php, accessed Dec. 10, 2015.

3. John Swansburg, "The Civil War's Most Chicken General," *Slate,* http://www.slate.com/articles/arts/books/2012/08/richard_slotkin_s_the_long_road_to_antietam_reviewed_.html, accessed Dec. 10, 2015.

4. Glenn David Brasher, *The Peninsula Campaign and the Necessity of Emancipation: African Americans and the Fight for Freedom* (Chapel Hill: University of North Carolina Press, 2012); Ethan S. Rafuse, *McClellan's War: The Failure of Moderation in the Struggle for the Union* (Bloomington: Indiana University Press, 2005); Donald Stoker, *The Grand Design: Strategy and the American Civil War* (New York: Oxford University Press, 2010).

5. James M. McPherson, *Battle Cry of Freedom: The Civil War Era* (New York: Oxford University Press, 1988), 423–27, 461–71; McPherson, *Ordeal by Fire: The Civil War and Reconstruction* (New York: Alfred A. Knopf, 1982), 236–39, 244–48 (quotations 238, 246). For some other noted examples, see Richard E. Beringer et al., *Why the South Lost the Civil War* (Athens: University of Georgia Press, 1986), 143–55 [a slightly more favorable assessment]; Stephen W. Sears, *George B. McClellan: The Young Napoleon* (New York: Ticknor and Fields, 1988); Sears, *To the Gates of Richmond: The Peninsula Campaign* (Boston: Houghton Mifflin, 1992); and Russell F. Weigley, *A Great Civil War: A Military and Political History, 1861–1865* (Bloomington: Indiana University Press, 2000), 122–26, 129–34.

6. Mike Davis, *Late Victorian Holocausts: El Niño Famines and the Making of the Third World* (London: Verso, 2001), 12–15, 17–18, 213–38; Bernard Mergen, *Weather Matters: An American Cultural History since 1900* (Lawrence: University Press of Kansas, 2008), 23–25, 40–41. The National Oceanic and Atmospheric Administration (NOAA) maintains an extensive webpage on ENSO; see "El Niño & La Niña (El Niño–Southern Oscillation)," Climate.gov, http://www.elnino.noaa.gov/lanina.html, accessed June 27, 2014. For ENSO and the Wilson's Creek campaign, see Rudi Keller, "MU Expert Studies Civil War Weather," July 11, 2011, *Columbia (MO) Daily Tribune,* http://m.columbiatribune.com/news/local/mu-expert-studies-civil-war-weather/article_6fe8c0e2-97bc-5f92-828f-708799996808.html, accessed June 21, 2014; and "The Science of Backward Weather Forecasting," May 6, 2010, *Mizzou Weekly* 31, no. 30, http://mizzouweekly.missouri.edu/archive/2010/31-30/the-science-of-backward-weather-forecasting/index.php, accessed June 21, 2014. See also Cary Mock, Columbia, SC, email messages to the author, Jan. 6, 2016.

7. Here I refer to my own research for a forthcoming book on the wider subject of Civil War weather.

8. Rafuse, *McClellan's War,* 175–93; Sears, *To the Gates of Richmond,* 7–9, 16–17. See also David W. Blight, ed., *When This Cruel War Is Over: The Civil War Letters of Charles Henry Brewster* (Amherst: University of Massachusetts Press, 1992), 99–100; William Child, *A History of the Fifth Regiment New Hampshire Volunteers in the American Civil War, 1861–1865. In Two Parts* (Bristol, NH: R. W. Musgrove, 1893), 44–46; Newton Martin Curtis, *From Bull Run to Chancellorsville: The Story of the Sixteenth New York Infantry together with Personal Reminiscences* (New York: G. P. Putnam's Sons, 1906), 91; Luther C. Furst Diary, 16, Harrisburg Civil War Round Table Collection, U.S. Army Military History Institute, Carlisle, PA [cited hereafter as HCWRTC, USAMHI]; Allan Nevins, ed., *A Diary of Battle: The Personal Journals of Colonel Charles S. Wainwright 1861–1865* (New York: Harcourt, Brace and World, 1962), 21, 25.

9. Rafuse, *McClellan's War*, 193–97; Sears, *To the Gates of Richmond*, 16–18.

10. William C. Davis, *Duel between the First Ironclads* (Garden City, NY: Doubleday, 1975), 60–65, 78–79.

11. Earl J. Hess, *Field Armies and Fortifications in the Civil War: The Eastern Campaigns, 1861–1864* (Chapel Hill: University of North Carolina Press, 2005), 71; Rafuse, *McClellan's War*, 195–96; Sears, *To the Gates of Richmond*, 18–20; Georgetown, District of Columbia, Mar. 1862, Reel 81, RG 27.5.7, National Archives and Records Administration–College Park [cited hereafter as NARA-CP]; Robert K. Krick, *Civil War Weather in Virginia* (Tuscaloosa: University of Alabama Press, 2007), 49, 51; William H. Stewart, *A Pair of Blankets: War-time History in Letters to the Young People of the South*, ed. Benjamin H. Trask (Wilmington, NC: Broadfoot, 1990), 45.

12. Child, *Fifth Regiment New Hampshire*, 46; Regis De Trobriand, *Four Years in the Army of the Potomac*, trans. George K. Douchy (Boston: Ticknor, 1889), 154–58; Thomas W. Hyde, *Following the Greek Cross; or, Memories of the Sixth Army Corps* (Boston: Houghton, Mifflin, 1894), 36–37; Nevins, *Diary of Battle*, 27; Oliver Willcox Norton, *Army Letters, 1861–1865. Being Extracts from Private Letters to Relatives and Friends from a Soldier in the Field during the Late Civil War, with an Appendix Retaining Copies of Some Official Documents, Papers and Addresses of Later Date* (Chicago: O. L. Deming, 1903), 59; Robert Hunt Rhodes, ed., *All for the Union: A History of the 2nd Rhode Island Volunteer Infantry in the War of the Great Rebellion, as Told by the Diary and Letters of Elisha Hunt Rhodes Who Enlisted as a Private in '61 and Rose to the Command of His Regiment* (Lincoln, RI: Andrew Mowbray, 1985), 59–60.

13. Blight, *When This Cruel War Is Over*, 101.

14. Georgetown, District of Columbia, Mar., Apr. 1862, Reel 81, RG 27.5.7, NARA-CP; Krick, *Civil War Weather*, 51, 54; De Trobriand, *Four Years*, 159, 163; Luther Dickey, *History of the Eighty-fifth Regiment Pennsylvania Volunteer Infantry 1861–1865* (New York: J. C. and W. E. Powers, 1915), 23; Furst Diary, 17, HCWRTC, USAMHI; Ed Malles, ed., *Bridge Building in Wartime: Colonel Wesley Brainerd's Memoir of the 50th New York Volunteer Engineers* (Knoxville: University of Tennessee Press, 1997), 57–58; Nevins, *Diary of Battle*, 28–30; Rhodes, *All for the Union*, 61; Mat Richards, Camp Northumberland, to Sophie, Mar. 30, 1862, M. Edgar Richards Correspondence, Box 97, Civil War Miscellaneous Collection, USAMHI [hereafter cited as CWMC, USAMHI]; James I. Robertson, ed., *The Civil War Letters of General Robert McAllister* (New Brunswick: New Jersey Civil War Centennial Commission by Rutgers University Press, 1965), 121, 128; Emil and Ruth Rosenblatt, eds., *Hard Marching Every Day: The Civil War Letters of Private Wilbur Fisk, 1861–1865* (Lawrence: University Press of Kansas, 1983), 11–14; David S. Sparks, ed., *Inside Lincoln's Army: The Diary of Marsena Rudolph Patrick, Provost Marshal General, Army of the Potomac* (New York: Thomas Yoseloff, 1964), 55, 59, 61–63; Russell C. White, ed., *The Civil War Diary of Wyman S. White, First Sergeant of Company F, 2nd United States Sharpshooters Regiment, 1861–1865* (Baltimore: Butternut and Blue, 1991), 46–48; Rafuse, *McClellan's War*, 196–204; Sears, *To the Gates of Richmond*, 23–35.

15. U.S. War Department, *The War of the Rebellion: A Compilation of the Official Records of the Union and Confederate Armies*, 70 vols. in 128 pts. (Washington, DC: Government Printing Office, 1884), ser. 1, 12(1):350 [hereafter cited as *OR*, all references to ser. 1]; Archie P. McDonald, ed., *Make Me a Map of the Valley: The Civil War Journal of Stonewall Jackson's Topographer* (Dallas:

Southern Methodist University Press, 1973), 8; Alonzo H. Quint, The *Record of the Second Mas-sachusetts Infantry, 1861–65* (Boston: J. P. Walker, 1867), 73; Georgetown, District of Columbia, Mar. 1862, Reel 81, RG 27.5.7, NARA-CP; Krick, *Civil War Weather,* 49, 51; Rafuse, *McClellan's War,* 202–7; James I. Robertson Jr., *Stonewall Jackson: The Man, The Soldier, The Legend* (New York: Macmillan, 1997), 339–47; Sears, *George B. McClellan,* 170–72; Sears, *To the Gates of Richmond,* 32–34, 39; Robert G. Tanner, *Stonewall in the Valley: Thomas J. "Stonewall" Jackson's Shenandoah Valley Campaign, Spring 1862* (Garden City, NY: Doubleday, 1976), 118–32.

16. *OR,* 11(3):39; Fortress Monroe, Va., Mar. 1862, Reel 522, RG 27.5.7, NARA-CP; Blight, *When This Cruel War Is Over,* 104; "Ultisols," U.S. Department of Agriculture Natural Re-sources Conservation Service, http://www.nrcs.usda.gov/wps/portal/nrcs/detail/soils/survey/class/?cid=nrcs142p2_053609, accessed Jan. 27, 2015; "Distribution Maps of Dominant Soil Orders," U.S. Department of Agriculture Natural Resources Conservation Service, http://www.nrcs.usda.gov/wps/portal/nrcs/detail/soils/survey/class/?cid=nrcs142p2_053589, accessed Jan. 29, 2015; Andrew McIlwaine Bell, *Mosquito Soldiers: Malaria, Yellow Fever, and the Course of the American Civil War* (Baton Rouge: Louisiana State University Press, 2010), 72–75; Joey Shaw, Auburn, Ala., email message to the author, July 3, 2015; Kathryn Shively Meier, *Nature's Civil War: Common Soldiers and the Environment in 1862 Virginia* (Chapel Hill: University of North Carolina Press, 2013), 45.

17. Fortress Monroe, Va., Apr. 1862, Reel 522, RG 27.5.7, NARA-CP; Hess, *Field Armies and Fortifications,* 71; Rafuse, *McClellan's War,* 203–4; Sears, *George B. McClellan,* 172; Sears, *To the Gates of Richmond,* 28–31.

18. De Trobriand, *Four Years,* 166. See also *OR,* 11(1):227, 297, 358.

19. Blight, *When This Cruel War Is Over,* 108.

20. A. B. Weymouth, ed., *A Memorial Sketch of Lieut. Edgar M. Newcomb, of the Nineteenth Mass. Vols.* (Malden, MA: Alvin C. Brown, 1883), 54–55 (quotation 55). See also De Trobriand, *Four Years,* 182.

21. Stephen W. Sears, ed., *The Civil War Papers of George B. McClellan: Selected Correspon-dence, 1860–1865* (New York: Ticknor and Fields, 1989), 236; Hess, *Field Armies and Fortifications,* 73–74; Rafuse, *McClellan's War,* 203–5; Sears, *George B. McClellan,* 174–76; Sears, *To the Gates of Richmond,* 24–27; Brasher, *Peninsula Campaign,* 87–89, 98–99, 107–11.

22. Richard F. Miller, *Harvard's Civil War: A History of the Twentieth Massachusetts Volunteer Infantry* (Hanover, NH: University Press of New England, 2005), 111.

23. Fortress Monroe, Va., Apr. 1862, Reel 522, RG 27.5.7, NARA-CP; Sears, *Papers of McClel-lan,* 229, 230. See also Child, *Fifth Regiment New Hampshire,* 51; De Trobriand, *Four Years,* 168; Betsy Fleet and John D. P. Fuller, eds., *Green Mount: A Virginia Plantation Family during the Civil War: Being the Journal of Benjamin Robert Fleet and Letters of His Family* (Lexington: University of Kentucky Press, 1962), 119; and Sears, *To the Gates of Richmond,* 41–43.

24. Rafuse, *McClellan's War,* 207–8; Sears, *George B. McClellan,* 174–76, 178–79; Sears, *To the Gates of Richmond,* 173–80; Hess, *Field Armies and Fortifications,* 73–74.

25. *OR,* 11(1):275; Hess, *Field Armies and Fortifications,* 73–84; Sears, *To the Gates of Richmond,* 48–50; Craig L. Symonds, *Joseph E. Johnston: A Civil War Biography* (New York: W. W. Norton, 1992), 148–49.

26. Mat Richards to Sophie, Steamer *Spaulding*, Apr. 21, 1862, M. Edgar Richards Correspondence, Box 97, CWMC, USAMHI. See also *OR*, 11(1):228, 11(3):116, 124.

27. Fortress Monroe, Va., Apr. 1861, Apr. 1862, Reel 522, RG 27.5.7, NARA-CP; Blight, *When This Cruel War Is Over*, 113, 116; Child, *Fifth Regiment New Hampshire*, 52; Dickey, *Eighty-fifth Pennsylvania*, 30; Nevins, *Diary of Battle*, 32, 34; Robertson, *Civil War Letters of General Robert McAllister*, 136–37, 142.

28. Guy R. Everson and Edward H. Simpson Jr., eds. *"Far, Far from Home": The Wartime Letters of Dick and Tally Simpson, Third South Carolina Volunteers* (New York: Oxford University Press, 1994), 117. See also Jubal Anderson Early, *War Memoirs: Autobiographical Sketch and Narrative of the War between the States*, ed. with an introduction by Frank E. Vandiver (Bloomington: Indiana University Press, 1960), 67; Susan P. Lee, *Memoir of William Nelson Pendleton, D.D.* (Philadelphia: J. B. Lippincott, 1893; reprint, Harrisonburg, VA: Sprinkle, 1991), 176–77; Carol Kettenburg Dubbs, *Defend This Old Town: Williamsburg during the Civil War* (Baton Rouge: Louisiana State University Press, 2002), 72.

29. *OR*, 11(1):606.

30. Mark DeWolfe Howe, ed., *Touched with Fire: Civil War Letters and Diary of Oliver Wendell Holmes, Jr., 1861–1864* (Cambridge, MA: Harvard University Press, 1947), 39.

31. Norton, *Army Letters*, 73. See also Fortress Monroe, Va., Apr. 1862, Reel 522, RG 27.5.7, NARA-CP.

32. Dickey, *Eighty-fifth Pennsylvania*, 31.

33. *OR*, 11(1):348.

34. Ibid., 275, 342–43, 383, 602; Fortress Monroe, Va., Apr., May 1862, Reel 522, RG 27.5.7, NARA-CP; Robertson, *Civil War Letters of General Robert McAllister*, 146; Hess, *Field Armies and Fortifications*, 86–91; Sears, *To the Gates of Richmond*, 57–68; Symonds, *Joseph E. Johnston*, 152–53.

35. Nevins, *Diary of Battle*, 58.

36. James Longstreet, *From Manassas to Appomattox: Memoirs of the Civil War in America*, ed. with an introduction by James I. Robertson (Bloomington: Indiana University Press, 1960), 71. See also "Diaries of John Waldrop, Second Company, and William Y. Mordecai, Second Company, Combined," *Contributions to a History of the Richmond Howitzers Battalion*, Pamphlet 3 (Richmond: Carlton McCarthy, 1884), 37; J. G. deRoulhac Hamilton, ed., *The Papers of Randolph Abbott Shotwell*, vol. 1 (Raleigh: North Carolina Historical Commission, 1929), 190; Sears, *To the Gates of Richmond*, 68–69.

37. Hamilton, *Papers of Randolph Abbott Shotwell*, 190. See also Dubbs, *Defend This Old Town*, 81.

38. Edwin Y. Brown, "4 and 5 May 1862 Description of the Battle of Williamsburg," 2–3 (quotation, 2), Edwin Y. Brown Papers, Digital Projects, Swem Library, College of William and Mary, http://transcribe.swem.wm.edu/items/show/2803, accessed Mar. 22, 2018; Dickey, *Eighty-fifth Pennsylvania*, 36, 37; Hamilton, *Papers of Randolph Abbott Shotwell*, 190; Nevins, *Diary of Battle*, 47; Dubbs, *Defend This Old Town*, 88; Sears, *To the Gates of Richmond*, 70; Symonds, *Joseph E. Johnston*, 153–54.

39. *OR*, 11(1):19, 20, 23, 234–35, 275, 286, 295, 300, 424, 429, 430, 435, 451, 458, 462, 469, 470, 475, 476, 477, 481, 492, 501, 502, 508, 509, 511, 516, 520, 532, 534, 538, 539, 541, 559, 560, 595, 597, 602; Fortress Monroe, Va., May 1862, Reel 522, RG 27.5.7, NARA-CP; Brown, "4 and 5

May 1862 Description of the Battle of Williamsburg," 7, 9; De Trobriand, *Four Years*, 191; Hamilton, *Papers of Randolph Abbott Shotwell*, 190, 197; Hyde, *Following the Greek Cross*, 50; Joseph E. Johnston, *Narrative of Military Operations, Directed, during the Late War between the States* (New York: D. Appleton, 1874), 120; Mary Lasswell, comp. and ed., *Rags and Hope: The Recollections of Val C. Giles Four Years with Hood's Brigade, Fourth Texas Infantry, 1861–1865* (New York: Coward-McCann, 1961), 94, 95; Longstreet, *From Manassas to Appomattox*, 72; Nevins, *Diary of Battle*, 49; Dubbs, *Defend This Old Town*, 88–172; Hess, *Field Armies and Fortifications*, 92–95; Sears, *Papers of McClellan*, 255–56; Sears, *To the Gates of Richmond*, 70–82.

40. *OR*, 11(1):23, 492; Brown, "4 and 5 May 1862 Description of the Battle of Williamsburg," 9; Blight, *When This Cruel War Is Over*, 130; De Trobriand, *Four Years*, 194, 204; Hamilton, *Papers of Randolph Abbott Shotwell*, 197; Hyde, *Following the Greek Cross*, 50–52; Edgar Warfield, *A Confederate Soldier's Memoirs* (Richmond: Masonic Home, 1936), 85.

41. Longstreet, *From Manassas to Appomattox*, 79.

42. Hamilton, *Papers of Randolph Abbott Shotwell*, 199–200.

43. *OR*, 11(1):605. See also Fortress Monroe, Va., May 1862, Reel 522, RG 27.5.7, NARA-CP.

44. Dickey, *Eighty-fifth Pennsylvania*, 43. See also *OR*, 11(1):23, 497, 498, 541, 566, 572.

45. Fortress Monroe, Va., May 1862, Reel 522, RG 27.5.7, NARA-CP; Longstreet, *From Manassas to Appomattox*, 79. See also Furst Diary, 19–20, HCWRTC, USAMHI; Nevins, *Diary of Battle*, 57; and Weymouth, *Memorial Sketch*, 59.

46. Sears, *Papers of McClellan*, 255, 256.

47. Blight, *When This Cruel War Is Over*, 122–23, 130. See also *OR*, 11(3):139; Child, *Fifth Regiment New Hampshire*, 57; Malles, *Bridge Building*, 66; Rhodes, *All for the Union*, 64; and Sears, *Papers of McClellan*, 256, 257.

48. *OR*, 11(1):185, 458.

49. Ibid., 24; Fortress Monroe, Va., May 1862, Reel 522, RG 27.5.7, NARA-CP; Blight, *When This Cruel War Is Over*, 125, 129; Child, *Fifth Regiment New Hampshire*, 58; Curtis, *First Bull Run to Chancellorsville*, 104; De Trobriand, *Four Years*, 213; "Diaries of Waldrop," 38; Dickey, *Eighty-fifth Pennsylvania*, 52, 53; Everson and Simpson, *"Far, Far from Home,"* 122; Fleet and Fuller, *Green Mount*, 124, 125; John B. Jenkins to Mary Benjamin, Cumberland Landing, May 17, 1862, John B. Jenkins Letters, Box 1, Folder 9, Henry C. Hoar Memorial Collection, 1861–87, Acc. 1992.46, Digital Projects, Swem Library, College of William and Mary, http://transcribe.swem.wm.edu/items/show/41, accessed Mar. 22, 2018; Laswell, ed., *Rags and Hope*, 98; Nevins, *Diary of Battle*, 60; Westwood A. Todd Reminiscence 722-z, 10, Southern Historical Collection, University of North Carolina at Chapel Hill [cited hereafter as SHC-UNC]; Rafuse, *McClellan's War*, 211–16; Sears, *Papers of McClellan*, 257, 267, 268, 271; Sears, *To the Gates of Richmond*, 87–110; Symonds, *Joseph E. Johnston*, 158–59.

50. *OR*, 11(1):24, 661, 11(3):174, 175, 184; Fortress Monroe, Va., May 1862, Reel 522, RG 27.5.7, NARA-CP; Blight, *When This Cruel War Is Over*, 134, 135, 137, 138; Dickey, *Eighty-fifth Pennsylvania*, 54–60; Furst Diary, 23, HCWRTC, USAMHI; Nevins, *Diary of Battle*, 68–71; Robertson, *Civil War Letters of General Robert McAllister*, 161–62; Sears, *Papers of McClellan*, 275–78; Joseph S. C. Taber Diary, 27, *Civil War Times Illustrated* Collection, USAMHI.

51. Nevins, *Diary of Battle,* 70, 71. See also Lee, *Memoir of William Nelson Pendleton,* 184; Spencer Glasgow Welch, *A Confederate Surgeon's Letters to his Wife* (New York: Neale, 1911), 10; and Sears, *To the Gates of Richmond,* 110–17.

52. *OR,* 11(1):33–34, 195, 240, 680, 682, 697, 698, 700, 702, 708, 710, 712, 717, 722, 736, 744; Miller, *Harvard's Civil War,* 127; Sears, *To the Gates of Richmond,* 117–20; Symonds, *Joseph E. Johnston,* 160–63.

53. Dickey, *Eighty-fifth Pennsylvania,* 63. See also Miller, *Harvard's Civil War,* 126.

54. Dickey, *Eighty-fifth Pennsylvania,* 64. See also *OR,* 11(1):873; Blight, *When This Cruel War Is Over,* 141; and Fleet and Fuller, *Green Mount,* 129, 130.

55. *OR,* 11(1):38, 112, 764, 813, 937, 11(3):685; Child, *Fifth Regiment New Hampshire,* 69, 76, 87; Curtis, *From Bull Run to Chancellorsville,* 111; Dickey, *Eighty-fifth Pennsylvania,* 67; Hyde, *Following the Greek Cross,* 63; Longstreet, *From Manassas to Appomattox,* 88; Malles, *Bridge Building,* 69–70; Norton, *Army Letters,* 82; Gustavus W. Smith, *The Battle of Seven Pines* (New York: C. G. Crawford, 1891), 18, 21, 144; James H. Wood, *The War: Stonewall Jackson, His Campaigns, and Battles, the Regiment, as I Saw Them* (Cumberland, MD: Eddy, n.d.), 81–82; Sears, *To the Gates of Richmond,* 117–21; Symonds, *Joseph E. Johnston,* 160–67.

56. Dickey, *Eighty-fifth Pennsylvania,* 67. See also *OR,* 11(1):895; Fortress Monroe, Va., May 1862, Reel 522, RG 27.5.7, NARA-CP; and Weymouth, *Memorial Sketch,* 66.

57. Furst Diary, 24, HCWRTC, USAMHI.

58. Longstreet, *From Manassas to Appomattox,* 91. See also Hamilton, *Papers of Randolph Abbott Shotwell,* 214.

59. *OR,* 11(1):41, 42, 243, 767, 778, 794, 795, 796, 802, 804, 943, 947, 958, 968, 988; Fortress Monroe, Va., May 1862, Reel 522, RG 27.5.7, NARA-CP; Blight, *When This Cruel War Is Over,* 141; Dickey, *Eighty-fifth Pennsylvania,* 67; Johnston, *Narrative,* 133–34, 136, 140, 142; Hamilton, *Papers of Randolph Abbott Shotwell,* 214; Lasswell, *Rags and Hope,* 101–3; Hess, *Field Armies and Fortifications,* 101–5; Sears, *To the Gates of Richmond,* 120–40; Symonds, *Joseph E. Johnston,* 166–72.

60. Hamilton, *Papers of Randolph Abbott Shotwell,* 216.

61. Sears, *To the Gates of Richmond,* 140–45.

62. Sears, *Papers of McClellan,* 286, 287. See also *OR,* 11(1):836; Fortress Monroe, Va., June 1862, Reel 522, RG 27.5.7, NARA-CP; "Diaries of Waldrop," 39; Dickey, *Eighty-fifth Pennsylvania,* 173; Brian K. Burton, *Extraordinary Circumstances: The Seven Days Battles* (Bloomington: Indiana University Press, 2001), 14; Sears, *To the Gates of Richmond,* 146–49.

63. Sears, *Papers of McClellan,* 291. See also *OR,* 11(1):46.

64. Sears, *Papers of McClellan,* 291, 294, 295, 297; *OR,* 11(3):223.

65. Weymouth, *Memorial Sketch,* 67–68. See also McPherson, *Battle Cry of Freedom,* 464; Rafuse, *McClellan's War,* 218–19; Sears, *George B. McClellan,* 196–201; and Sears, *To the Gates of Richmond,* 146–50, 158–59.

66. Blight, *When This Cruel War Is Over,* 146.

67. Dickey, *Eighty-fifth Pennsylvania,* 173.

68. Sears, *Papers of McClellan,* 288, 307. See also Fortress Monroe, Va., June 1862, Reel 522, RG 27.5.7, NARA-CP; "Diaries of Waldrop," 39–40; Austin C. Dobbins, ed. *Grandfather's Journal:*

Company B, Sixteenth Mississippi Infantry Volunteers, Harris's Brigade, Mahone's Division, Hill's Corps, A.N.V., May 27, 1861–July 15, 1865 (Dayton, OH: Morningside House, 1988), 85–88; Fleet and Fuller, *Green Mount*, 139; Richard Waldrop to Mother, Ashland, Va., June 26, 1862, Richard Woolfolk Waldrop Papers 02268-z, SHC-UNC.

69. Sears, *Papers of McClellan*, 288, 300.

70. Lee, *Memoir of William Nelson Pendleton*, 188; Sears, *To the Gates of Richmond*, 151–56, 167–74.

71. Krick, *Civil War Weather*.

"YOUR GOLDEN OPPORTUNITY IS GONE"

George Gordon Meade, the Expectations of Decisive Battle,
and the Road to Williamsport

Jennifer M. Murray

N EAR 3:00 ON THE MORNING of June 28, 1863, Col. James Hardie, a
staff officer to Gen. in Chief Henry Halleck, arrived at the tent of Maj.
Gen. George Gordon Meade. The Army of the Potomac had been maneuvering
and marching north for weeks while Gen. Robert E. Lee's Army of Northern
Virginia crossed the Potomac River into Maryland and marched on into Pennsylvania. A clash with the Confederate invaders seemed imminent. Meade,
commanding the Union V Corps, had positioned his troops slightly south of
Frederick, Maryland. Surprised at the colonel's untimely arrival, the general
presumed that he had been relieved of command. Instead Hardie presented
Meade with an order from Pres. Abraham Lincoln placing the Pennsylvanian
in charge of the Army of the Potomac effective immediately.[1] Lest the newly
appointed commander be unaware of the momentous circumstances that lay
before him, Halleck summarized: "Considering the circumstances, no one
ever received a more important command."[2]

Over the course of the ensuing three weeks, Meade would lead the Army of
the Potomac to its most significant victory to date. The Battle of Gettysburg, July
1–3, proved a pivotal Union victory. Upon hearing of the repulse of Lee's forces,
Northern civilians and newspapers rejoiced in Meade's great victory. When the
commanding general returned to Frederick just days after the battle, scores of
residents clamored to catch a glimpse of the victorious general, and several
ladies presented him with wreaths and bouquets.[3] Meade's decline in prominence, however, came as rapidly as his assent to command. By July 14, a mere
eleven days following the battle's climatic assault known as Pickett's Charge,
Lee's beleaguered army rested in relative safety south of the Potomac River.

71

Events from July 4 to July 14 offer an occasion to move beyond a mere re-counting of familiar details of the operational and tactical maneuvers of the two armies and probe important, if not timeless, questions of the definitions of victory and defeat, the expectations of decisive battle, and the dynamics of civil-military relations. At the confluence of these questions stood Meade, whose performance during the campaign endures as one of the most controversial of the war. To be sure, disappointment in his inability to *destroy*, not merely *defeat*, the Southern army spread throughout the North and quickly defined the atmosphere in Washington, D.C. Detractors found Meade's leadership overly cautious, culminating in dilatory action at Williamsport, Maryland, in the final days of the campaign. Upon hearing of Lee's escape across the Potomac, Lincoln, coveting a battle of annihilation, wrote to his commanding general, "Your golden opportunity is gone, and I am distressed immeasurably because of it."[4]

The pursuit to Williamsport offers an opportunity to probe definitions of victory and defeat and explore how military and civilian actors understood these meanings. As importantly, the Federal pursuit and the desire for decisive victory must be situated within a broader military history context, particularly within traditions of eighteenth- and nineteenth-century armies. Dissatisfaction with Meade's conduct and the seemingly hallowed victory at Gettysburg rests in misplaced expectations of a battle of annihilation or the ability of the Army of the Potomac to execute a relentless pursuit culminating with the destruction of the Confederate army. Meade's contemporaries as well as scores of historians have judged the general's actions and crafted his legacy on his inability to deliver a conclusive blow to Lee's retreating army. Criticism stems from a narrow interpretive assessment; few of Meade's detractors have placed the pursuit within a broader historical context. Using such a wider perspective illustrates two critical points that more accurately, and objectively, contextualize Meade's leadership during the Gettysburg Campaign. First, a broader study of military history readily shows the difficulty commanders face in achieving a decisive battlefield victory. Second, executing a successful pursuit is one of the most complex operations for an army and, like decisive battlefield victories, are incredibly rare. From this wider context, then, Northerners, including President Lincoln, expected Meade to accomplish a rare military feat.[5]

The quest for a "decisive" military victory preoccupied nineteenth-century Americans, both civilians and soldiers. Yet decisive battlefield victories are incredibly uncommon, both within American and European military history. The Napoleonic Wars offer a few examples. In December 1805 Napoleon achieved a decisive victory at Austerlitz against Austrian and Russian forces. There allied forces suffered approximately 33 percent casualties, and Napoleon extracted an armistice that effectively ended the Third Coalition. He later described this battle as the "most splendid of all I have fought."[6] Still, Napoleon's "decisive" victory at Austerlitz proved only temporary. Coalition forces eventually regrouped, closing out the Napoleonic Wars with another "decisive" victory nearly a decade later. On June 18, 1815, combined armies led by Britain's Duke of Wellington and Prussian general Gebhard Leberecht von Blücher defeated Napoleon at Waterloo, Belgium. With approximately 25,000 casualties, the Grand Armee disintegrated.[7] Napoleon never fought another battle, living the balance of his life on Saint Helena, where he died in 1821. Meanwhile, Louis XVIII was restored to the throne in France, and Europe sought to achieve stability after decades of warfare.

Successful, conclusive pursuits are even more difficult to achieve than a decisive battlefield victory. Historically, few generals proved skilled enough to couple battlefield victory with an aggressive, relentless pursuit that resulted in the annihilation of the adversary. The best example of a brilliantly conducted and executed pursuit occurred at the Battle of Jena-Auerstadt in October 1806. On October 14 Napoleon's army engaged Prussian forces commanded by Prince Frederick Hohenlohe near Jena. Meanwhile, thirteen miles away at Auerstadt, Marshal Louis-Nicholas Davout achieved a stunning victory against overwhelming numbers. The morning after these dual victories, Napoleon launched one of the most decisive pursuits in military history. Spreading his forces out over one hundred miles, the French army drove the Prussians approximately 300 miles. By November 7, or within three weeks of his battlefield victory, Napoleon had destroyed the Prussian forces, which surrendered 140,000 men and 200 guns. Further reflecting the annihilation of the enemy, Napoleon's men seized 250 battle flags.[8]

Similarly, an examination of American military history finds few examples of decisive battlefield victory coupled with effective pursuit. The Battle of Saratoga in October 1777 during the American Revolution offers one such example. After his battlefield defeat on October 7, Lt. Gen. John Burgoyne initiated a retreat of his British army northward the following morning. Maj. Gen. Horatio Gates's American forces pursued. On October 17, ten days after their battlefield victory, the Americans had surrounded the British. Burgoyne surrendered his entire army, consisting of approximately 3,500 soldiers, or one-fifth of all British forces in North America. The vitality and viability of the revolution seemed assured after Saratoga, leading European nations to recognize this new American government. Just months after Gates's victory, the French formed an alliance with the United States.[9] As Britain now faced a world war, its military altered strategy and focused on quelling the rebellion in the southern colonies. The Battle of Cowpens, fought in South Carolina on January 17, 1781, offers another example of a battlefield victory followed by an aggressive pursuit. Brig. Gen. Daniel Morgan's combined Continental and militia forces defeated Lt. Col. Banastre Tarleton's British regulars. As Tarleton's forces fled the field, the mounted militiamen and Continental dragoons pressed the redcoats nearly twenty miles, rounding up additional prisoners of war and capturing wagons en route. Morgan's victory represented one of the most decisive of the American Revolution and, coupled with a pursuit, proved another step on the British march to Yorktown.[10] This level of destruction of the enemy army, however, proved an exception in warfare.

Nineteenth-century theorists speculated on tenets that made engagements conclusive. In *On War,* for example, Prussian military theorist Carl von Clausewitz considered the nature of war, including its means and ends. Clausewitz states, "The military power must be destroyed, that is, reduced to such a state as not to be able to prosecute the War."[11] Indeed, a decisive battle of this sort would serve as the culminating point of a conflict's escalating violence. In its simplest forms, a decisive battle need be so grand, with results so clear, that the adversary would capitulate because further resistance would be futile. To be sure, the decisive battles already considered—Austerlitz, Waterloo, Saratoga—generated decisive military and political consequences. Yet in the Civil War, by the summer of 1863, Americans had yet to see a battle with even the slightest comparable results.

Civil wars, and particularly wars waged by democracies, pose unique challenges. Beginning in April 1861, civilians and leaders wrestled with the military and political implications of an internecine war, escalating levels of violence, and the blurring lines of home front and battlefront. The coveted yet elusive battle of annihilation must be framed within the context of the Civil War's levels of violence and a democratic population's toleration of such destruction. At the outbreak of hostilities, the belief that the conflict would be short, decided in fact in one grand battle, permeated the national culture.

Charles Royster in *The Destructive War* argues that as the war progressed, both Northern and Southern civilians readily cast aside their expectations for a short war, embraced the escalation of violence, and eagerly sought this climatic, final clash. The population yearned for decisive battle, accepting such unparalleled destruction as the vindication of their respective cause, the primacy and triumph of the martial superiority of their soldiers, and the perpetuation of their national objectives. The media fed this frenzy for a decisive battle, calling for engagements comparable to Waterloo and Austerlitz.[12]

The nature of the Civil War compounded the challenge of destroying the enemy. For instance, the dominance of citizen-soldier armies led by a cadre of professional officers made a battle of annihilation incredibly difficult to achieve. Neither North nor South had a meaningful advantage over their adversary. Drawn from a similar citizen-soldier tradition, led by an officer corps educated at West Point, and often relying on shared military doctrine, Northern and Southern forces advanced through the war at an equal pace, neither gaining a significant advantage over the other. In his study of West Pointers in the Civil War, Wayne Hsieh concludes that the armies possessed "rough equilibrium" in rank-and-file soldiers, trained and professional leaders, and doctrine. Consequently, because of this Old Army tradition and citizen-soldier base, Hsieh states, "The general equilibrium of competence among Civil War armies more than anything else contributed to the climate of military indecision that predominated until spring of 1865."[13]

By June 1863 the Army of the Potomac had already sequenced through a string of commanding generals, six to be precise, and none of whom lasted more than one year. In fact Meade represented the third man to lead the army since the beginning of the year.[14] Expectations of decisive battle strained the relationship between Lincoln and his commanding generals. Clearly the president assumed his role as commander in chief with an active hand. "War is not merely a political act," Clausewitz posited, "but also a real political instrument."[15] Lincoln wielded the political instrument and played a central part in the war's military trajectory. The turnover rate of Army of the Potomac commanders is the clearest testament of this. Indeed, in his study of civil-military relations, Eliot Cohen argues, "Lincoln did not merely find his generals; he controlled them." Continuing, he offers, "Finding the right generals was only a prerequisite for strategic success; directing them proved for Lincoln, as for other war statesmen, the critical matter."[16]

Lincoln's active role in the Gettysburg Campaign emerged immediately. With the Army of Northern Virginia on the offensive, the change in high command occurred at a critical time. Meade's operational orders came with parameters, though with some flexibility and discretion. His primary objective was the protection of Washington, D.C. Within that operational confine, Halleck instructed, "Your army is free to act as you may deem proper under the circumstances as they arise."[17] Consequently Meade determined to march his army toward the Susquehanna River, keeping Washington and Baltimore protected, and offer battle if Lee turned toward Baltimore or attempted to cross the Susquehanna.[18] Thus in keeping with his instructions, he put the Army of Potomac, numbering approximately 90,000 men, in motion. The seven infantry corps spread out like a fan, covering a front approximately twenty-five miles wide, and moved north toward Pennsylvania. By June 30 the army straddled the Mason-Dixon Line, with Meade's headquarters in Taney-town, Maryland. Meanwhile, Union cavalry had pressed into Pennsylvania, occupying positions at Gettysburg and Littlestown as well as at Manchester and Mechanicsville, Maryland.[19]

The events of the first three days in July 1863 are well known and an oft-recited part of America's historical canon. At 7:30 in the morning of July 1, an Illinois cavalryman fired the opening shot of the Battle of Gettysburg. Over the next two days, Union and Confederate troops struggled over now-iconic places—McPherson's Ridge, Little Round Top, Devil's Den, the Peach Orchard, and Culp's Hill among them. Still, by the evening of July 2 and after a mounting casualty toll estimated at 16,500 combined men, neither side could claim decisive victory.[20] On the third, and what would be the final, day of the battle, Federal soldiers along Cemetery Ridge successfully repulsed a large-scale frontal assault, popularly termed Pickett's Charge. The Gettysburg Campaign had been costly to the Southern forces. Lee's army suffered approximately 28,000 casualties, a loss representing one-third of his command. The pouring rain on July 4, Independence Day, hampered any further operations. That night Lee directed his units to head toward Hagerstown, Maryland, via the Fairfield Road. Although badly wounded and strategically defeated, the Army of Northern Virginia was neither crippled nor annihilated. Edwin Coddington, author of the definitive volume on the campaign, argues, "All in all, on July 4 Lee's army, instead of being ripe for the plucking, still had the determination and capacity to punish severely, if not wreck any incautious or unskillful foe who might pursue it."[21] As important, although in retreat, Lee continued to hold the strategic initiative. Meade had to protect Washington and Baltimore per his original instructions, therefore any movement had to be carefully considered.

Although Gettysburg had brought the Federal army victory, it came at a high cost. The Army of the Potomac sustained approximately 23,000 casualties. Yet with the defeat of the heretofore seemingly invincible Lee, the nation eagerly awaited the final, culminating blow to the Army of Northern Virginia. Events over the course of the next ten days, however, leading to the unimpeded crossing of the Confederates across the Potomac River at Falling Waters, diminished the Federal victory at Gettysburg and irrevocably sullied Meade's reputation. President Lincoln and the nation sought more than the defeat of Lee's forces; they yearned for their destruction. Perceptions of victory between civilian and military individuals quickly came apparent. In a congratulatory order to his army, Meade championed the gallantry of his soldiers. Then, in words soon to be subject to scrutiny, he declared, "our task is not yet accomplished, and the commanding general looks to the army for greater efforts to drive from our soil every vestige of the presence of the invader."[22] The language of Meade's congratulatory order, and his presumed intent, quickly caught the ire of Lincoln. The president evaluated the Pennsylvanian's intentions and movements as being to "get the enemy across the river again without a further collision."[23]

Meade indeed worked to drive the Confederate army from Union soil, though certainly not with the relentless aggression displayed by Napoleon's forces against the Prussians at Jena. Once Meade decided to maintain his position along Cemetery Ridge, however, he placed himself in a position of reaction to Lee's movements. Before engaging in a pursuit, Meade needed additional intelligence on the enemy's position and movements. On the morning of July 5, advance elements of the Union VI Corps began moving westward to "find out the position and movements of the enemy."[24] Near Fairfield, eight miles west of Gettysburg, its lead brigade engaged in a small skirmish with the rear guard of Lt. Gen. Ambrose Powell Hill's corps.[25] Upon learning of this encounter, Meade made a critical decision. Already uncertain as to Lee's intentions and forced to consider the possibility that the Confederate commander was retiring westward into the mountains to secure a defensive position, Meade halted his army, which had been ordered to converge upon Middletown, Maryland.[26] The following morning he ordered a reconnaissance again.[27] Meanwhile, orders went out to all corps commanders to suspend their planned movement to Middletown.[28] Finally, by midafternoon, with enough intelligence on Confederate movements, Meade issued orders for his troops to resume the march into Maryland. The Army of the Potomac had been idle for nearly thirty hours, giving Lee the advantage of time to concentrate his army near Hagerstown unmolested, with the exception of Federal cavalry nipping at the edges of his columns and skirmishing with the screening Confederate cavalry.[29]

By the afternoon of July 6, Union soldiers were once again on the move. Meade reported 55,000 effectives and added a request that "every available reinforcement" be sent to Frederick, Maryland.[30] The march to Middletown was a long and tedious one. Located seven miles west of Frederick, Middletown sat prominently between the Catoctin Mountains and South Mountain. Soldiers from the XII Corps began their march from Littlestown, Pennsylvania, at 4:00 A.M. and, "destitute of shoes, and all greatly fatigued by the labor and anxiety of a severely contested battle," still managed to cover twenty-nine miles that day.[31] Weather complicated the situation when it began to pour rain again, slowing the columns to a crawl on "almost impassable" roads.[32] Still, as instructed, by July 8 Meade's army had converged on Middletown. The general himself kept pace with his army, moving his headquarters from Gettysburg to Frederick, a distance of thirty-three miles.[33] That evening Meade penned a letter to his wife, sharing with her the strain of command. Over the course of the previous ten days, he wrote, "I have not changed my clothes, have not had a regular night's rest, and many nights not a wink of sleep, and for several days did not even wash my face and hands, no regular food, and all the time in a great state of mental anxiety."[34]

Meanwhile, the Army of Northern Virginia inched closer to the Potomac River. Although the weather had also complicated and slowed the Confederate retreat, Lee's forces began arriving near Hagerstown on the afternoon of July 6, with the very last of the weary troops stumbling in the following morning. The Virginian noted in his official report that Federal forces "offered no serious interruption" to the army's retreat to Hagerstown. The frequent and heavy rains had swollen the Potomac River to a depth of thirteen feet, however, making it too dangerous to affect a crossing. Adding to Lee's woes, Union troops from Frederick had previously destroyed the lone Confederate pontoon bridge at Falling Waters. Thus when the Army of Northern Virginia reached Williamsport, Lee had no choice but to halt his troops, initiate construction of new pontoon bridges, and prepare for an anticipated Federal assault.[35]

As Union and Confederate soldiers maneuvered closer to the Potomac River, news of the Federal victory at Gettysburg spread quickly throughout the North. While civilians eagerly awaited further word from the battlefront, newspapers churned out scores of columns and headlines on the fighting in Adams County. Comparing the Union victory to that of the Duke of Wellington over Napoleon, the *Philadelphia Inquirer* headlined, "VICTORY! Waterloo Eclipsed!!"[36] Ranking Gettysburg to Waterloo, a battle in the recent memory of 1863 Americans and one with indisputable military and political implications, offered a dangerous comparison and further fueled Northern expectations for a decisive, complete triumph over Lee. Other parallels to Napoleon's own victories soon followed. Liking the battle-ridden Gettysburg landscape to Austerlitz, the local newspaper reported, "The sun of Austerlitz is not more memorable than that which flung its dying rays over the battle fields of Gettysburg on the evening of the third day of successful battle." Reports of "decisive" Union success permeated the headlines and columns. "The victory won by Gen. Meade is so decisive, and so glorious in its results," claimed Gettysburg's *Star and Banner*.[37] Quickly Meade became a conquering hero. Upon arriving in Frederick, the town's residents lined the streets to catch a glimpse of the victorious general. Just moments after his arrival, a group of ladies greeted the commander with wreaths and bouquets.[38]

For a nation starved for battlefield success, July brought the North two resounding victories. While Meade battled Lee's seemingly invincible Army of Northern Virginia, Maj. Gen. Ulysses S. Grant's forces launched a campaign to capture Vicksburg and reopen the Mississippi River. After a nearly two-month siege, Lt. Gen. John C. Pemberton surrendered his approximately 30,000 Confederate defenders of that Mississippi port town. The strategic implications were monumental: Union control of the Mississippi River cut off the western states of the Confederacy and brought the surrender of an entire Confederate army. On the evening of July 7, Washington's residents gathered to celebrate the Federal victories. The occasion prompted a few words of congratulations from the commander in chief. Lincoln championed the successes of Grant's and Meade's armies to eager listeners, but the president simultaneously reflected on military disappointments, almost foreshadowing the events to come. "There are trying occasions, not only in success, but for the want of success," he cautioned.[39]

Lincoln and his advisors eagerly followed Meade's pursuit and anticipated news of a culminating blow. Elated with the news of Grant's success at Vicksburg, the president desired similar decisive results from Meade. *Defeating* Lee's forces was not enough; the Army of Northern Virginia needed to be *destroyed*. Lincoln pressed this viewpoint on July 7, writing, "Now, if General Meade can complete his work, so gloriously prosecuted thus far, by the literal or substantial destruction of Lee's army, the rebellion will be over."[40] Halleck prodded Meade forward, promising him reinforcements and declaring his movements "perfectly satisfactory."[41] The army commander responded that he expected to "try the fortunes of war" with Lee on the north side of the Potomac, but he outlined his constraints as well. "I wish in advance to moderate the expectations of those who, in ignorance of the difficulties to be encountered, may expect too much," he cautioned.[42] Days later Meade complained to his wife of these expectations heaped upon him as he struggled to maneuver his army. "My success at Gettysburg," he lamented, "has deluded the people and the Government with the idea that I must always be victorious." Still, the general forecasted another engagement. "I expect in a few days," he continued, "if not sooner, again to hazard the fortune of war."[43]

The fortunes of war were to come into play at Williamsport. With the Army of Northern Virginia concentrated around Hagerstown, Lee and his subordinates surveyed the area and selected a position that best allowed them to secure the routes to the primary crossing sites at Falling Waters and Williamsport on the Potomac River. By the morning of July 11, the Confederates had established a nine-mile-long defensive position on a series of slight ridges between Hagerstown and Williamsport. Held with approximately 50,000 effectives, it offered several tactical advantages. Engineered with artillery emplacements and two lines of infantry entrenchments, the Confederate position also protected the vital road junctions, covering the National Road, the Hagerstown–Williamsport Turnpike, the Williamsport–Boonsboro Road, and the Hagerstown–Downsville Road. Still, with the high river level and the loss of the sole pontoon bridge, the situation remained precarious.[44]

Shortly after Lee's forces abandoned Hagerstown, Union troops marched into its streets on July 12. Moving on, the forces formed a line of battle within two miles of the Confederate position.[45] Accounting for reinforcements that poured in from the surrounding areas, the Army of the Potomac amounted to approximately 80,000 effectives, 30,000 more men than available to Lee.[46] With his forces deployed, Meade, accompanied by Brig. Gens. Andrew Humphreys and Gouverneur Warren, briefly surveyed Lee's line. The engineering background of all three generals informed their observations of a strong, well-entrenched position with no apparent points of weakness. More importantly, the Potomac River had begun to fall.[47] The rapidly declining water levels would facilitate Lee's escape, so if Meade were to "hazard the fortune of war" and attempt a conclusive contest, he needed to act immediately and decisively. As the commanding general deliberated his next course of action, he issued orders to his corps commanders to hold their positions and "be prepared to meet an attack from the enemy."[48]

By July 12 the Confederate retreat and Union pursuit had reached its culminating point. Nearly thirty hours of stagnate operations six days earlier had cost Meade the advantage, allowing Lee's forces to hold the strategic and tactical advantage at Williamsport. While presented with intelligence on the enemy position and of the Potomac's decreasing water levels, assured to facilitate Lee's crossing, Meade remained cautious. Finally, after days of maneuvering and with Lee's back pressed to the river, he offered Halleck a plan: "It is my intention to attack them to-morrow," Meade declared, then couched his aggressive tone with caution, "unless something intervenes to prevent it, for the reason that delay will strengthen the enemy and will not increase my force."[49] Something intervened.

Near 8:00 that evening, Meade held a council of war. The command structure of the Army of the Potomac had changed considerably since his first council just ten days prior. This inexperience among the army's senior leadership cannot be overstated.[50] Meade later recalled that he advocated an attack on the Confederate position, stating that he was "in favor of moving forward and attacking the enemy and taking the consequences." As the generals deliberated, however, his apparent preference for an offensive did not guide the council. Here, as he had in the campaign's earlier councils, the commanding general allowed his subordinates to vote on the proposed course of action. In a telegraph to Halleck the following day, Meade reported that "five of six" of his generals were "unqualifiedly opposed" to an attack. Unwilling to act against the consensus of his subordinates and reluctant to face uncertainty in this operational environment, Meade acquiesced to the majority vote. His decision to exercise cautious leadership and yield the initiative and timing to the enemy cast significant strategic implications.[51]

The following day, July 13, Meade and his staff again reconnoitered the

Confederate line. Fog and rain prevented a thorough assessment of the enemy position and, Meade later reported, "not much information was obtained."[52] That evening he telegraphed Washington and informed Halleck that a majority of his corps commanders had opposed an assault. Meade further justified his delay: "Under these circumstances, in the view of the momentous consequences attendant upon a failure to succeed, I did not feel myself authorized to attack until after I had made a more careful examination of the enemy's position, strength, and defensive works." He informed the general in chief that forces would reconnoiter the area, and if they detected a weak point in the enemy line, the army would "hazard an attack."[53] Halleck wasted no time in responding to this apparent lethargy, urging an attack before Lee could cross the Potomac. Frustrated with Meade's method of leadership by council, Halleck added: "Act upon your own judgment and make your generals execute your orders. Call no council of war. It is proverbial that councils of war never fight."[54]

Thus with effectively the same intelligence and reconnaissance information already gained, Meade prepared for an offensive, albeit a halfhearted effort. At 9:00 P.M. headquarters issued orders for a "reconnaissance in force" to commence at 7:00 the following morning. Meade's plans proved cautionary. His "reconnaissance in force," not an all-out attack, engaged only a fraction of the Army of the Potomac in what appeared to be only a test of the Confederate line and not the full assault that Halleck and Lincoln sought.[55]

Meanwhile, capitalizing on Meade's hesitations, Lee began moving the Army of Northern Virginia across the river.[56] By sunrise on July 14, the majority of the Confederate army and its baggage trains were safely on the south side of the Potomac. At 6:35 A.M., thirty minutes before the planned reconnaissance in force, Maj. Gen. Oliver Otis Howard reported that the Confederates had evacuated their position west of Hagerstown.[57] Other reports soon followed. As intelligence confirmed that Lee had maneuvered his army across the river, Meade issued orders for a pursuit. At 8:30 A.M. headquarters instructed the four corps originally ordered to lead the reconnoitering party to form the advance. Staff officers continued to issue orders to the corps commanders to "overtake" and "strike" Lee's forces before they crossed the river.[58] But it was too late. Save for a few units acting as a rear guard near Falling Waters, the Army of Northern Virginia lay safely on the south side of the Potomac. Although the Army of the Potomac continued to pursue Lee's forces into northern Virginia, the Gettysburg Campaign had concluded with a lethargic sigh rather than a climatic struggle. The ten days' chase from Pennsylvania had resulted in a combined casualty rate of 6,000 soldiers. Union cavalry, the primary force in contact with the enemy, suffered the most casualties, approximately 1,000 men.[59]

Meade's caution tested relations with the commander in chief and thus strained civil-military affairs. At 1:00 P.M. Halleck telegraphed ordering the general to initiate an "energetic pursuit" and noting Lincoln's "dissatisfaction" with the strategic situation. Frustrated with the seemingly unrealistic objectives of the administration, ninety minutes later Meade caustically responded by asking to be relieved of command. Halleck denied the request and again urged an "active pursuit."[60] Still aggrieved two days later, Meade wrote to his wife, "no man who does his duty, and all that he can do, as I maintain I have done, needs *spurring*." Constrained by the weakened condition of the army, he articulated annoyance with being "urged, pushed and *spurred* to attempting to pursue and destroy an enemy nearly equal to my own." Certainly attuned to the rather toxic political environment of the Army of the Potomac, he confided to her, "This has been the history of all my predecessors, and I clearly saw that in time my fate would be theirs—this was the reason I was disinclined to take the command, and it is for this reason I would gladly give it up."[61]

Frustrations and disappointment in Meade's actions at Williamsport defined deliberations in Washington. Upon hearing the news of Lee's escape, Lincoln decried to Secretary of the Navy Gideon Welles: "There is bad faith somewhere. Meade has been pressed and urged, but only one of his generals was for an immediate attack. . . . What does it mean, Mr. Welles? Great God! What does it mean?"[62] Lincoln quickly drafted a strongly worded, if not condescending, letter to the army commander. The president freely expressed his "deep distress" at Lee's escape, then criticized the Federal pursuit, going so far as to declare that Meade had failed to recognize the momentous implications of his actions. "Again, my dear general," Lincoln chided, "I do not believe you appreciate the magnitude of the misfortune involved in Lee's escape." The president continued, "He was within your easy grasp, and to have closed upon him would, in connection with our other late success, have ended the war—as it is, the war will be prolonged indefinitely."[63] Lincoln never sent the letter. A week later, in a message to General Howard, the president offered a similar sentiment, writing that he was "deeply mortified" by Lee's "escape" at Williamsport. To Lincoln, the Confederate "escape" had profound strategic implications—"the substantial destruction of his army would have ended the war, and . . . such destruction was perfectly easy." Yet the president closed his letter to Howard by articulating his gratitude for the Federal victory at Gettysburg and pronouncing his faith and confidence in Meade as a "brave and skillful officer, and a true man."[64]

Both of these letters offer clear expressions of how Lincoln viewed the Gettysburg Campaign and its conclusion at Williamsport. His rhetoric cannot be overstated. Lincoln believed that defeat of Lee's forces before they crossed into Virginia not only would have delivered a culminating blow to the Army of Northern Virginia but also would have ended the war. To the president's understanding, however elementary, if Meade had destroyed Lee's army, the Civil War would have ended in July 1863. But Lincoln's disappointment was bound to unreasonable expectations and simplistic understandings of the complexity of military operations. Decisive victories rarely occur. Certainly battles of annihilation, like Jena-Auerstadt or Austerlitz, did not characterize the Civil War. While euphoria over the Confederate surrender at Vicksburg spread across the Union in July 1863, Grant's significant achievement did not end the war in the western theater; there too the war continued to drag on.

Meade's decision not to attack Lee at Williamsport quickly became one of the most scrutinized decisions of the campaign. In the spring of 1864, the Joint Committee on the Conduct of War investigated Meade's leadership during June and July 1863. Established by the Thirty-Seventh Congress on December 10, 1861, the joint committee was tasked with oversight of military objectives, campaigns, and commanders and, amid accusations of disloyalty, to root out those who may be traitors to the Union.[65] Chaired by Sen. Benjamin Wade, an Ohio Republican, the committee investigated a myriad of instances during the course of the war. While their investigations often proved little more than political grandstanding, for they investigated military incidents well after the fact, the hearings did work to deepen political and personal animosities and shape generals' reputations.

Wade and the committee seized on the discontent and speculation surrounding Meade's conduct at Gettysburg. Their investigation centered on several allegations, the most sensational being that Meade had not wanted to fight at Gettysburg but had preferred to abandon the battlefield. His dilatory actions at Williamsport also came under scrutiny.[66] Testifying before the committee on three occasions, March 5 and 11 and again on April 4, Meade worked hard to deflect blame for the inactivity at Williamsport. He lamented the lack of comprehensive intelligence and insisted that a failed attack there would have exposed Washington, thereby risking "all the fruits" of the Federal victory at Gettysburg.[67] The general stated his willingness in "attacking the enemy and taking the consequences," but he couched such seemingly decisive, authoritarian decision making with a statement of deferential authority. Speaking of the decision of his subordinates during the council of war on July 12, Meade testified, "I left to their judgment, and would not do it unless it met with their approval."[68]

In the months following the campaign, various individuals speculated as to the outcome had the Army of the Potomac attacked Lee at Williamsport. Predictably Meade found both critics and supporters of his actions. Testifying to Congress, General Warren, Meade's chief engineer, stated that had Union forces attacked, they would have cut the Confederate army "all to pieces."[69] Andrew A. Humphreys offered one of the most objective, balanced assessments of Meade's leadership. Underscoring the strength of Lee's position, he concluded, "had we made an attack we should have suffered severely." Col. Charles Wainwright, commanding the artillery brigade of the I Corps, supported Meade's actions. In his diary entry of July 14, Wainwright described the strength of the Confederate position. He took careful note of the meticulous construction of the parapets and the selection of their locations to achieve deadly crossfire. Attuned to the viperous political atmosphere within the army and the heightened public pressure and expectations, Wainwright sympathized with the commanding general's predicament. "People at home of course," the colonel wrote, "will now pitch into Meade, as they did McClellan after Antietam, for letting him escape. My own opinion is that under the circumstances and with the knowledge General Meade then had he was justified in putting off his attack until today."[70] Maj. Gen. John Sedgwick, a senior commander in the Army of the Potomac, testified before the committee that Lee occupied a "very strong position" and that if Meade had urged an assault, the Union army would have "received a severe repulse."[71]

Cautious, deliberate decision making characterized operations after Gettysburg. "The pursuit of a beaten Army commences at the moment that Army, giving up the combat, leaves its position," wrote Clausewitz.[72] Meade's decisions on July 4 cost the Federals momentum and placed the initiative with the vanquished. His order for the army to halt on July 5–6 for nearly thirty hours afforded Lee valuable time to march closer to the Potomac River. At the Williamsport council of war, Meade sought advice from his corps commanders, three of whom were newly in place. In an environment ripe with generals inexperienced with their respective level of command, Meade failed to exercise decisive leadership. Army commanders are expected to give orders, not solicit and then concede to the advice of subordinates. Halleck tersely reminded him of the responsibility of a commanding general: "act upon your own judgment and make your generals execute your orders."[73] Thus in the end, the council of war at Williamsport bought the Army of the Potomac only time, meaningless time under the circumstances. Nothing that Meade and his accompanying generals witnessed during their reconnaissance on July 13 had convinced them not to press the Confederate line. Knowing as much, or as little, about the enemy position as he had on July 12, Meade ordered a "reconnaissance in force" by a portion of his army instead of a more coordinated assault by his entire force meant to break the Confederates.[74]

Meade proved capable in *defeating* the attacking enemy force and thus fulfilled his army's strategic objective by protecting Washington and Baltimore. Yet he was unable to *destroy* Lee's forces. Still, placed within context from military campaigns prior to Gettysburg, Meade's inability to achieve a decisive battlefield victory and then execute a relentless pursuit resulting in the complete destruction of the enemy was not uncommon. Few generals have demonstrated the ability to fight battles resulting in the complete annihilation of the foe. Crushing victories such as Austerlitz or Waterloo or relentless pursuits leading to the capitulation of the enemy as occurred after Jena-Auerstadt or Saratoga are incredibly rare in military history. While Lincoln and the Northern public sought a battle of annihilation, this proved an elusive chimera. Still, Meade had brought the Army of the Potomac its most significant victory to date and struck a severe blow to the fighting capabilities of Lee's Army of Northern Virginia. To be sure, his pursuit was not without flaws; his leadership not consistently decisive. The fact that Meade could not couple battlefield victory with decisive pursuit resulting in the complete annihilation of Lee's command is less of a damning testament to his leadership than an observation of a broader reality in military history. Consequently, the Gettysburg Campaign closed with the Army of Northern Virginia back on its native soil, recovering, and the end result so fervently wished for in Washington unfulfilled.

NOTES

1. George Gordon Meade [GGM] to Margaretta Meade [MM], June 29, 1863. Folder 11, Box 1, Ser. 1, George Meade Collection, Historical Society of Pennsylvania, Philadelphia [hereafter cited as Meade Collection, HSP]. Little scholarship exists on Civil War leadership and decision making. Among the existing works in the scant historiography are Steven E. Woodworth, *Jefferson Davis and His Generals: The Failure of Confederate Command in the West* (Lawrence: University Press of Kansas, 1990); W. J. Wood, *Civil War Generalship: The Art of Command* (New York: Da Capo, 1997); and Albert Castel and Brooks Simpson, *Victors in Blue: How Union Generals Fought Confederates, Battled Each Other, and Won the Civil War* (Lawrence: University Press of Kansas, 2011).

2. Henry Halleck to GGM, June 27, 1863, U.S. War Department, *The War of the Rebellion: A Compilation of the Official Records of the Union and Confederate Armies*, 70 vols. in 128 pts. (Washington, D.C.: Government Printing Office, 1880–1901), ser. 1, 27(1):61 [hereafter cited as *OR*, all items from ser. 1].

3. GGM to MM, July 8, 1863, *The Life and Letters of George Gordon Meade, Major-General United States Army*, ed. George Gordon Meade, vol. 2 (New York: Charles Scribner's Sons, 1913), 132–33 [hereafter cited as *L&L*].

4. Abraham Lincoln to GGM, July 14, 1863, Abraham Lincoln, *The Collected Works: The Abraham Lincoln Association, Springfield, Illinois*, ed. Roy P. Basler et al., 9 vols. (New Brunswick, NJ: Rutgers University Press, 1953–55), 5:327–28.

5. Although historians have produced an unprecedented amount of scholarship on the Battle of Gettysburg, less attention has been devoted to the decision making of the Union high command. This is not surprising, but it in fact reflects the dearth of scholarship on Meade himself. For example, the general's definitive biography, Freeman Cleaves's *Meade of Gettysburg* (Norman: University of Oklahoma Press, 1960), is over fifty years old. More recent treatments of the battle, namely Allen Guelzo's *Gettysburg: The Last Invasion* (New York: Alfred C. Knopf, 2013), offers a scathing, unbalanced critique of Meade's generalship. Moreover, of the voluminous amount of literature on the battle, the majority concentrates on the fighting of July 1–3, paying less attention to the events of the subsequent ten days that terminated with the Confederate army successfully crossing the Potomac River. For a fine narrative of the campaign's closing days, see A. Wilson Greene, "From Gettysburg to Falling Waters: Meade's Pursuit of Lee," in *The Third Day at Gettysburg and Beyond*, ed. Gary W. Gallagher, 161–201 (Chapel Hill: University of North Carolina Press, 1994). More recently, Kent Masterson Brown's *Retreat from Gettysburg: Lee, Logistics, and the Pennsylvania Campaign* (Chapel Hill: University of North Carolina Press, 2005) and Eric Wittenberg's *One Continuous Fight: The Retreat from Gettysburg and the Pursuit of Lee's Army of Northern Virginia, July 4–14, 1863* (New York: Savas Beatie, 2008) offer thorough discussions of the events from July 4–14. Other works to address Meade include Ethan Rafuse's *George Gordon Meade and the War in the East* (Abilene, TX: McWhiney Foundation, 2003) and Richard Sauers's *Meade: The Victor of Gettysburg* (Washington, D.C.: Potomac Books, 2003).

6. Napoleon Bonaparte, *A Diary*, ed. R. M. Johnston (New York: Houghton Mifflin, 1994), 116.

7. Robert Doughty et al., *Warfare in the Western World: Military Operations from 1600 to 1914*, vol. 1 (Boston: Houghton Mifflin, 2007), 222, 290.

8. Ibid., 226.

9. Richard M. Ketchum, *Saratoga: Turning Point of America's Revolutionary War* (New York: Henry Holt, 1997).

10. Lawrence Babits, *Cowpens: A Devil of a Whipping* (Chapel Hill: University of North Carolina Press, 1998), 133–37. British losses totaled 300 dead and wounded, with an additional 500 captured, while Morgan lost approximately 70 men.

11. Carl Von Clausewitz, *On War,* trans. Michael Howard (Princeton, NJ: Princeton University Press, 1989), 20.

12. Charles Royster, *The Destructive War: William Tecumseh Sherman, Stonewall Jackson, and the Americans* (New York: Knopf, 1991), 253–54.

13. Wayne Hsieh, *West Pointers and the Civil War: The Old Army in War and Peace* (Chapel Hill: University of North Carolina Press, 2009), 159.

14. Meade replaced Maj. Gen. Joseph Hooker, who had commanded the Army of the Potomac since January 1863. Hooker took over from Maj. Gen. Ambrose Burnside, who led the army between November 1862 and January 1863. For additional reading on the Army of the Potomac, see Jeffery D. Wert, *The Sword of Lincoln: The Army of the Potomac* (New York: Simon and Schuster, 2005).

15. Clausewitz, *On War,* 17.

16. Eliot Cohen, *Supreme Command: Soldiers, Statesmen, and a Leadership in Wartime* (New York: Free Press, 2002), 18, 38.

17. Halleck to Meade, June 27, 1863, *OR,* 27(1):61.

18. Meade to Halleck, June 28, 1863, ibid., 61–62.

19. Harry W. Pfanz, *Gettysburg: The First Day* (Chapel Hill: University of North Carolina Press, 2001), 45. The Army of the Potomac occupied the following positions: the I Corps at Marsh Creek; XI Corps at Emmitsburg; III Corps near Bridgeport, along the Monocacy River east of Emmitsburg; II Corps at Uniontown; V Corps in Union Mills; XII Corps at Littlestown; and VI Corps in Manchester, Maryland. Mechanicsville, Maryland, is now Thurmont.

20. Edwin B. Coddington, *The Gettysburg Campaign: A Study in Command* (New York: Simon and Schuster, 1968), 442.

21. Ibid., 536.

22. Seth Williams, General Orders No. 68, July 4, 1863, *OR,* 27(3):519.

23. Lincoln to Halleck, July 6, 1863, ibid., 567; Gideon Welles, *Diary of Gideon Welles,* vol. 1 (Boston: Houghton Mifflin, 1911), 363 (July 7, 1863).

24. Williams to Commanding Officer VI Corps, July 4, 1863, *OR,* 27(3):517.

25. "A. T. Torbert, Hdqrs. First Brig., First Div., Sixth Army Corps," Aug. 13, 1863, *OR,* 27(1):669–70; Coddington, *Gettysburg Campaign,* 549–50; Brown, *Retreat from Gettysburg,* 259–62.

26. Williams, Circular, July 5, 1863, *OR,* 27(3):532–33.

27. Meade to John Sedgwick, July 6, 1863, ibid., 554.

28. Williams, Orders, July 6, 1863, ibid. The Cumberland Valley lies beyond the South Mountain range and was the primary route of advance and withdrawal for Lee's army.

29. Brown, *Retreat from Gettysburg,* 262.

30. Meade to Halleck, July 5, 1863, *OR,* 27(1):79. Maj. Gen. John Sedgwick oversaw the

movement of his VI Corps as well as the I and III Corps; Maj. Gen. O. O. Howard directed the V and XI Corps' movements; Maj. Gen. Henry Slocum oversaw the movement of his XII as well as the II Corps.

31. Henry Slocum, "Reports of Maj. Gen. Henry W. Slocum, U.S. Army, Commanding Twelfth Army Corps," ibid., 761; Meade to Halleck, July 8, 1863, ibid., 85; Coddington, *Gettysburg Campaign,* 554–55. Slocum's XII Corps marched from Littlestown, Pennsylvania, to Walkersville, Maryland.

32. Meade to Halleck, July 8, 1863, *OR,* 27(1):84; Andrew Humphreys, "Report of Brig. Gen. Andrew A. Humphreys, U.S. Army, commanding Second Division," Aug. 16, 1863, ibid., 536. Meade made his headquarters in Frederick, Maryland. Close proximity to that town afforded several strategic advantages to the Federal army, including access to the Baltimore and Ohio Railroad and hard-surfaced roads.

33. "Itinerary of the Army of the Potomac and Co-Operating Forces, June 5–July 31, 1863," ibid., 146.

34. GGM to MM, July 8, 1863. *L&L,* 132.

35. Robert E. Lee, Jan. [?], 1864, *OR,* 27(3):322; Brown, *Retreat from Gettysburg,* 256; Coddington, *Gettysburg Campaign,* 539–41; Testimony of GGM, Mar. 5, 1863, *Report of the Joint Committee on the Conduct of the War,* vol. 4 (Wilmington, N.C.: Broadfoot, 1999), 335–36 [hereafter cited as *JCCW*]. Brown finds the two-day period of July 5–6 as one of the most important phases of the retreat. As Lee moved his forces west through Monterey Pass, his soldiers fortified the mountain passes before turning south toward Hagerstown. This action further confused Meade, who seemed unsure if Lee was retreating or moving west to a superior position within the mountains. Maj. Gen. William H. French's troops, without instruction from Meade, advanced to Falling Waters and destroyed the Confederate pontoon bridge.

36. *Philadelphia Inquirer,* "VICTORY! Waterloo Eclipsed!!" July 6, 1863.

37. *Star & Banner* (Gettysburg, PA), "The Battles of Gettysburg," July 9, 1863.

38. GGM to MM, July 8, 1863, *L&L,* 132–33.

39. Lincoln, "Response to a Serenade," July 7, 1863, Lincoln, *Collected Works,* 5:319.

40. Lincoln to Halleck, July 7, 1863, ibid.

41. Halleck to Meade, July 5, 1863, *OR,* 27(1):79; Halleck to Meade, July 7, 1863, ibid., 82–83.

42. Meade to Halleck, July 8, 1863, ibid., 84.

43. GGM to MM, July 10, 1863, Folder 10, Box 1, Ser. 1, Meade Collection, HSP.

44. Brown, *Retreat from Gettysburg,* 310–11; Coddington, *Gettysburg Campaign,* 565–69; E. P. Alexander, *Fighting for the Confederacy: The Personal Recollections of General Edward Porter Alexander,* ed. Gary W. Gallagher (Chapel Hill: University of North Carolina Press, 1989), 270–72; Ewell, "Report of Lieut. Gen. Richard S. Ewell, C.S. Army, commanding Second Army Corps, 1863," *OR,* 27(2):448.

45. Brown, *Retreat from Gettysburg,* 316–18.

46. Coddington, *Gettysburg Campaign,* 559; 569; Abstract Returns of the Army of the Potomac, July 10, 1863, *OR,* 27(1):152. While the combat effective number of 80,000 appears impressive, various reinforcement units were certainly not of equal quality to the veteran units of the Army of the Potomac. Some reinforcement units were poorly trained and inadequately armed.

47. Ranald S. MacKenzie to Warren, July 12, 1863, *OR*, 27(3):669.

48. Williams, Circular, July 12, 1863, ibid., 670.

49. Andrew Humphreys, *From Gettysburg to the Rapidan: The Army of the Potomac, July 1863–April 1864* (New York: Charles Scribner's Sons, 1883), 6; Meade to Halleck, July 12, 1863, *OR*, 27(1):91.

50. Testimony of GGM, Mar. 5, 1864, *JCCW*, 336; Testimony of Andrew Atkinson Humphreys, Mar. 21, 1864, ibid., 396; Andrew A. Humphreys, "Journal of Movements of the HdQrs Army of the Potomac from July 8, 1863–June 23, 1864," July 8, 1863, Andrew A. Humphreys Papers, Original War Papers, vol. 16, Historical Society of Pennsylvania, Philadelphia [hereafter cited as AAH Papers, HSP]; Humphreys, *From Gettysburg to the Rapidan*, 6.

51. Testimony of GGM, Mar. 5, 1864, *JCCW*, 336; Testimony of John Sedgwick, Apr. 8, 1864, ibid., 463; Meade to Halleck, *OR*, 27(3):91. Maj. Gen. John Newton, commander of the I Corps, was sick, and Brig. Gen. James Wadsworth represented the corps in his stead. Brig. Gen. William Hays now commanded the II Corps, and General French the III Corps. The command structure of the V, VI, XI, and XII Corps remained the same, with Maj. Gens. George Sykes, Sedgwick, Howard, and Slocum in command of their respective corps. Also present at the council were Maj. Gen. Alfred Pleasonton, commanding the Federal cavalry, and Generals Warren and Humphreys, respectively Meade's chief engineer and his chief of staff. There are some discrepancies in how many of the generals opposed or favored the proposed offensive. Meade reported to Halleck on July 13 that five of his six generals opposed the assault, a clear majority. In his testimony to the JCCW, however, Meade recalled that two of his generals, Wadsworth and Howard, favored the attack. While not considered members of the council, Pleasonton and Humphreys also favored an offensive. Allen Guelzo argues that this council of war is "portrayed as the moment when a suddenly offensive-minded Meade was restrained by his timid corps commanders" and suggests that Meade did not want to hazard an offensive. Guelzo, *Gettysburg*, 439–40.

52. Testimony of GGM, Mar. 5, 1864, *JCCW*, 336.

53. *OR*, 27(1):91.

54. Halleck to Meade, *OR*, 27(1):92.

55. Williams, Circular, July 13, 1864, *OR*, 27(3):675.

56. Lee, Jan. [?], 1864, *OR*, 27(2):323.

57. Oliver Otis Howard to Humphreys, July 14, 1863, *OR*, 27(3):683; H. R. Wright to Headquarters, VI Corps, Aug. 21, 1863, *OR*, 27(1):666–67. Longstreet's and Hill's men crossed at Falling Waters and Ewell's corps at Williamsport.

58. Williams, Circular, July 14, 1863, *OR*, 27(3):686; Humphreys to Hancock, July 14, 1863; and Humphreys to Sykes, July 14, 1863, vol. 39, AAH Papers, HSP.

59. Wittenberg, *One Continuous Fight*, 343–44.

60. Halleck to Meade; Meade to Halleck; and Halleck to Meade, all July 14, 1863, *OR*, 27(1):93–94.

61. GGM to MM, July 16, 1863, Folder 10, Box I, Ser. 1, Meade Collection, HSP.

62. Welles, *Diary of Gideon Welles*, July 14, 1863, 370.

63. Lincoln to Meade, July 14, 1863, Lincoln, *Collected Works*, 5:327–28. For additional reading on the relationship between Meade and Lincoln, see Gabor Boritt, "'Unfinished Work':

Lincoln, Meade, and Gettysburg," in *Lincoln's Generals*, ed. Gabor S. Boritt, 81–120 (New York: Oxford University Press, 1994).

64. Lincoln to Howard, July 21, 1863, *L&L*, 138. Lincoln's letter to Howard is also reproduced in Lincoln, *Collected Works*, 5:341.

65. Bruce Tap, *Over Lincoln's Shoulder: The Committee on the Conduct of the War* (Lawrence: University Press of Kansas, 1998), 22–24.

66. The argument that Meade did not want to fight at Gettysburg has been a hotly debated and controversial theory among contemporaries and historians. Some of this contention has centered on arguments laid out by "Historicus" (presumed by many to have been Daniel Sickles) and were also promoted by Meade's detractors. The Historicus letter is reproduced in *OR*, 27(1):128–36. For additional reading on the Meade-Sickles controversy, see Richard A. Sauers, *Gettysburg: The Meade-Sickles Controversy* (Washington, D.C.: Brassey's, 2003); and James A. Hessler, *Sickles at Gettysburg* (New York: Savas Beatie, 2009).

67. Testimony of GGM, Mar. 5, 1864, *JCCW*, 336.

68. Ibid.; Thomas J. Ryan, *Spies, Scouts, and the Secrets in the Gettysburg Campaign: How the Critical Role of Intelligence Impacted the Outcome of Lee's Invasion of the North, June–July, 1863* (El Dorado Hills, CA: Savas Beatie, 2015), 440. Hooker established the Bureau of Military Intelligence in early 1863, appointing Col. George H. Sharpe to its command. The bureau was responsible for the gathering, analysis, and dissemination of intelligence. Its records are housed in the National Archives.

69. Testimony of G. K. Warren, Mar. 9, 1864, *JCCW*, 381; Testimony of Andrew Humphreys, Mar. 21, 1864, ibid., 397.

70. Charles Wainwright, *A Diary of Battle: The Personal Journals of Colonel Charles S. Wainwright, 1861–1865* (New York: De Capo, 1998), 261–62.

71. Testimony of John Sedgwick, Apr. 8, 1864, *JCCW*, 462.

72. Clausewitz, *On War*, 235.

73. Halleck to Meade, July 13, 1863, *OR*, 27(1):92.

74. Williams, Circular, July 13, 1864, *OR*, 27(3):675.

"THE FARCE WAS COMPLETE"

Braxton Bragg, Field Orders, and the Language of
Command at McLemore's Cove

Andrew S. Bledsoe

D EBATES ABOUT THE art of command during the Civil War occupy a
unique place in the scholarship on the military history of that conflict.
Even more than is usual, historians tend to approach this subject with their
own sets of preconceptions, motivations, and intellectual or occupational bi-
ases. Some employ a method that is both pragmatic and, to many in the academy, old fashioned. Following the practice of military professionals, scholars
mine the past for practical illustrations to implement in contemporary martial
settings. Approaching the history of war as parable, they view past operations
as case studies and consider command decisions in all their complexity as
object lessons to distill and incorporate into doctrine for future application.[1]
Alternatively, those interested in taking an institutional approach to the art
of command need look no further than the origins, nature, and composition
of the forces of the day. The Civil War represented a moment of evolution for
these institutions, as massive and hastily mobilized citizen-armies faced off in
a war of unprecedented scale and destructiveness. Commanders were responsible for armies of massive size and astonishing (for the time) mobility; bound
by complicated strategic, tactical, and political considerations; forced to adapt
to unique circumstances of the moment; and subjected to immense stresses.
Generals had to negotiate these obstacles without much in the way of a staff
system or other institutional supports to aid with command and control, logistics, standardization, and operational planning. Historians, relying on these
various approaches, should assess the contingent nature of military operations
within the constraints of all available evidence and employ the full arsenal of

interpretive tools at their disposal to bring order to complexity while orienting actions within their proper institutional, historical, and cultural contexts.

Sometimes lost in the process, however, is an easily forgotten but inescapable fact—that perhaps more than any other factor, the ineffable and unpredictable human element remains the most essential variable affecting the art of command. Armies are, after all, composed of and led by human beings, with all of humanity's fallibility and frailties that alternatively aid or impede the effectiveness of the best-laid plans. Moreover, command of Civil War armies at the tactical or operational levels was often a matter of problem solving, and commanders had to "see" the problem themselves in order to arrive at a satisfactory solution. An officer's sphere of influence dictated his ability to manage his forces and dictate their actions through orders. This arrangement often turned on the nature of a commander's relationships with his subordinates; his ability to issue orders with clarity, precision, and appropriateness; and his army's capacity or willingness to execute those instructions. Implicit within this complicated arrangement is the possibility—often probability—of intervening human error, exhaustion, disruption, confusion, limitations of character, aptitude, or simple chance. Evaluating the art of command in a particular historical moment begs a careful balance of multiple methods, and the historian's multifaceted and granular approach is particularly suitable for such a complicated process.

The challenges for historians evaluating the art and language of command during the Civil War are much like those faced by the commanders themselves. Effective military leaders must impose order and coherence upon complexity and uncertainty while creating an organized portrait of the context, conditions, and environment in which their decision making takes place. Historians of command, unencumbered by the impediment of combat's physical, mental, and emotional stresses, have the immense benefit of hindsight. Consequently, it is important to approach any analysis of the art of command with a degree of humility, even empathy, remembering that precise courses of action and clear solutions after thoughtful deliberation were not always possible during military operations. Historians must always recognize that conclusions arrived at from the comfortable perch of the calm present often do not allow for the dynamism and abstractions of war's reality. Military action is an interconnected and complicated process, and the reductive nature of distilling war to problems and solutions ignores the intervention of causation, contingency, complexity, and chance, all which frustrate and disrupt conclusions. As Prussian military theorist Carl von Clausewitz famously observed:

> Everything in war is simple, but the simplest thing is difficult. The difficulties accumulate and end by producing a kind of friction that is inconceivable unless one has experienced war. . . . Countless minor incidents—the kind you can never really foresee—combine to lower the general level of performance, so that one always falls far short of the intended goal. . . . The military machine—the army and everything related to it—is basically very simple and therefore seems easy to manage. But we should bear in mind that none of its components is of one piece: each part is composed of individuals, . . . the least important of whom may chance to delay things or somehow make them go wrong. . . . This tremendous friction, which cannot, as in mechanics, be reduced to a few points, is everywhere in contact with chance, and brings about effects that cannot be measured, just because they are largely due to chance.[2]

Historians, like military leaders themselves, must account for the unaccountable in analyzing the art of command. This is the "friction" and "fog of war" Clausewitz warned of, the inescapable degradation of effectiveness endemic to armies engaged in prolonged military operations as well as the natural uncertainty brought on by faulty, limited, or distorted intelligence, human weakness, and the element of randomness that all contribute to warfare's unpredictability. In short, to understand the variegated factors that influence historical contingency, historians of the art of command should draw upon every available tool of analysis to inform their assessment of decisions and events, including those of military professionals, planners, and thinkers.

The affair at McLemore's Cove, also known as the Battle of Davis's Cross Roads or the Battle of Dug Gap, occurred on September 9–11, 1863, in northwestern Georgia as part of the Chickamauga Campaign, in concert with Federal efforts to capture Chattanooga, Tennessee.[3] At McLemore's Cove Gen. Braxton Bragg and his Confederate Army of Tennessee permitted two vulnerable Federal divisions to escape entrapment and possible destruction, thus altering the opening sequence of the entire campaign. An immense lost opportunity for the Confederates, this operation serves as an object lesson on the power of contingency to shape historical events, on the difficulty of managing and commanding field armies during the Civil War, and a valuable window into the command problems and troubled relationships between Bragg and his subordinates during the summer of 1863. Historians, military professionals, and the participants themselves have explained this failure in numerous ways, including Federal acumen, Unionist civilian help, Confederate paralysis under pressure, faulty planning and intelligence, Bragg's ineptitude, the venomous command culture within the Army of Tennessee's senior officer corps, and even cowardice.[4] While each of these reasons has merit, the ultimate failure to isolate and destroy the Army of the Cumberland's vulnerable elements at Mc-Lemore's Cove did not stem entirely from faulty intelligence, a dysfunctional command structure, or indecisive and incompetent leadership, as various orthodox explanations propose. Even taken together, these disparate explanations only partially account for what actually happened; further, they do not actually answer the essential question of why and how that failure happened and what it reveals about the art of command in this specific instance.

A breakdown in Bragg's use of written words is at the core of the fiasco at McLemore's Cove, and the events, relationships, and written orders of September 9–11 reveal an unfolding debacle that forced the general and his subordinates into a torpor of muddled thinking, indecision, insubordination, and inaction. To comprehend how faulty language disrupted command and control, led to the Army of Tennessee's missteps at McLemore's Cove, and set events in motion that led to the dire consequences that followed, we must first understand why militaries emphasize the importance of employing written words effectively. In April 1894 and November 1895, some thirty years after the Civil War, U.S. Army major Eben Swift delivered a series of lectures on field orders at the Infantry and Cavalry School at Fort Leavenworth, Kansas, the precursor to the modern U.S. Army Command and General Staff College. Swift's lectures represented some of the army's first serious efforts to systematize the ways in which commanders in the field delivered orders to subordinates, distilling the lessons of the Civil War as well as the innovative methods of the German General Staff. After studying the means and methods by which historical leaders such as Napoleon Bonaparte, Ulysses S. Grant, and others had exercised command over their troops in the field, Swift concluded that prior to the German General Staff's reforms of command communications during the Franco-Prussian War (1870–71), generals usually devised their own individualized methods for crafting and disseminating written field orders to subordinates. Civil War generals were among the worst perpetrators of what Swift called "strange ideas . . . among officers who represented the best trained element of the arm[ies]." These orders were "often filled with insignificant details, useless suggestions, and unwarranted interference with subordinates."[5] Swift's lectures and the professional military literature they inspired had an immediate and lasting effect on the methods of crafting and delivering field orders, leading ultimately to the venerable five-paragraph field-orders format currently enshrined in U.S. Army doctrine.[6]

In military parlance, field orders are written or verbal instructions articulated to convey the will of the commander to his subordinates and deal with tactical, operational, or strategic considerations concomitant to specific military operations. Civil War–era armies moved at the impetus of language, and military operations during that conflict usually began with general orders or letters of instruction governing the movements, administration, or logistical needs of large bodies of troops across time and space for extended periods. When circumstances required a greater level of operational or tactical specificity, officers would then issue field orders managing the offensive and defensive operations of smaller components within their command. Civil War field orders could be either written or verbal, and other than containing the date, time, and place of origination, followed almost no standard format. In fact Union and Confederate commanders followed the Napoleonic tradition of issuing free-form field orders, which Swift found utterly inadequate and considered "an important element in bringing about his [Napoleon's] final defeat."[7]

Field orders, then and now, have several principal purposes. First, field orders enable commanders to direct subordinates toward accomplishing a specific objective. Second, they empower the commander to curate information and coordinate action effectively among multiple subordinates and other elements. Third and finally, they provide the means to communicate a clear course of action with precision, clarity, and timeliness to achieve an ultimate objective.[8] Effective field orders, according to Swift, should convey enough information and instruction necessary to fulfill these purposes. When composing these communications, commanders must ensure that they have made a careful estimate of the situation by evaluating all available intelligence, including the known strengths and positions of both friendly and enemy forces as well as intervening circumstances such as terrain, weather, supply considerations, and known or suspected enemy intentions. Commanders then formulate a plan of action based on their estimate of the situation. Once they have determined what their course will be, they must then draft field orders sufficient to enable subordinates to execute the plan of action.[9] These instructions should ideally consist of five simple paragraphs containing the following elements:

1. *Information on the enemy and on supporting troops.* If intelligence about the enemy is uncertain, then commanders should provide subordinates with their most accurate estimation of the enemy's strength, position, and intentions as well as the strength, location, and status of friendly forces.

2. *The commander's plans, or an "intimation of the end in view."* Commanders should provide subordinates with enough information about the operation's general goals to carry out their specific role without overwhelming them with superfluous detail.

3. *The commander's detailed tactical disposition for carrying out his plans.* Commanders should assign subordinates their necessary tasks, notify them of the timetable for completion, and place them in the best position and circumstances to complete the mission.

4. *The destination of the trains.* When relevant, commanders must see to it that subordinates understand the logistical factors pertinent to the mission, including supply, reinforcements, and marching orders.

5. *The commander's location.* In order to ensure effective communication, subordinates must always be informed of the commander's location, his headquarters, or the locations and schedule of his staff.[10]

Swift urged commanders to include the date, hour, minute, and manner of issue in written field orders. While such instructions could be verbal or written, the latter was much preferred for clarity's sake. Verbal orders are inherently unreliable and ought to be avoided. In extremely urgent circumstances, he urged commanders to employ multiple means of transmission to ensure delivery and to send copies of field orders to superiors.[11] Couriers ought to deliver field orders, though staff officers authorized to clarify questions that may arise should handle particularly important dispatches. Written field orders were especially necessary, maintained Swift, when a force was scattered across a broad geographic space, as was often the case in operations. Commanders must allow time for the transmission of formal orders from higher to lower units as well; his rule of thumb was one hour for dispatches within brigades and one and a half hours for divisions. Because the complexity of transmitting orders only increases once movement has begun, he urged that all commanders apprise all of their subordinates of the general plan for an operation "so that in case of unforeseen developments they may continue to act in conformity with such [a] plan without waiting for further orders."[12]

Orders ought to be brief, Swift continued, because "short sentences are easily understood; conjecture, expectations, reasons for measures adopted and detailed instructions for a variety of possible events, are little calculated to raise the confidence of troops, and should therefore be avoided."[13] Along with concision, precision, clarity, and thoroughness, he explained that a dispatch "must be so positive in its terms that the responsibility can be placed with ease." Ambiguity, vagueness, or uncertainty have no place in field orders, Swift added, and commanders should take care to leave subordinates no room for interpretation if possible. "The line must be clearly drawn between an order which is to be strictly construed and one where discretion is allowed." He proposed a simple way to test for clarity: "Imagine yourself in the place of the recipient of your order, and ask yourself if you could obey without asking a question"; if not, then the dispatch is insufficiently clear.[14] Above all, Swift urged, "orders must not be couched in uncertain terms." Ambiguity not only sowed the seeds of confusion but also provided leaders with the opportunity to avoid action, shirk responsibility, or exercise undue caution to the detriment of the operation. "The commander should accept the entire responsibility and shift none of it to the shoulders of his subordinates," he declared. "Precise orders give confidence in dangerous undertakings. The more difficult the situation, the clearer and more definite should be the order."[15] To Swift, phrases like "as far as possible," "as well as you can," and so forth "tend to divide responsibility between the commander and his subordinate." Equivocal field orders reflected weakness and uncertainty, and "commanders will frequently choose such forms of expression in order to shift the responsibility in case of failure."[16] Though the Civil War preceded Swift's reforms by a generation, when superimposed upon the McLemore's Cove operation, these principles serve as a stark reminder of the command-and-control shortcomings of those armies and illustrate the link between these problems and the subsequent evolution in thinking that emerged among U.S. military reformers in the years that followed.

With these considerations in mind, it is through the lens of the experiences of Bragg and his subordinates during the operations at McLemore's Cove that language of command and its limits during the Civil War become clear. Following the Battle of Stones River in early 1863, Maj. Gen. William S. Rosecrans and his Army of the Cumberland prepared for a new campaign into the Confederate heartland from their winter quarters in Murfreesboro, Tennessee. Rosecrans had at his disposal some 50,000 men organized into four infantry corps along with a corps of cavalry.[17] Opposing him was Bragg's Army of Tennessee, with infantry corps under Lt. Gen. Leonidas Polk, Lt. Gen. Daniel Harvey Hill, and Maj. Gen. Simon Bolivar Buckner and a reserve corps under Maj. Gen. W. H. T. Walker, along with two cavalry corps under Maj. Gen. Joseph Wheeler and Brig. Gen. Nathan Bedford Forrest.[18] Rosecrans spent much of the winter and spring of 1863 refitting his battered army and laying plans to eject Bragg from Middle Tennessee and capture Chattanooga, an essential node in the Confederate logistical web and the gateway into northern Georgia. Rosecrans's well-developed war of maneuver paid off brilliantly that summer in the Tullahoma Campaign. By August 1863 he had Bragg's army in retreat and the city of Chattanooga in his sights.

Besides the precarious strategic position of the Army of Tennessee that summer, other concerns beset the Confederates under Bragg. As previously noted, Bragg suffered from a dysfunctional command relationship among his chief subordinates, a predicament for which he was not solely to blame, but for which he had neither a solution nor the faculties to resolve. The enmity within the command structure of the Confederacy's western army had a lengthy history, and after a hollow tactical victory at Stones River, the already unruly generals of the Army of Tennessee were in a seditious frame of mind. A vocal bloc of anti-Bragg generals, including Polk, Buckner, Lt. Gen. Edmund Kirby Smith, and Lt. Gen. William J. Hardee, waged a bitter campaign against their commander. Bragg was either inexcusably oblivious to their open hostility or, more likely, simply unwilling to confront their insolence, and he did little to counter his critics or impose his authority upon their machinations.[19]

The Federals, on the other hand, glowed with confidence that summer. After the ease with which he had outgeneraled Bragg thus far, Rosecrans believed he had the measure of the Confederate commander. Moreover, he intended to maintain the initiative he had seized during the Tullahoma Campaign and to continue the war of maneuver that had served him so well. With the Confederates pinned in and around Chattanooga, Rosecrans knew that he could strike Bragg at the time and place of his own choosing and decided a hasty pursuit was in order. Staging from Winchester, Tennessee, on August 16, Rosecrans ignored the advice of his best corps commander, Maj. Gen. George H. Thomas, and split his army into multiple columns for a headlong turning movement through the mountain gaps southwest of Chattanooga.[20] Initially all went according to plan, and elements of the Army of the Cumberland crossed the Tennessee River at multiple points over a five-day period without significant Confederate resistance, swinging south into Georgia and using the Lookout Mountain range to screen their approach to the city.[21] On the evening of September 7, Bragg ordered the Army of Tennessee to pull out of Chattanooga altogether and fall back on Rome, Georgia, to concentration its strength. By placing his various columns among the jagged mountains and out of easy supporting distance of one another, Rosecrans had made a serious mistake. Recognizing this, Bragg hoped to locate and attack one of the isolated Federal corps, break it up, and then place the bulk of his army between Rosecrans's remaining forces. Such an eventuality would not only disrupt the Federals' turning movement and recover Chattanooga for the Confederacy but also place Bragg's concentrated forces in a favorable position to defeat Rosecrans's dispersed army in detail.[22]

During the day on September 9, Confederate cavalry commander Brig. Gen. William T. Martin reported to Bragg that a force of some 5,000 Federals had entered McLemore's Cove via Stevens's Gap in the valley's western wall. Martin's troopers had located Maj. Gen. James S. Negley's Second Division, an advance element of Thomas's XIV Corps. Brig. Gen. Absalom Baird's First Division trailed Negley in support; together these two units numbered a little more than 8,000 men.[23] The Army of Tennessee had overwhelming numerical superiority in the area of operations, and with a bit of luck and good plan-

ning, Bragg was on the verge of achieving tactical surprise over an isolated
and unwitting enemy force. Geography also seemed to favor the Confederates. McLemore's Cove lay between Lookout Mountain on the east and Pigeon
Mountain on the west. The valley itself was about seven miles wide on its
northern end, with the mountains converging about eighteen miles to the
south. Entry to the cove was restricted to a few gaps through these mountains: Stevens's and Cooper's (or Frick's) Gaps through the western side, and
Worthen's, Catlett's, Dug, and Bluebird Gaps through the eastern wall. The
Federals' anticipated route would take them east via Stevens's Gap, through
Bailey's and Davis's Cross Roads, and then through Dug Gap directly into La-
Fayette. By choosing this course, the Federals had blindly entered a natural
chokepoint straight into the teeth of superior forces with no alternative escape
routes. A Confederate victory in the cove would disrupt the entire Federal
effort. Here, perhaps, were the seeds for a change of momentum in the West
that had eluded the Confederacy for so long.[24]

Between 5:00 P.M. and 10:00 P.M. on September 9, Bragg ordered Maj.
Gen. Thomas C. Hindman to report personally to army headquarters at Lee
and Gordon's Mills and to prepare his division of 7,697 men to move out.[25]
Hindman's Division was part of Polk's Corps and the nearest available unit
for the operation. Bragg expressed no initial qualms about giving Hindman
this critical assignment, nor did the commanding general hesitate to cut his
superior, Polk, completely out of the impending operation. Though new to the
army, Hindman had a reputation for flamboyance and aggressiveness from his
service at Shiloh and in the Trans-Mississippi, and Bragg much preferred him
to the insubordinate Polk or the unreliable Maj. Gen. Benjamin F. Cheatham,
whose division, also part of Polk's Corps, was nearby.[26] With veteran brigades
under Brig. Gen. James Patton Anderson, Brig. Gen. Zachariah C. Deas, and
Brig. Gen. Arthur M. Manigault, Bragg was hopeful that Hindman would
be up to the task. Unfortunately, he misread his new division commander's
sensibilities. Hindman got off on the wrong foot with his troops, imposing
harsh discipline and alienating his officers and enlisted men alike almost as
soon as he took charge.[27] Worse, despite his reputation for boldness, Hindman
actually had a tendency toward excessive caution when faced with unknown
or challenging circumstances, as demonstrated by his reticence during the
1862 Battle of Prairie Grove.[28] New to his division and probably forewarned
by his peers about Bragg's reputation for scapegoating subordinates, the gen-

eral must have understood that his assignment was fraught with personal and professional peril. It is unclear whether Hindman came to the Army of Tennessee predisposed to disobedience and difficulty, but certainly his subsequent performance did him no credit in that regard.[29]

Because Hindman remained a largely unknown quantity, Bragg ordered corps commander D. H. Hill, also new to the army, to support the operation. Hill was a querulous Carolinian with a strong combat reputation. While he had distinguished himself in Virginia and elsewhere under Gen. Robert E. Lee, Hill possessed a brittle personality and an antagonistic streak that tended to alienate friend and foe alike. By the summer of 1863, Lee had had enough and sent him West, where he took over Hardee's old corps. Pres. Jefferson Davis approved the transfer without consulting Bragg, which probably irked the irascible army commander. Though the two generals were old acquaintances from their West Point days, they clashed practically from the moment of their first encounter in July. Hill quickly picked up the instinctive habit of questioning Bragg's every move and by September had fallen in with Polk's clique of anti-Bragg officers.[30] On September 9 his headquarters were at La-Fayette, about fourteen miles from Lee and Gordon's Mills and army headquarters. Hill's greatest asset at that time was that the army's most dependable division, that of Maj. Gen. Patrick R. Cleburne, was part of his corps. But Hill had posted Cleburne's troops along Pigeon Mountain, the eastern wall of McLemore's Cove and proximate to the Federals' anticipated line of approach but some distance from Negley's and Baird's position. So Hill and Hindman would have to do, with Cleburne serving as insurance.

When Hindman arrived at Bragg's tent at Lee and Gordon's Mills on the night of September 9, the army commander instructed him to march his division "immediately to Davis's Cross-Roads, on the road from LaFayette to Stevens' Gap," a thirteen-mile journey from start to finish. Upon reaching the crossroads in the heart of the cove, Hindman would establish "communication with the column of General Hill, ordered to move to the same point." Bragg would direct Hill to send Cleburne's Division over Pigeon Mountain through Dug Gap, where it would enter McLemore's Cove from the eastern end to link up with Hindman, approaching from the north. Once the juncture with Cleburne was established, Hindman would "take command of the joint forces, or report to the officer commanding Hill's column according to rank." With this unified force, Hindman would "move upon the enemy" if in command or, presumably, follow the orders of the senior officer in charge. With these two divisions approaching from the north and the east, Bragg hoped to strike the Federals in McLemore's Cove in the front and flank. The enemy would have only a single escape route —back through Stevens's Gap by way of Bailey's Cross Roads. As Bragg explained his plan to Hindman, he shared the intelligence that Martin's cavalry had brought in early that afternoon. The enemy was "reported to be 4,000 or 5,000 strong," Bragg relayed, and "encamped at the foot of Lookout Mountain at Stevens Gap." He then cautioned Hindman "in passing" that "another column of the enemy is reported to be at Cooper's Gap; number not known." This vague estimate reflected Bragg's own uncertainty about the Federals' strength and precise location, and while it may have been his best guess given the limited intelligence his cavalry and scouts had obtained, the warning to an uncertain, perhaps hostile, subordinate likely did more harm than good. Bragg lacked concrete information on the enemy's whereabouts, and his offhand mention of possible enemy forces at Cooper's Gap, three miles north of Stevens's Gap on what would be Hindman's right flank, apparently stuck in the division commander's mind, becoming a preoccupation that would dramatically affect his subsequent performance.[31]

After the initial conference with Bragg, Hindman huddled with the general's chief of staff, Brig. Gen. William W. Mackall, to clarify questions about the operation and receive his formal written orders. Meanwhile, Bragg dispatched a copy of those orders, along with additional instructions, to Hill at LaFayette. He ordered the corps commander to "send or take, as your judgment dictates, Cleburne's division to unite with General Hindman at Davis's Cross-Roads to-morrow morning." Bragg unnecessarily reminded him that "a cavalry force should accompany your column" and that Hill should "open communication with Hindman with your cavalry in advance of the junction." He noted that "Hindman starts at 12 o'clock to-night, and he has 13 miles to make," adding that "the commander of the column thus united will move upon the enemy encamped at the foot of Stevens' Gap, said to be 4,000 or 5,000."[32]

The mishaps that followed were not entirely Bragg's fault. Yet the general and his staff committed a series of serious and inexcusable errors in composing these initial orders that created conditions instrumental in the operation's ultimate failure. Personality clashes and army politics played important roles in these mistakes. Bragg created an unnecessarily complicated and uncertain command arrangement, partially to preclude Polk and Cheatham's involvement. He assigned Hindman, a division commander, to take charge of what was in essence an ad-hoc understrength corps eventually composed of units from three separate and existing commands. Moreover, he apparently expected him to answer directly to him while also consulting with Hill in La-Fayette, all while coordinating with Cleburne's borrowed division. Later Bragg also inserted Buckner, another corps commander, into this leadership equation while retaining Hindman in nominal but informal overall charge of the operation. He defined none of these command relationships explicitly, nor did he explain his reasoning for this odd arrangement; rather, he seems to have expected his subordinates to work out these details themselves as the situation unfolded. Further, Bragg granted Hill broad discretion to act—or not—as the Carolinian saw fit throughout the early stages of the operation. The general's provision, "If unforeseen circumstances should prevent your movement, notify Hindman," permitted Hill enough latitude to decide on his own whether he wished to go to Hindman's aid in the cove or to simply do nothing. Bragg also neglected to inform either Hill or Hindman of his overall operational intent or what he expected each subordinate to do with respect to achieving his desired goal. Beyond ordering Hindman to "move upon the enemy" thought to be encamped at Stevens's Gap, Bragg's written orders simply failed to convey a clear sense of the ultimate goal for the McLemore's Cove operation or of his expectations for his generals.

Bragg also did not account for the inherent lag in the operation's timing from the moment he issued his initial set of orders. The courier bearing the September 9 directive for Hill had to make a fourteen-mile night journey from Lee and Gordon's Mills to LaFayette. Assuming that Hill acted promptly upon receipt of these orders, Cleburne's troops would still have had to make the trek to Davis's Cross Roads, rendezvous with Hindman, and coordinate an attack, all leading to more delays. Bragg made no specific provisions for these considerations of time and space in his orders. Hill and Cleburne were certain to be delayed until midday on September 10, or perhaps even later, and until that time Hindman would have to operate independently and without immediate support. Bragg also neglected to require Hindman or Hill to send regular updates on their progress and status, ensuring that the commanding general would be the last to know of any new developments. He could have joined Hill in LaFayette on the evening of the ninth, instead of the tenth, as he would do later. Also Bragg created these orders knowing that no reliable field-telegraph system was in place to help him maintain contact with the various elements during the operation. The primary responsibility of the army's telegrapher, Capt. Edward H. Cummings, was to maintain contact with commanders in other districts and to provide information to the Confederate War Department in Richmond, not to facilitate communications between army headquarters and subordinate units in a tactical or operational sense. Bragg relied exclusively on mounted couriers and staff officers to maintain communications and relay his field orders during the operation. Given that he hoped to coordinate Hindman's effort through Lee and Gordon's Mills, Hill's headquarters at La-Fayette, and McLemore's Cove itself, he sorely needed a telegraph network or a more reliable system of couriers. The absence of an effective and efficient command-and-control apparatus ensured that there would be delays in transmitting information and clarifications during the entire campaign.[33]

With these problems saturating the command atmosphere, Hindman started his march from Lee and Gordon's Mills toward Davis's Cross Roads at about 1:00 A.M. on September 10, an hour after his initial conference with Bragg and Mackall. His shortest path to McLemore's Cove would have been via Crawfish Spring, but that route was deemed insecure and too far from friendly lines in case of a crisis. Hindman instead decided to take a circuitous three-mile detour along the LaFayette Road to avoid alerting any Federal cavalry pickets. Marching first to a Dr. Peter Anderson's house, his division took roads through Worthen's Gap and into McLemore's Cove itself, all in the dark of night and with no clear sense of the enemy threats lurking in and beyond the mountains. During a pause, friendly locals told Hindman that Federal columns had been sighted near Davis's Cross Roads, three or four miles south, and also at Stevens's Gap, six miles to the southwest. Dug and Catlett's Gaps, the civilians said, were blocked by trees and rocks that Confederate cavalry had positioned earlier to slow any potential enemy advance into the cove. Hindman was also deeply concerned about the unknown Federal force at Cooper's Gap that Bragg had mentioned in his initial briefing. If credible, this report placed enemy forces of uncertain size along Hindman's right, directly on his line of march. He had hoped the gaps in the mountains would serve as escape routes for his division should some unforeseen disaster occur, but with Dug and Catlett's Gaps now impassable, only Worthen's Gap remained viable. Even worse, there was still no word from Hill about Cleburne's departure or estimated time of arrival.[34]

Hoping to gather more information about the rumored force at Cooper's Gap, Hindman sent one of Martin's attached cavalry regiments to gather information. While the horsemen reconnoitered, at 6:00 A.M. Hindman drafted a message to Hill outlining his concerns. The general was anxious about the whereabouts of Cleburne's column and the timing of their scheduled rendezvous at Davis's Cross Roads. He also worried that Catlett's Gap, his favored avenue of retreat, was blocked, which would also prevent or delay Cleburne's efforts to provide support. Hindman then warned Hill of the unknown Federal forces lurking near Davis's Cross Roads and at Bailey's Cross Roads and cautioned that another enemy force had been seen near Cooper's Gap. Given these fears, the normally audacious Hindman reached a rather timorous conclusion: "I deem it inexpedient," he informed Hill, "to move beyond this place till I learn that you are in motion and that we can safely unite."[35]

Meanwhile, between 4:25 A.M. and 5:00 A.M., Hill received Bragg's message and a copy of Hindman's orders. He ignored his instructions to open up communications with Hindman and did not notify the division commander that Cleburne would not, in fact, march for Davis's Cross Roads. Consequently, Hill ensured that Hindman would remain paralyzed in the cove, waiting for reinforcements that were not coming. He dashed off an immediate reply to Bragg, reciting his own litany of reasons why he would not send Cleburne to Hindman's aid. The eleven miles between LaFayette and Davis's Cross Roads were too far to transit in time to help, Hill avowed. Hoping to slow the advancing Federals, Martin's retreating cavalrymen had felled trees and blocked the road through Dug Gap, he added, which made it impossible to pass. In any case, Cleburne was supposedly sick in bed and unfit to lead his men, and anyway his division was scattered along Pigeon Mountain. Finally, Hill claimed that he had not received Bragg's orders until 5:00 A.M. on the tenth and that it was then far too late for him to do anything about them. The corps commander was firm in his conclusion: "Under the circumstances, I have not ordered the movement, as it could not possibly be simultaneous. Either Hindman should be stopped or the movement postponed till to-night."[36]

Hill's excuses for inaction were utterly specious. In fact, the distance from his headquarters to Davis's Cross Roads was only five miles, an easy morning march and well within his men's capabilities. While Dug Gap was blocked, Martin estimated that his cavalrymen could have cleared away the obstructing timber in two hours or less. Also, contrary to Hill's assertion, Cleburne was not sick at all, something that the corps commander should have known and could have discovered simply by sending a staff officer to inquire.[37] Cleburne was one of the ablest division commanders in the Army of Tennessee and his troops among its best; there is little doubt that they could have prepared to march into the cove on short notice had Hill simply ordered them to do so. He did not. Finally, his reply to Bragg's orders was marked 4:25 A.M., some thirty-five minutes *earlier* than 5:00 A.M., the time he claimed to have actually received them. Hill never satisfactorily explained this temporal discrepancy, nor did he ever answer for his failure to act in the early morning hours of September 10.[38]

Despite the flawed nature of Bragg's 11:45 P.M. instructions, Hill could and should have complied with the spirit of the orders, first by sending Cleburne to Davis's Cross Roads, then by dispatching a courier to Hindman and Bragg updating both generals on the situation. Unfortunately, he was not inclined to interpret his orders with even a modicum of cooperative spirit. Furthermore, Bragg's ambiguous language in his 11:45 A.M. dispatch gave Hill a fig leaf to justify his inaction, as did Bragg's inexcusable inclusion of the discretionary provision regarding "unforeseen circumstances" preventing his participation. In the strictest construction of this order, Hill's only absolute obligation was to send a message to Hindman letting him know that the unanticipated had occurred and no reinforcements were forthcoming from his corps. Yet rather than fulfill even that most rudimentary requirement in his instructions, Hill simply declined to move entirely, advised Bragg to call of the operation, and neglected to notify Hindman, then marching his division into harm's way, of these critical changes to the plan.[39]

Hindman, of course, knew none of this in the predawn hours of September 10, and his troops continued trudging down the Cove Road toward Davis's Cross Roads. Near dawn the general ordered his division to halt at Morgan's house for a breather. With no word yet from either Hill or Cleburne, Hindman found himself on the horns of a dilemma. To remain in place indefinitely would have violated Bragg's orders to move upon the enemy. On the other hand, to advance incautiously into McLemore's Cove with no word of Cleburne's location or timetable; with unknown enemies to his front, right, and possibly rear; and with his lines of retreat blocked or threatened would have been reckless. Despite his reputation as an aggressive leader, Hindman had demonstrated a propensity to act cautiously when under the shadow of the enemy, and this characteristic again reared its ugly head. The general decided on a compromise course: he would advance as Bragg had ordered, but he would move very slowly in the hopes that Cleburne would have time to catch up and reinforce him before any encounter with the enemy.[40] Hindman ordered his division to deploy for battle about three miles from Davis's Cross Roads, then settled in anxiously to await support.

At 8:00 a.m. on the tenth, Bragg received Hill's message recommending that he postpone the operation. Sensing a choice opportunity about to slip away, Bragg refused to resign himself to failure. Rather than canceling the mission and recalling Hindman, he called on the next available troops to take Cleburne's mission. These forces happened to be Buckner's two-division corps, which by then had arrived near Anderson's house along the Worthen's Gap Road. Buckner and Bragg had a tempestuous relationship dating back to the ill-fated Kentucky Campaign of 1862. Following the Battle of Perryville, the Kentuckian Buckner had joined with other anti-Bragg generals in publicly criticizing their commander's performance. He also apparently harbored a grudge against Bragg for subsuming his control over the Department of East Tennessee in the summer of 1863 and believed that Bragg's command authority over his corps was limited in nature and his orders subject to interpretation.[41] Further, the Kentuckian found himself placed under Hindman's temporary authority for the operation, which likely irked him. Bragg either failed to appreciate Buckner's antipathy toward him, as well as his peculiar notions about the command relationship between them, or simply chose to ignore them. Thus after receiving Hill's response, Bragg ordered Buckner to "execute without delay the order issued to General Hill," enclosing copies of Hill's and Hindman's original orders. Buckner's two divisions would replace Cleburne's single division in Bragg's plan; beyond this, nothing else would change.[42] A little over eight hours had passed since Bragg issued his initial orders for the attack, and by 11:00 a.m. on the tenth, Buckner still had not moved from Anderson's house. The general informed Hindman via courier that he would send all of his cavalry, that his divisions would "come very soon to support you," and that his "infantry are somewhat wearied, but I will move them forward as rapidly as I can."[43]

At this time too Hill sent a message to Hindman repeating the earlier excuses he had provided Bragg for declining to send Cleburne to Davis's Cross Roads. He also explained that the commanding general had seen fit to allow him to exercise his own discretion as to whether to participate in the operation. By 12:20 P.M. Hindman received reports that Negley's Federals were advancing on Dug Gap and preparing to fight. If Hill's hunch was correct and the Federal movement in the cove was merely a ruse to draw the Confederates' attention, it was certainly a convincing gambit.[44] In fact, the Federal presence in McLemore's Cove was no feint; Negley and Baird represented the lead elements of Thomas's XIV Corps, the middle prong of Rosecrans's trident of columns. Hill wasted much of September 10 fretting over the attack he anticipated would fall upon the Confederates from their southern flank. Oddly enough, his decision to do nothing came even after his cavalry scouts had reported that "the enemy [are] perfectly careless 4 miles from Dug Gap. They have no idea that we have any forces in this section, and I am sure the whole division can be captured in three hours, wagons & all."[45]

At 1:30 P.M. Hill sent Hindman a peculiar message reflecting his own ambivalence about the McLemore's Cove operation. He forwarded to the division commander a copy of a letter to Bragg's chief of staff, marked for Hindman's "information and guidance," in which he informed the commanding general: "I am moving Cleburne's division out to Dug Gap. Should the Yankees be attacking there in force, it would be a good time for Hindman to attack in rear." Hill's oblique 1:30 P.M. suggestion did not contain additional positive orders for Hindman; rather, it couched any potential action as a mere conditional suggestion that an attack might be helpful if the rumors of a Federal attack on Dug Gap proved true. When Hindman read this odd missive, he interpreted Hill's suggestion to mean that he ought to continue to hold position until Cleburne's Division arrived. Then, if enemy forces were assaulting Dug Gap, it "would be a good time" for the Confederate divisions to attack the Federals in concert. Since Cleburne's troops were still nowhere to be found by midafternoon, Hindman simply remained in place and waited.[46]

Hindman was still waiting at Morgan's house with his forces when Buckner and his two division commanders, Maj. Gen. Alexander P. Stewart and Brig. Gen. William Preston, joined him at around 4:45 P.M. With the addition of these troops, Confederate strength in McLemore's Cove now numbered about 17,000 men, more than the original plan had included and more than enough to confront Negley's and Baird's outnumbered divisions. Moreover, the Federals at Davis's Cross Roads were only about four miles away, easily within striking distance despite the late afternoon hour, and apparently had little idea of Confederate strength or location. But rather than take action and begin planning to attack with Buckner, Hindman decided to confer with the new arrivals instead. It is unclear what exactly transpired between the generals that afternoon, but one historian asserts that Buckner gradually "gained personal ascendancy over Hindman, a fact later admitted by the latter," resulting in yet more uncertainty and inaction.[47]

By late afternoon on September 10, Bragg still had heard nothing from Hindman. At 5:00 P.M. Bragg detached a company of engineers to clear the obstructions at Catlett's Gap. At 6:00 P.M. he sent an alarming message to Hindman, notifying him that "Crittenden's corps marched from Chattanooga this morning in this direction, and that it is highly important that you should finish the movement now going on as rapidly as possible." This warning, much like the earlier warning of unknown Federal troops at Cooper's Gap, resonated in Hindman's thinking. News of Maj. Gen. Thomas L. Crittenden's feared movement may have been Bragg's most accurate assessment of the enemy's position and intentions, and the commanding general doubtless hoped it would spur Hindman to greater urgency. Between 6:00 P.M. and 7:30 P.M., Bragg decided to relocate from his headquarters at Lee and Gordon's Mills to get closer to the action and had his staff begin packing up to join Hill at La-Fayette. Perhaps thinking his message to Hindman had not been clear enough, at 7:30 P.M. he dispatched another, writing: "The enemy is now divided. Our force at or near LaFayette is superior to the enemy. It is important now to move vigorously and crush him."[48] Bragg's decision to send two redundant orders within an hour and half of each other was ill advised. They did nothing to clarify the tactical or operational situation and merely added to the command complexity confronting the befuddled Hindman. Clearly Bragg was concerned about Hindman's silence and inaction, but the vaguely ominous intimation about Crittenden only stoked Hindman's anxiety about his vulnerable flank and rear.

From 4:45 P.M. to 8:00 P.M., Hindman and Buckner sat idle at Morgan's house. Finally at 8:00 P.M., Hindman convened a formal council of war with Buckner and their subordinate generals to gauge their opinion on the overall situation and compose a response to Hill's oblique suggestion. During this council, Bragg's redundant messages arrived, and Hindman had them read aloud to the group. The report that Crittenden was advancing south from Chattanooga alarmed both him and Buckner. From that moment, Hindman's primary focus was no longer on the Federal troops just a few miles in front of him at Davis's Cross Roads, nor on the other enemy force reported to be closing on Dug Gap. A mortal threat, he believed, came from Crittenden moving south, falling on his right or rear, and leaving him with no viable escape route. Feeling the noose tightening around him, in a message to Bragg marked 7:00 P.M., though actually written at 9:10 P.M., Hindman repeated Hill's earlier assessment that Federal activity at Davis's Cross Roads and Dug Gap must be a feint to draw attention away from Rosecrans's main effort, which both Hindman and Hill were convinced would be at Alpine farther south. "Unless something unforeseen prevents," Hindman reassured Bragg, "I expect to make the attack at daylight." He then explained that he would likely not make the strike at all because of the threat Crittenden posed to his flank and rear. Hindman would only strike the Federals at Davis's Cross Roads, he declared, if he could ascertain whether or not the "main body" of Rosecrans's army had moved from its presumed position threatening Alpine. "If it has not," Hindman concluded, "my force will probably be insufficient, and I will be attacked in rear from Stevens' Gap while attacking the column going east." Here Hindman implied that he intended to disregard the order to attack because the threats Bragg had hinted at throughout the operation made such a course too hazardous.[49] Buckner and the rest of the war council agreed, deciding that the best course of action would be to wait until morning. If circumstances remained unchanged, Hindman planned to pull out of the cove along his line of entry, turn northward to face Crittenden, and attack. This conclusion required him to countermand Bragg's original orders without authorization and to disregard a known enemy threat in his front in favor of turning back to face a rumored threat in his rear, all without permission.

Hindman must have realized that so drastic a change to Bragg's plan was tantamount to insubordination, but he apparently thought it necessary to get Hill's support for his proposal in writing. At 8:00 P.M. he dispatched a message to the corps commander requesting further clarification and seeking tacit approval for this new course. Posing the matter as a series of interrogatories, Hindman put the matter to Hill thus:

> The question which I am trying to solve to-night is: What force of the enemy is at or about Stevens' Gap to attack me in rear while co-operating with you? Probably the greater part of that force would be drawn

toward Dug Gap at the sound of your artillery, thus enabling me to move by way of Davis's Cross-Roads without too great risk. Can you at an early hour to-morrow make a real attack on the head of the enemy's column, so as to induce him to mass his forces while I strike him in rear? In this connection, can you force your way through them and effect a junction with me about Davis's Cross-Roads, while I force my column to the same point? Please answer these questions specifically. It may be that the enemy is in such force at Stevens' Gap that I may find it imprudent to expose my rear to their attacks.[50]

Hindman decided that he ought to let the commanding general know about his new plan too, and at 10:15 P.M. he sent a message to Bragg along with a copy of the 8:00 P.M. interrogatories for Hill. In his message to Bragg, Hindman informed the commander that he and his generals were all in agreement to withdraw from McLemore's Cove the next morning. If "General Hill responds negatively to the questions propounded to him, or if the enemy on our flank prove to be in such force as to render it too hazardous," he maintained, then the best option would be "to move rapidly against Crittenden, Cheatham co-operating, and Hill if possible, and thus crush that corps of the enemy."[51] Hindman, with Buckner's approval, had decided to override Bragg's express orders despite clear and repeated exhortations to carry them out.

To make matters even worse, Hindman chose to send Maj. James Nocquet, a French-born officer on Buckner's staff, perhaps at Buckner's suggestion, to deliver his message and "confer" with Bragg and Hill about the situation. Hindman instructed him to explain to the commanding general why his orders had been countermanded. "He understands the situation here as fully as I do," Hindman maintained of Nocquet, and would be able to clear up any confusion for Bragg. In reality, Nocquet was an abysmal choice for an envoy to headquarters. The major had a checkered career, having served on the staffs of several generals, including a brief stint as chief engineer for Bragg, before being relieved for incompetence. The Frenchman's English was very poor, and he unlikely understood the complicated operational situation in McLemore's Cove at all or be capable of explaining where things stood to Bragg and Hill.[52] Nocquet's mission seemed doomed from the start. Sometime after 10:15 P.M., the major departed for LaFayette bearing at least three written messages: the 9:10 P.M. (marked 7:00 P.M.) message from Hindman to Bragg; the 8:00 P.M.

interrogatories from Hindman to Hill, with a copy for Bragg; and the 10:15 P.M. letter of explanation from Hindman to Bragg.

Around midnight on September 11, Nocquet reported to army headquarters, where the commander was conducting a conference with Hill, Walker, Martin, and Brig. Gen. St. John R. Liddell. According to Lt. Col. David Urquhart, a staff officer in attendance during Nocquet's audience, the Frenchman "stated that General Hindman had heard that the enemy were moving in a particular direction, and that General Hindman thought it advisable to modify the orders he had received." Here, then, was clear evidence that Hindman had decided to disobey orders. Exasperated at this bit of news, Bragg spread out his maps in front of Nocquet and told him, "Major, I wish you to tell me nothing but what you know as a fact." The envoy replied that he could only relay the information that he had heard from Hindman; beyond that, he could not vouch for its reliability. Furious at this inadequate reply, the general "then turned to him and said his information amounted to nothing, and he would not modify his orders to General Hindman, and to return at once to General Hindman and tell him to carry out his orders." Bragg later recalled ordering Nocquet to return to Hindman and tell him "that my plans could not be changed, and that he would carry out his orders."[53] To ensure compliance, Bragg insisted that his own chief of staff send additional written orders "to attack the enemy if he lost his command in carrying out the order."[54] General Mackall reminded the commander that yet another order to attack would be redundant, but Bragg insisted. The communication, marked September 10, 12:00 P.M. by mistake (midnight of the eleventh would have been the correct designation), stated: "Crittenden's corps is advancing on us from Chattanooga. A large force from the south has advanced within 7 miles of this. Polk is left at Anderson's to cover your rear. General Bragg orders you to attack and force your way through the enemy to this point at the earliest hour that you can see him in the morning. Cleburne will attack in front the moment your guns are heard."[55]

Bragg couched these orders in the worst possible terms, given both the operational situation and Hindman's state of mind. He prefaced his midnight orders with yet another warning about the Federal threats converging on La-Fayette without providing any substantive intelligence as to location or estimated strength. These warnings, based as they were on little more than blind conjecture, could only alarm rather than inform and had precisely the wrong effect. Bragg's well-intentioned reassurances that Polk would defend Hindman's rear against Crittenden's approach could not counterbalance the worrisome addendum instructing the general to "force your way through the enemy to this point," LaFayette.[56] Moreover, Bragg needlessly employed language that emphasized potential enemy threats ancillary to the main objective rather than the expeditious completion of that objective. In so doing he unwittingly changed the primary focus of the operation altogether.[57]

At 4:20 A.M. on the eleventh, Hindman, still at the Morgan family's house, finally received Bragg's midnight orders. Once again their imprecision and lack of clarity served to fuel the sense of dread that had been growing in Hindman since the operation began. The impression he took from them was that his command faced an existential crisis. In his interpretation Bragg had just warned Hindman that he was about to be surrounded on all sides, and to survive he would have to cut his way through a cordon of concentrating enemy columns. As Hindman later explained, his reading of the communication "was that the general commanding considered my position a perilous one, and therefore expected me not to capture the enemy, but to prevent the capture of my own troops, forcing my way through to La Fayette, and thus saving my command. . . . This idea only was conveyed by the language used."[58] In other words, Bragg's written language conveyed an operational picture much different than the one he had described in detail to Hindman face to face on September 9 at Lee and Gordon's Mills. If the commanding general's written orders were to be believed, something drastic had changed, and Hindman was about to be caught in a vice and crushed by a superior enemy force. At a minimum the situation seemed to be evolving beyond Bragg's control. The message had a note of alarm in it that unsettled Hindman and must have raised dark uncertainties in his mind. Worse, there was no way to confirm or alleviate these suspicions, for Nocquet had still not yet returned from his disastrous conference with Bragg. Hoping that the major might be able to shed additional light on the situation, Hindman began preparing for a dawn movement to "save" his beleaguered command. Notifying his and Buckner's divisions to be ready to move at 7:00 A.M., Hindman sent out yet more cavalry scouts to feel for the enemy while he waited for sunrise.[59]

About two hours later, at 6:30 A.M., Nocquet finally returned. Hindman's version of the report he received on the meeting with Bragg is jaw dropping. According to Hindman, the major informed him that Bragg had granted authorization to "execute my [Hindman's] own plans" and that "he [Bragg] would sustain me" in those plans, whatever they might be. Further, Nocquet reported, Hill also expected that Hindman would be a morning attack and he fully intended to support such an effort.[60] Nocquet's statement that Hindman had carte blanche to act as he chose was ludicrous on its face, for nothing could have been further from the truth. In fact, Bragg had repeatedly issued both written and verbal nondiscretionary orders for Hindman to attack, even if it meant the destruction of his entire command and, by all accounts except Nocquet's, told the major exactly that. Certainly prior to the morning of the eleventh, Bragg had not authorized Hindman to execute any plan other than the one he had been ordered to carry out on the ninth and repeatedly thereafter. At a minimum Hindman disobeyed orders when countermanding his commander's original plan without authorization. He should never have postponed or canceled the ordered assault without explicit written orders to do so. That Hindman believed that he had the discretion to change Bragg's plans based on Nocquet's report reflects the ramshackle nature of command and control in the Army of Tennessee. The ease with which he engaged in this degree of gross insubordination also hints at the pernicious influence of anti-Bragg sentiment among the army's general officers.[61]

As Nocquet was reporting his fantastical version of his conference to Hindman, Bragg, Hill, and their respective staffs reached the summit of Pigeon Mountain, overlooking McLemore's Cove, to await what they thought was the coming battle. Cleburne's men soon had Dug Gap cleared and stood ready to move at the first sound of Hindman's guns. Bragg, "waiting in great anxiety," remembered that "several couriers and two staff officers were dispatched at different times, urging [Hindman] to move with promptness and vigor."[62] By 7:00 A.M. Hindman's force was on the move, but things quickly went awry. Deploying his three divisions for the advance on Davis's Cross Roads, Hindman decided to shift Buckner's troops, initially in the rear, to the front of the marching column. This required a complicated reshuffling of units along thickly wooded and cramped confines on the lone road to the objective, resulting in yet more delays and disorganization. Not until 11:00 A.M. was the long-awaited movement toward the crossroads finally underway.[63]

Soon thereafter, according to Hindman, he received a stunning new message from Bragg that altered the entire complexion of the operation. In an 11:00 A.M. dispatch, the general told Hindman: "If you find the enemy in such force as to make an attack imprudent, fall back at once on La Fayette by Catlett's Gap, from which obstructions have now been removed. Send your determination at once and act as promptly."[64] This dispatch exists only in Hindman's report, a document drafted a month after the operation as the division commander prepared his defense for a possible court-martial. No other record of this dispatch has survived, and the original document is long lost. Given the self-serving nature of the message as well as its curious provenance, some historians have questioned its existence altogether, with the implication that it may be a fabrication.[65] Without addressing the 11:00 A.M. message's legitimacy and taking Hindman at his word, it is clear that Bragg knew of his subordinate's concerns about the closing Federal threats, and the commanding general was anxious for more information about where things stood. Still, Bragg's supposedly explicit authorization for Hindman to call off the advance and retreat should he believe an attack "imprudent" is a shocking turn. In Bragg's version of events, at midnight he had ordered Hindman to attack at dawn even if it mean the loss of his entire command, but now after another half day of delays, he was prepared to leave the entire fate of the operation to Hindman, with no explanation for his change of heart.[66]

Apparently Bragg never seriously considered making the eight-mile ride from Dug Gap down into the cove in order to assume personal control to attempt to correct this fiasco, instead relying on a succession of couriers and aides to emphasize his growing impatience. By noon he decided to send another of his staffers, Capt. S. W. Presstman, to find out what was happening.[67] When Presstman arrived in the cove, Hindman and Buckner were still mulling over the 11:00 A.M. dispatch. Everything from Bragg to that point had indicated that the commanding general wanted Hindman to attack at all costs. Now something had changed: a retreat was not only conceivable but also perfectly acceptable. Presstman could be of little help; the captain could only repeat the substance of the most recent orders and confirm that Catlett's Gap was now open in case of a retreat. Hindman claimed to have sent a message to Bragg asking for clarification and then returned to discussing what to do with Buckner and the other officers.[68] At around 1:00 P.M. another peevish message from the commanding general arrived. "The enemy, estimated 12,000 or 15,000, is forming line in front of this place," Bragg wrote to Hindman. "Nothing heard of you since Captain Presstman, engineer, was with you. The general is most anxious and wishes to hear from you by couriers once an hour. A line is now established from your headquarters to ours." This message gloomily concluded: "The enemy are advancing from Graysville to La Fayette. Dispatch is necessary to us." Nothing in this dispatch mentioned the original and repeated orders to attack; Bragg only expressed his desire for regular updates along with a warning that the enemy was still advancing on LaFayette. It seemed to Hindman that the general had finally given up on the idea of striking the Federals in McLemore's Cove and was resigned to confronting threats elsewhere.[69]

After consulting with Buckner and Anderson, at 2:45 P.M. Hindman sent a careful but conclusive update to Bragg:

> Since my last dispatch I have received certain information that a large force of the enemy moved from Stevens' Gap toward Davis's Cross-Roads last night and this morning. The strength of this force is put by citizens at 11,000. I have previously reported a similar movement of a considerable force. My information is still imperfect as to the strength of the enemy on the road to Dug Gap, but I believe it superior to mine. In this opinion Generals Buckner and Anderson concur, and they also agree with me that any farther advance would be imprudent. Our judgment is influenced also by the apprehension that our rear is insecure upon information derived from you. I shall therefore retire by Catlett's Gap to La Fayette. The orders are now given.[70]

Bragg's last positive orders had been the 11:00 A.M. bombshell granting Hindman discretion to withdraw back LaFayette through Catlett's Gap if "the enemy [was] in such force as to make an attack imprudent." Hindman included liberal estimates of enemy strength at both Davis's Cross Roads and Dug Gap, emphasizing his belief that the Federals greatly outnumbered him. He also specifically included the term "imprudent," then reminded Bragg of the threat Crittenden posed to his rear, using the tortured phrase "upon information derived from you." Finally, Hindman was sure to mention that Buckner and Anderson completely agreed with his assessment and backed his decision. With two Federal corps approaching from his flanks and rear, with an uncertain force at his front, and with a flurry of contradictory messages from the commanding general, Hindman decided that he had had enough of the whole business in McLemore's Cove and that it was time to retreat.

Before he could send this final dispatch, however, at around 3:00 P.M. Capt. Taylor Beatty, another staff officer, conveyed Bragg's wishes that "the attack which was ordered at daybreak must be made at once or it will be too late." But Hindman was already in the process of ordering his withdrawal and told Beatty that "his information was of so various a character that he had vacillated" and that Bragg's orders had always been discretionary, both patent falsehoods.[71] Regardless, the alerted Federals had already managed to begin their withdrawal from McLemore's Cove, leaving Bragg, Hill, Hindman, Buckner, and the rest of the bewildered Army of Tennessee to bicker among themselves about yet another squandered opportunity. That evening Bragg finally rode down from Pigeon Mountain to join Hindman and the others at Davis's Cross Roads. By most accounts the meeting was highly unpleasant, with the army commander demanding to know where the enemy had gone and receiving no good explanation from Hindman. Captain Beatty, gauging the mood of the army's generals that night, concluded: "The bird had flown and the farce was complete."[72]

There is more than enough blame to go around for the Army of Tennessee's failure; besides, military misadventures of this nature are never entirely monocausal. Bragg conceived the operation in McLemore's Cove brilliantly, and under ideal conditions it should have worked. War, however, rarely presents commanders and armies with ideal conditions, and the general's difficult subordinates failed him catastrophically. Even so, Bragg must bear a large proportion of blame for his mistakes throughout the operation, errors that reflect poorly on his ability to understand and manage his principal commanders. If he was unmindful of the antipathy and hesitancy simmering among Hill, Buckner, and Hindman, it displays a deplorable lack of awareness, and he should bear the ultimate responsibility for failing to compensate for these problems. On the other hand, if Bragg suspected that his generals resented him and realized that it could lead them to interpret his orders in uncharitable ways, then he should have taken affirmative measures to mitigate or preclude the possibility of disobedience or resistance through the careful use of language. He should also have been willing to assume greater control of the situation in McLemore's Cove personally when he sensed things beginning to go wrong. Certainly by the time he knew that Hill had declined to send reinforcements into the cove and Hindman had repeatedly balked at attacking, Bragg should have intervened. When he chose to move his headquarters to La-

Fayette on the evening of the tenth, Bragg took the partial measure of placing himself only a few miles' ride from Hindman and Buckner, certainly close enough to manage the operation himself. The general understood the urgent need for haste as well as the growing confusion descending upon the operation. When his personal presence might have made a great deal of difference, instead Bragg continued to use couriers and staff officers to relay orders and demand updates.

Bragg also contributed to an unnecessary environment of command complexity and uncertainty in McLemore's Cove. He set up a complicated and ambiguous command arrangement by throwing together a joint force from across multiple corps and failing to delineate clear lines of authority between his various subordinates. He created the conditions under which strong-willed, insubordinate, or hostile leaders like Hill and Buckner could prey upon Hindman's hesitancy and exert undue influence over the operation. He failed to apprise his subordinates of the "intimation of the end in view," or his overarching operational objectives, in writing. Bragg also sent too many messages that did too little to accomplish these goals and, in fact, exacerbated existing problems. The general's orders contained far too much faulty, misleading, or disruptive and dangerous information sharing that served mainly to distract Hindman from attacking the Federals in McLemore's Cove. Over the course of September 9–11, some eleven written and verbal messages flew back and forth between Bragg and Hindman; most of these contained speculation, redundant instructions, and ambiguous, vague, or imprecise directives. In his exchanges with Hindman, Bragg included several unhelpful estimates of the enemy's strength and location based on faulty intelligence, rumor, and speculation more detrimental than helpful in achieving his ultimate objectives. In addition, he exchanged at least five written messages with Hill and two with Buckner. Hill and Hindman exchanged at least four missives, and while Buckner and Hindman communicated in writing just once, they held lengthy personal conferences and councils of war in an echo chamber of their own devising, without Hill's or Bragg's information or input, and with the additional handicap of Nocquet's misinformation. Finally, a number of couriers, aides, and other messengers delivered verbal instructions, demands, and requests for clarification between Bragg and his various subordinates. The accretion of complexity these communications created led to interruptions, misinterpretations, misunderstandings, command paralysis, and plentiful opportunities for

Bragg's recalcitrant subordinates to engage in outright disobedience. Bragg's unartful orders led to cumulative confusion during what ought to have been a straightforward operation. The confluence of these factors led to a missed opportunity with far-reaching consequences for the operation, the campaign, and ultimately the entire war.

By integrating various methods of analyses of the art of command with the historian's embrace of context, language, setting, human interaction, and perspective, we see that the failure at McLemore's Cove resulted from Bragg's inability to conceive, create, and promulgate field orders suitable to fulfill his operational objectives. Moreover, the unreliable and haphazard command-and-control methods customary to Civil War armies served as subtext to these failures, amplifying the existing problems within the Army of Tennessee's leadership. Bragg's command language also reveals his greatest leadership weakness—his inability or unwillingness to account for the human element in the evolving and often dysfunctional command relationship between himself and his subordinates. Understanding how words failed Bragg during these early days of the Chickamauga Campaign has the potential to open new vistas into difficult personalities; thorny relationship dynamics; daunting tactical, operational, and strategic problems; leadership; causation; and contingency in war.

NOTES

1. Donald R. Jermann, *Civil War Battlefield Orders Gone Awry: The Written Word and Its Consequences in 13 Engagements* (Jefferson, NC: McFarland, 2012), 11.

2. Carl von Clausewitz, *On War*, ed. and trans. Michael Howard and Peter Paret (Princeton, NJ: Princeton University Press, 1976), 119–20.

3. CWSAC Battle Summaries, "Davis's Cross Roads," American Battlefield Protection Program, https://www.nps.gov/abpp/Battles/ga003.htm, accessed June 26, 2016.

4. Glenn Tucker, *Chickamauga: Bloody Battle in the West* (New York: Bobs-Merrill, 1961), 60–71; Thomas Lawrence Connelly, *Autumn of Glory: The Army of Tennessee, 1862–1865* (Baton Rouge: Louisiana State University Press, 1971), 189–90; Peter Cozzens, *This Terrible Sound: The Battle of Chickamauga* (Urbana: University of Illinois Press, 1992), 70–75; William Glenn Robertson, "The Chickamauga Campaign, McLemore's Cove: Rosecrans' Gamble, Bragg's Lost Opportunity," *Blue & Gray* 23, no. 6 (Spring 2007): 6–26, 42–50; Steven E. Woodworth, "'In Their Dreams': Braxton Bragg, Thomas C. Hindman, and the Abortive Attack in McLemore's Cove," in *The Chickamauga Campaign*, ed. Woodworth (Carbondale: Southern Illinois University Press, 2010), 50–67, 65–66; David A. Powell, *The Chickamauga Campaign: A Mad Irregular Battle, from the Crossing of the Tennessee River through the Second Day, August 22–September 19, 1863* (El

Dorado Hills, CA: Savas Beatie, 2013), 155–60; Earl J. Hess, *Braxton Bragg: The Most Hated Man of the Confederacy* (Chapel Hill: University of North Carolina Press, 2016), 153–59.

5. Eben Swift, *Orders* (Fort Leavenworth, KS: Staff College Press, 1907), 9–10.

6. Matthew L. Smith, *The Five Paragraph Field Order: Can a Better Format be Found to Transmit Combat Information to Small Tactical Units?* (Fort Leavenworth, KS: School of Advanced Military Studies, U.S. Army Command and General Staff College, 1989), 4–6.

7. Swift, *Orders*, 6–8.

8. Ibid., 9–10.

9. Eben Swift, *Field Orders* (Fort Leavenworth, KS: Staff College Press, 1907), 1–5; Smith, *Five Paragraph Field Order*, 3–5.

10. Swift, *Field Orders*, 5–9; Smith, *Five Paragraph Field Order*, 4.

11. Swift, *Orders*, 44–45.

12. Swift, *Field Orders*, 2–3.

13. Ibid., 4.

14. Swift, "Field Orders, Messages and Reports," *Journal of the United States Cavalry Association* 10, no. 36 (Mar. 1897), 224–27.

15. Swift, *Field Orders*, 4–5.

16. Ibid., 5.

17. U.S. War Department, *The War of the Rebellion: A Compilation of the Official Records of the Union and Confederate Armies*, 70 vols. in 128 pts. (Washington, D.C.: Government Printing Office, 1880–1901), ser. 1, 23(1):410–17, 585 [hereafter cited as *OR*, all items from ser. 1].

18. *OR*, 30(2):11–20.

19. Connelly, *Autumn of Glory*, 73, Kenneth W. Noe, *Perryville: This Grand Havoc of Battle* (Lexington: University Press of Kentucky, 2001), 57, 127–28, Woodworth, *Jefferson Davis and His Generals: The Failure of Confederate Command in the West* (Lawrence: University Press of Kansas, 1990), 162–68.

20. Thomas B. Van Horne, *The Life of Major-General George H. Thomas* (New York: Charles Scribner's Sons, 1882), 104–8.

21. Powell, *Chickamauga Campaign*, 74.

22. Connelly, *Autumn of Glory*, 171–75; Robertson, "Chickamauga Campaign, McLemore's Cove," 14.

23. Robertson, "Chickamauga Campaign, McLemore's Cove," 22, 42.

24. Woodworth, *Jefferson Davis and His Generals*, 230.

25. Robertson, "Chickamauga Campaign, McLemore's Cove," 19.

26. Historian William Glenn Robertson argues that Bragg deemed Polk "utterly unsuited for the mission," that Cheatham was "despised by Bragg as a drunkard," and that Hindman was "the only choice, but seemingly a strong one. . . . Thus a strong and experience[d] division, with an aggressive commander at its head," coupled with "an equally experienced division led by Hindman's best friend in the army" gave Bragg reason for confidence in Hindman. Robertson, "Chickamauga Campaign, McLemore's Cove," 19.

27. Powell, *Chickamauga Campaign*, 141–42.

28. Woodworth, "'In Their Dreams,'" 58–59.

29. Connelly, *Autumn of Glory,* 177; Diane Neall and Thomas W. Kremm, *Lion of the South: General Thomas C. Hindman* (Macon: Mercer University Press, 1997), 164.

30. Connelly, *Autumn of Glory,* 155.

31. *OR,* 30(2):28.

32. Ibid.

33. Robert Lewis Johnson, "Confederate Staff Work at Chickamauga: An Analysis of the Staff of the Army of Tennessee" (M.M.A.S. thesis, U.S. Army Command and General Staff College, 1992), 74. For the Federal employment of telegraphy during the Chickamauga Campaign, see Philip J. Baker Jr., "Command and Control Mechanisms in the Chickamauga Campaign: The Union Experience" (M.M.A.S. thesis, U.S. Army Command and General Staff College, 1989), 45–50.

34. Robertson, "Chickamauga Campaign, McLemore's Cove," 20.

35. *OR,* 30(2):138.

36. Ibid., 300.

37. Irving A. Buck, *Cleburne and His Command* (New York: Neale, 1908), 107, 110, 290–93.

38. Daniel Harvey Hill, "Chickamauga—The Great Battle of the West," in *Battles and Leaders of the Civil War,* ed. Clarence Buel and Robert Johnson, 4 vols. (New York: Century, 1885), 3:638.

39. William G. Robertson says that Hill was "frozen in a defensive mindset" and "looking south rather than west," unable to reconcile "Bragg's sudden interest in mounting offensive operations in the Cove" with his own operational assessment. Robertson, "Chickamauga Campaign, McLemore's Cove," 20.

40. Woodworth, "'In Their Dreams,'" 59.

41. Connelly, *Autumn of Glory,* 156–58.

42. *OR,* 30(2):28.

43. *OR,* 30(4):633.

44. *OR,* 30(2):300.

45. A. H. Johnson to D. H. Hill, 10:00 A.M., Sept. 10, 1863, D. H. Hill Papers, Library of Virginia, Richmond, microform.

46. *OR,* 30(2):28, 137–38, 292–93, 300.

47. Robertson, "Chickamauga Campaign, McLemore's Cove," 22, 47; Woodworth, "'In Their Dreams,'" 60–61.

48. *OR,* 30(2):301.

49. Ibid., 302.

50. Ibid., 301.

51. Ibid., 302.

52. Powell, *Chickamauga Campaign,* 145–49.

53. Braxton Bragg, "The Battle of Chickamauga," *Southern Historical Society Papers* (1883), 11:49–65, 53–54.

54. *OR,* 30(2):311.

55. Ibid., 294–95.

56. Ibid.

57. Jermann, *Civil War Battlefield Orders Gone Awry,* 147–48.

58. *OR*, 30(2):295.

59. Robertson, "Chickamauga Campaign, McLemore's Cove," 43–44.

60. *OR*, 30(2):295.

61. Woodworth, *Jefferson Davis and His Generals,* 233.

62. Bragg, "Battle of Chickamauga," 54.

63. Robertson, "Chickamauga Campaign, McLemore's Cove," 43–44.

64. *OR*, 30(2):296.

65. Woodworth, "'In Their Dreams,'" 64.

66. *OR*, 30(2):311.

67. Ibid., 296.

68. Powell, *Chickamauga Campaign,* 152–53.

69. *OR*, 30(2):296.

70. *OR*, 30(4):636.

71. Robertson, "Chickamauga Campaign, McLemore's Cove," 45–46.

72. *OR*, 30(2):74; Powell, *Chickamauga Campaign,* 153, quoting Taylor Beatty Diary, Southern Historical Collection, Louis Round Wilson Special Collections Library, University of North Carolina at Chapel Hill.

THE LOOTING AND BOMBARDMENT
OF FREDERICKSBURG
"Vile Spirits" or War Transformed?

John J. Hennessy

FOR FIVE DAYS IN DECEMBER 1862, the Union's Army of the Potomac loomed over and in the streets of Fredericksburg. The first day the army bombarded the riverside town. Then, upon entering its ancient streets, the soldiers looted it. They entered abandoned houses, and a quest for food and warmth soon turned to evil frolic. Soldiers turned households inside out like old socks, filling streets and sidewalks with everything from pianos and featherbeds to dresses and children's toys. On December 13 the battle raged, and virtually every public building in town filled with wounded. Two days later the Army of the Potomac loaded their maimed and retreated back across the Rappahannock River, defeated more thoroughly than it ever had been before. The Confederates who cautiously crept back into town found devastation unlike anything they had ever seen, from a cause unprecedented in America.[1]

In newspapers across the land, opinionators and witnesses naturally offered the standard shallow narratives of battle with the requisite shallow analysis of generalship and strategy (the process continues still), all mingled with fulsome praise for the "stout hearts" that confronted the Confederates' "immense fortifications."[2] But perceptive readers quickly recognized something different about the commentary on the battle at Fredericksburg. The *Philadelphia Inquirer*'s editor wrote gingerly "that some outrages were committed in Fredericksburg." Witnesses—soldiers mostly—wrote more plainly. "Hundreds and thousands of dollars' worth of property was destroyed," Lt. William Walton of the 34th New York told his hometown newspaper, "and what was a short time since a wealthy city, is now nothing but a poverty stricken place."[3]

This seemed to be warfare of a different sort—certainly far removed from the polite, orderly imaginings of most Americans before the Civil War began. In the giddy days of 1861, most foresaw a struggle determined solely by the acts of armies against armies, where the respective societies would sit back, watch, pray for victory, but accept the outcome. When again and again battle-field contests yielded only ambiguous verdicts, the Federal government—and more slowly the people of the North—recognized the need for war and war-fare beyond their initial storybook visions. In 1862 the war's trend was unmis-takable: bigger, harsher, more destructive. Each month, every battle, every presidential proclamation, every victory, and every failure revealed something new about the conflict.[4]

For Union generals, questions of "war policy" and "war aims" competed for time and energy with their traditional roles as strategists and tacticians. Sometimes reluctantly, sometimes not, they became the instrument for imple-menting emerging policies on the method and purpose of war, policies that would determine the consequences on Southern civilians, the economy of the Confederacy, and most visibly of all, the institution of slavery. Questions about the nature and purpose of the war would cause raucous debate and divisions in the Union war effort, ones that offered the Confederacy its greatest hope for peace by political rather than military resolution. These questions of policy would, in the public's mind, always dwell in the shadow of the military calcu-lus, but they nonetheless would help determine the outcome and, perhaps just as important, the enduring legacy of war in a reunited nation.[5]

But this—Fredericksburg? How did what happened there fit the narrative of a war in transformation? How did the town itself become a battlefield? Was the bombardment and looting a symbol of emerging Union policy? Was the fate of Fredericksburg a proper and deserved remedy for Southern re-calcitrance, or simply an army run amok—the work of "vile spirits" (as one resident wrote)—seeking soothing revenge against what they saw as one of the Confederacy's most rabidly nationalistic bastions?[6]

⁓

Fredericksburg's journey into the abyss of war began in the spring of 1862, when a Union command under Maj. Gen. Irvin McDowell, the vanquished loser at Bull Run, arrived there. McDowell intended his stay to be short: re-store the crossings of the Rappahannock at Fredericksburg and then, at the appointed moment, descend southward on Richmond, adding a northern front to Maj. Gen. George B. McClellan's westward advance against the Confederate capital. His command swelled to 41,000 men in advance of the movement. But just days before McDowell was to move, Maj. Gen. Thomas J. "Stonewall" Jackson and his small Confederate army in the Shenandoah Valley spoiled the plan. Jackson's bold dash down the Valley inspired a far-flung and ultimately unsuccessful response from Pres. Abraham Lincoln. Instead of moving south, pieces of McDowell's command rushed westward to snare Jackson (they failed). For the next three months, McDowell's command would lay scattered across northern Virginia; thousands hovered at Fredericksburg until the end of August.[7]

McDowell recognized that no army could carry into the field all that it needed—and indeed, Union policy across the South recognized this fact. Water, wood, forage for animals, lumber, and bulk supplies of corn and wheat all would come from the nearby countryside—from local civilians. Soon after his arrival near Fredericksburg, McDowell prescribed (and largely enforced) the process by which supplies could be taken from area residents. Seizures could only occur when approved by division or brigade commanders. In every case, he ordered, enough must be left behind to sustain the family affected. Receipts would be made in duplicate on a printed form, signed, and one copy given to the civilian. The document committed that remuneration would be paid at the end of the war so long as the claimant could demonstrate his or her loyalty to the United States from the date on the certificate forward, presumably giving even the most rabid secessionist some incentive for a philosophical transformation. As Union railroad man Herman Haupt described it, "General McDowell claimed the privilege, as he frequently said, of being the only plunderer in the Army of the Rappahannock."[8]

While Fredericksburg's residents found the presence of a Union occupying force noxious, they could hardly claim malevolence. McDowell went to pains to ensure the good behavior of his men. He reminded them that local civilians had no practical redress for wrongs done by the army; this, he commanded, "heightens our obligation to protect the helpless." When some soldiers despoiled a tomb in the cemetery at Falmouth's Union Church, the general ordered a team of bricklayers to make repairs. Not only did McDowell prohibit wanton foraging, he actively sought to protect local residents against it. He permitted, and sometimes required, the placement of guards at houses and farms (those of unionists received the most enthusiastic protection). A soldier trying to tour the grounds at Chatham, the home of secessionist J. Horace Lacy and for a time McDowell's headquarters, encountered a phalanx of guards "stationed everywhere around his house and lands, with the strictest directions to preserve his fences, trees, and even lawns, intact." More evidence of McDowell's determination to see private property protected emerged when, after troops took some of Lacy's fence rails, he ordered the fences rebuilt.[9]

McDowell even reassured his enemies, writing to Confederate brigadier general J. R. Anderson, whose small command watched his troops from a distance: "You cannot be more anxious than I am that this war should be conducted with the least amount of suffering to the innocent and the non-combatants. I know of few, if any, who labor as incessantly and untiringly to this end as I have done and am doing."[10]

No wonder that by midsummer he would boast to his wife, "I find that I am respected and always have been, by my enemies." The locals noted his efforts. Weeks into the occupation, diarist Betty Herndon Maury—daughter of former U.S. naval officer Matthew Fontaine Maury and now a thoroughly converted Yankee hater—conceded: "I am much struck with the superior discipline of these Yankee soldiers over ours. I have not seen a drunken man since they have been here." When schoolteacher Jane Beale attended services at the Presbyterian church on June 22, she feared the "trial" of being in the presence of Union soldiers "would be too great to bear," but, she recorded that day in her diary, "their deportment was quiet and reverential, and I almost forgot they were our enemies."[11]

Despite McDowell's conciliatory practices and the relative good behavior of his men, local civilians grew to despise the presence of the Union army, if not the blue-clad soldiers themselves.[12] Troops swarmed through the town and patrolled its edges, preventing passage in and out. The flag of the United States appeared over streets, hung from buildings, trees, and, according to one resident, even the horns of oxen. In return, Federal soldiers suffered snubs, curses, taunts, and spitting. Local women refused to walk under the U.S. flag, and occasionally, one soldier told his hometown newspaper, they "resorted to indecencies which I cannot write or get printed in a respectable northern newspaper." On May 23 young Lizzie Alsop scrawled her antipathy on the pages of her diary: "Ah! They little know the hatred in our hearts towards them,—the GREAT scorn we entertain for Yankees." Soldiers returned the hostility. One man from New York concluded, "the idea of restoring the majority of the present generation of Virginia to a condition of sanity and reason, might as well be abandoned." The women, he wrote, "are little more to be respected than she wolves, or rattlesnakes."[13]

Nothing provoked angrier reaction among the white citizenry than the army's disruption of slavery. On this topic McDowell issued few orders. Rather, the enslaved people of central Virginia acted for themselves. During the summer of 1862, more than 10,000 men, women, and children left their places of bondage, determined to find freedom within the Union lines at Fredericksburg. It was one of the largest, most concentrated exoduses of the war. By groups and families, they came, and as government policy and political realities dictated, the army accepted them. In town many slaves embarked on the northward journey, but some soldiers urged others to remain with their owners and demand wages. Schoolteacher Jane Beale thought the practice insidious: "It fixes upon us this incubus of supporting a race, who were ordained of high Heaven to serve the white man and it is only in that capacity they can be happy useful and respected." Still, the alternative—that her slaves would leave—seemed worse. "I can but hope that no evil influences will be brought to bear upon their minds inducing them to place themselves and me in a more unhappy position than that which we now occupy," she wrote. "We cannot now tell 'what a day may bring forth.'"[14]

While McDowell administered his occupation of central Virginia according to prevailing policies (perfectly consistent with McClellan's light-handed touch on the Peninsula), both he and his practices came under scrutiny by the press, public, soldiers in the field, and authorities in Washington. The problem was not that the general was too harsh, but he was too lenient. The rumbles came first within the army itself from men exasperated with both the hostility of secessionists and the restraint of the army. An anonymous soldier wrote to the *Salem Register* complaining that the army was "protecting [the Confederates] in their treason, . . . treating them more like those whose favor we were endeavoring to gain." He suggested instead a few illustrative hangings: "it would do more for our cause than this 'if you please' and 'by your leave' business." In July the *New York Herald* carried a dispatch complaining bitterly about the administration of the occupation of Fredericksburg by McDowell appointee Capt. John Mansfield, an officer in the 2nd Wisconsin. The paper declared that Mansfield "punishes a Union soldier worse for plucking a bud from a 'secesh' rose-tree, than he would for stealing a horse from a loyal man."

An officer serving in the Valley proclaimed, "We are the most timid and scrupulous invaders in all history."[15]

Similar debates raged in the press and in the upper echelons of the army and the government, most notably between McClellan, his proxies, and their philosophical opponents in Washington. McClellan's missive to Lincoln on July 7, 1862—the Harrison's Landing Letter—amounted to a defense of the status quo: "It should not be, at all, a War upon population; but against armed forces and political organizations. Neither confiscation of property, political executions of persons, territorial organization of states or forcible abolition of slavery should be contemplated for a moment." Private property should be "strictly protected," the general declared. The property that must be taken for military use must be paid; "pillage and waste should be treated as high crimes." Arrests of civilians must "not be tolerated." Military government, McClellan concluded, "should be confined to the preservation of public order and the protection of political rights.[16]

McClellan's was no argument against the past, for most of what he advocated was already embodied in policy practiced by McDowell. Rather, his was an argument against the future, for that summer he, McDowell, and anyone else watching sensed change in Virginia's hot summer air. That change had arrived on June 26, when Maj. Gen. John Pope received command of all Union forces in central and northern Virginia (including McDowell's), creating the new Army of Virginia. Soon thereafter, Pope penned a letter that conveyed his willingness to wage war much differently than had McDowell and McClellan. "War means desolation and death," he wrote, "and it is neither humanity nor wisdom to carry it out upon any other theory. The more bitter it is made for the delinquents, the sooner it will end."[17]

Pope swiftly issued a series of general orders that would govern the treatment of civilians within the expansive area of his command, directives that reflected not just the general's boisterous personality but also evolving government policy toward Southern civilians. The Confederates took great offense at General Orders No. 11, issued July 22, stipulating that all disloyal male citizens within Union lines would be arrested immediately and required to take the oath of allegiance. If they refused, they would be "conducted South beyond the extreme pickets of the army" and treated as spies—hanged—if they dared to return. Southerners viewed this as a virtual assault on the institution of family; the *Macon Telegraph* proclaimed, "Gen. Pope is imitating and excelling [Maj. Gen. Benjamin] Butler." The Richmond government promised retribution against Pope and his officers should any civilians he executed under his order. But in the end they need not have worried. While the document signaled a dire future for families in Union-held areas, implementing it proved so onerous for the army that troops made only sporadic efforts to arrest citizens, much less dispatch them South (though probably hundreds appeared to take the oath voluntarily).[18]

Two of Pope's other orders received far more attention, both from within his own army and from the Confederates. General Orders No. 5 set the conditions by which his troops could seize supplies and material from local civilians. In their procedures the orders were nearly identical to McDowell's. But one sentence marked Pope's approach as different (and to some, odious). At every opportunity the army would "subsist upon the country in which their operations are carried on," dispensing with trains "as far as possible." Under McDowell and McClellan, the bounty of the land merely supplemented the army's immense efforts to supply itself. Under Pope, Virginia would become an immense larder, the army's principal source of food and fodder, with all the hardships that implied for the civilians who lived there.[19]

There was more. McDowell had acted energetically to prevent uncontrolled foraging in central Virginia, issuing orders and warnings and arresting those who even intruded on private property, much less disturbed it. Pope removed those controls. In General Order No. 13, issued July 25, Pope prohibited his commanders from posting guards to protect homes and property. "Soldiers were called into the field to do battle against the enemy," he explained, "and it is not expected that their force and energy shall be wasted in protecting private property of those most hostile to the Government." Instead, the general expected his men to abide by the Articles of War and army regulations prohibiting pillage and plunder; the processes in place should, he apparently concluded, provide enough deterrent to prevent things from spinning out of control. Confederate newspapers shared none of Pope's optimism. The *Richmond Examiner* proclaimed, "The North now is avowedly embarked on a war of plunder, rapine, and oppression, without shame and without compunction."[20]

If any doubt existed that these orders reflected not Pope's personality, but emerging government policy, that uncertainty vanished on July 22, when President Lincoln signed an executive order permitting all armies "to seize and use any property, real or personal, which may be necessary or convenient for . . . supplies or for other military purposes."[21]

Pope's aggressive language that summer and the rapid rate of orders from both the army and the government seemed to bespeak an enthusiasm for a new style of warfare soldiers in the field quickly embraced. From the Shenandoah Valley to Fredericksburg, Union soldiers perceived themselves unshackled from the conventions of McDowell and McClellan. The correspondent of the New York World noted a "decided revolution in the feelings and practices of the soldiery. . . . Men at home who would have shuddered at the suggestion of touching another's property, now appropriate remorselessly whatever comes within their reach." A detachment of Union cavalry near Sperryville, Virginia, spent nearly two weeks on outpost duty, yet as one soldier wrote, "the expense to Uncle Sam has been but little." Virtually every man returned with a new horse, and the regiment drew only some sugar and coffee for rations. The rest of their larder, the cavalryman continued, "came through [Order] No. 5." Another soldier summarized the situation in early August: "Most of the destruction is perfectly wanton, and not necessary," calculated only to turn local civilians into "our bitterest enemies."[22]

While enlisted men adjudged Pope's and Lincoln's orders by how they helped fill their stomachs and bring hardship to recalcitrant rebel citizens, officers and politicians viewed the orders through a different lens—their effect on discipline within the ranks, and thus the army's ability to function in the field. Civilians flocked to the army seeking protection. "The country," wrote McDowell, "has been laid waste, houses plundered and rifled. . . . Men claimed that now they were to live off the country! That it all belonged to them, and that they could take whatever they wanted." The army, he concluded, "is becoming, and that too rapidly, a mere band of marauders & theives [sic], and the Officers are becoming alarmed." In such chaos McDowell saw redemption for his former conciliatory policies. "I did not expect so soon to be vindicated!" he trumpeted to his wife. "It is wrong, and all wrongs bring their own punishment—ours is showing itself as I before said, in the deterioration of our army!" An editorialist for New York's most conservative newspaper, the New York World, similarly found fault not with the policy, only its execution. "It must be regulated better than it has been thus far. Unless the discipline of the army is to be destroyed, and the morals of the men corrupted, stricter orders against plundering must be enforced."[23]

At first glance, nothing in Pope's orders violated the principles that had guided conscientious armies worldwide for decades. Union general in chief Henry W. Halleck, a lawyer, had written a treatise on the rules of war in 1861 that would legally sustain Pope in 1862. The problem lay not in the orders' nature, but in their implementation. For three unrestrained weeks, the soldiers of Pope's army scoured central Virginia without system and with little restraint. Pope realized quickly, as he wrote, that the directives had been either "entirely misinterpreted or grossly abused" by the troops. The general's high public profile and his boastful and aggressive proclamations caused his men to perceive his written orders in a way he had not intended. The confusion lingered for weeks, much to the misfortune of the area residents and much to the detriment of both Pope's and his army's reputation in the South.

In his treatise Halleck writes, "the commanding officer who permits indiscriminate pillage, and allows the taking of private property without a strict accountability, whether he be engaged in offensive or defensive operations, fails in his duty to his own government, and violates the usage of modern warfare." Pope clearly violated this maxim, and on August 14 he took corrective action by issuing General Orders No. 19, decrying "pillage and outrage" as "disgraceful." He established a system of patrols intended not to find Confederates, but to round up unauthorized foragers. "It is to be distinctly understood that neither officer nor soldier has any right whatever, under the provisions of that order [No. 5], to enter the house, molest the persons, or disturb the property of any citizen whatsoever." The directive of August 14 had its desired effect. In any event, the Army of Virginia was soon so occupied by Lee's Army of Northern Virginia that few Union soldiers had time for foraging, authorized or not.[24]

Unmistakably, though, the atmospherics in Virginia had changed in that summer of 1862, and Fredericksburg felt the change as acutely as did their neighbors in the Piedmont. Soon after Pope's arrival, Union authorities arrested nineteen of the town's most prominent white men as "hostages"—retaliation for Confederate arrests of unionists that spring. Daily from Union camps departed groups of wagons, scouring the countryside for "potatoes and other garden sass." "It is quite time that they should be brought to a realizing sense of the destiny that awaits all rebels," wrote a soldier of the 2nd Wisconsin of the civilians he had been prohibited from bothering all summer. Residents shuddered under the flood of soldiers wanting food. A woman near Port Royal, on the Rappahannock below Fredericksburg, mildly resisted two determined Union foragers for breakfast but then let them in; soon thirty men crowded her house. She lamented, "What shall the end of these things be?"[25]

McDowell's command commenced a slow removal from Fredericksburg in early August 1862, destined to join Pope's campaign against Lee. (Union troops would fully evacuate Fredericksburg on September 1). Before he departed, Union brigadier general John Gibbon, a conservative and a North Carolinian with brothers in Confederates service, mused at the future of the town and the people he had come to know that summer. He saw no brightness. "Poor creatures," Gibbon wrote to his wife, "they have seen but little of the horrors of war. . . . If they ever do see really what war is, they will sigh for the times they are now passing though."[26]

—⁕—

On November 21, 1862, the *Virginia Herald* churned out the last issue of a newspaper to be produced in Fredericksburg for two and one-half years. The fragile sheet recounted no distant news of war, but war come home. The Army of the Potomac, now under the command of Maj. Gen. Ambrose Burnside, had arrived opposite the town a few days earlier, on November 17. A too-feisty Confederate battery opened fire on the distant Federals from the fields just north of town, which prompted a noisy response from Union guns on the heights above Falmouth. For a time that Monday afternoon, artillery shells flew through the northern reaches of Fredericksburg. One plunged through a paper mill, inspiring a rapid exit by the women who worked there. Young George Timberlake, son of the sheriff, had come to that area to watch the excitement. A fragment from one of the Yankee shells lacerated his foot—the first battle casualty in the town's history (and the only one that day).[27]

Two days later young Timberlake's neighbor Jane Beale recorded an even more frightening scene: "Watched with trembling hearts the long line of Yankees pouring over the Chatham hills," she wrote. Union forces had been gone for nearly three months. But now, Beale wrote, "they come in countless numbers and our hearts sink within us."[28]

Like his predecessors, Burnside bore the responsibility of both maneuvering his army against enemy forces in quest of victory and implementing policies with respect to civilians. Regarding the latter, not much had changed since Pope's short stint in command. His General Orders No. 19 seemed to have brought the problem of wanton plundering under control.[29] Neither Mc-Clellan nor Burnside had issued any additional significant directives on the topic of foraging. The army still held the right of seizure, and poultry, pigs, cows, corn, and fences succumbed wherever Union troops appeared (potential plunder did not fare well at the hands of passing Confederates either). But increasingly—and especially after the harvest—pickings grew thin. Pope's idea of a Union army subsisting off the trampled land of central Virginia exploded as fantasy. A newspaper correspondent with the army declared the region northwest of Fredericksburg "skinned completely out." When part of the III Corps pulled up at a house in war-worn Stafford County, across from Fredericksburg, the Federals found a typical scene: "As far as we can see this section of the country looks as if a grasshopper would have to handle himself pretty lively to find enough grass to survive." Even orderly foraging could not spare Virginians from "reaping a fearful retribution."[30]

Burnside's arrival opposite Fredericksburg presented to him a new problem: the over-enthused fire from that lone Confederate battery marked the town as occupied and hostile—subject to assault under the prevailing rules of war. If Burnside had had the necessary pontoon bridges, he might have responded to the provocation by crossing the Rappahannock River on November 18 or 19 with virtually no opposition. But those materials were days away, which meant Union forces could threaten the town only from a distance, with artillery. So on November 21 Burnside's man at the front, Maj. Gen. Edwin Vose "Bull" Sumner, composed a letter to Mayor Montgomery Slaughter and the Common Council of Fredericksburg demanding the surrender of their town. If they chose to defy the request, the U.S. Army would give residents sixteen hours to evacuate (until 9:00 A.M. the following morning), then, wrote Sumner, "I will proceed to shell the town." All of this comported with military law and policy most anywhere, but something else was also at work: Burnside tried to use the threat of bombardment as leverage to achieve a military objective—the uncontested occupation of Fredericksburg and the road network leading south toward Richmond. (He naturally did not mention that the bridging materials the army would need to cross the river at Fredericksburg had not yet arrived.)[31]

Sumner's ultimatum commenced a tense exchange between the leaders of the Confederate and Union armies. Lee, Maj. Gen. James Longstreet, and division commander Maj. Gen. Lafayette McLaws (all newly arrived at Fredericksburg) calculated military necessity, humanity, and the perceived perfidy of their foes. The three Confederate generals opted not to give the Union army any pretense to open fire on the town—any "excuse for the exercise of the natural brutality," as McLaws wrote. But neither would they surrender Fredericksburg or permit Federal forces to occupy it. Recognizing the possible consequences of his decision, Lee also suggested that the women and children of the town be evacuated—an unprecedented measure in Virginia's war thus far.[32]

Lee communicated his terms through Mayor Slaughter, who composed a straightforward response to Sumner, neither defiant nor pleading. The mayor promised that Union troops would not be fired upon from the town, that the mills and manufactories would no longer furnish materiel to the Confederates, and that the railroad through town would no longer move supplies for the Confederate army. Most notably, Slaughter included Lee's declaration: while Confederate troops "will not occupy the town, they will not permit yours to do so."[33]

This was no mere prideful impudence on the mayor's part, and Union officers knew it. They had spent the day scanning westward with their glasses and saw plainly the Confederates placing batteries and constructing earthworks on the heights behind town. Burnside and Sumner required only a few hours to come to an answer. Before midnight Sumner sent a return message to Mayor Slaughter. The promises the mayor had made were enough, the general wrote, and in order to spare hardship for the civilian population, the town would not be bombarded.[34]

The reprieve for Fredericksburg spun on the rules of war. Lee knew the Union threat to bombard Fredericksburg had been justified under those rules; now he had removed the pretexts that might have warranted the bombardment. Burnside agreed, and with few exceptions, for the next eighteen days, the guns overlooking Fredericksburg remained silent. The rules of war had won out at Fredericksburg—for now.

───※───

Fredericksburg now lay between glowering armies, each committed for the moment to leave the town untouched, but each willing to turn it into a battlefield should circumstances warrant. The residents understood this well enough, and when Lee recommended they leave, they quickly commenced a mass exodus. Of all the notable aspects of the Fredericksburg Campaign as it relates to civilians, none caused stronger reaction among Southern soldiers and distant citizens than the image of civilians driven from their homes. The evacuation began under the immediate threat of Union bombardment but continued beneath the uncertain prospect of battle.[35]

Most civilians fled along the roads leading into the countryside of Spotsylvania County, destination uncertain. They trudged along cold and muddy routes, children in tow, carpetbags slung over shoulders, handcarts bumping along. They found shelter with friends and strangers, in improvised camps, or in barns, mills, churches, or abandoned slave cabins; by late 1862 probably more than half of the region's enslaved people had fled to Union lines, freeing up shelter prized by these refugees. Lee called it a "piteous site." Alexander McNeill of the 2nd South Carolina wrote of what he saw on November 27: "Wagons loaded with furniture pass our camp constantly. . . . My heart has been made to bleed freely when called to witness the sufferings of the weak and helpless inhabitants of this unfortunate country." A Georgian claimed that the sight simply steeled the soldiers for the work to come. "We will restore your homes to you," the men yelled as the civilians passed. "God bless you."[36]

"There is not even a shadow of an excuse for such an outrage on humanity," wrote Major General McLaws on November 22. But his indignation overlooked an important fact: the evacuation of civilians took place not because the Union army had violated the accepted rules of war, but because both armies remained committed to those rules. By the time of the battle, only about 900 of Fredericksburg's 5,000 residents remained in town. South Carolinian McNeill concluded, "Virginia is truly unfortunate in being the theatre upon which this monster war is enacted."[37]

For the next two weeks, General Lee and his army monitored Union movements along more than twenty-five miles of the Rappahannock, from Port Royal upstream to United States Ford. Midpoint within that zone lay Fredericksburg, a place Lee could hardly afford not to watch closely. And so in late November he nominally violated his own pledge by sending Brig. Gen. William Barksdale's brigade of Mississippians into the town. Each night those men set to work building earthworks and preparing cellars to resist any Union crossing. No doubt the Federals noticed, but Burnside neither protested nor unleashed his artillery on the town, adjudging the Confederate presence there as nothing different than their presence elsewhere along the Rappahannock line. Burnside, meanwhile, considered crossing his army above and below Fredericksburg, but after two weeks of inaction he concluded that Lee would expect least the most obvious: a crossing at Fredericksburg itself. That decision, with Lee's previous declaration that the Army of Northern Virginia would resist any attempt by the Union army to cross there, ensured Fredericksburg's most difficult days were nigh.[38]

At about 5:15 on the frigid morning of December 11, the boom of two Confederate cannon echoed through the Rappahannock valley—the prearranged signal that the Union army's attempt to cross the river had begun.[39]

From backyards and basements, Barksdale's Mississippians opened fire at two developing crossing sites opposite the town, where under darkness Union engineers had managed to get pontoon bridges more than halfway across the river. Their fire from upper Sophia Street struck the bridge builders opposite Hawke Street with, as one Confederate claimed, "stunning effect." The Union engineers required no orders to know what to do next: all of them rushed for shore. "Some fell into the boats, dead. Some fell into the Stream and some onto the bridge, dead." A few wounded crawled along on hands and knees. "In a few moments," Col. Wesley Brainerd remembered, "all of us were off the bridge, all except the dead."[40]

Burnside and his chief of artillery, Brig. Gen. Henry Hunt, had anticipated such enemy action, and they had already arranged artillery and distributed orders to the various battery commanders to open fire if the Confederates resisted. At both crossing sites Union cannon on the heights—about fifty guns—responded instantly to the rebel defenders. Theirs was an intense, focused, purposeful fire intended to quell the Confederate infantry positioned in riverside houses. But between the predawn mist building over the river, the darkness, and the smoke from the guns, battery commanders could see nothing of their intended targets. The boom of cannon echoed through the valley for a few minutes. Solid shot tore into the riverside homes of Fredericksburg. Men watched from afar in awe.[41]

The artillery fire—perhaps five hundred total rounds—stopped. But in the darkness, no Union soldier could tell whether the barrage had done any good. Indeed, no one in either army knew what would be required for artillery to subdue infantry hidden in a town, for no army had attempted such a thing in this war. After an hour, as the sky brightened, the engineers again rushed onto the bridge. Again the Confederate infantry on upper Sophia Street opened fire. And again the engineers retreated, finding cover behind lumber piles and tool wagons. This time two Union infantry regiments along the riverbank supporting the engineers returned fire, but that did nothing to tip the balance. Union artillery joined in once again, though at a more leisurely intensity.[42]

And so it would go that day. At 9:00 A.M. General Hunt called up more guns to add to the line, swelling the number overlooking the two crossings to about seventy (with another forty-nine within range if called upon). They opened yet again on the Confederate hiding places opposite the bridges, firing solid shot and explosive shells with percussion fuses. No wind disturbed the gunsmoke or the morning mist, and few on the Union side of the river could see the effect of the bombardment. But the sound—men remembered the sound. "There was one continual roar from the guns and the shot & shell made such a screaching [sic] through the air that the sound was almost deafening," wrote a soldier from Massachusetts. At 10:00 and again at 11:00 A.M., the guns slackened their fire, and the engineers emerged yet again. Some fell; the rest rushed for cover again. The effect of the bombardment was, concluded one officer, "ridiculously out of proportion to the noise and weight of metal thrown into the place, and we were all greatly disappointed."[43]

As midday approached, Union bridge builders and Southern sharpshooters stood at a noisy, smoky, destructive stalemate. Glimpses into town revealed the Confederates moving troops through the streets, strengthening their hold at the crossing sites.[44] The situation inspired Burnside to intervene with General Hunt. His chief of artillery was of a mind common in the Army of the Potomac—convinced, as had been his friend George McClellan, that the war must be prosecuted with restraint without inflicting undue damage on Southern civilians, Southern property, or Southern "institutions" (slavery). His management of the bombardment that morning had reflected such views. Though his gunners could see little and had so far achieved just as much, Hunt insisted that the fire be confined to the crossing sites. Now at about noon, Burnside ordered otherwise. Hunt recorded the moment in his report: "All the batteries that could be brought to bear were now, by order of General Burnside, turned upon the town." At least two of Hunt's subordinates recalled the intent of Burnside's orders: set the town on fire and burn it down.[45]

This was a general bombardment, not the targeted, purposeful (albeit ineffective) barrages of the morning. When a short time later Hunt took it upon himself to order the firing stopped, Burnside just as quickly countermanded him and ordered the barrage to resume. On the afternoon of December 11, Fredericksburg rocked and burned in a way no American town ever had.[46]

In the morning most batteries used solid shot to batter the buildings near the crossings. In the afternoon some switched to explosive shells in their quest to start fires. That morning about seventy guns had fired into Fredericksburg. That afternoon eighty-seven cannon joined in—likely the largest artillery action of the war so far.[47] The sun had by then burned off the mist that had so obscured the morning's action. With the view cleared, thousands of Union soldiers gathered on Stafford Heights to watch.[48]

The Union guns merged into a crescendo, defeating those who attempted to count the shells exploding within Fredericksburg. Witnesses on both sides ventured a consistent estimate—one hundred shells each minute, more than one per second. A Union cavalryman wrote enthusiastically of "a scene so exciting and grand," relating to neighbors back home in Pennsylvania the "roar of so many cannon, the hissing shells, as they went tearing and crashing among whole streets of buildings. . . . The whole scene was beautiful to behold, yet terrible to contemplate."[49]

Within a few minutes, smoke rising from Fredericksburg marked the fires the commanding general had desired. The flames raged fiercest along Caroline Street in the center of town, and soon only the steeples of the downtown churches could be seen through the smoke (those churches still stand today). That area had been gutted by a windswept fire decades ago, but on this day the wind failed Burnside—else the day would have been far more destructive. Still, the site of a town ablaze inspired the pens of many who witnessed it. A Minnesotan saw the underside of the hanging clouds of smoke glowing red, "the color of a red-hot iron." He noted, "I was reminded of a Sunday school picture I had once seen of the burning of Sodom." Looking over at the still-burning town the next day, an officer of the 140th New York saw in the spectacle both a changing war and hope for the future: "At the present time we are witnessing a splendid sight, as the city of Fredericksburg is on fire. . . . I call it beautiful because it is just the way that I wish to see our Generals operate, for then I begin to think that they mean business."[50]

Beyond the outskirts of town, the Confederates watched the spectacle too. Artilleryman E. Porter Alexander remembered the smoke rising in straight columns, unbent by wind, then spreading out over the town "like a great black canopy." He wrote, "The White winkings of the bursting shells reminded me of a constant swarm of fire-flies." General Lee had known that his decision to dispute the Union crossing would turn Fredericksburg into a battlefield. But he did not expect this, an attempt at wholesale destruction while civilians huddled in their basements. He likely watched the bombardment from his headquarters a mile southwest of town on a hill that now bears his name. John Esten Cooke noted that it was not the bombardment itself but apparently its general nature that caused Lee to comment bitterly: "These people like to make war on the defenseless. It just suits them."[51]

For an hour or more the tumult continued. Then about 2:00 P.M. the gunners stopped their work on Stafford Heights. One Union artillery officer peered through the smoke: "The city was fired in four places," he recorded. "But the most distressing sight was the women and children that we saw running from the burning buildings and seeking shelter in more secure places." Along the riverbank below the Lacy house, soldiers emerged too. The New York engineers jumped up from their hiding places and dashed for the bridges. Confederate troops in town—shell shocked and begrimed, but most of them alive—poked out of their hiding places, unleashing yet another deadly fusillade on the bridge builders. Once again the beleaguered engineers rushed back to cover. Stalemate again, this one against the backdrop of a town ablaze.[52]

The day had illustrated vividly the limitations of artillery, so Hunt suggested trying a different solution. He resurrected an idea suggested by one of the engineers that morning: put infantry from Brig. Gen. Oliver Otis Howard's division of the II Corps in the boats and have them storm across the river to establish a bridgehead on the Fredericksburg shore. Where tradition had failed, improvisation worked. Under the eyes of thousands of anxious Union soldiers, men of the 7th Michigan and the 50th New York Engineers crowded into seven boats, rowed madly across the Rappahannock, and landed at the foot of Hawke Street. Wrote one of the onlookers: "The bullets showered into them, but on they kept. We were almost wild with excitement, cheering and yelling." The Michiganders scrambled up the riverside bank and launched themselves into town. A fierce battle in the streets followed—something much like modern battles in Fallujah and Ramadi—with Union soldiers breaking in back doors while Confederates escaped out the front, or Confederates being hauled out of basements as prisoners. Howard's men quickly carved out enough space for the engineers to work safely. Within thirty minutes the bridge builders lashed the final boat in place, completing the first bridge. Moments later the rest of Howard's division marched across and into town. The fighting in the streets continued until dark, when Barksdale's Mississippians withdrew, their mission fulfilled. They had gained Lee most of a day by their resistance, allowing the Confederate commander to consolidate his ever-strengthening position on the heights behind the town.[53]

The end of the fighting that evening marked the end of the hardest day in Fredericksburg's history. Cruel though it was, the bombardment of December 11 violated no rules of war. When Lee decided to dispute the Union crossing at Fredericksburg (by any measure a military necessity), he cast the town as a battlefield. General in Chief Halleck's own prewar treatise on law and war recognized the legitimacy of property destruction under such circumstances: "if such destruction is necessary in order to cripple the operations of the enemy, or to insure our own success, it is justifiable." Still, there could be no denying that by expanding the scope of the bombardment beyond the likely hiding places of Confederate defenders, Burnside crossed a threshold that Hunt, Lee, and many others recognized. "The general rule by which we should regulate our conduct toward an enemy," Halleck had written in his treatise, "is that of moderation." The bombardment of December 11 amounted to a denial of the restrained practice of warfare that had governed the high command of the Army of the Potomac since its beginning. The question remained, where would it all lead? That answer would come more quickly than anyone then imagined.[54]

─·──

As the firing in the streets died away that cold December night, Union soldiers coming across the bridges encountered sights that few Americans had ever witnessed. "Oh! But that was a long and gloomy night," wrote Lieutenant Walton of Howard's division. Darkness competed with "the lurid light of burning buildings" to frame scenes of horror. "The ghastly dead" (Union and Confederate) lay on sidewalks, in gardens and yards, and in the streets. Near the docks, men of the IX Corps encountered a sharply dressed Confederate sergeant dead, his face mostly shot away—"a ghastly object seen in the dim light of a distant fire." Occasionally a civilian would appear, "frightened inhabitants hurrying away from great danger," Walton recorded. Some disappeared toward

Confederate lines on Marye's Heights behind the town, while others headed toward the Union bridges. Safety trumped allegiance.[55]

The city itself seemed wounded. Fires still burned on Caroline Street, but most remarkable of all was the damage to surviving buildings. "The houses were all vented with shells," Charles Davis of the 1st Minnesota told his homefolk a few days later. Dozens of soldiers went about town counting holes in homes—the notable numbers ranged from thirty-two to more than one hundred. "Trees were cut off, chimneys torn down, buildings burned, or knocked to pieces, the churches well perforated with holes," wrote another man, all the products of "the terrible storm of the iron hail which swept through the streets." Lieutenant Walton of the 34th New York predicted: "Years and years will pass away, but scores will be numbered ere that city ceases to wear its scars and recovers from that one day's bombardment. . . . The city is one wreck and ruin."[56]

It seemed that every building in town suffered damage (many attics still bear the scars), and this may well have been true. But the number of structures that succumbed entirely to the Union bombardment certainly marked Burnside's effort to burn Fredericksburg a failure. Of the approximately 830 taxable structures on government roles, 69 likely were victims of the December 11 bombardment—either burned or damaged so badly that they had to be pulled down. Thus Burnside's quest for total destruction brought about the loss of only about 8 percent of the taxable buildings in town.[57]

As the first Union troops into Fredericksburg, the men of Howard's division would set the example for most who followed. These Northerners came with adrenaline and rage into a town famous as a cauldron of secessionists. (In fact Fredericksburg was by no means exceptional in its support for the Confederacy, but as the one Virginia town the Union army and press acquired extended access to in 1862, its fame and image as a hostile place grew as hundreds of newspapers carried descriptions of the town and its people.) That afternoon its houses and homes had given protection to Confederates bent on killing Union soldiers and disrupting plans for the defeat of Lee's army and the restoration of the Union. The dead of Col. Norman Hall's brigade lay scattered on Sophia and Caroline Streets. The night was cold, the ground damp, and a nervous uncertainty of looming battle hovered over all.[58]

Something else added to this complicated salad of emotion and circumstance. Around these men stood empty homes and businesses abruptly abandoned by their owners—the very people who had, most Union soldiers imagined, welcomed Confederate infantrymen into their basements and backyards that morning. One of Howard's soldiers claimed that the ladies of Fredericksburg had declared their preference for desolation rather than surrender to the Northerners. Now they had both; "we have accommodated them," he wrote, "for there is not a building left untouched in the whole city." In those secessionist structures so ravaged by Union artillery, Howard's infantrymen—and indeed the rest of the army—saw sanction for what was to come. As one soldier put it, "Having come into its possession by capture, instead of surrender, they argued that the place and all it contained belonged to them." After Howard's men cleared the town of Confederates, posted pickets, and returned to their bivouacs, they individually or in small groups headed toward the houses—the empty, battered, unguarded memorials to the perfidy of Southern civilians.[59]

Some headed toward the residences to escape the cold, find some food, and claim a featherbed for sleep. Indeed, much of Hall's brigade apparently intended to quarter in the houses for the night. Lt. John G. B. Adams of the 19th Massachusetts took quarters in the chamber of a young lady, her "little finery . . . scattered about the room." Nervous that the girl might return at any time, he refused to undress and slept still wearing his boots. Downstairs, meanwhile, members of his company prepared a meal of "roast duck, biscuits, and all kinds of preserves, . . . [served] on the best china." Two days hence, Adams would earn the Medal of Honor on the fields beyond Fredericksburg.[60]

The civility of Adams's billet contrasted mightily with what unfolded elsewhere in town. Lt. Henry Ropes of the 20th Massachusetts, a regiment whose officer corps was imbued with Harvard educations, declared his understanding and intent in a single sentence: "As the City was defended against us, of course it was given up to pillage." Another man of the Harvard regiment noted that officers chose to place no guards at the houses. "The men had free access," he wrote, and they soon availed themselves of the uncommon opportunity—some with a vengeance.[61]

"The boys ransacked everything," wrote Charles Davis of the 1st Minnesota.

Houses, once the Homes of Elegance & comfort now stripped of everything. Articles of apparel, bed clothing, furniture and letters now all strewed around the floor. Every one took what they wanted & carried off what they pleased. The destruction was complete. Private soldiers were sitting around the streets in spring bottomed chairs or lying down on feather beds. The best quality of dinner or tea sets were far more plenty & abundant among the men than the tin ware allowed by the Army Regulations. Everything in the way of eatables was taken by the men & if not used was thrown away.[62]

Capt. George Macy of the 20th Massachusetts registered amazement but no disapproval of his men. He left a long list of remarkable scenes: "Soldiers making coffee in silver pitchers, cleaning guns with lace undersleeves," he wrote. "Nothing seemed to be revered—houses torn to pieces, beautiful paintings, pianos, in fact everything which wealth and luxury gives was there in abundance." And then he promised his correspondent, "I have a little trophy for you which I will send." The men in Brig. Gen. Alfred Sully's brigade found "flour, honey, preserves, potatos [sic], wine, whiskey, & tobacco by the wholesale," along with a fiddle. After "getting a little tight," a diarist wrote, the brigade had a dance. "Sully's brigade is a gay old crowd tonight," he recorded. "The boys sit around the fires in rocking chairs." Howard's men suffered the most on December 11, but as the first looters they got the best when it came to food and booty.[63]

For those few hundred residents trapped in town, that night offered a nightmarish slice of the worst of war and human nature. Mamie Wells, part of a unionist family living on Sophia Street, remembered vividly "the pounding at our doors; the peering in the cellar windows by eyes red with intoxication; the oaths and curses; the ringing of axes and hammers; breaking in the tenantless houses; the firing of the buildings opposite; the insults heaped upon the occupants; the streets literally packed with soldiers in a complete state of moral demoralization." Reflecting back on the night years later, she wrote: "I ask myself: How did we live through them? And I sometimes wonder if it is not all a dream—so incomprehensible does such human depravity appear."[64]

Amid the chaos, a notable pattern emerged. Those civilians who dared to remain in their houses reaped a reward their absent neighbors did not: rampaging Union soldiers usually left occupied dwellings alone. The Wells family had a succession of officers stay upstairs in their shell-battered home, including "a colonel from Philadelphia" Mamie Wells identified as "Ormes"— almost certainly Brig. Gen. Joshua Owen, whose troops bivouacked nearby. Union soldiers did not loot the Wells house. Instead of looting homebound civilians, those who came in contact them marveled at their fortitude: "How can one be surprised that they are determined never to give up?" A personal encounter with civilians so deeply affected by war left some men wondering at the war's moral compass. "I never felt so much disgusted with the war as I did that day," wrote artilleryman Tully McCrae. He wished for the war's end to put a "stop to all this terrible suffering."[65]

Over the next four days, about 30,000 Union troops would come into Fredericksburg on their way into or out of battle. The scenes would be broadcast by letters, newspapers, and sketch artists across the nation, North and South: soldiers dressed as women; a man milking a cow into his canteen while sitting in someone's parlor; mirrors smashed for the joy of it; pianos pulled into the streets, then invariably smashed; whole libraries broken up, to be either sent north or tossed in the streets; beeswax poured down the tubes of the organ in one of the churches on Princess Anne Street; a soldier moving swiftly along with arms full of baby clothes; fine furniture smashed turned into firewood; soldiers with arms white from dives into flour barrels. One unfortunate fellow mistakenly fried up some flapjacks not in lard, but a medical ointment. Another mistook plaster for flour and produced inedible flapjacks of notable texture. Soldiers read to each other love letters found in secret spaces, then scattered them. One man looted a stuffed alligator, another toted a stuffed monkey nailed upright to a board. Virtually every soldier sought some prize to send home. By the day of the combat on December 13, few trinkets were left to be had. The 30,000 Federals made thorough work of the contents of Fredericksburg's 830 buildings. "Soldiers lived and fared well during our short stay," wrote an officer in the IX Corps. "They found an abundance on all hands." An officer in the V Corps admitted to being a vandal himself but found justification in the presumption that the city would be destroyed anyway. A man of the IX Corps described in great detail the looting for his hometown newspaper, then concluded, "secession families have been made to feel the awful horrors of a war brought on by their treason."[66]

Officers' widespread approval of (or at least ambivalence to) the looting of Fredericksburg surely had much to do with the government's evolving policies with respect to the property of rebellious Southerners. Two confiscation acts, the Preliminary Emancipation Proclamation, and Pope's orders for foraging, with the Emancipation Proclamation itself just weeks away, all made clear that Union armies and their commanders had a charge beyond the straightforward destruction of Confederate armies in the field. These measures all aimed at property and diminishing the South's ability to wage war. No one proclaimed the looting of Fredericksburg as justified under any government policy (though many claimed it was justified under the rules of war). But certainly soldiers saw the event in the context of a movement toward a harsher war at a moment when the forces of anger, opportunity, and chaos coincided. In a letter home to Herkimer, New York, after the looting, Lieutenant Walton acknowledged the irony of cruel injustice within what he considered a just war for a virtuous cause. "Do our friends cry out against this?" he asked. Yes, he responded, and "so do we—it is wrong, essentially wrong, *but it is War*. It has always been thus, since man raised hand against brother." Walton concluded, "It will always be thus until the Millennium dawns."[67]

Some voices within the army did rise in protest against the pillaging, and a few commanders acted affirmatively to restrain it. A soldier of the V Corps called the army's behavior "disgraceful." "What Uncle Sam's balls had spared, Uncle Sam's boys finished," he wrote. "One thing is certain, if we are not brave in the field, we are valiant at the trencher." Rush Hawkins, a brigade commander in the IX Corps, posted guards between his and Howard's boisterous men in the upper part of the town—though with apparently little effect. Howard counseled the colonel, "Soldiers are not expected to be angels." Brig. Gen. Thomas Francis Meagher, commander of the Irish Brigade and perhaps the officer least qualified to claim purity and innocence, went to pains to assert in his report that his command "scrupulously abstained from any act of depredation." Quartermaster John McGonigle of the 122nd Pennsylvania constructed his sentences carefully when writing to his hometown newspaper after the battle, reporting that the men in his regiment undertook "no wanton destruction practiced . . . no hacking, hewing, burning and destroying, from purely vicious motives." This was not to say that they did not engage in lesser acts of looting and plunder—"an infuriated soldiery . . . cannot be wholly restrained," McGonigle admitted. Col. John D. Wilkins of the 3rd U.S. Infantry—maybe the crustiest officer under Burnside—declared his disapproval to his wife. "I am ashamed to be considered an officer belonging to" the Army of the Potomac. "Such wholesale, unnecessary destruction I have never seen." A chaplain in the III Corps conceded that the pillage may have been lawful, but, he wrote, "it jostled my New England prejudices."[68]

The spirit of restraint (as espoused by McClellan) still lived in the army and indeed would never depart it altogether. Many soldiers foresaw that this brutish behavior would simply make the Confederates fight harder. A IX Corps man who witnessed the looting wondered, "When will discipline become a part of the United States army?" He answered his own question: "God only knows, but while these things are tolerated they will rebound upon us as sure as justice follows crime." To those who complained about army guards protecting Southerners' property, he offered, "it is better to spare the men for that than to suffer the demoralization that is sure to follow." The old Regular Wilkins also foresaw retribution and a more difficult struggle to come. "If they were not embittered before," the colonel wrote, "the sight of that city is enough to make them fight like tigers in defense of their own homes, now threatened with a similar fate."[69]

No soldier looked more disapprovingly on the fate of Fredericksburg than the army's provost marshal general, Brig. Gen. Marsena Patrick, the army's great advocate of restrained war. The former military governor of Fredericksburg rode into town the morning of December 12. "The Soldiery were sacking the town!" he wrote in his diary. "Every house and Store was being gutted!" He attacked the disorder with passion, likely concerned equally with the immorality of the moment and its effect on the discipline of the army (his bailiwick). Patrick especially combated those trying to haul booty back across the river. He unhorsed a mattress and bedding, though it took a whack of his sword on the rider to do it. Patrick watched as officers trotted along with mantle ornaments hanging off their saddles. Maj. Gen. Darius Couch, II Corps commander, posted guards at the crossings to prevent the hauling of prizes back to camp. But few beyond Patrick made any attempt to halt the looting at its source. Moreover, few noted the essential pessimism embodied by those trying to carry loot back to camps that they would return to only if the army were defeated.[70]

Despite the efforts of Patrick and a few voices of restraint, officers of the Army of the Potomac generally watched the looting in tolerant silence. Some even encouraged it. When the nine-month troops of Col. Peter Allabach's brigade stacked their arms on the sidewalks of Fredericksburg, Allabach announced: "Boys, I know you are tired. I have tried to have you relieved all day, but could not. You have liberty to go into cellars and houses, to build fires and make coffee, if you do not expose your fires, so as to attract the enemies' shells." One of these men admitted, "This is just what we wished."[71]

General Howard, a righteous and pious man, had an opportunity to impose discipline when he came upon a group of drunken men singing and dancing in the streets: "I remarked . . . this was unusual preparation for the battle that all were expecting on the morrow." One of the soldiers assured him, "Ah, general, let us sing and dance to-night; we will fight the better for it to-morrow!" Howard, who called them a "hilarious group," let the party go on.[72]

Voices of approval even extended to officers within the command of Provost Marshal General Patrick. Col. John Crocker and his regiment, the 93rd New York, were subject to Patrick's orders in his efforts to enforce law and regulation. But citizen-soldier Crocker saw the looting differently than did his Regular Army boss. The colonel was "quite indifferent as to waste" and explained why: "Men who are present at such a cannonade as that was, seeing their comrades shot down by a cowardly foe, who take shelter behind the buildings of a city contrary to their own pledge, become so excited they cannot restrain themselves. They seem to become as infuriated as tigers and so they act." According to Crocker, Burnside's unwillingness to stop the pillage was "right and perfectly justified. The cursed Rebels brought it all on themselves by their maddened folly."[73]

In July and August 1862, soldiers presumed intent from Pope's aggressive language and orders and embarked on three weeks of barely restrained foraging. Then the army commander and his subordinates took relatively swift action to restore order and function to the army. In December under Burnside, the soldiers likewise perceived unspoken approval of pillaging—the unrestrained destruction of a Confederate town by the artillery of a Union army. But this time the high command made only feeble attempts to bring the men under control. Why the difference?

Certainly, unlike July, soldiers and officers alike recognized the unique circumstances of Fredericksburg. Maj. Charles Howard, aide to and brother of General Howard, probably reflected the views of his brother and many others in the hierarchy of the Army of the Potomac. He clearly knew well the Articles of War, for he conceded the situation would have been improved had the town's loot "been seized and confiscated by Government," as the articles required. But, Howard claimed, circumstances rendered that course impossible. By resisting, the enemy "necessitated the devastation" that visited Fredericksburg during the bombardment. That destruction in turn led directly to the looting: "It was the natural and unavoidable consequence when in the darkness of the night the soldiers entered building after building and saw all kinds of property before them to be wasted or appropriated according to their will." Clearly many officers at least understood the motives of looting soldiers, and some sympathized.[74]

That may have been true in July and August too, but a crackdown in Pope's army came nonetheless. Almost unanimously, officers then cited the effect unrestrained foraging had on the army itself, undermining its discipline and thus its ability to function in the field. In the open spaces of the Piedmont, foraging could and did disconnect soldiers from the army entirely.

In the close spaces of Fredericksburg, looting had a less significant effect on the army's ability to function. "Although I heard no formal permission to plunder, I have heard no one forbidding the men to do it," a man of the II Corps remembered. Officers released soldiers to move about or sleep in houses but required them to stack arms, stay relatively close, and be prepared to respond when called.[75] And apparently they did. While General Patrick grumbled that "many were left behind" when the army went into action on the thirteenth, few other officers offered this complaint. Though looting created chaos in the streets of Fredericksburg, it seems not to have affected the ability of various regiments, brigades, and divisions to function properly, and at something close to their expected strength and efficiency. So the officers let the soldiers go.[76]

On December 13, during and after the catastrophic fighting in the fields just west of town, the town became a refuge to defeated Union soldiers. For two more days thereafter, they churned through the streets, surrounded now by the wounded and by hospitals, with dead populating sidewalks and yards. Confederate artillerists fired their guns down the east–west streets, rendering the intersections the most perilous places in town. Most regiments had occasional work to do somewhere on the battlefield outside town, but always they retired to the safety of the buildings, protectors against Confederate artillery fire. Invariably the soldiers stacked their arms and looked for comfort, food, or trinkets among the residences and businesses. To the very last hours of the army's occupation of Fredericksburg, the troops continued their search for loot, though by the end, little of value could be found.[77]

On December 15 the Army of the Potomac gathered its wounded (but not its dead) and retreated back across the Rappahannock. It and the Northern populace had witnessed defeat before, though rarely like this—a one-sided slaughter, the most disastrous battle of the war save for the embarrassment at Bull Run in 1861. In the fighting's aftermath Union soldiers railed at their officers, the home front, and even the war itself. Col. Patrick Guiney of the 9th Massachusetts declared himself "indignant." "I feel now too deeply that our troops—our brave troops—are not—and seemingly not to be, skillfully led," he wrote. A V Corps soldier started his recrimination before he even left town on the fifteenth. "Shame oh shame on our Generals," he wrote. "To think they would lead an army of men into a place like this to fight, and then give it up. . . . It is perfectly disgusting." Yet another soldier wrote gloomily: "Oh how dreadful is this War, so unholy and unjust—none can realize it unless they have been in the midst of it. . . . Oh there is so much suffering that I cannot feel contented."[78]

One of the Harvard officers in the 20th Massachusetts offered perhaps the most succinct summary of all: "Nothing but murder. Good bye."[79]

Northern newspapers shied not from carrying lengthy and detailed descriptions of the bombardment and looting of Fredericksburg, but those accounts received little comment.[80] Instead uproar over defeat quickly seized the attention of congressmen and editorialists. The Joint Committee on the Conduct of the War came en masse to Burnside's headquarters just days after the battle. They asked not a question about what had happened in Fredericksburg's streets or under the artillery's guns. Any concerns about the morality of the army or its behavior toward civilian property yielded to relentless questions about the conduct of the battle. Commentary within the ranks and across the North savaged the army's leadership, sometimes even the army itself. "You have no idea of the depression there is in this army," a civilian visitor wrote to a Waterbury, Connecticut, newspaper. A Canadian observer declared flatly (and wrongly), "Our men would not fight."[81]

The day after the retreat, division staff officer Major Howard offered a prediction: "There will undoubtedly be a great clamor in the South and among Rebels of the North against the sacking and pillage of Fredericksburg." He was right.

News of Fredericksburg's fate and its residents' struggles ignited outcry across the South, but few felt the outrage more acutely than the Confederate soldiers who bore personal witness to the destruction. Lt. Channing Price of Brig. Gen. J. E. B. Stuart's staff described the town as a "perfect wreck," with "houses burnt & battered fences & boarding of every description torn down." Dozens wrote home about the ruin left behind by Yankee looters and cannoneers: streets covered with glass; pews thrown out windows onto sidewalks;

dead pets and livestock; and clothes, dressers, pianos, and beds littering the streets, many wantonly smashed. One man counted 132 shell holes in a single house. "Words are too inadequate to give a just accurate account of their work," wrote Quartermaster James Beaty of Mississippi. Soldiers of the Army of Northern Virginia would lead a fundraising effort that eventually raised nearly $250,000 from across the South for the relief of what became widely known as the "Fredericksburg sufferers"—the residents of that battered town.[82]

Engulfed by the wreckage—"the rifled tenements of our friends, and in many instances helpless widows and children"—a man of the 10th Georgia dismissed the sympathy he typically felt when viewing Union dead in the aftermath of battle. "All sympathetic feelings [for our enemies] vanish," he wrote, "and regrets arise that their mutilated carcasses do not lie cross and pile upon every field." Some found consolation in triumph. "No victory of the war has ever done me so much good," declared Confederate engineer Lewis Blackford, whose family had for two decades lived in Fredericksburg. "I hate them [the Yankees] worse than ever. . . . It seems to me that I don't do anything from morning to night but hate them worse and worse." Wrote Lieutenant Price, "If we desire a bloody revenge, we have gotten it." When during a truce a Union officer apologized to Eliza Slaughter, wife of the mayor, for damage done to her house, she pointed to a dozen blue-clad corpses in her yard: "I am repaid for all I have suffered by the sight of these."[83]

The damage inflicted on the town chiseled more deeply the commitment of white Southerners to the Confederacy and their perception of their enemies as unworthy. The bitterness endured through the war and even beyond, with the people of Fredericksburg having more cause to resent than most. In May 1865 Lizzie Alsop, whose home on Princess Anne Street had fared better than many, watched Union troops on their return march to Washington. The contrast between Union victory and Southern suffering almost overwhelmed her. "Oh it is very hard to endure such misery patiently," she confided to her diary. "I feel as if I never could forgive them all they have done to us; the desolation, the grief all over our land." A month later her feelings had intensified. "I hate them more every hour of my life," she wrote. "Look at the misery in every household . . . and then tell me whether it were human to forgive them? I never can!" Literally the same day, young Mary Caldwell wrote in her diary, reflecting on the war, Yankees, and suffering, and concluded, "As for the bygones, I never wish them to be bygones."[84]

Those in the North who opposed the abandonment of conciliation toward the South would have predicted the profound bitterness and deeper rebel commitment that followed Fredericksburg. They would also have predicted the break in discipline within the army that begot the ravaging. But in the aftermath of defeat and amid the tumult of political discourse and debate swirling around and through the Union war effort in late 1862, few in the army, in Congress, or in the North showed much interest in challenging the actions at Fredericksburg. No record has been found of a single soldier disciplined for looting there. Indeed, after just a couple weeks of chatter, the topic virtually disappeared from both public and private discourse.[85]

The questions, however, remain: What of the bombardment and looting of Fredericksburg as it related to the prevailing rules and philosophy of war? Did Fredericksburg portend a Union war effort gone brutal?

War theorists, including the North's own general in chief at the time, would have judged the events at Fredericksburg variously. What would they say about the bombardment of the Confederates' hiding places in and around civilian structures at the crossing sites? Almost certainly they would judge this as clearly consistent with the rules of war. Lee knew this. His orders for civilians to evacuate the town reflected his certainty of the Union response to his defense of the crossings.

What of Burnside's decision to expand the bombardment in an attempt to burn the town down? As noted earlier, Halleck's *Rules Regulating the Intercourse of States in Peace and War* prohibits "useless destruction" but condones action against property "to cripple the operations of the enemy, or to ensure our own success." There is little doubt that Burnside viewed the generalized bombardment of the town as necessary. Confederate troops moved through the streets to reinforce the defenders at the crossing sites. His initial targeted bombardment intended to splinter riverside hiding places with solid shot and percussion shells. It had failed to quell Confederate resistance and could do nothing to stop the free movement of enemy troops through the streets. Burning the town seemed a logical alternative, though that ultimately failed too. One suspects that if Burnside ever presented his case for bombardment to Halleck, the general in chief would have accepted the argument, albeit with a tinge of regret from the theorist.[86]

As it related to the taking of private property, Halleck's treatise reflects the thoughts of theorists long preceding him: "Private property taken from the enemy on the field of battle, in the operations of a siege, or in the storming of a place which refuses to capitulate, is usually regarded as legitimate spoils of war." Officers and soldiers in Fredericksburg often justified the looting by referring to this age-old concept, but in doing so they overlooked something else. "The right to private property taken in such cases," writes Halleck, "must be distinguished from the right to permit the unrestricted sacking of private houses [and] the promiscuous pillage of private property." He later adds for emphasis, "Waste and useless destruction [are] forbidden alike by the law of nature, and the rules of war."[87]

Theorists would have adjudged the seizure of property in Fredericksburg justified but the sacking of the town as an affront to custom and discipline. With few exceptions—notably the cauldron of World War II—Americans have always had an uncomfortable relationship with wartime violence against civilians. This was especially so during the early years of the Civil War, and the writings of Halleck and his predecessors both sustained and reflected that thinking. Halleck's treatise espouses restraint: "The general rule by which we should regulate our conduct toward an enemy, is that of moderation, and on no occasion should we unnecessarily destroy [the enemy's] property." Failure to abide the principle would simply permit enemies to "assert the dignity" of their cause. Union armies tightly embraced the idea of war in moderation during the first year of the Civil War. But Pope and his orders had challenged that devotion, and Fredericksburg to some eyes threatened the concept of "moderation" entirely.[88]

Fredericksburg was the first wanton, sanctioned, large-scale destruction inflicted on an American town by an American army. But while it symbolized a war intensifying in violence and scope, it did not usher forth a new era of destruction. Events in Virginia would demonstrate much of what happened here to be born of a unique concoction of circumstances—a mix of geography, morale, resentment, and leadership. Indeed, the development and distribution of a new set of instructions for the operation of armies in the field in 1863 (the "Lieber Code") included no bending of the moral or legal precepts that would have made the looting of Fredericksburg acceptable.[89]

But to most, Fredericksburg was no case study in military law. Rather, the campaign took place in the context of an evolving Union war effort. Through that lens, it became evident to all—no matter their political views—that what happened there had benefited no one (the army included) and diminished the Confederates not at all. For Union soldiers, the rampage in town became inextricably linked with the disastrous battle that followed; there would be few fond remembrances of either. But perhaps the best indicator of how the men and their officers came to view their actions is this: they never repeated them. In that sense the looting at Fredericksburg helps bring into relief the relative restraint of the Union war effort at large.[90]

The mosh of defeat, dysfunction, debate, and despair after Fredericksburg carried the men of the Army of the Potomac—and their nation—to a point of crisis. Artilleryman George Breck of New York mused, "No wonder the patriot begins to exclaim, with an emphasis never before uttered, 'My country, my country, how long must this terrible sacrifice of human life continue!'" Col. John Wilson of Albany's 43rd New York seemed mystified: "I cannot believe that such a great country as this, such a government, such a Nation, will be permitted to be torn asunder and totally disabled; to be wrecked, and thrown to the winds; to be made the object of mockery of the whole world."

From the chaos of Fredericksburg, the army confronted the cold of an uncertain winter.[91]

NOTES

1. A note on source material: This essay is based almost entirely on sources written during or soon after the event. In reviewing items written after the war, it quickly became apparent that writers often minimized or even dismissed the events that were so plainly and vividly described in 1862. Indeed, the contrast between wartime and postwar sources relating to the looting and bombardment of Fredericksburg would itself make an excellent case study in the evolution of memory and forgetting.

2. "The Fredericksburg Disaster"—a letter from 'J.F.' [of the Irish Brigade]," Dec. 23, 1862, *Irish American Weekly*, Jan. 17, 1863.

3. "The Progress of the Decisive Campaign," *Philadelphia Inquirer*, Dec. 16, 1862; Letter of "W.S.W." [Lt. William S. Walton, 34th New York], *Herkimer (NY) County Journal*, Dec. 25, 1862.

4. Two outstanding analytical narratives of the Battle of Fredericksburg are George C. Rable, *Fredericksburg! Fredericksburg!* (Chapel Hill: University of North Carolina Press, 2002); and Francis Augustín O'Reilly, *The Fredericksburg Campaign: Winter War on the Rappahannock* (Baton Rouge: Louisiana State University Press, 2003).

5. The most obvious case study of a general caught in the crosswinds of a changing war is George B. McClellan, and the most balanced work on this topic is Ethan Rafuse, *McClellan's War: The Failure of Moderation in the Struggle for the Union* (Bloomington: Indiana University Press, 2005).

6. "The Army of the Rappahannock (From Our Own Correspondent)," *Richmond Examiner,* Dec. 18, 1862. The *Examiner's* correspondent in the town was former resident James B. Sener, a part owner of the *Democratic Recorder,* who relocated to Richmond when war forced Fredericksburg's local papers out of print. Sener's dispatches from Fredericksburg to the *Examiner* in late 1862 and into 1863 are outstanding and underutilized sources for life in that war-torn town.

7. For McDowell's strength at Fredericksburg, see Irvin McDowell to his wife, June 15, 1862, McDowell Letters, Fredericksburg and Spotsylvania National Military Park (hereafter referred to as FSNMP), copy.

8. The general order governing foraging, dated May 7, 1862, appears in "McDowell Court of Inquiry," U.S. War Department, *The War of the Rebellion: A Compilation of the Official Records of the Union and Confederate Armies,* 70 vols. in 128 pts. (Washington, D.C.: Government Printing Office, 1880–1901), ser. 1, 12(1):51 [hereafter cited as *OR,* all items from ser. 1]. Haupt testified to the requirement to leave sufficient supplies for the subsistence of the affected family. Ibid., 77. See also Davis Tillson's testimony, ibid., 80. For an expression of support for McDowell's practices in the field, see "The Intent and Spirit of the War," *Springfield (MA) Republican,* May 21, 1862.

9. Letter of "C" (20th New York State Militia), Apr. 29, 1862, *Kingston (NY) Argus,* May 7, 1862. Edmund Schriver, McDowell's chief of staff, testified to the rebuilding of Lacy's fences. *OR,* 12(1):105. See also unattributed correspondence, *Philadelphia Sunday Dispatch,* Jan.18, 1863.

10. In late 1862 the government—at McDowell's request—convened a court of inquiry to examine the general's acts in the field. The proceedings of that court include a trove of material reflecting on the army's interactions with civilians in and around Fredericksburg. For the quotes here, see *OR,* 12(1):48, 52, 53. By far the best modern treatment of the Union occupation is Edmund Raus, *Banners South: A Northern Community at War* (Kent, Ohio: Kent State University Press, 2005). The book chronicles the experiences of the 23rd New York, part of McDowell's command.

11. Irvin McDowell to his wife, July 21, 1862, McDowell Letters, FSNMP, copy; Carolyn Carpenter, ed., "The Civil War Diary of Betty Herndon Maury," *Fredericksburg History and Biography* 9 (2010): 74; Kerri S. Barile and Barbara P. Willis, eds., *A Woman in a War-Torn Town: The Journal of Jane Howison Beale, Fredericksburg, Virginia, 1850–1862* (Virginia Beach: Donning, 2011), 84; For more praise of McDowell's protection of local property, see Betty Churchill Jones Lacy, "Memoirs of a Long Life," n.d., FSNMP.

12. Two untoward incidents punctuated McDowell's tenure in the Fredericksburg region. On May 3 two Union deserters murdered Robert Eden Scott, a prominent Unionist and legislator from Fauquier County. Lincoln had offered him a cabinet post, but the Virginian had declined and remained on his farm. According to friend William Wallach, Scott's death "did more to destroy the remaining Union feeling existing in that section of Virginia than any other event of the war . . . up to that time." About the same time, a Union soldier raped a young woman near Potomac Creek Bridge in Stafford County. Authorities never found the man who committed the crime, but the offense inspired McDowell to remind his soldiers that the punishment for rape would be death. For the reaction to Scott's murder, see testimony of William Wallach, McDowell Court of Inquiry, *OR,* 12(1):48, 51. For Confederate reaction to the murder, see "The Late Robert

E. Scott," *Richmond Dispatch*, May 9, 1862. For McDowell and the response to the rape, see McDowell Court of Inquiry, *OR*, 12(1):52, 78.

13. Carpenter, "Diary of Betty Herndon Maury," 75; Elizabeth Maxwell Alsop Wynne Diary, May 23, 1862, Virginia Historical Society, Richmond; Letter of Fred Burritt (23rd New York), May 10, 1862, *Elmira (NY) Weekly Advertiser and Chemung County Republican*, May 24, 1862; "From the 76th Regiment," *Courtland (NY) Gazette and Banner*, June 26, 1862. For additional commentary on civil-military relations in Fredericksburg, see "From the Cromwellian Regiment [76th New York]," *Utica (NY) Daily Observer*, June 19, 1862; and Letter from "Camp Near Fredericksburg [from a member of the 5th Pennsylvania Reserves]," June 1, 1862, *The Huntingdon (PA) Globe*, June 11, 1862.

14. The figure of 10,000 former slaves was recorded by W. W. Wright, the superintendent of the railroad between Fredericksburg and Aquia Landing—the route by which most slaves traveled. See *OR*, 12(3):815; and Barile and Willis, *Woman in a War-Torn Town*, 74. For additional testimony of the evolving relationship between slaves and masters in Fredericksburg, see "Letters from the Army," [letter of Lt. N. T. Colby, 23rd New York, May 1, 1862], *Corning (NY) Journal*, May 8, 1862.

15. "From McDowell's Corps," *Salem (MA) Register*, June 2, 1862; "More about Capt. Mansfield's Tenderness to the Rebels," *New York Herald*, July 23, 1862; *Life and Letters of Wilder Dwight* (Boston: Ticknor and Fields, 1868), 233. The *New York Times* also printed a lengthy and stinging indictment of McDowell's administration at Fredericksburg: "The Conduct of the War: McDowell's column—An Army for the Protection of Rebel Property," July 14, 1862. In late 1862 McDowell would request and receive a court of inquiry, where his supposed leniency with civilians came under intense scrutiny.

16. McClellan's Harrison's Landing letter has often been interpreted by historians as an overreach in the realm of civil-military relations. Historian Ethan Rafuse effectively disputes this in "General McClellan and the Politicians Revisited," *Parameters* (Summer 2012): 71–85.

17. Pope letter quoted in Wallace J. Schutz and Walter N. Trenerry, *Abandoned by Lincoln: A Military Biography of General John Pope* (Urbana: University of Illinois Press, 1990), 177. The best treatment of evolving Union war policy under Pope appears in Mark Grimsley, *The Hard Hand of War: Union Military Policy toward Southern Civilians, 1861–1865* (Cambridge: Cambridge University Press, 1995), 85–91.

18. *OR*, 12(2):52; "Infamous Order of Gen. Pope," *Macon (GA) Telegraph*, July 31 1862. For an accurate assessment of the order by a Union artilleryman, see "Artillerist," "Our Army Correspondence," July 26, 1862, *Columbia (PA) Democrat*, Aug. 2, 1862. The *New York Herald* of August 1, 1862, carried the Confederate response to Pope's orders, "Important Declaration by the Rebels." For a discussion of General Order No. 11, see John J. Hennessy, *Return to Bull Run: The Campaign and Battle of Second Manassas* (New York: Simon and Schuster, 1993), 17.

19. *OR*, 12(2):50.

20. *OR*, 12(3):509; *Richmond Examiner*, Aug. 4, 1862.

21. *OR*, 11(3):362–63. McClellan delayed distributing this order to his army for more than two weeks, then added a thousand-word cover, cautioning his troops not to perceive the order as "a pretext for military license."

22. "Effect of General Pope's Orders," *Boston Daily Advertiser*, Aug. 7, 1862; "Army Correspondence: From the Connecticut Cavalry," *Norwich (CT) Morning Bulletin*, Aug. 18, 1862; Washington Roebling to his father, Aug. 24, 1862, Washington Roebling Papers, Rutgers University Library, New Brunswick, NJ. See also Grimsley, *Hard Hand of War*, 90–92; Hennessy, *Return to Bull Run*, 19–20.

23. Irvin McDowell to "My Dear Nelly," Aug. 14, 1862, McDowell Letters, FSNMP, copy; "Effect of General Pope's Orders," *Boston Daily Advertiser*, Aug. 7, 1862.

24. *OR*, 12(3):573; Henry W. Halleck, *International Law: Or, Rules Regulating the Intercourse of States in Peace and War* (New York: D. Van Nostrand, 1861), 461. For a sharp order to Brig. Gen. Adolph von Steinwehr, who had apparently sanctioned unbridled foraging, see *OR*, 12(3):577. For the best modern discussion of Union war policy as it related to the rules of war, see Grimsley, *Hard Hand of War*, esp. 11–17.

25. Letter of William P. Andrews, July 19, 1862, in Charles A. Cuffel, *History of Durrell's Battery in the Civil War* (Philadelphia: Craig Finley, 1903), 51; Letter of "C" (2nd Wisconsin), July 25, 1862, "[Edwin B.] Quiner Scrapbooks: Correspondence of the Wisconsin Volunteers, 1861–1865, Volume 3," Wisconsin Historical Society, http://content.wisconsinhistory.org/cdm/ref/collection/quiner/id/33964.

Copies of letters in the Quiner collection relating to the Iron Brigade have been transcribed and can be found at "1862 July, the Second Wisconsin," Second Wisconsin Volunteer Infantry, http://www.secondwi.com/fromthefront/2d%20wis/1862/1862_july.htm. Rebecca Campbell Light, ed., *War at Our Doors: The Civil War Diaries and Letters of the Bernard Sisters of Virginia* (Fredericksburg: American History Co., 1998), 43. For reference to the arrest of hostages, see John Hennessy, "For All Anguish, for Some Freedom: Fredericksburg in the War," *Blue and Gray Magazine* (Winter 2005), 12.

26. John Gibbon to his wife, July 21, 1862, Box 1, John Gibbon Papers, Historical Society of Pennsylvania, Philadelphia. Similarly McDowell told his wife, "What suffering is coming to these people." McDowell to "My dear Nelly," July 21, 1861, McDowell Letters, FSNMP, copy.

27. "Fredericksburg Threatened: Burnside's Army in Front," *Virginia Herald*, Nov. 21, 1862; "From Fredericksburg," *Richmond Examiner*, Nov. 19, 1861.

28. Mary Campbell Knox Moncure, "A War Time Sketch," *The Spur: Life in Virginia, Past and Present* (Feb. 1956): 5; Barile and Willis, *Woman in a War-Torn Town*, 105.

29. The army's provost marshal general, Marsena Patrick, recorded that on the army's return to Virginia from Maryland in early November, he deployed patrols to stop what he called "plundering and marauding." Nevertheless, unauthorized plundering clearly differed in scale and effect from that under Pope. It seems to have had no widespread effect on the army's operations, though it certainly kept Patrick fretting. See David S. Sparks, ed., *Inside Lincoln's Army: The Diary of Marsena Rudolph Patrick, Provost Marshal General, Army of the Potomac* (New York: Thomas Yoseloff, 1964), 171, 172.

30. "Letter from Falmouth, Va.," Nov. 18, 1862, *Philadelphia Inquirer*, Nov. 21, 1862; Ruth L. Silliker, ed., *The Rebel Yell and Yankee Hurrah: The Civil War Journal of a Maine Volunteer* (Camden, ME: Down East Books, 1985), 53; Letter of Macauley (44th New York), *Rochester Democrat and American*, Sept. 5, 1862. For a good description of efforts to control plundering and soldiers'

determination to get what they wanted regardless, see "Our Army Correspondence" (5th Pennsylvania Reserves), *Columbia (PA) Spy*, Nov. 15, 1862.

31. Sparks, *Inside Lincoln's Army*, 179; *OR*, 21:783; "From Fredericksburg—the surrender of the town demanded," *Richmond Dispatch*, Nov. 24, 1862. The latter article includes a letter from a "prominent citizen" of town—perhaps the mayor himself, but almost certainly at least a member of the common council, given the detailed knowledge he communicated.

32. Clifford Dowdey and Louis Manarin, eds., *The Wartime Papers of R.E. Lee* (Boston: Little Brown, 1961), 341; John C. Oeffinger, *A Soldier's General: The Civil War Letters of Major General Lafayette McLaws* (Chapel Hill: University of North Carolina Press, 2002), 162; Sparks, *Inside Lincoln's Army*, 179–80; William Teall to his wife, Nov. 21, 1862, William Teall Papers, Tennessee State Library and Archives, Nashville. Teall was on Sumner's staff, witnessed Patrick's return that evening, and recorded several details not found elsewhere.

33. *OR*, 21:783–84; Sparks, *Inside Lincoln's Army*, 179–80; Teall to his wife, Nov. 21, 1862, Teall Papers; Sparks, *Inside Lincoln's Army*, 180. The correspondent of the *New York Herald* wrote a detailed account of the events of November 21, widely published in Northern newspapers, as in "Affairs at Fredericksburg," *Boston Advertiser*, Nov. 25, 1862.

34. *OR*, 21:785. The *Richmond Examiner* of November 28, 1862, offered extensive commentary and praise for Fredericksburg and its mayor.

35. Thomas R. R. Cobb to his wife, Nov. 22, 1862, Thomas Reade Roots Cobb Papers, University of Georgia Library, Athens; *OR*, 21:788. For civilians preparing for travel by train, see Matilda Hamilton Diary, Nov. 25, 1862, Virginia Historical Society, Richmond; Moncure, "War Time Sketch," 5; and Oeffinger, *Soldier's General*, 163.

36. "Our Army Correspondence," *Southern Watchman* (Athens, GA), Dec. 31, 1862; Dowdey and Manarin, *Wartime Papers of R. E. Lee*, 343; Alexander McNeill to "My Dear Wife," Nov. 27, 1862, Alexander McNeill Papers, FSNMP, copy. The privately owned McNeill letters have recently been published: Mac Wyckoff, ed., *The Civil War Letters of Alexander McNeill, 2nd South Carolina Regiment* (Columbia: University of South Carolina Press, 2016). Contemporary commentary from Southern soldiers on the plight of refugees is extensive. See, for example, Robert E. Lee to his wife, Nov. 22, 1862, in Dowdey and Manarin, *Wartime Papers of R. E. Lee*, 343; Gen. Thomas R. R. Cobb to "Darling," Nov. 22, 1862, Cobb Papers; and Charles W. Turner, ed., *Captain Greenlee Davidson, C.S.A.: Diary and Letters, 1861–1863* (Verona, VA: McClure, 1975), 62.

37. Oeffinger, *Soldier's General*, 163; Alexander McNeill to "My Dear Wife," Nov. 27, 1862, McNeill Papers, copy. The estimate of the number of residents remaining in town is derived in part from an analysis of voting turnout during the war years as embodied in the minutes of the Fredericksburg Town Council. See John Hennessy, "To Go or Not to Go: Fredericksburg's Refugees and Those Who Stayed Behind," Jan. 4, 2012, *Mysteries and Conundrums* (blog), https://npsfrsp.wordpress.com/2012/01/04/to-go-or-not-to-go-fredericksburgs-refugees-and-those-who-stayed-behind/. The extended period of quiet prior to December 11 inspired many residents to return to their homes only to be driven out again by the Union bombardment. See, for example, Barile and Willis, *Woman in a War-Torn Town*, 107. The Wells family on Sophia Street decided to remain in their house throughout because a family member was sick. Rebecca Campbell Light, *Between Two Armies at Fredericksburg: The Benjamin Franklin Wells Family Papers* (Fredericksburg:

American History Co., 2010), 121. Light's book includes the memoir of Mamie Wells, which is the only known account of a resident of Fredericksburg who remained in town throughout the battle.

38. Lafayette McLaws, "The Confederate Left at Fredericksburg," in *Battles and Leaders of the Civil War*, ed. Robert U. Johnson and Clarence C. Buel, 4 vols. (New York: Century, 1887–88), 3:86.

39. *OR*, 21:258, 259; O'Reilly, *Fredericksburg Campaign*, 63–64; Clark Baum to his wife, noon, Dec. 11, 1862, FSNMP, transcript; Letter of Arthur T. Williams (50th New York Engineers), n.d., in *I Will Try to Send You All the Particulars of the Fight: Maps and Letters from New York State's Civil War Newspapers, 1861–1863*, ed. David S. Moore (Albany: Friends of NYS Newspaper Project, 1995), 107. The three-quarter moon rose in Washington, D.C., the night of December 10 at 10:53 P.M. The night was largely clear. Sunrise on December 11 in Richmond was at 7:14 A.M. McLaws, "Confederate Left at Fredericksburg," 86; *OR*, 21:578, 601–2.

40. *OR*, 21:602; Ed Malles, ed., *Bridge Building in Wartime: Colonel Wesley Brainerd's Memoir of the 50th New York Volunteer Engineers* (Knoxville: University of Tennessee Press, 1997), 112.

41. The reports of Union artillery officers are fairly complete. Based on them, it appears that fifty-two light guns participated in this first fusillade, ranging from the Washington farm on the south to guns in what is today Pratt Park, to the north of the Lacy House (Chatham). Seven siege guns of Maj. Thomas Trumbull's 1st Connecticut Heavy Artillery also opened fire, though Trumbull admitted that he could see nothing of Fredericksburg from his position on the ridge overlooking the Washington farm. The reports of Hunt and Tompkins are most valuable. *OR*, 21:181–82, 191, 193, 195, 199.

42. Williams letter, n.d., in Moore, *Will Try to Send You All the Particulars*, 107; Malles, *Bridge Building in Wartime*, 113. Waterman's and Seeley's reports document the brevity of this first bombardment and the rate of fire: Seeley's battery fired twenty-five rounds, while Waterman claimed his guns fired between three and six rounds each. *OR*, 21:194, 196.

43. *OR*, 21:182–83; Letter of John L. Smith (35th Massachusetts), Dec. 23, 1862, FSNMP, typescript; Josiah M. Favill, *The Diary of a Young Officer* (Chicago: R. R. Donnelley and Sons, 1909), 209.

44. For references to Confederate troops moving through the streets, see Letter of J. B. Wheeler (50th New York Engineers), n.d., *Cohoes (NY) Cataract*, Dec. 20, 1862; and "From the Second Delaware," *Delaware Statesman and Journal* (Wilmington), Jan. 2, 1863.

45. *OR*, 21:183. The intent to set the town on fire is referenced by both Col. Charles Tompkins and Capt. Richard Waterman. See ibid., 191 (Tompkins), 195 (Waterman).

46. For a discussion of the conflict between Hunt and Burnside, see Edward G. Longacre, *The Man behind the Guns: A Biography of General Henry Jackson Hunt* (South Brunswick, NJ: A. S. Barnes, 1977), 131.

47. The seven batteries on the Union right under Lt. Col. William Hays did not participate in the bombardment of Fredericksburg. Some of those units fired that afternoon, though at distant Confederate batteries, not the town. The number of guns that participated in the bombardment is calculated by a tally that meshes the reports of battery and battalion commanders with Hunt's careful record of the number of guns in each battery as recorded in his report. For reference to

the direction and rate of fire of batteries on the Union north flank, see, for example, Diedrichs report (fired fifty-three rounds that afternoon), *OR,* 21:201, Harn (forty-three rounds), ibid., 202, and King (zero) and Durell ("a few"), ibid., 208.

48. *OR,* 21:182–184, 191, 195.

49. For references to one hundred shots per minute, see Letter of J. B. Wheeler, *Cohoes (NY) Cataract,* Dec. 20, 1862; Channing Price to his mother, Dec. 17, 1862, Channing Price Papers, Southern Historical Collection, University of North Carolina at Chapel Hill; Gary W. Gallagher, ed., *Fighting for the Confederacy: The Personal Recollections of General Edward Porter Alexander* (Chapel Hill: University of North Carolina Press, 1989), 171. "Army Correspondence: From the 8th Penna Cavalry," *Columbia (PA) Spy,* Jan. 17, 1863.

50. Steven J. Keillor, ed., *No More Gallant a Deed: A Civil War Memoir of the First Minnesota Volunteers* (Minneapolis: Minnesota Historical Society Press, 2001), 231; "From the 140th Regiment: Letter from True Blue," *Rochester Evening Express,* Dec. 22, 1862. For the extent of smoke and the visibility of spires, see Letter from Adjutant, 140th NY, n.d., *Rochester Democrat and American,* Dec. 27, 1862; and "A Chelsea Volunteer's Account of the Battle of Fredericksburg," *Chelsea (MA) Telegraph and Pioneer,* Dec. 17, 1862.

51. John Esten Cooke, "Fredericksburg," *Philadelphia Weekly Times,* Apr. 26, 1879. Cooke recorded that Lee fully expected the Union army to fire on Fredericksburg if his men offered resistance from its streets.

52. *OR,* 21:183.

53. Letter of J. B. Wheeler, *Cohoes (NY) Cataract,* Dec. 20, 1862; Catherine S. Crary, ed., *Dear Belle: Letters from a Cadet & Officer to his Sweetheart, 1858–1865* (Middletown, CT: Wesleyan University Press, 1965), 173. For by far the best summation of the fighting in the streets of Fredericksburg, see O'Reilly, *Fredericksburg Campaign,* 83–101.

54. Halleck, *International Law,* 464, 466. While McClellan is the most obvious case study of an adherent to what has become known a policy of "conciliation," a more succinct example can be found in the story of his most favored subordinate, Fitz John Porter. See John Hennessy, "Conservatism's Dying Ember: Fitz John Porter and the Union War, 1862," in *Corps Commanders in Blue,* ed. Ethan Rafuse, 14–60 (Baton Rouge: Louisiana State University Press, 2014). See also Grimsley, *Hard Hand of War,* 92–94.

55. Letter of "W.S.W.," *Herkimer (NY) County Journal,* Dec. 25, 1862; S. Millett Thompson, *Thirteenth Regiment New Hampshire Volunteer Infantry in the War of the Rebellion* (Boston: Houghton Mifflin), 38. See also John H. Merrell Diary, Dec. 11, 1862, Special Collections Department, University of California at Los Angeles, 13. For reference to civilians crossing into Union lines, see Oliver Otis Howard, *Autobiography of Oliver Otis Howard,* 2 vols. (New York: Baker and Taylor, 1907), 1:325; and Stephen W. Sears, ed., *For Country, Cause & Leader: The Civil War Journal of Charles B. Haydon* (New York: Ticknor and Fields, 1993), 297.

56. Charles Davis (1st Minnesota) Letter Fragment, n.d., Charles Edward Davis Papers, U.S. History Civil War Collection, Brown University, Providence, RI; "From the 15th Regiment, C.V.," *Waterbury (CT) American,* Jan. 23, 1863; Letter of "W.S.W.," *Herkimer (NY) County Journal,* Dec. 25, 1862. For reference to widespread damage to virtually every building, see John M. Priest, ed., *From New Bern to Fredericksburg: Captain James Wren's Diary* (Shippensburg, PA: White Mane,

1990), 94; and "From the Army of Gen. Hooker—the Scene Near Fredericksburg," *Boston Traveler*, Mar. 12, 1863.

57. The calculation of buildings lost in the bombardment is derived from an analysis of the town's property-tax records for 1865, the first attempt at tax collection since 1862. The tax collector noted those buildings "burned" (fifty-one), "shelled and pulled down" (seventeen), and "pulled down and burned" (sixteen). Another seventeen buildings were listed as "damaged by shells" but apparently not sufficient enough to warrant demolition. Of the eighty-three buildings listed as lost, fifteen were in locations unlikely to have been touched by the Union bombardment of December 11. Instead those structures likely succumbed during the fighting on December 13—in fact most probably perished at the hands of Confederate artillery fire. "Fredericksburg Research Resources," http://resources.umwhisp.org/fredburg.htm.

58. Letter of "W.S.W.," *Herkimer (NY) County Journal*, Dec. 25, 1862.

59. Ambrose Cole to "Mrs. Jane Cole," Dec. 27, 1862, Ambrose Cole Letters, FSNMP; Letter of David Chamberlain (4th Michigan), Dec. 23, 1862, *Hudson (MI) Gazette*, n.d., FSNMP, typescript. In a piece widely reprinted, the *New York Herald* likewise offered an indictment of the secessionist proclivities of Fredericksburg residents. See *Daily State Sentinel* (Indianapolis), Dec. 18, 1862; *Weekly Wisconsin Patriot* (Madison), Dec. 27, 1862; and *Savannah Republican*, Jan. 10, 1863. For other references to the nexus between the guilt of Southern civilians and the looting that followed, see Letter of Herbert C. Mason, [date illegible], FSNMP, copy; and "From the Nineteenth Regiment, *Cambridge (MA) Chronicle*, Dec. 27, 1862.

60. John G. B. Adams, *Reminiscences of the Nineteenth Massachusetts Regiment* (Boston: Wright and Potter Printing, 1899), 51. Adams identified the home he used as that of a namesake music teacher, R. W. Adams, who lived in the former home of Martha Crump on Sophia Street, just below the ruins of the Chatham Bridge. For the use of houses as quarters, see also "From the Nineteenth Regiment."

61. Henry C. Ropes to John Ropes, Dec. 20, 1862, Boston Public Library; Letter of Herbert C. Mason, [date illegible], FSNMP, copy.

62. Davis Letter Fragment, n.d., Davis Papers.

63. Hazel C. Wolf, ed., "Campaigning with the First Minnesota: A Civil War Diary," *Minnesota History* 25, no. 3 (Sept. 1944): 36 (Dec. 11, 1862); George N. Macy to his former colonel, William R. Lee, Dec. 20, 1862, USAMHI, typescript. Sully himself confirmed the drunken condition of his brigade on December 11: "The soldiers, breaking into the liquor stores, got drunk and all in all it was a frightful scene." It may have been, but there is no evidence that Sully undertook any effort to curtail it. Landon Sully, *No Tears for the General: The Life of Alfred Sully, 1821–1879* (Palo Alto, CA: American West, 1974), 159.

64. Light, *Between Two Armies at Fredericksburg*, 146–47.

65. Crary, *Dear Belle*, 176; Cyrus Bacon Diary, Dec. 15, 1862, Michigan State Archives, Lansing; Porter Farley, "Reminiscences of the 140th Regiment New York Volunteer Infantry," in *Rochester in the Civil War*, ed. Blake McKelvey (Rochester, NY: Rochester Historical Society Publications, 1944), 205. Among many others, Mamie Wells stated, "every unoccupied house was plundered." Letter of an unidentified woman [very likely Mamie Wells], n.d., *Richmond Dispatch*, Jan. 2, 1863, quoted in Light, *Between Two Armies at Fredericksburg*, 157–59. Capt. James Wren of

the 48th Pennsylvania recorded staying at the Wells house for two nights. Priest, *From New Bern to Fredericksburg*, 120–22.

66. "J.H.C." (John H. Canfield), "From the Connecticut Brigade," n.d., *Hartford (CT) Evening Press*, Dec. 23, 1862; Samuel S. Partridge (13th New York) to "My Dear Ed," Dec. 17, 1862, Samuel S. Partridge Papers, FSNMP, typescript; Letter of "Adjutant," *Rochester Democrat and American*, Dec. 25, 1862; "Letter from Lieut. Col. N. Coryell" (89th New York), *Havana (NY) Journal*, Jan. 3, 1862; Peter Messent and Steve Courtney, eds., *The Civil War Letters of Joseph Hopkins Twichell: A Chaplain's Story* (Athens: University of Georgia Press, 2006), 197; J. Gregory Acken, *Inside the Army of the Potomac: The Civil War Correspondence of Captain Charles Francis Adams Donaldson* (Mechanicsburg, PA: Stackpole, 1998), 182. For excellent, expansive descriptions of the looting of Fredericksburg, see Rable, *Fredericksburg! Fredericksburg!*, 174–89; and O'Reilly, *Fredericksburg Campaign*, 102–26.

67. Letter of "W.S.W.," *Herkimer (NY) County Journal*, Dec. 25, 1862.

68. "Our Army Correspondence," letter of "Adjutant," Dec. 18, 1862, *Rochester Democrat and American*, Dec. 27, 1862; Matthew J. Graham, *The Ninth Regiment, New York Volunteers (Hawkins' Zouaves): Being a History of the Regiment and Veteran Association from 1860 to 1900* (New York: N.p., 1900), 386; Letter of "J.T. McG," [John T. McGonigle], *Lancaster Daily Express*, Dec. 23, 1862; Col. John D. Wilkins to his wife, Dec. 18, 1862, John Wilkins Papers, Schoff Collection, Clements Library, University of Michigan, Ann Arbor; Messent and Courtney, *Letters of Joseph Hopkins Twichell*, 197.

69. "From the 89th Reg't N.Y.S.V.," *Bloomville (NY) Mirror*, Jan. 6, 1863. See also Crary, *Dear Belle*, 176; and Wilkins to his wife, Dec. 18, 1862, Wilkins Papers. Another Regular, Cyrus Bacon of the 14th U.S. Infantry, also asserted the virtue of the professionals: "I am proud of one thing, that it is not the Regulars who have sacked the city. Our regiment took but little. The men, for the reason that they were kept to their places by order." But Bacon also conceded a moment of personal weakness (as did many other officers): "I took a couple of books and having no opportunity to return them, I burned them up. I would not take such disgraceful evidence to camp with me." Bacon Diary, Dec. 15, 1862.

70. Sparks, *Inside Lincoln's Army*, 189; Darius Couch, "Sumner's Right Grand Division," in Johnson and Buel, *Battles and Leaders*, 3:108; *OR*, 21:241.

71. Nathaniel Brown to "Dear Cousin" [Albert M. Given], Dec. 23, 1862, FSNMP, typescript.

72. Howard, *Autobiography*, 1:325; David K. Thomson, ed., *We Are in His Hands Whether We Live or Die: The Letters of Brevet Brigadier General Charles Henry Howard* (Knoxville: University of Tennessee Press, 2013), 78.

73. Letter of John S. Crocker, Dec. 11, 1862, Brockett Collection, Department of Manuscripts and University Archives, Cornell University, Ithaca, NY.

74. Thomson, *We Are in His Hands*, 78–79. The Articles of War were established by an act of Congress in 1806. The article referenced here is No. 58. See *The Public Statutes at Large of the United States of America, from the Organization of the Government in 2789, to March 3, 1848. Arranged in Chronological Order*, vol. 2 (Boston: Charles C. Little and James Brown, 1848), 366.

75. James Wright of the 1st Minnesota recalled, "Lieutenant Ball was considerate and gave us all the liberty he could—only asking that we would be within call and get into line promptly

if there should be an alarm, and men were not to take off their accouterments or their shoes." Keillor, *No More Gallant a Deed*, 233.

76. Sparks, *Inside Lincoln's Army*, 189; Thomas Francis Galwey, *The Valiant Hours*, ed. W. S. Nye (Harrisburg, PA: Stackpole, 1961), 58. As examples of managing troops in the streets and the general inclination for troops to stay close to their assigned bivouacs, see Amos Judson, *History of the Eighty-Third Regiment Pennsylvania Volunteers* (Erie, PA: B. F. H. Lynn, 1865), 106–7; M. H. McNamara, *The Irish Ninth in Bivouac and Battle* (Boston: Lee and Shepard, 1867), 167–69; Thompson, *Thirteenth Regiment New Hampshire*, 38; Charles Page, *History of the Fourteenth Regiment, Connecticut Volunteer Infantry* (Meriden, CT: Horton Printing, 1906), 79; Nathaniel Brown to "Dear Cousin" [Albert M. Given], Dec. 23, 1862, FSNMP, typescript; Favill, *Diary*, 210; and Michael A. Flannery and Katherine H. Oomens, eds, *Well Satisfied with My Position: The Civil War Journals of Spencer Bonsall* (Carbondale: Southern Illinois University Press, 2007), 68.

77. The reports of most officers make clear that the army continued to function and provide the needed security on the battlefield. See, for example, Butterfield's report for the V Corps, *OR*, 21:400–401; and David T. Hedrick and Gordon Barry Davis, eds., *I'm Surrounded by Methodists: Diary of John H. W. Stuckenberg* (Gettysburg: Thomas, 1995), 43–44.

78. Christian G. Samito, ed., *Commanding the Irish Ninth: The Civil War Letters of Colonel Patrick R. Guiney, Ninth Massachusetts Volunteer Infantry* (New York: Fordham University Press, 1998), 156; Linda Foster Arden and Dr. Walter L. Powell, eds., *Letters from the Storm: The Intimate Civil War Letters of Lt. J. A. H. Foster, 155th Pennsylvania Volunteers* (Chicora, PA: Firefly, 2010), 31; Orsell Cook Brown (44th New York) to "Sister Ollie," Dec. 14, 1862, Orsell Cook Brown Papers, New York State Library, Albany. Testimonials to Union morale after Fredericksburg are many. For good summaries, see Rable, *Fredericksburg! Fredericksburg!*, 339–43; and A. Wilson Greene, "Morale, Maneuver, and Mud," in *The Fredericksburg Campaign: Decision on the Rappahannock*, ed. Gary W. Gallagher (Chapel Hill: University of North Carolina Press, 1995), 171–79.

79. Robert Garth Scott, ed., *Fallen Leaves: The Civil War Letters of Major Henry Livermore Abbott* (Kent, Ohio: Kent State University Press, 1991), 154.

80. An example of the limited comment on the looting is found in "The Progress of the Decisive Campaign," *Philadelphia Inquirer*, Dec. 16, 1862.

81. "Important Testimony," *Daily National Intelligencer* (Washington, D.C.), Jan. 1, 1863, reprinted from the *Waterbury (CT) American;* "A New Account of the Battle of Fredericksburg," reprinted in *Macon (GA) Telegraph*, Feb. 9, 1863.

82. R. Channing Price to his mother, Dec. 17, 1862, R. Channing Price Papers, Southern Historical Collection, University of North Carolina at Chapel Hill; James R. Hagood (1st South Carolina), "Memoir," 98, University of South Carolina, Columbia; James W. Beaty to Miss Lucy, Dec. 16, 18, 1862, James Beatty Papers, Alderman Library, University of Virginia, Charlottesville. The fundraising effort on behalf of Fredericksburg civilians was widely publicized across the South. Mayor Slaughter led a small committee responsible for distributing the funds based on claims filed by residents who suffered losses to the looters. Those claims survive in the Historic Court Records of Fredericksburg, Collection MP-MP-P, FSNMP, typescripts. Likewise at FSNMP are the papers of Mayor Montgomery Slaughter relating to the raising and distribution of the relief fund. Funds not distributed were invested by the town in Confederate war bonds.

83. "Letter from the Tenth Georgia Regiment," *Augusta (GA) Daily Constitutionalist,* Dec. 27, 1862; Price to his mother, Dec. 17, 1862, Price Papers; Letter of Benjamin Lewis Blackford, Dec. 23, 1862, Blackford Family Papers, Alderman Library, University of Virginia, Charlottesville. Francis Charles Lawley's narrative, written from Richmond on December 20, 1862, appeared in *The Times* of London on January 23, 1863, and was reprinted widely in the United States.

84. Wynne Diary, May 18, June 26, 1865, Virginia Historical Society; Russell P. Smith, ed., "I Should Look Forward to the Future: The Diary of Mary G. Caldwell, Part 2," *Fredericksburg History and Biography* 12 (2013): 80.

85. "The Progress of the Decisive Campaign," *Philadelphia Inquirer,* Dec. 16, 1862. The writer of this article asserted, "Our troops should make war upon Rebels and the Rebellion, not upon women and children, nor upon looking-glasses, dressing-cases, and furniture generally."

86. Halleck, *International Law,* 212. For a discussion of the roots of policy, see Grimsley, *Hard Hand of War,* 15–22.

87. Halleck, *International Law,* 211, 464.

88. Ibid., 466.

89. Francis Lieber, *Instructions for the Government of Armies of the United States in the Field* (New York: D. Van Nostrand, 1863). For a discussion of Leiber's Code, see D. H. Dilbeck, *A More Civil War: How the Union Waged a Just War* (Chapel Hill: University of North Carolina Press, 2016), 69–86.

90. The restrained nature of the Union war effort is argued in both Dilbeck, *A More Civil War,* and Mark Neely, *The Civil War and the Limits of Destruction* (Cambridge, MA: Harvard University Press, 2007).

91. Letter of Lt. George Breck (Reynolds's New York Battery), n.d., *Rochester Union and Advertiser,* Dec. 24, 1862 (Breck's outstanding letters have been made available online; see "What a Sacrifice of Human Life Is This!," *1st Artillery Regiment (Light), Battery L: George Breck Columns,* transcribed by Bob Marcotte, last modified Aug. 17, 2006, New York State Military Museum, Unit History Project, https://dmna.ny.gov/historic/reghist/civil/artillery/1stArtLt/1stArtLtBatL-BreckChap14Sacrifice.htm); Letter of Col. John Wilson, Dec. 23, 1862, in Rufus W. Clark, *Heroes of Albany* (Albany: S. R. Gray, 1866), 175. For comprehensive (and to some degree companion) treatments of the next several months in the army's history, see Greene, "Morale, Maneuver, and Mud," 171–217; and John J. Hennessy, "We Shall Make Richmond Howl: The Army of the Potomac on the Eve of Chancellorsville," in *Chancellorsville: The Battle and its Aftermath,* ed. Gary W. Gallagher, 1–35 (Chapel Hill: University of North Carolina Press, 1996).

---◆---

GUERRILLA WARFARE AS SOCIAL STIMULUS

Brian D. McKnight

---◆---

O
N TOP OF A SMALL HILL in Fentress County, Tennessee, lies the Travisville Cemetery. Today the main road lies well below the cemetery, but at
the time of the Civil War, it ran alongside the graveyard, which was passed by
everyone traveling between Travisville and Pall Mall. On September 29, 1861,
warring parties came together near the base of the hill and produced a single
casualty, a local man named James Saufley. Little is known about Saufley or
the events surrounding his death, but something was certainly curious about
it. He was buried in the cemetery's first row next to the road, with a tomb-
stone that read, "Killed by James Ferguson of 1st Ky Cav U.S.A. 29 Sept 1861."
Not only did the marker identify Saufley's killer by name, but his friends also
turned it toward the road, effectively inviting passersby to exact vengeance on
the man's behalf.[1]

In most books that examine guerrilla warfare, particularly that of the Civil
War, the focus is on guerrilla warfare as a military event. It is true that Saufley
died in one of only a handful of actions in the region, but the influence of his
death would not be exclusively of the military variety. Indeed, even those who
buried him recognized the value of retributive violence as an element of the
societal conflict that would soon wrack the region. As the conventional war
proceeded, ended, and was commemorated, the memory of this community
war was replaced by that of a military conflict that offered the familiarity
of commanders, battles, and victories. Such interpretations often leave out
regions like the Upper Cumberland plateau and men like James Saufley. Recently, as interest began to return to these borderland regions and the community war endemic there, the primary interpretive lens was military, which
fails to tell the entire story. By only viewing irregular participants through a
traditional military perspective, scholars lose sight of the broader scene at

ground level. The dirty underbelly of war involves not only military action but also civilian and societal response. Indeed, guerrillas are as much purveyors of armed violence as soldiers in armies, but viewing them only in that way is myopic. While armies also institute regime change and provide security for populations, guerrilla warriors occasionally play a similar role. During the Civil War, one of the leading motivations for and byproducts of guerrilla violence was in fact social change.

Furthermore, this violence was not a means unto itself, it was a means to an end. And it was that end that holds the great question: How were decent citizens to survive in a world whose rules of order no longer functioned as such? For many of the Civil War's borderlanders, their fight was to maintain their society rather than to free the slaves or save the Union. When Wayne Wei-siang Hsieh lamented that "this new wave of Civil War revisionism with its focus on 'dark history' runs the real risk of replacing an overly triumphalist and emancipationist narrative with one fixated on waste and folly," he was thinking about battlefields strewn with glory sacrificed for a great political cause. For scholars of the Civil War's dirty underbelly, his abstract phrase "waste and folly" describes real civilian sacrifices that, if further explored, reveal people with actual names and dependent families.[2] Hsieh finds the separation of the war's violence and the principle of emancipation troubling, but that is largely because he is trying to define the terms and paradigms others use in their studies. Similar criticisms have been lodged by Gary W. Gallagher and Kathryn Shively Meier, who worry that "the analytical risk of overemphasizing the dark side is that readers who do not know much about the war might infer that atypical experiences were in fact normative ones."[3] Scholars of the Civil War borderlands would counter that there is also a significant risk in those who know little about the war in contested regions overemphasizing a formal martial history that suggests a reality that was not true in large areas of the nation at that time. Along that borderland, large numbers of Virginians, Tennesseans, and Kentuckians, among others, might have had an opinion about the issues of slavery and emancipation, but their physical presence in a contested region required them to prioritize safety and security over lofty political concerns. They may have cheered victories and expressed disappointment at news of defeats, but their primary focus was on direct, local threats. While the Civil War gave Philadelphians and Bostonians an opportunity to advocate for emancipation and military officers their opportunity for battlefield glory, Appalachians and other borderlanders were plunged into widespread conditions of deprivation and fear.

Embracing the unique nature of these borderlands, this chapter examines the inherently relational nature of warfare and how communities responded to the guerrilla threats that seemingly surrounded them. In some cases, like that of Saufley, it appears that the community, or at least some of its members, hoped that a violent response would remove a proven threat. Others sought to avoid violence in a variety of ways that included both formal and informal attempts at neutrality. In one powerful example of an effort to protect a community from extralegal violence, a collection of the most notorious guerrilla figures from Overton and Fentress Counties in Tennessee and Clinton County in Kentucky met and agreed on what became known as the "Livingston Compromise." Under its terms, the men declared that the home counties of others were off limits to their periodic raids.[4] Not surprisingly, the arrangement did not last very long, but the efforts to establish the initial agreement speaks volumes about how these men viewed the idea of a guerrilla war being brought to their doorsteps. As individuals respond to stressors, so do the communities they constitute. These neighborhoods illustrate the broader concerns of their citizens and attempt to bind together what destructive forces were working to fragment and scatter.

This chapter also addresses the power of fear, whether real or imagined, as a motivator of men and women who have no idea what the future might hold. In southwestern Virginia this anxiety caused a man to kill a Union deserter who was completely dependent on the goodwill of the small community in which he was hiding.[5] Champ Ferguson notoriously claimed that he killed dozens of men because if he had not done so, they would have killed him. In taking "time by the forelock," as he put it, he believed that he was able to save his own life on these numerous occasions.[6] This concept of preventative violence places the community only one justifiable event away from descending into a state of full-scale anarchy in which "each man feels an impulse to kill his neighbor lest he be first killed by him."[7] Just as communities have to come together to maintain their safety and security, they also have to deal with the variety of reasons that drives these events and the powerful influence of an unknown future.

If there was a single deleterious effect of the Civil War on local communities, it was the shuttering of those institutions that traditionally provided social stability. While enjoying the protection afforded by the White House, even Abraham Lincoln understood the nature of guerrilla warfare. He wrote to Charles Drake, an emancipationist and Radical Republican, that warfare brought about uncertainty: "Deception breeds and thrives. Confidence dies, and universal suspicion reigns. Each man feels an impulse to kill his neighbor, lest he be first killed by him. Revenge and retaliation follow. And all this . . . may be among honest men only. But this is not all. Every foul bird comes abroad, and every dirty reptile rises up. These add crime to confusion. . . . Murders for old grudges, and murders for self, proceed under any cloak that will best cover for the occasion."[8]

Lincoln understood that, at its roots, guerrilla warfare cuts at the social sinews, replacing stability with instability, and realigning priorities at the individual and community levels. In order to do this, civil and religious institutions must be marginalized if not completely removed. In Appalachia, an exemplar of the Civil War guerrilla conflict, most contested communities went years without those institutions of security. For the most part, locals primarily reacted to insults and depredations by either stifling their dissatisfaction and attempting to find a middle way, behaving extralegally and taking the fight to the aggressors, or reaching out to the state for sanctioned self-defense against depredations.

In the contested borderlands, local institutions suffered under the weight of the war. For an upstart entity such as the Confederate States, traditional civil authority promised little help. By destroying these foundational elements of society, the Confederacy gained credibility among sympathetic elements of the local populace and alienated those who would likely never join the Southern cause anyway. Along the shared borders of Kentucky, Tennessee, and Virginia, many courthouses were put to the torch. By burning the administrative center of a county, the community would see the destruction of their dominant symbol of traditional authority, removing its reminding presence from their daily existence.

In addition to the deeds, wills, and other documents that meant so much to those who valued social and political stability, tax records, delinquencies, and indictments were also lost, giving those on the community's margins reason to support a new regime. In Lebanon, Kentucky, John Hunt Morgan's July 1863

raid resulted in the burning of the courthouse, which reportedly held indictments against several of Morgan's men.[9] When Confederates entered Barbourville, Kentucky, they removed the tax books and destroyed them in an attempt
to befriend many of the county's indebted citizens.[10] In Booneville, Kentucky,
Confederate soldiers strewed public documents in the street before burning
them.[11] Local citizens recognized this element of warfare and sought to either
prevent or hasten the destruction of such papers. In Hardinsburg, Kentucky,
citizens rescued county records from the courthouse before fire could destroy
them.[12] Worried that men from nearby Kentucky might burn the Lee County,
Virginia, courthouse, the clerk removed all public records and stored them
twelve miles away in the private home of a respected citizen to prevent their
destruction.[13]

A second byproduct that compromised stability was the closing of churches
and schools. As the war grew and hostilities expanded into communities, such
institutions in contested regions closed their doors, usually because it was
no longer safe to travel the public roads or be away from home. Edward O.
Guerrant, a member of Brig. Gen. Humphrey Marshall's staff who had spent
the preceding year in Virginia, noticed the absence of these activities. Near
Crockettsville, Kentucky, Guerrant wrote, "While grazing my horse, the children came laughing, from school—! From School—!! Ah! its memories! Today
how beautiful they are! How prized! How lost! So strange to see a schoolhouse
& school children."[14]

Under constant threat and without the protection of civil authorities or the
comfort of churches, borderlanders began to realize that if they were to survive the war with their lifestyles intact, they were going to have to take matters
into their own hands. Understanding the power of violence as a result of their
own exposure to it, many in these communities embraced violent response
as a way to resist their transgressors. One petitioner to Kentucky's governor
explained this rationale: "The warfare of guirillas upon citizens of Kentucky
and especially upon discharged soldiers justly condemns every guerrilla to
outlawry and death whenever wherever & by whomsoever taken. It is a matter
of self defence upon the part of every citizen who slays a guerilla at any time
as well as defence of society."[15]

During the summer of 1863, eastern Kentucky was besieged by Confederate guerrillas. Among the more notorious were brothers Sid and Dave Cook.
Both had gotten their starts in the 2nd Kentucky Mounted Rifles but by spring

had transitioned into a partisan unit raised under the authority of Brig. Gen. John S. Williams. They spent the summer conducting raids throughout eastern Kentucky, primarily focusing on robbing stores and banks rather than fighting for the greater cause of the conflict, and became locally known as "Cook's Guerrillas." Throughout 1863 and 1864, Cook's Guerrillas struck dozens of targets in Carter, Greenup, Morgan, and Johnson Counties, including the robbery of a bank in Ashland on September 26, 1863.[16]

The Cooks carried with them a reputation that prompted men to get out of their way. That October they struck the Pennsylvania Iron Furnace in Greenup County. Less than a month later, after being robbed twice by Dave Cook, W. L. Geiger moved to Ashland, where he could enjoy the relative safety of town life. In the meantime pressure increased on local unionists to bring guerrilla activity under control. After having been shot by his own brother in a dispute, Dave Cook was taken prisoner by unionists who then sent him off to prison, where he died. By the summer of 1864, Sid Cook led a raid on Paintsville, Kentucky, and by January 1865 Cook's Guerrillas were at Castle's Woods, in Russell County, Virginia, where they robbed the locals and used their ill-gotten gains to pay for the services of prostitutes.[17]

As a community, the crossroads town of Castle's Woods had endured warfare on a daily basis since the beginning of the conflict, and its citizens were not new to heavy-handed treatment from soldiers. In January 1865, with the war obviously winding down and Confederate fortunes in visible decline, concerned locals, with the assistance of a few fed-up soldiers, rose up in opposition to Cook's brand of authoritarianism. After setting fire to the brothels, a violent clash ensued that resulted in Cook being killed by a fellow Confederate soldier, Cleve Boyd.[18] In Castle's Woods the exhaustive nature of the war and poor behavior of its actors drove local citizens to rise up against their tyrants.

Violence was not the only response to guerrilla depredations. When Confederate raider Capt. Jake Bennett arrived in Owensboro, Kentucky, with not quite two dozen men, he did so in the hopes of stealing U.S. currency supposedly deposited there. Bennett herded the townspeople into the square and ordered the vaults opened, but no one moved. He threatened to burn their courthouse, but still no one stepped forward. Finally a townsman suggested that the boats tied up at the docks may hold Union supplies and that the captain and his men might be better served by investigating them. Ultimately Bennett's exploration of the docks resulted in his men killing several black

Union soldiers detailed with guarding the boats. This incident, however, also represents the kind of ingenuity that townspeople leaned upon to save themselves and their property from guerrilla attacks.[19]

At the same time that citizens defended their rights to eliminate guerrillas "whenever wherever & by whomsoever taken," they acknowledged the acceptable possibility that they might unwittingly harm the innocent.[20] Near Hayesville, Kentucky, in late 1864, two Dickens brothers arrived at the Rinehart home in search of their stolen mule. The Dickenses were strangers from the next county to the south and so were not surprised when two other men rode up to the Rinehart house and exchanged pleasantries with them. The men offered to take the Dickens brothers to Mr. Rinehart, who was away from home that afternoon, and the four men rode off. After a short distance, the brothers grew suspicious of their guides' intentions and refused to go any farther. At this point the men turned on the brothers, relieved them of their guns, and shot them both, inflicting serious wounds. The Dickens brothers rode together in the direction of a Louisville & Nashville Railroad crew more than a half mile away. As the brothers approached, one worker, Michael Foley, a discharged Union veteran of the 9th Kentucky Cavalry, stepped forward to receive the fast-riding strangers. As they came nearer, Foley noticed that they carried with them the hallmarks of guerrillas: pistol belts, scabbards, and a "rebel saddle." The Dickenses demanded to know if the workers were Union men and explained that they had been "bush-whacked." With the community under recent threats from a guerrilla unit, Foley did not believe their story and told them to ride away. Three hundred yards later they met John Mauser, who also deemed them guerrillas and watched the brothers ride off. Just down the road, the two stopped at the home of Charles Prewitt, where one of them dismounted and entered the house while the other, Merritt, remained in the saddle. In the meantime Foley had left his work crew, spoken with Mauser on the road, and was convinced that he should arrest the brothers as guerrillas. Foley took a gun from Mauser's house and rode up to Merritt Dickens, still on his horse. He announced his intention of taking the stranger to the town jail even though he steadfastly stuck to his story of being a Union man. Finally, the wounded and unarmed man agreed to go with Foley. For the second time that afternoon, Merritt Dickens was in the custody of a threatening individual, and just as he had done before, he spurred his horse in an attempt to escape. He made it only back to the Prewitt house, where he refused to believe Foley's promises that he would be released if his story could be confirmed. Soon thereafter, Foley shot him dead. The veteran then ordered "a loyal citizen and law abiding man to guard the house and not let the other guerrilla escape." He then went looking for the local guerrilla hunters, but returned with them to the Prewitt place too late. While Foley was gone, the other Dickens brother had provided an account of the day's events to a local woman serving as his nurse as he began slipping toward death.

Upon the community's realization that two innocent men had died due to an overzealous citizen, logic might suggest that the regrettable events would be forgiven and forgotten. But the residents turned on Foley, jailing him, releasing him, and then confining him a second time. As was later determined, "during the whole of the ten days which had elapsed since the shooting of the two Dickenses, no effort had been made to ascertain and bring to justice the two men who had actually murdered them before Foley saw them." Furthermore, Mr. Rinehart, who was almost certainly known by the killers, was called but failed to appear and testify at the inquest. While Foley's attorneys portrayed the miscarriage of justice as an intentional effort to protect the real offenders, it is more likely that the fever of the times called for punishment despite true culpability. In the end Gov. Thomas Bramlette granted Foley a pardon, arguing that "due caution being used to avoid mistakes[,] no one should be held criminally liable for killing [a man] supposed to be a guerrilla."[21]

It became clear to borderland citizens that organization could help them resist those who threatened their safety and security. Home-guard units were established as a way to maintain some degree of local civil control over the use of armed force. Guerrillas thrived on the isolation of their targets, and if a community could come together and form a unifying presence, it could more effectively resist harassment and depredation. The use of home guards was undertaken very early in the war in some sections and remained popular throughout the conflict, particularly in areas with no predictable militia presence.

A look into the records of the Civil War governors of Kentucky illustrates the rapid mobilization of home-guard units within the state as a way to combat local guerrilla activity. In Johnson County Col. Burgess Preston raised 101 men and had 55 of them in camp in Paintsville to be drilled. His main problem, however, was the availability of firearms. He confessed that his company had "about 45 guns 10 enfield a few shot guns and the balance old guns that the Rebeles left Scatered about in the country" and that "thare is a good meny Reble Gerrillars in this country and I think the company might be in agrat [a great] deal of danger in camp without being beter [better] armed."[22]

Cades Cove, Tennessee, was one of those communities targeted because of its isolation. Confederates from nearby North Carolina often raided the cove, stealing livestock and harassing the largely unionist citizenry. By the spring of 1864, most of the men remaining in the neighborhood were old and responsible for the entire community's security. Overwhelmed, they organized themselves into a home-guard unit. In Durwood Dunn's standard work on Cades Cove, he writes, "they revived an older sense of community among the cove people which enabled them to act collectively to defend themselves." Dunn attributes their willingness to take a public stand against the raiders to several factors. The Federal presence in Knoxville had not made an impression on the people of the cove. Raiders still came, and residents still lost their property. More importantly, they lost livestock and stores of food, which meant they would be doomed to another winter of starvation diets if they did not act. Dunn also sees the raiders' attack on the town's Primitive Baptist church as being catalytic. Having a long and comfortable relationship with the idea of fatalistic deprivation, Primitive Baptists could suffer as individuals and find biblical comfort in doing so, but they would not permit an assault on their church. Finally, these concerns found redress with solid local leadership. Russell Gregory developed an early alert system by which locals could warn the community of approaching guerrillas, thereby giving every citizen an important role in the cove's protection.[23]

Gregory's system of having women and children watch the main passes into Cades Cove from North Carolina paid dividends. Lt. Charles G. Davis, a Union prisoner from Camp Sorghum in Columbia, South Carolina, visited Cades Cove while fleeing imprisonment. He recalled: "A girl was on duty as a sentinel. She gave the alarm with a horn. When she blew the horn we were looking down the Cove. In an instant it was alive." He further elaborated: "I remember asking the girl on guard what she would do if a stranger should demand the horn . . . before she could have used it. . . . Her reply was that she should tell him to go to 'Hell!'" This girl or another sentry sounded several alarms over the latter months of the war, but one was particularly important. Upon hearing that the Confederates had entered Cades Cove in the spring of 1864, Gregory and the other old men felled trees across the roads at the other end of the cove, through which the invaders would have to funnel any stolen livestock. He and his neighbors hid among the downed trees and limbs, waiting for the Carolinians to arrive. Once the raiders drew close, the residents unleashed a short burst of gunfire and quickly drove the strangers out of their community without any of the bounty they had gathered. The result was an overwhelming sense of accomplishment, and the Carolinians—having seen that these men and women were prepared to resist them violently—turned to less effective and less frequent night raids rather than the daylight attacks that had been so effective up to that point. Gregory had helped his neighbors develop a response to atrocity, and the citizens of Cades Cove no longer passively accepted Confederate depredations—even after Gregory was killed in his bed only two weeks after this pivotal event.[24]

Like their peers in Cades Cove, other Appalachian communities responded to direct threats by organizing citizens into ad hoc military bands. Patsy Keel Boggs remembered her father's role in the local Civil War. Having a quick temper and physical prowess to back it up, David Smith grew frustrated by "bushwhackers" who refused to formally join the fight. Several local men, along with deserters from both sides, were actively avoiding service by "laying out in the woods, dodging the guards sent to arrest them." One evening David and his brother Flournoy, hearing owls hooting suspiciously early, stepped onto the front porch. At the next hoot a shot rang out from the woods and hit Flournoy in the arm. David jumped off the porch and tried to run around the back of the house, but Harrison "Hare" Bowman ran down the hill to get a better shot, hitting David in the side, the ball lodging near his spine. Smith's wife, Priscilla, came to his aid and covered him with her body as Bowman moved in for a fatal shot. As Bowman readied himself, Priscilla talked him out of firing, and he went away.

By March or April 1865, David Smith had recovered and began pursuing not only his attackers but also all the local men hiding out. Joining a handful of Confederate soldiers seeking out the bushwhackers, he led the men to an isolated valley, Alley's Creek, where they found their targets along with a Federal deserter. Three of the bushwhackers were killed—including Hare Bowman, the man who had tried to kill Smith—and the deserter was found hiding under a log. The still ten-year-old Boggs remembered, "They pulled him out and . . . put a gun to his head and his brains flew everywhere."[25]

By the end of January 1862, the Battle of Mill Springs had brought the

Civil War too close for comfort for the residents of central Kentucky and the Tennessee border region. Tensions were heightened and lines of loyalty even more blurred as locals began to guard against anything that might threaten their daily existences. In either February or March, concerned local residents gathered together to try to map a safe path forward between the warring parties. They met in Monroe, Tennessee, a small town on the road between securely unionist Albany, Kentucky, and securely Confederate Livingston, Tennessee. The group of men who met that day were unlikely allies: Avowed unionists "Tinker Dave" Beatty and his two sons met with steadfast Confederates Winburn Goodpasture and three others. They were joined by several more moderate men from the surrounding counties whose primary goal was to end the state of open warfare that had existed up to that point in the region. The resulting compromise stated that "horse stealing, and raiding about, was a bad business" and "proposed putting a stop to it" by arranging "for both parties to go home, lay down their arms, and go to work." One participant remembered that "the Home Guard was not to pester the [Confederate] soldiers, and we were to be protected, all faring alike."[26] Despite the fact that the compromise fell apart within weeks, there is much to be appreciated in people with competing loyalties banding together in an attempt to provide civil security for their region.

Along the Border South, individuals and communities rose up to resist their assailants by publicizing their crimes. Writing from Winchester, Kentucky, James M. Ogden informed Governor Bramlette about Claiborne Lisle of Clark County, explaining, "There is not . . . between Heaven and Hell such a traitor & rebel scoundrell as this same Claiborne Lisle." Expounding to include the status of Lisle's relatives, Ogden wrote, "there is a large family of them here & viler traitors never breathed." With a close cousin killed "while with Morgan's horse thieves," a brother "convicted as a rebel spy" but his sentence forgiven by Lincoln, another brother who took advantage of Edmund Kirby Smith's invasion to rob a "good Union man," and yet another brother who had been indicted in court for treason and had stolen a "Government horse," Lisle was certainly surrounded by anti-Union sentiment.[27]

Ogden made clear that while the entire family was trouble, their undisputed leader was Claiborne Lisle. Identifying him as "very adroit, cunning, and dangerous" and with "a considerable property," Ogden suggested that he "be 'arbitrarily' arrested & held in custody till [the] close of the war," warning the governor that Lisle "is as mean a man & as bad a traitor as can be found any where." Writing confidentially, he further declared if his identity were revealed, he would "certainly be assassinated & have his house burned down."[28] Interestingly, Odgen wrote Bramlette not to initiate Lisle's arrest, but to protest his potential pardon—as he saw it, it was the governor's responsibility to keep Lisle shelved for as long as possible.

Standing on the opposite side of the fence from the Lisles was John Hale of Harrodsburg. Hale had been a Union soldier early in the war before returning home and raising a militia regiment for the protection of the citizens of Mercer County, Kentucky. With the end of hostilities, Hale remained on guard against partisan depredations, but on September 3, 1865, he was arrested by a mob of fourteen men. The group declared in town their intent to hold the veteran, and one of them, a local man named Roberts, ran to a nearby livery stable and retrieved a rope with the hope that the others would hang the captive. Instead, the men took Hale out of town and held him for twenty-four hours, threatening him with the noose. Reconsidering their position, they decided to release him, but only if he promised not to prosecute them for the unlawful arrest. Hale agreed and was released. Back in town immediately after being let go by the mob, he confronted Roberts about his rabble rousing. When Roberts reached into his pocket, Hale drew a pistol and promised to shoot him.[29] Things calmed down in Harrodsburg for a few days until September 9, when a policeman named Bowen attempted to arrest Hale for breach of peace. As Hale argued with Bowen, Lt. William Bishop of Company B, 5th U.S. Colored Cavalry, stepped forward and claimed that he had been ordered to protect Hale and refused to allow his arrest. Bishop told Bowen that he was there to ensure that local Union men were protected and that Hale had been "abused sufficiently" the previous week.[30]

The ending of a war often requires the tying up of loose ends. In Wise County, Virginia, in February or March 1865, the last lawless bands were rooted out. One such group was hiding in the area and stealing from the locals. A witness later wrote of these men: "I don't know whether they had much preference for either side or not. But they seemed to want to live on what they could get from the citizens that had nothing to spare." The band of "six or eight of them, well armed," remained on the community's outskirts for months until local men sought out Lt. Col. Clarence Prentice, who dispatched a squad to break up the group. Having an established camp, the bandits were easily found by Prentice's men, who quietly surrounded them, and "the whole camp was killed out." Henry Keel remembered, "That fight put an end to the depredations."[31]

Guerrilla warfare remained a part of local communities long after the last shots of the war were fired, but the residents themselves responded less actively than during the war. Writing in July 1865 in response to Governor Bramlette's plan to muster out the state-guard units, E. B. Treadway warned, "we have not yet established Civil Courts or even yet put down all the Gurrillas in the counties of Harlan, Perry, Breathitt, Letcher, &c. there are reported to be three Bands of Gurrillas in those counties."[32] J. B. Cassady wrote similarly that without protection from guerrillas, "at least Some of us will be ruined if we are not Spedily relieved from the desperation of these out laws."[33] Besieged by the return of the guerrilla threat, often in the form of returning former Confederates, war-weary communities sometimes struggled to form local units to defend themselves. Within two months of Lee's surrender at Appomattox, the Owingsville sheriff could get no one to join a posse to bring in a local bandit.[34] A few months later John W. Tuttle of Monticello declared, "the *possecomitatus* system would prove impracticable and ineffectual as a means of apprehending these thieves cut-throats and scoundrels" and urged the governor to consider appointing "a squad of Volunteer Militia of this County organized under some one of approved courage, energy and zeal for the execution of the laws or if not they earnestly ask that a small detachment of State troops already organized armed and mounted may be sent here to their assistance."[35]

As one studies the role of guerrilla warfare during the Civil War, it is easy to classify it as a military function and move on to the next question. But when viewing the irregular war from the ground up, it becomes obvious that social and community history can be very helpful in reconstructing the story. Furthermore, the guerrilla story must also be understood through those who were affected by it, with the knowledge that they had as much influence over the guerrillas as the guerrillas had over them. At numerous points during the conflict, individuals and communities rose up to resist irregular actors and often did so with great effect. Not only did they halt ongoing depredations, they even went so far as forcing influential politicians to take firmer stands than they would have naturally preferred. In the past few decades much good work has been done to provide breadth and context to the guerrilla experience in the Civil War. The myth of powerlessness is ripe for reconsideration.

Brian D. McKnight

NOTES

1. Aaron Astor, *The Civil War along Tennessee's Cumberland Plateau* (Charleston, SC: History, 2015), 116; Brian D. McKnight, *Confederate Outlaw: Champ Ferguson and the Civil War in Appalachia* (Baton Rouge: Louisiana State University Press, 2011), 41.

2. Wayne Wei-siang Hsieh, "Go to Your Gawd like a Soldier: Transnational Reflections on Veteranhood," *Journal of the Civil War Era* 5, no. 4 (Dec. 2015): 551.

3. Gary W. Gallagher and Kathryn Shively Meier, "Coming to Terms with Civil War Military History," *Journal of the Civil War Era* 4, no. 4 (Dec. 2014): 492.

4. Astor, *Civil War along Tennessee's Cumberland Plateau,* 125; McKnight, *Confederate Outlaw,* 62.

5. Patsy (Keel) Boggs Reminiscence, Sept. 28, 1941, in *Pioneer Recollections of Southwest Virginia,* ed. Elihu Jasper Sutherland (Clintwood, VA: H. S. Sutherland, 1984), 38.

6. *Nashville Union,* Oct. 21, 1865.

7. Abraham Lincoln to Charles D. Drake and Others, Oct. 5, 1863, *Abraham Lincoln, Speeches and Writings, 1859–1865: Speeches, Letters, and Miscellaneous Writings, Presidential Messages and Proclamations* (New York: Literary Classics of the United States, 1989), 523.

8. Ibid.

9. James A. Ramage, *Rebel Raider: The Life of General John Hunt Morgan* (Lexington: University Press of Kentucky, 1986), 165.

10. K. S. Sol Warren, *A History of Knox County, Kentucky* (Barbourville, KY: Daniel Boone Festival, 1976), 172.

11. Robert Perry, *Jack May's War: Colonel Andrew Jackson May and the Civil War in Eastern Kentucky, East Tennessee, and Southwest Virginia* (Johnson City, TN: Overmountain, 1998), 64.

12. *Louisville Weekly Journal,* Dec. 28, 1864.

13. James W. Orr, *Recollections of the War between the States, 1861–1865* (N.p., 1909), 13; Bonnie Ball, "Impact of the Civil War upon the Southwestern Corner of Virginia," *Historical Sketches of Southwest Virginia* 15 (Mar. 1982): 3.

14. William C. Davis and Meredith L. Swentor, eds., *Bluegrass Confederate: The Headquarters Diary of Edward O. Guerrant* (Baton Rouge: Louisiana State University Press, 1999), 246.

15. "To his Excellency Thos. E. Bramlette," Dec. 21, 1864, Office of the Governor, Thomas E. Bramlette: Governor's Official Correspondence File, Petitions for Pardons, Remissions, and Respites, 1863–67 [hereafter cited as Petitions for Pardons], BR12-138 to BR12-143, Kentucky Department for Libraries and Archives, Frankfort [hereafter cited as KDLA].

16. John David Preston, *The Civil War in the Big Sandy Valley of Kentucky,* 2nd ed. (Baltimore, MD: Gateway, 2008), 180–81.

17. James Pritchard and Jeffrey C. Weaver, "The 7th Battalion Confederate Cavalry—Virginia," http://files.usgwarchives.net/va/military/civilwar/rosters/va7th.txt.

18. Ibid.

19. Randy Mills, "Confederate Raider . . . Criminal . . . Hero: Captain Jake Bennett's Civil War," unpublished manuscript in author's possession.

20. "To his Excellency Thos. E. Bramlette," Dec. 21, 1864.

21. Ibid.

22. Burgess Preston to Thomas E. Bramlette, Aug. 5, 1864, 37th–76th Regiments Enrolled Militia Primary Source Documents (1861–66), Box 81, KDLA.

23. Durwood Dunn, *Cades Cove: The Life and Death of a Southern Appalachian Community, 1818–1937* (Knoxville: University of Tennessee Press, 1988), 134–35.

24. Ibid., 135–38.

25. Boggs Reminiscence, Sept. 28, 1941, in Sutherland, *Pioneer Recollections of Southwest Virginia,* 37–38; Henry Keel Reminiscence, Oct. 28, 1925, ibid., 183–84.

26. Winburne W. Goodpasture Testimony, Aug. 22, 1865; James Beatty Testimony, Aug. 9, 1865; Rufus Dowdy Testimony, Aug. 26, 1865; and Marion Johnson Testimony, Aug. 9, 1865, Proceedings of the Trial of Champ Ferguson, RG 153, Records of the Office of the Judge Advocate General (Army), 1792–1981, Court-Martial Case Files, Textual Archives Services Division, National Archives and Records Administration, Washington, D.C.; Statement of John J. McDonald, John Boles, Sen., H. Stover, and John Winingham, n.d., in J. D. Hale, *Sketches of Scenes in the Career of Champ Ferguson and His Lieutenant* (N.p., 1870), 7–8; Astor, *Civil War along Tennessee's Cumberland Plateau,* 125.

27. James M. Ogden to Thomas E. Bramlette, Feb. 5, 1864, Petitions for Pardons, BR9-328 to BR9-329, KDLA.

28. Ibid.

29. William F. Bishop to Major Brown, Sept. 25, 1865, Office of the Governor, Thomas E. Bramlette: Governor's Official Correspondence File, Military Correspondence, 1863–67, BR5-221 to BR5-222, KDLA; John D. Hale Affidavit, Sept. 23, 1865, Office of the Governor, Thomas E. Bramlette: Governor's Official Correspondence File, Apprehension of Fugitives from Justice Papers, 1863–67, BR7-166 to BR7-169, KDLA.

30. William F. Bishop to Major Brown, Sept. 25, 1865; Hale Affidavit, Sept. 23, 1865; Chas A. Hardin Statement, Sept. 23, 1865; and M. V. Bowen Statement, Sept. 23, 1865, Office of the Governor, Thomas E. Bramlette: Governor's Official Correspondence File, Apprehension of Fugitives from Justice Papers, 1863–67, BR7-166 to BR7-169, KDLA.

31. E. A. Dunbar to Dear Nephew, June 11, 1923, in Sutherland, *Pioneer Recollections,* 119–20.

32. E. B. Treadway to Thomas E. Bramlette, July 14, 1865, Active Militia Records—Capital Guards, North Cumberland Btn., and Three Forks Btn., Box 77, Folder 865 Three Forks Battalion KSG "Officer Correspondence," Kentucky Department of Military Affairs, Frankfort.

33. J. B. Cassady to Thomas E. Bramlette, May 8, 1865, Guerrilla Letters, Document Box 1, Folder G. L. 1865, ibid.

34. B. D. Lacy to Daniel W. Lindsey, June 7, 1865, Active Militia Records—Capital Guards, North Cumberland Btn., and Three Forks Btn., Box 76, Folder 864–65, 1st Regt Capital Guards Co. F, Frankfort Btn, Correspondence, ibid.

35. John W. Tuttle to Thomas E. Bramlette, Nov. 8, 1865, Guerrilla Letters, Document Box 1, Folder G. L. 1865, ibid.

III

THE
SOLDIERS' WAR

THE LIMITS OF AMERICAN EXCEPTIONALISM
Military Occupation, Emancipation, and the Preservation of Union

Andrew F. Lang

T HE CONCEPT OF AMERICAN EXCEPTIONALISM—the idea that the
United States has enjoyed a distinct past and unique historical development—has long-endured concentrated historiographical scrutiny. But the
end of the Cold War and the rise of globalization influenced a generation of
scholars seeking to pull American history out of its protective exceptionalist
shell, which presented an inimitable founding, a distinctive democratic political culture, and an economic system that downplayed class tensions. Histories
that focused solely on the nation-state, these historians suggested, ignored the
powerful global influences on the historical evolution of the United States. A
new era of American historiography thus discouraged what appeared to be a
tired national provincialism in favor of seeing the United States as "a nation
among nations." Comparative approaches, transnational histories, and Atlantic
studies now place the United States as part of the wider world, offering a rich
counterpoint to a once-isolated historical narrative.[1]

The project of decentering national histories, however, sometimes "fail[s]
to recognize that American exceptionalism is as old as the nation itself and,
equally important, has played an integral part in the society's sense of its own
identity." If professional consensus no longer portrays an exceptional American past, those who *lived* that past certainly regarded their country as separate
and distinct from the rest of the world. This manifest sense of national destiny was especially pronounced during the nineteenth century, particularly
during the Civil War era. Indeed, the conflict unfolded as a contest between
two competing visions of American exceptionalism, each rooted in divergent
conceptions of the nation. The mass of citizens who remained loyal to the
Union—the subject of this chapter—celebrated the United States as the bea-

con of democracy in a world consumed by oligarchy, tyranny, and aristocracy. The common American, as a citizen of a republican government that fiercely guarded individual liberty, enjoyed the freedom to rise or fall economically, socially, or politically. In this construction of American exceptionalism, the Union served as a bulwark against the Confederacy's undemocratic cornerstone of slaveholding privilege, a culture that reeked of European hierarchy and arbitrary class distinctions. The war against secession and slaveholding thus fought to preserve the promise of American egalitarianism, individualism, and democracy.[2]

Seeing the Union's war as a problem of American exceptionalism compels historians to take seriously the concept as contemporaries understood it and not as a validation or refutation of exceptionalism's legitimacy. To that end, this study evaluates the sensibilities of white Federal soldiers who served as forces of military occupation in the wartime Confederacy. Preserving the Union ultimately meant defeating Confederate armies, removing secessionists from power, and enforcing emancipation, all of which remained contingent on the triumph of U.S. military forces. Occupation functioned as a critical component in this war effort, advancing the process of African American freedom and smothering the rebellious spirit of disunion.[3]

As they served throughout the war-torn South, witnessed the death of slavery, and interacted with black and white civilians, Northern volunteers noted the transformative social changes and upheavals happening in the wake of the movements of Union forces. They acknowledged that the collapse of the region's slaveholding aristocracy and the liberation of enslaved people necessarily strengthened the Union's exceptional disposition. Yet in confronting the aftermath of emancipation and the repressive conditions of white slaveholding, these soldiers witnessed how the power of military occupation at once collapsed forces that threatened American uniqueness while also creating cavernous vacuums in which those very threats took new form. They questioned whether the inclusion of black and white Southerners, conditioned by the evils of slavery and seen as uncivilized, indolent, and apathetic, would ultimately delegitimize all that made the Union worth preserving in the first place.[4]

The Civil War's cultural, social, and political problems were directly attached to and influenced by military institutions and concepts. Union soldiers connected their particular forms of service—military occupation, in this instance—to the rapid changes in American life wrought at the points of their armies' bayonets. This is not merely a story about if white Federals supported emancipation—the literature now recognizes that most did, albeit for conflicting reasons—nor the Union army's transition from a limited war of conciliation to a "hard war" against the slaveholding republic. Instead this study addresses how and why soldiers recognized that only military power could preserve their exceptional nation while at the same time grew ambivalent, and even fearful, about what a preserved Union would resemble when the armies departed. Nineteenth-century American exceptionalism had long drawn sustenance from anxieties about the future. These men stood on the front lines of a changing Union, one occasioned by a contest of arms, and one that might well look very different in the wake of war.[5]

Military occupation brought Union soldiers into close proximity with slavery and African Americans. Despite early civil and military policies that prohibited slavery's destruction, the South's premiere social and economic institution deteriorated through a lengthy war of invasion and occupation, African Americans' unswerving quest for freedom, and white soldiers' growing commitment to emancipation in a war for Union. Federal armies offered refuge to the enslaved who actively pursued freedom, undermining the Confederacy by utilizing emancipation as a military tool in the quest for national preservation. U.S. forces, composed of loyal volunteers who reflected the broad swath of moderate antislavery opinion, thus acted as the central vehicles in collapsing American slavery. Ultimately the Union military extended the arm of federal emancipation policy, assuming the role of an occupying institution that governed evolving social relations in the South.[6]

Soldiers in the ranks helped enact the policy and processes of military emancipation. As William Augustus Willoughby, a volunteer in the 10th Connecticut, wrote in January 1863 from occupied eastern North Carolina, the Emancipation Proclamation "will encourage our arms and weaken the *Rebels.*" Zenas T. Haines, who served in the 44th Massachusetts Volunteers, declared: "There is likely one item of compensation to the Government for holding these posts upon the enemy's soil. It is, indeed, due to the freedmen that we provide these harbors of refuge for those who escape from the rebel lines."

New Yorker William H. Root agreed, writing from Bayou Boeuf, Louisiana, "The negroes are now free according to the proclamation," but "their freedom here is conditional with the stay of our troops in this portion of the country." Despite an exhausting raid near New Bern, North Carolina, Charles Hill of the 5th Massachusetts cited the army as the central institution in undermining slavery, "my hatred [of which] has not been lessened by this expedition." He explained, "If it (the expedition) has not been fruitful in any other direction it has given freedom to a good number of slaves and that is worth something."[7]

Other soldiers looked with awe at African Americans' enthusiastic embrace of freedom as the institution of slavery collapsed. "They appear like birds who have been long caged," James Henry Smith, a New York volunteer, wrote from Florida, "& who have sudenly been set at Liberty." Just three weeks before the Emancipation Proclamation went into effect, Amos Collins of the 32nd Iowa explained how slavery had already been shattered in parts of Missouri. Writing about the arrival of fifteen "intelligent contrabands" behind the lines, he asserted that "they prized their freedom more than a new suit of clothes." Later, after speaking with the freedpeoples' former master, Collins explained that emancipation "is quite expensive to the rebels, when the slaves can get into the federal lines and thus obtain their freedom." He believed that "to carry on a war against the government that has heretofore protected them in their enjoyment of this vanishing property . . . is teaching them a lesson that they will not forget soon."[8]

While they supported emancipation as a pragmatic means to assist the war effort, some Union soldiers questioned the rapidity with which military occupation brought social dislocation and destabilization to the South. While detesting the Southern slavocracy, believing that it spawned an unscrupulous, oligarchic, and aristocratic ruling class, these soldiers worried that the combination of rebellion, invasion, occupation, and emancipation—with a powerful army responding to and directing the course of each—collapsed order and stability. Even as Federal armies helped produce a new birth of freedom that portended a more secure Union, occupiers questioned what would come in the wake of black liberation, sensing that military emancipation thrust freedom onto a people presumably unprepared to meet the standards of white American liberty.[9]

Part of the problem stemmed from Union soldiers' complex racial worldviews. It is difficult, if not impossible, to ascribe a universal Northern posture toward African Americans, yet "if there was one attitude, it was an ambivalence compounded of pity, affection, disgust, and hatred." While Union soldiers perceived African Americans through a variegated lens, two constants appeared in their assessments of black Southerners: ubiquity and difference. Andrew H. Minnick of the 69th Indiana Volunteers described the "Nigroes coming through [Memphis] this morning as thick as bees and as black as tar." The occupiers associated the South with teeming throngs of enslaved peoples who embodied the region's distinct character. "Negroes crowd in swarms to our lines," one soldier wrote from the Atlantic coast, while another described the "odd race of people" who populated Louisiana. New Yorker William H. Nichols looked upon black Southerners with incredulity. "We passed through a contraband camp," he described, "and darkeys of every age, color, and sex flocked to the road to behold us pass. A more varried set of beings I have never before seen."[10]

The stark racial constructs of Southern society resulted from centuries of slavery, creating a permanent racial underclass and fostering what some soldiers considered degrees of racial inferiority. Thomas Wentworth Higginson, a Massachusetts abolitionist who commanded African American soldiers in the 1st South Carolina Volunteers (U.S.), considered freedpeople to be docile children who had been deprived of opportunities to mature. Others offered considerably harsher critiques, believing that slavery had transformed African Americans into a slothful, apathetic people who were not fit for freedom. "The negroes are pretty much all lazy and shiftless. They do not seem to appreciate the pleasures of liberty," Joseph Fiske wrote in 1863 from Beaufort, North Carolina. William Thompson Lusk worried that emancipation would convince former slaves that their days of work were complete "and that henceforth they are to lead that life of lazy idleness which forms the Nigger's Paradise." And Chauncey Cooke, a soldier stationed at Helena, Arkansas, believed that "whites would be liars and thieves too if they had been slaves for two hundred years."[11]

Fiske, Lusk, and Cooke rooted their sentiments in abject racism, yet their comments extended far beyond notions of white supremacy. Their interactions with enslaved and freedpeople fostered the sense that there existed a deeply troubling quality about the American South. Slavery, as many Northerners had long argued, contradicted the principles of free labor, which celebrated individual initiative and rewarded a persistent work ethic. Fiske, Lusk, and

Cooke implied that black Southerners, by virtue of a lifetime of bondage, had been deprived of their natural rights. The peculiar institution, they alleged, fostered laziness and indolence, corrupting both black and white. To many white Northerners, slavery reflected the antithesis of progress and efficiency, discipline and enterprise. A slaveholding region, defined by languor and sloth and governed by oligarchic rule, contradicted Northern ideals of ingenuity, egalitarianism, and individualism.[12]

While they seemed to recognize that the injustices of slavery stripped the unalienable rights of life, liberty, and the pursuit of happiness from it victims, Union soldiers like Fiske, Lusk, and Cooke also considered armies of occupation to have occasioned an abrupt freedom. Because they had long enjoyed the fruits of republican liberty and democratic privilege, some soldiers struggled to interpret how a formerly enslaved people responded to freedom, the conditions of which had been created by an active army at the vanguard of social change. Three soldiers who served in Louisiana implied that the apparent destabilization caused by occupying armies created vacuums in which freedpeople allegedly abused their freedom rather than engaging in a thoughtful process of self-improvement and industry. "They don't care," Lawrence van Alstyne, an officer in the 90th U.S. Colored Troops, wrote in October 1863 from Brashear City. "Someone has always thought for them and will have to think for them for some time to come." Massachusetts volunteer Frank Peck suggested that the formerly enslaved, whom he encountered on an expedition in the Lafourche countryside, lacked ambition. Although employed by the federal government to work on sugar plantations, "when that sugar is gathered, where they will go," he pondered, "I shouldn't wish to say." Edward Lewis Sturtevant claimed that freedpeople near New Orleans "can hardly be made to work, [and] need strict watch to prevent from stealing. They [t]hink liberty means liberty to be idle."[13]

In these confessions soldiers acknowledged the necessity of wartime emancipation in preserving the Union while also questioning what the *aftermath* of liberation would bring. This discourse at once reflected the present and foreshadowed the troubled future of mid-nineteenth-century race relations. The processes of military emancipation, while liberating to hundreds of thousands of black Southerners and necessarily catastrophic to the slaveholding aristocracy, exposed the uncertain implications of incorporating a previously enslaved people into the mainstream of American life. If preservation of the

Union meant upholding the nation's individualistic, free-labor, democratic promise, then how would a formerly enslaved people allegedly unaccustomed to such egalitarian traits thrive in a white republic? Could black freedom be reconciled with the nation's long-established economic and political cultures, which stressed initiative, self-reliance, and the responsibility of civic virtue? Although these questions later formed the basis of Republican Reconstruction, Union soldiers also probed these uncertainties during the war. Witnessing the transformative social dislocation wrought by military occupation and emancipation, they asked how formerly enslaved African Americans would be introduced to the world of freedom and a reunited nation of free northerners and southerners, black and white. These inquiries had not framed the initial debates on emancipation, but rather were unexpected outgrowths of its repercussions.[14]

Slavery threatened the very core of American exceptionalism, yet so too did any pretense of racial equality, which many Union soldiers regarded as distinct from emancipation. The experience of domestic military occupation revealed that notions of "inferior" races and cultures would not be left behind when the war ended. Rather, all—Northern soldiers, white Southerners, and freedpeople—would be integrated into the same Union. Articulating this dichotomy, Illinoisan Adolphus P. Wolf "hope[d] the time will come when they [the enslaved] are all free. But I do not want to see them turned loose in the northern states." Charles Francis Adams Jr., a volunteer officer in the 1st Massachusetts Cavalry, agreed. He supported emancipation, believing black freedom to be long overdue, especially since slavery had sparked the terrible war in which the nation was engaged. "Slavery may perish and no one regret it," he wrote from the Union-occupied South Carolina Sea Islands in April 1862, "but what is to become of the unfortunate African?" Adams celebrated the "many good qualities" of the local black population: they were "good tempered, patient, docile, willing to learn and easily directed." He was not wholly optimistic, however, regarding the demeanor of black Southerners. "[T]hey are all slavish," he wrote of the freedpeoples, "and all that the word slavish implies. They will lie and cheat and steal; they are hypocritical and cunning; they are not brave and they are not fierce." Adams did not blame African Americans for their presumably depraved characters: "these qualities the white man took out of them generations ago, and in taking them deprived the African of the capacity for freedom."[15]

Although he endorsed abolition, Adams remained unsure how the former slaves would become assimilated into the American economic system. White Northerners, he explained, had long been imbued in the cultures of republicanism, material progress, free labor, and individual liberty; recently enslaved peoples lacked such formative exposure. "My views of the future of those I see about me here are not therefore encouraging," he acknowledged. Adams could not conceive how African Americans might transition from the backward world of slave-based agriculture into a progressive industrial setting that required initiative and economic training. "Will they be educated and encouraged and cared for," he asked, "or will they be challenged to compete in the race, or go to the wall, and finally be swept away as a useless rubbish?"[16]

Adams could not answer these questions, "but one thing I daily see and that is that no spirit exists among the contrabands here which would enable them to care for themselves in a race of vigorous competition. The blacks must be cared for or they will perish, and who is to care for them when they cease to be of value." Adams believed that the United States would emerge from the war as a beacon of industry, progress, and liberty for the entire world to emulate. Yet for African Americans, "the gift of freedom may prove [their] destruction. Still the experiment should and must be tried and the sooner it is tried the better."[17]

The ways in which Adams attempted to reconcile the problem of black freedom with his version of American exceptionalism reflected the concerns of Union occupiers as they participated in the process of emancipation. Although few soldiers could ignore black Southerners' yearnings for freedom, the aftereffects of liberation appeared just as troublesome as the institution of slavery itself. Charles Enslow Calvin, a volunteer in the 77th Illinois, built on Adams's sentiments nearly a full year after Pres. Abraham Lincoln's proclamation went into effect. Calvin had spent much of the war occupying various portions of Mississippi, placing him in one of the South's most concentrated slaveholding regions. He came to hate the institution, arguing that it was immoral for one human to enslave another. By November 1863, while stationed near Frankfurt, Kentucky, Calvin attempted to organize his thoughts on emancipation. "In the first place I advocate the entire abolition of slavery," and an in allusion to the Declaration of Independence, he favored "equalizing the negro with the white man so far as life, liberty, and the pursuit of happiness is concerned."[18]

Yet Calvin wavered in the very next sentence, pausing to reconsider the idealism of his initial statement. "I do not believe that with all the education that might be bestowed upon the African race that they could be brought on equal terms with the Anglo-Saxon race in regard to intellect." In fact, he declared, "I do not believe in having them in the North." Calvin suggested that because enslaved peoples had for generations been natives of the South, acclimated to the region's climate and inculcated in particular labor practices, "therefore I say keep them in [that] part of the country." Yet he believed that as free laborers, African Americans were entitled to a wage and, as potential citizens, eligible for a proper education. Yet within one generation, Calvin explained, southern blacks would be elevated above their present condition "so far that they would want to be in a country where they could have their own government." Reviving the old colonizationist argument, Calvin imagined that "the United States [would] buy them some country [where they] would gladly go there by their own choice." Finally, writing seven months later from Baton Rouge, he declared, "it will not be the best policy to have [African Americans] come North among us and let them have all the rights and privileges that we as white people and a superior race do."[19]

Far less hesitant than Calvin, Edward Lewis Sturtevant, who served in the 24th Maine Volunteers, emphasized what he considered the troubling implications of emancipation and racial equality. "For the sake of our Country," he wrote from New Orleans in May 1863, "I desire that this blot [slavery] be stripped from our national union." Describing how slavery ensnared and cursed all who practiced the institution, Sturtevant advocated "[f]ree[ing] every slave—teach[ing] them—educat[ing] them." Subsequently, however, "send them from the country." He explained that in the aftermath of emancipation, white and black could not live together, both having been conditioned by their respective experiences of freedom and bondage. Sturtevant further outlined what he perceived to be the distinction between liberty and equality. "Give all a fair chance," he instructed. "Let the Anglo Saxon be developed by itself, and the African by itself." Both races, Sturtevant implied, claimed natural rights of freedom, moral progress, and self-initiative, yet each embodied disparate capacities for their pursuit and maturation. "We do not desire to live with the negro," he concluded, "and the negro with our intelligence, should not desire to live with us. Intercourse only demoralizes us, and benefits him not. A white man could not associate with a negro on a footing of social equality and be protected."[20]

Soldiers such as Adams, Calvin, and Sturtevant endorsed the necessity of emancipation in the present while articulating a vision of the future grounded in skepticism and fear. The aftermath of emancipation fostered profound ambivalence. Preservation of the Union, these troops suggested, partly meant safeguarding the culture of self-sufficiency and maintaining the obligations of individual liberty, both of which seemed grounded in conceptions of whiteness. Yet although exceptional in its political and egalitarian promise, the Union seemingly could not withstand the inclusion of a people who had lived all their lives enveloped in slavery's enervating atmosphere. "So much for emancipation," New York volunteer Peter Yawyer scoffed. "The negroes concluded that they had worked for nothing long enough and as for working wages they cant be depended upon," he wrote from Baton Rouge on the day Lincoln's proclamation went into effect. "When they get a dollar or two they think they have money enough."[21]

Preserving the Union through occupation and emancipation created a paradox. The fate of republican self-government and free-labor egalitarianism depended on the elimination of slavery. Yet the very people who benefited most from emancipation—African Americans—were presumed unfit for, and were even thought to threaten, the very institutions that defined American uniqueness. How would black freedom integrate itself within national (white) traditions and customs, especially when that freedom had been occasioned so suddenly by U.S. military forces? The experience of occupying the South instilled within Union soldiers a sense that their nation was rapidly changing. They wanted to preserve American exceptionalism through military victory, but the very armies charged to achieve that end had created a new nation entirely in occupation's wake. Even as they witnessed the fruits of emancipation, they feared that such sweeping change would, in the end, only create more instability and uncertainty.

The perceived crisis of American exceptionalism not only related to emancipation but also extended to Union soldiers' perceptions of the white South. The occupiers wrote at great length about its stark class polarities, labeling poor whites and elite slaveholders oppositional inhabitants of the region. Both groups seemed burdened by debilitating laziness, backward lifestyles, and uncivilized comportment, all of which sprung from the presence of and reliance on slavery. And yet, although both groups were white, Union soldiers labeled them in the same manner as African Americans, launching an ironic discourse in the sphere of wartime occupation. White nineteenth-century contemporaries used racial difference to demarcate society, drawing distinctions between social fitness and unfitness, equality and inequality.[22] Poor white Southerners and wealthy landed elites, however, inverted Union occupiers' preconceived notions about race and culture. If African Americans, based on centuries of slavery and racial insubordination, were ill equipped for the promises of republican liberty and the free-labor market, then why did so many white Southerners appear just as unqualified?[23]

The basis of this question shocked the soldiers, who of course also were white. And thus concerns regarding the fate of Union grew broader: although the war sought to preserve the nation, how could a postwar United States flourish with the inclusion of black *and* white southerners who, by virtue of their regional and cultural distinctiveness, threatened the very essence of the American character? In addition to African Americans who appeared lazy and unappreciative of their liberty, so too did poor whites seem helpless and estranged by a class of wealthy elites who subsisted exclusively on the arbitrary, unfair privilege of slaveholding. Race and culture thus merged within the mind of the Union soldier, exposing an unanticipated wartime crisis.

When they encountered poor white Southerners, Union occupiers saw a single, unique, and depraved people. Following William T. Sherman's famed March to the Sea, Charles Carleton Coffin served with the occupation forces in Savannah, Georgia, where he considered local whites to be "below the colored people in ability and force of character. They are a class from which there is little hope." He believed that lack of aptitude precluded personal ambition, erasing any desire "to rise to a higher level of existence." Coffin even described the poor whites' dialect as "a mixture of English and African," which he believed was the language of regression. Blaming centuries of slavery for fostering cultural inferiority, he claimed that "the poor whites were in bondage as well as the blacks, and to all appearance will remain so." Coffin concluded that Union victory in the war would not bring these disadvantaged whites into the fold of American uniqueness, simply because they did not possess the attributes necessary to live in a progressive nation molded in the North's image.[24]

The appearance of poor whites inspired curious glances from Northerners unaccustomed to, as one soldier described, "inhabitants [who] are a lazy, lousy, dirty engnorant set of vagabonds." Moreover, disadvantaged residents of occupied communities appeared to be malnourished and crude. Stationed in North Carolina, Richard Kirtland Woodruff described how he "had grown so accustomed [to] the sickly/sallow wobegone looking countences, & at the same time a look sour enough to curdle milk in three minutes, & a voice that . . . [he would] not undertake to describe." By 1864 Illinoisan Rankin P. McPheeters's morale suffered from being in close proximity to people so different from Northerners. "Would you blame me," he asked his wife, "for having the blues, in this God forsaken Country, cut off & shut up from the rest of the world, surrounded on all sides by as low degraded set of human beings as ever lived[?]"[25]

Some soldiers were stunned to discover the uncivilized and backward conditions in which poor whites lived and presented themselves. "I had often heard of the beauty of southern ladies," a soldier in the 17th Connecticut wrote from Saint Augustine, Florida, "[but I] find it much exaggerated. The men are tall, slim, and homely specimens of humanity, . . . and the women look as if they were very nearly related to the men," he chronicled. "The principle accomplishments of both sexes consists of drinking whiskey chewing and smoking tobacco and taking snuff." In 1862 a New Englander stationed in New Orleans observed the civilians' odd "outward appearance, especially their dress [which] is ten years behind the times." Two years later another soldier wrote from the Crescent City that local churchgoers "were dressed in their best which was poor enough and sadly out of style. . . . [T]hey are so wretchedly homely." He even added, "Every body here uses rain water to drink and cook with and it is the best they have."[26]

Soldiers stationed in North Carolina especially noted local women's odd habit of using tobacco, a practice that challenged Northern perceptions of femininity. David Day of the 25th Massachusetts Volunteers reported that women in New Bern "have a filthy habit of snuff chewing or dipping as they call it, and I am told it is practiced more or less by all classes of women." He described how "they take a small stick or twig about two inches long . . . and chew one end of it until it becomes like a brush," which was then dipped into the tobacco and inserted into the mouth. Day claimed that many local women "can squirt the juice through their teeth as far and as straight as the most accomplished chewer among the lords of creation." George O. Jewett, stationed in coastal Carolina, accused white women of gender *and* racial transgressions if they abused tobacco. "The women here, both black and white 'dig' snuff like thunder," he observed. "It will do for niggers, but for white women, faugh!" Military occupation in the rural South seemed to test the cultural, gender, and racial limits of whiteness.[27]

Interactions with poor white Southerners forced the occupiers to reshape their interpretations of national uniqueness, instilling fear that the South deprived the nation of its exceptional character. And as Jewett suggested, poor whites resembled the lowest form of society, on par only with African Americans. "Everything is unlike new england," another soldier agreed. "The inhabitants" of New Orleans "are all kind of some Nig." Union soldiers thus sought refuge, trapped within a region of presumably regressive and lazy people buttressed by degenerative institutions. Everywhere they turned they encountered the opposite of their Northern world. The South, they believed, had robbed its inhabitants, both black and white, of the Revolution's promise. Personal liberty, individualism, and republican virtue, they claimed, did not exist in the land of Dixie. The experience of occupation fueled sentiments of moral and cultural superiority while also inculcating concern for the nation's future. The fate of the Union hung in the balance, not merely because of secession and rebellion but also because of the traits of regression and inability shared by poor whites and black freedpeople.[28]

The citizen-soldiers who occupied the wartime South struggled to comprehend how the region, while populated by white Americans, could be so backward in its cultural disposition. Northern volunteers considered themselves dedicated to progress and industry, virtuous notions that guided individual interests in support of the common good. Yet the white South seemed to undermine such established ideals. "I suppose the difference," Charles Hill of the 5th Massachusetts surmised from the Atlantic coast, "is owing to the difference in climate. The natives here all seem to lack in energy." Fellow Bay State volunteer David Day went further to explain the sectional disparities. "Perhaps they are not wholly to blame for [their condition]," he pondered. "The same principle that will oppress a black man, will a white one. They are entirely cut off from the means of acquiring land or an education." Day condemned the slaveholding aristocracy not only for confiscating the best lands on which to create wealth and prosperity but also for monopolizing all forms of intellectual development. The majority of white Southerners, he concluded, were "in rather a bad fix; poor, shiftless and ignorant. . . . They do not seem to have any intelligent idea about anything."[29]

Occupying the South exposed Union soldiers to a static region that seemed lost in time, devoid of vitality to chart an alternate course. Day's comments implied that the South appeared like much of the European world: rural and hierarchical, governed by an elite landed gentry that ruled over an unfree labor system, and inhabited by a broad class of people unable and unwilling to rise above their place in society. Wisconsinite Clement Abner Boughton applauded, however, the abundant resources of Hunstville, Alabama, especially the copious, active water supply that could be used for industrial transformation: "water power or sites for factorys are to be seen on every stream whare all the cotton of the south might be manufactured. But," he concluded, "slavery has prevented" any kind of innovation. "As long as [the] men of the south could get their living by negro labor they would not set their heads to work to make any improvements so that the same labor would be dispenced with as Yankees of the north did."[30]

Slavery imposed devastating limitations to the use of an otherwise rich and bountiful landscape. Iowan William Legg Henderson commended central Alabama's "diversity of timber. . . . And yet with all those natural advantages the Southern Country is a Century behind the North in Architecture, Mechanics & Civilization." Charles H. Smith of the 8th Maine Volunteers expanded on these beliefs, linking the free-labor ideal to the opportunities that existed, but that had been wasted, in Southern agriculture. He expected that "if the war was over and this place was inhabited by northern people I would like to live" in Beaufort, South Carolina. Wagering that "one northern man with his horse and plow would do as much as 50 negroes in a day," Smith scoffed at the notion that white men could not labor effectively and independently in the South. "I would not risk myself to do as much as any negro that I ever see work." But as currently constituted, the South is "at least 100 years behind the north in improvements and all this difference is caused by slavery."[31]

Commentary about the power of slaveholding framed a broader critique that Union soldiers leveled against the white South. The aforementioned soldiers considered that dependence on slavery had stripped the region of any economic diversification, any chance at moral and material improvement, and any use of the land other than large-scale plantation agriculture.

Acquiring thousands of acres and managing armies of slaves afforded opulent lifestyles for the precious few planters fortunate enough to exploit land and people to their personal advantage. Poor and middling whites were left with the agricultural scarps, evolving into mediocre, lazy civilians devoid of economic opportunity. Themselves drawn from a sizeable cross-section of rural and agricultural life, Northern volunteers thus bristled at the catastrophic effects wrought by slaveholding. As he traversed Virginia, a soldier in the 14th Vermont protested how slavery had "impoverished the land, and reduced the people to the lowest state of misery and degradation, and has at last culminated in this wicked rebellion." Flabbergasted at the blatant misuse of land and resources, Union soldiers filled pages of diaries, letters, and even post-war regimental histories to voice their marked opposition to a society that so clearly undermined the Union's free-labor ideal of individual initiative and personal improvement.[32]

Charles Harvey Brewster, who volunteered in the 10th Massachusetts and served in Virginia, believed that slaveholding had abused a region that otherwise could have flourished among the leading societies of the world. The South instead seemed to retrograde, governed by the calculating decision made long ago to order white independence on black slavery. "This country is a constant wonder to all Yankees," Brewster remarked. "To think that we are in the oldest part of the United States and yet the country is almost all forest." Based on the romantic, imagined lives that proslavery defenders had long projected, Brewster likely expected the South to be a thriving, bustling center of activity and energy. "There is no reason why this should not be as thickly settled and thriving as any county on the face of globe," he wrote, undoubtedly surprised. "The soil is good the climate too, and everything grows here that we could wish, and it would be a magnificent region, but for the curse of slavery which has blighted it." Brewster wrote from the Virginia Peninsula, a place that at once embodied America's glorious, revolutionary past and now stood to threaten its promising, exceptional future.[33]

If slavery had abused the land and barred the South's entrance into modernity, it also had created a culture of dependence not only among its victims but also among its administrators. Rufus Kinsley, who soldiered in the 8th Vermont, served in Louisiana, and loathed slaveholders, looked with awe at the rich cotton districts of the lower Mississippi River valley. "This country is rich beyond comprehension," he wrote, holding the region's natural resources

Andrew F. Lang

in high regard. Like Brewster, Kinsley noted that white Southerners had crafted their entire worldview and existence on an arrogant faith in slavery's everlasting life. And now "an air of gloom at present overshadows everything. Desolation reigns supreme. Hunger stands guard at every door." Kinsley harbored little sympathy for white Southerners whose power, opulence, and prestige had collapsed in their martial effort to defend slavery through war. Yet his commentary suggested an ambivalent aura, one that accused hypocritical slaveholders of being unable to live independently from their bondsmen's forced toil. "Starving women, who have rolled in wealth, creep forth from their princely palaces, earned for them by the victims of tyranny, to receive at the hands of charity the Government pittance" made possible only by Union armies. An arbitrary liberty, contingent solely on slaveholding, had now fallen to a pitiful dependence on public largesse.[34]

Recognizing how the terrible swift sword had cut down so fiercely the South's entire basis for existence, Kinsley underscored military occupation's unique influence in reshaping societies. The Union army's presence shattered slavery, rendering the South destitute and chaotic. Freedom had been expanded, but precisely what kind of liberty existed in a postemancipation society in which the formerly enslaved were allegedly unprepared for independence and former slaveholders had been deprived of their capricious lifestyles? Frankly, Kinsley did not care. "Sad, and desolate, and fearful as it is, this is a picture on which I love to look." Much like his president, this soldier viewed the Civil War and its immense destruction as a sacrosanct cleansing, or as he called it, a "harvest." The war "is the legitimate fruit of the seed we have sown." All realms of life were directed by "a law of compensation, so accurately adjusted by Infinite wisdom, that no action or purpose can fail to receive its reward." Union armies that waged this presumably holy war spread the "seed[s] as shall bear to us National honor and permanent peace."[35]

Kinsley undoubtedly celebrated the military power behind destabilizing the South, rendering it impotent, and fracturing future rebellions against the Union. At its most basic level, military occupation sought to transition a conquered region from its prewar condition into a new postbellum order. Unlike Kinsley, many other Northern soldiers witnessed what they considered the startling speed at which societal transformation had taken place, asking whether any nation so conceived in personal liberty—and dedicated to the proposition of white equality—could seamlessly incorporate people allegedly

198

unbefitting of those exceptional national qualities. Kinsley might well have answered that a sustained military occupation would have been necessary to ensure that this transition, occasioned by war, occurred indefinitely.

In March 1861, one month prior to the bombardment on Fort Sumter, Gen. in Chief Winfield Scott had presaged Kinsley's intuition, offering an assessment with which the future soldier would not have been pleased but with which most Americans would have agreed. Scott warned against a protracted war of occupation, fearing that Union forces might become mired indefinitely in the Confederacy. The general believed in the possibility of conquering the rebellious South, yet he argued that such a task would take several years and could be accomplished only by an army numbering 300,000 men. Such an invasion would result in an "enormous waste of human life to the North" and create "fifteen devastated Provinces! not to be brought into harmony with their conquerors; but to be held for generations by heavy garrisons," sustained with the exorbitant cost of indefinite maintenance and regulation.[36]

And herein lay the root of soldiers' concerns as they witnessed the rise of emancipation and the fall of the slaveholding elite to the Union's armed legions. The United States was exceptional because it presumably *was not* an invading and occupying nation, one that transformed societies at the point of the bayonet. And yet preservation of the Union and its democratic promise *mandated* that fundamental change had to take place under the duress of military actors able to alter Southern ways of life, permanently changing existing social and cultural relations. But would loyal citizens be willing to use the army indefinitely, as Scott wondered, to shape the aftermath of emancipation and reform the South's decrepit conditions, both of which witnessing Northern soldiers feared could undermine their conception of American exceptionalism? With force and tenacity Americans answered this question during Reconstruction, a moment that not only ensured the nation's lasting peace but also allowed former Confederates to fill critical voids once held by the Union's armies of occupation.[37]

NOTES

1. Portions of this essay were previously published in Andrew F. Lang, *In the Wake of War: Military Occupation, Emancipation, and Civil War America* (Baton Rouge: Louisiana State University Press, 2017). The definition of "American exceptionalism" is adopted from Michael Kammen,

"The Problem of American Exceptionalism: A Reconsideration," *American Quarterly* 45 (Mar. 1993): 6. For examples of Cold War–era historiography that framed an exceptional American past, see Daniel J. Boorstin, *The Genius of American Politics* (Chicago: University of Chicago Press, 1953); David M. Potter, *People of Plenty: Economic Abundance and the American Character* (Chicago: University of Chicago Press, 1954); and Louis Hartz, *The Liberal Tradition in America* (New York: Harcourt, Brace, 1955). For historiographic critiques of American exceptionalism, see Ian Tyrrell, "American Exceptionalism in an Age of International History," *American Historical Review* 96 (Oct. 1991): 1031–55; and Godfrey Hodgson, *The Myth of American Exceptionalism* (New Haven, CT: Yale University Press, 2009). For transnational approaches to American history, see Thomas Bender, ed., *Rethinking American History in a Global Age* (Berkeley: University of California Press, 2002); Bender, *A Nation among Nations: America's Place in World History* (New York: Hill and Wang, 2006); and Ian R. Tyrrell, *Transnational Nation: United States History in Global Perspective since 1789* (Basingstoke, UK: Palgrave Macmillan, 2007).

2. Kammen, "Problem of American Exceptionalism," 6 (quotation), 1–43; Earl J. Hess, *Liberty, Virtue, and Progress: Northerners and Their War for the Union* (New York: New York University Press, 1988), 1–80; Gary W. Gallagher, *The Union War* (Cambridge, MA: Harvard University Press, 2011), 1–6, 36–37, 40–49, 50–54, 60–69, 70–78, 116–19, 132, 139, 156–59, 160–62.

3. For recent studies of military occupation during the Civil War, see Stephen V. Ash, *When the Yankees Came: Conflict and Chaos in the Occupied South, 1861–1865* (Chapel Hill: University of North Carolina Press, 1995); Mark Grimsley, *The Hard Hand of War: Union Military Policy toward Southern Civilians, 1861–1865* (New York: Cambridge University Press, 1995); Judkin Browning, *Shifting Loyalties: The Union Occupation of Eastern North Carolina* (Chapel Hill: University of North Carolina Press, 2011); Joseph W. Danielson, *War's Desolating Scourge: The Union's Occupation of North Alabama* (Lawrence: University Press of Kansas, 2012); Timothy B. Smith, *Corinth, 1862: Siege, Battle, and Occupation* (Lawrence: University Press of Kansas, 2012); Michael D. Pierson, *Mutiny at Fort Jackson: The Untold Story of the Fall of New Orleans* (Chapel Hill: University of North Carolina Press, 2008); Judkin Browning, "'I Am Not So Patriotic as I Was Once': The Effects of Military Occupation on the Occupying Soldiers during the Civil War," *Civil War History* 55 (June 2009): 217–43; Earl J. Hess, *The Civil War in the West: Victory and Defeat from the Appalachians to the Mississippi* (Chapel Hill: University of North Carolina Press, 2012); William A. Blair, *With Malice toward Some: Treason and Loyalty in the Civil War Era* (Chapel Hill: University of North Carolina Press, 2014); and Andrew F. Lang, "Republicanism, Race, and Reconstruction: The Ethos of Military Occupation in Civil War America," *Journal of the Civil War Era* 4 (Dec. 2014): 559–89.

4. On the scholarly debate about when, how, and why Union soldiers came to support emancipation, see Chandra Manning, *What This Cruel War Was Over: Soldiers, Slavery, and the Civil War* (New York: Alfred A. Knopf, 2007), 86–90, 118–19, 121, 150–55, 191–92, 218–19; Gallagher, *Union War*, 40–41, 78–82, 101–10, 112–14, 142–45; Hess, *Liberty, Virtue, and Progress*, 96–102; Reid Mitchell, *Civil War Soldiers* (New York: Viking, 1988), 117–25; Randall C. Jimerson, *The Private Civil War: Popular Thought during the Sectional Conflict* (Baton Rouge: Louisiana State University Press, 1988), 34–49; James M. McPherson, *For Cause and Comrades: Why Men Fought in the Civil War* (New York: Oxford University Press, 1997), 118–30; Grimsley, *Hard Hand of War*,

120–41; Steven J. Ramold, *Across the Divide: Union Soldiers View the Northern Home Front* (New York: New York University Press, 2013), 55–86; Browning, "'I Am Not So Patriotic as I Was Once,'" 225–26; Danielson, *War's Desolating Scourge,* 93–99; and Peter C. Luebke, "'Equal to Any Minstrel Concert I Ever Attended at Home': Union Soldiers and Blackface Performance in the Civil War South," *Journal of the Civil War Era* 4 (Dec. 2014): 509–32. For the best treatments of the Union army's role in "military emancipation," see James Oakes, *Freedom National: The Destruction of Slavery in the United States, 1861–1865* (New York: W. W. Norton, 2013), 143–44, 207–10, 213–14, 327–28, 345–92, 414–15, 419–22, 427–28, 438, 443, 475, 547; and Gallagher, *Union War,* 141–50. The most comprehensive analysis of Union soldiers' interactions with Southerners is Grimsley, *Hard Hand of War.*

5. For endorsements interpreting Civil War history from the vantage point of military institutions and concepts, see Gary W. Gallagher and Kathryn Shively Meier, "Coming to Terms with Civil War Military History," *Journal of the Civil War Era* 4 (Dec. 2014): 487–508, esp. 490–91; and Earl J. Hess, "Where Do We Stand? A Critical Assessment of Civil War Studies in the Sesquicentennial Era," *Civil War History* 60 (Dec. 2014): 371–403.

6. See note 4.

7. William Augustus Willoughby to My Dear Wife, Jan. 22, 1863, in *Yankee Correspondence: Civil War Letters between New England Soldiers and the Home Front,* ed. Nina Silber and Mary Beth Sievens (Charlottesville: University Press of Virginia, 1996), 98; Zenas T. Haines letter, May 23, 1863, in *In the Country of the Enemy: The Civil War Reports of a Massachusetts Corporal,* ed. William C. Harris (Gainesville: University Press of Florida, 1999), 174; William H. Root Diary, May 19, 1863, in L. Carroll Root, ed., "The Experiences of a Federal Soldier in Louisiana in 1863," *Louisiana Historical Quarterly* 19 (July 1936): 654; Charles Hill to My Dear Martha, Nov. 5, 1862, Charles Hill Letters, DL0283, John L. Nau III Civil War Collection, Houston, TX (hereafter cited as JLNC); George W. Whitman to Mother, Mar. 16, 1862, in *Civil War Letters of George Washington Whitman,* ed. Jerome M. Loving (Durham, N.C.: Duke University Press, 1975), 48; Gallagher, *Union War,* 101–10, 141–50; Ash, *When the Yankees Came,* 149–53.

8. James Henry Smith to Dear Father and Mother, Mar. 12, 1862, Smith Letters, William Gladstone Collection, U.S. Army Military Heritage Institute, Carlisle, PA (hereafter cited as USAMHI); Amos S. Collins to My Dear Annie, Dec. 11, 1862, DL0534, Collins Letters, JLNC.

9. On Union soldiers' desires to punish slaveholders, see Gallagher, *Union War,* 67–69; and Ramold, *Across the Divide,* 72–73.

10. Mitchell, *Civil War Soldiers,* 117 (1st quotation); Andrew H. Minnick to Dear Father & Mother, Dec. 11, 1862, Federal Soldiers' Letters, 1861–65, Collection, Unit 3, no. 03185, Southern Historical Collection, Louis Round Wilson Special Collections Library, University of North Carolina at Chapel Hill; William H. Nichols, to Dear Friends, May 22, 1864, William H. Nichols Letters and Diaries, Civil War Miscellaneous Collection, USAMHI; Ash, *When the Yankees Came,* 31–33, 94, 101, 153–56.

11. Joseph Emery Fiske letter, Jan. 1863, in Joseph Emery Fiske, *War Letters of Capt. Joseph E. Fiske* (Wellesley, MA: Maugus, n.d.), 22; William Thompson Lusk to Elizabeth Freeman Adams Lusk, Nov. 13, 1861, *War Letters of William Thompson Lusk* (New York: privately published, 1911), 101; Chauncey Herbert Cooke to his parents, Aug. 3, 1863, in Chauncey Herbert Cooke, *Soldier*

Boy's Letters to his Father and Mother, 1861–5 (Independence, WI: News-Office, 1915), 55; Thomas Wentworth Higginson, *Army Life in a Black Regiment* (1870; repr., New York: Penguin, 1997), 13–14; Mitchell, *Civil War Soldiers*, 121.

12. Hess, *Liberty, Virtue, and Progress*, 4–20, 24–26; James M. McPherson, "Antebellum Southern Exceptionalism: A New Look at an Old Question," *Civil War History* 50 (Dec. 2004): 418–33.

13. Lawrence van Alstyne, *Diary of an Enlisted Man* (New Haven, CT: Tuttle, Morehouse, and Taylor, 1910), 197 (Oct. 19, 1863); Frank Peck to My Dear David, Dec. 4, 1862, Peck Correspondence, Montgomery Family Papers, Library of Congress, Washington, D.C. (hereafter cited as LC); Edward Lewis Sturtevant to Dear Mary, Mar. 21, 1863, Sturtevant Letters, Historic New Orleans Collection, Williams Research Center, New Orleans (hereafter cited as HNOC).

14. For interpretations on Union soldiers' conflicting thoughts on the aftermath of emancipation, see Ramold, *Across the Divide*, 55–56, 66–75; Mitchell, *Civil War Soldiers*, 129–31; and Browning, "'I Am Not So Patriotic as I Was Once,'" 223–27.

15. Adolphus P. Wolf to Dear Parents, May 20, 1863, Wolf Letters, Civil War Times Illustrated Collection, USAMHI; Charles Francis Adams Jr. to Henry Brooks Adams, Apr. 6, 1862, in *A Cycle of Adams Letters, 1861–1865*, ed. Worthington Chauncey Ford, 2 vols. (Boston: Houghton Mifflin, 1920), 1:130; Paul Quigley, *Shifting Grounds: Nationalism and the American South, 1848–1865* (New York: Oxford University Press, 2012), 30–33; Thomas R. Hietala, *Manifest Design: American Exceptionalism and Empire* (Ithaca, NY: Cornell University Press, 2003), 170–72.

16. Charles Francis Adams Jr. to Henry Brooks Adams, Apr. 6, 1862, in Ford, *Cycle of Adams Letters*, 1:130–33.

17. Ibid., 1:132–33.

18. Charles Enslow Calvin to wife, Nov. 15, 1863, Charles Enslow Calvin Letterbook, 1862–63, LC.

19. Ibid.; Charles Enslow Calvin to My Dear Wife, June 6, 1864, ibid. (last quotation); Mitchell, *Civil War Soldiers*, 129–30.

20. Edward Lewis Sturtevant to Dear Mary, May 4, 1863, Sturtevant Letters, HNOC. See also David D. Roe, ed., *A Civil War Soldier's Diary: Valentine C. Randolph, 39th Illinois Regiment* (DeKalb: Northern Illinois University Press, 2006), 141 (Feb. 10, 1863); and Charles O. Musser to Dear Father, Sept. 12, 1864, in *Soldier Boy: The Civil War Letters of Charles O. Musser*, ed. Barry Popchock (Iowa City: University of Iowa Press, 1995), 150.

21. Peter Yawyer to Dear Brother, Jan. 1, 1863, Peter H. Yawyer Letter, Louisiana and Lower Mississippi Valley Collections, Hill Memorial Library, Louisiana State University, Baton Rouge (hereafter cited as LSU); van Alstyne, *Diary of an Enlisted Man*, 197 (Oct. 19, 1863); Henry Anderson to unknown, May 21, 1863, Anderson (Henry) Letter, LSU.

22. Hietala, *Manifest Design*, 132–72.

23. For Union soldiers' perceptions of poor and elite white Southerners, see Mitchell, *Civil War Soldiers*, 107–17; and Browning, "'I Am Not So Patriotic as I Was Once,'" 221–23, 227–33.

24. Charles Carleton Coffin, *The Boys of '61; or, Four Years of Fighting* (Boston: Estes and Lauriat, 1885), 432–33. See also John W. De Forest, *A Union Officer in the Reconstruction*, ed. James H. Croushore and David M. Potter (New Haven, CT: Yale University Press, 1948), 52–54, 152–54;

and Stephen V. Ash, "Poor Whites in the Occupied South, 1861–1865," *Journal of Southern History* 57 (Feb. 1991): 39–62, esp. 46–49.

25. Ira Russell to Dear Wife, Jan. 9, 1863, Ira Russell Letters, David W. Mullins Special Collections Library, University of Arkansas, Fayetteville; Richard Kirtland Woodruff letter, Oct. 19, 1863, DL0172.018, JLNC; Rankin M. McPheeters to Annie McPheeters, Jan. 11, 1864, McPheeters Family Collection, USAMHI.

26. J. Henry Blakeman to [Wife], Aug. 27, 1864, J. Henry Blakeman Letters, Lewis Leigh Collection, USAMHI; Charles F. Sherman to Dear Cousin, Dec. 8, 1862, Charles F. Sherman Civil War Letters Collection, HNOC; John Warner Sturtevant to Dear Friends at Home, Apr. 11, 1864, DL0948.3, Sturtevant Letters, JLNC.

27. David L. Day, *My Diary of Rambles with the 25th Massachusetts Volunteer Infantry: With Burnside's Coast Division; 18th Army Corps, and Army of the James* (Milford, MA: King and Billings, 1884), 54 (Apr. 20, 1862); George O. Jewett to Dear Deck, June 1, 1862, Jewett Collection, LC; Browning, "'I Am Not So Patriotic as I Was Once,'" 227–33; William L. Shea, *Fields of Blood: The Prairie Grove Campaign* (Chapel Hill: University of North Carolina Press, 2009), 92–108.

28. Sam to Danice, Feb. 28, 1863, Sam (Union Soldier) Letter, LSU; Hess, *Liberty, Virtue, and Progress,* 78–79; Mitchell, *Civil War Soldiers,* 90–91, 94–101.

29. Charles Hill to My Very Dear Martha, Jan. 6, 1863, DL0442, Hill Letters, JLNC; Day, *My Diary of Rambles,* 54 (Apr. 20, 1862); Ash, *When the Yankees Came,* 24–25, 34–35.

30. Clement Abner Boughton to C[larence] E. Boughton, May 24, 1862, Clement Abner Boughton Papers, James S. Schoff Civil War Collection, William L. Clements Library, University of Michigan, Ann Arbor; McPherson, "Antebellum Southern Exceptionalism," 418–33, esp. 430–33; C. Stuart McGehee, "Military Origins of the New South: The Army of the Cumberland and Chattanooga's Freedmen," *Civil War History* 34 (Dec. 1988): 323–43.

31. "Henderson Journal 06, November 8, 1864–May 14, 1865," Apr. 23, 1865, William Legg Henderson Civil War Diaries, Civil War Diaries and Letters Digital Collection, University of Iowa Libraries, Special Collections Department, Iowa Digital Library, http://digital.lib.uiowa.edu/cdm/compoundobject/collection/cwd/id/26810/rec/2; Charles H. Smith to Dear Wife, Feb. 28, 1863, Smith Letters, Civil War Miscellaneous Collection, USAMHI. The classic study on free labor is Eric Foner, *Free Soil, Free Labor, Free Men: The Ideology of the Republican Party before the Civil War* (New York: Oxford University Pres, 1970). For an important critique of free labor, see Jonathan A. Glickstein, *American Exceptionalism, American Anxiety: Wages, Competition, and Degraded Labor in the Antebellum United States* (Charlottesville: University of Virginia Press, 2002).

32. Adam Wesley Dean, *An Agrarian Republic: Farming, Antislavery Politics, and Nature Parks in the Civil War Era* (Chapel Hill: University of North Carolina Press, 2015), 101–7 (quotation, 103); Gallagher, *Union War,* 66–70; Ash, "Poor Whites in the Occupied South," 47. For a recent study that places Northern opposition to Southern plantations in an international context, see James L. Huston, *The British Gentry, the Southern Planter, and the Northern Family Farmer: Agriculture and Sectional Antagonism in North America* (Baton Rouge: Louisiana State University Press, 2015). See also Andre M. Fleche, *The Revolution of 1861: The American Civil War in the Age of Nationalist Conflict* (Chapel Hill: University of North Carolina Press, 2012), 60–79, 107–31.

33. Charlie Brewster to Dear Mother, Apr. 23, 1862, in *When This Cruel War Is Over: The Civil*

War Letters of Charles Harvey Brewster, ed. David W. Blight (Amherst: University of Massachusetts Press, 1992), 120; Mitchell, *Civil War Soldiers*, 97–101.

34. David C. Rankin, ed., *Diary of a Christian Soldier: Rufus Kinsley and the Civil War* (Cambridge: Cambridge University Press, 2004), 105–6 (Aug. 31, 1862).

35. Ibid., 106. For Union soldiers who saw the necessity of cleansing the South via military power, see Ash, *When the Yankees Came*, 171–73; and Ash, "Poor Whites in the Occupied South," 47.

36. Winfield Scott to William H. Seward, Mar. 3, 1861, in Scott, *Memoirs of Lieut.-General Scott, LL.D.*, 2 vols. (New York: Shelden, 1864), 2:627.

37. On the culture of antimilitarism, see Gallagher, *Union War*, 124; and Mark Wahlgren Summers, *The Ordeal of the Reunion: A New History of Reconstruction* (Chapel Hill: University of North Carolina Press, 2014), 4, 5, 13. On the problem of military occupation during Reconstruction, see Gregory P. Downs, *After Appomattox: Military Occupation and the Ends of War* (Cambridge, MA: Harvard University Press, 2014); Lang, "Republicanism, Race, and Reconstruction." 559–89; and Andrew F. Lang, *In the Wake of War: Military Occupation, Emancipation, and Civil War America* (Baton Rouge: Louisiana State University Press, 2017), chs. 8–9. In *Manifest Design*, Thomas Hietala offers a strong case for the inherent militarism of antebellum American territorial expansion.

"THEY MET THEIR FATE WITHOUT A SIGH"

An Analysis of Confederate Military Executions

Kevin M. Levin

N HIS 1912 MEMOIR *War Stories*, Berrien M. Zettler devotes a section to describing in detail the executions on December 9, 1861, of two men who served in the Louisiana "Tiger Rifles." The two soldiers had "overpowered" an officer and threatened to kill him, "and for this they had been court-martialed and condemned to be shot." According to Zettler, the executions attracted around fifteen thousand men; so many crowded into the site that "the sentinel threatened repeatedly to put his bayonet into those of us in front if we did not stand back." The prisoners finally came into sight on a wagon, which also contained their coffins. Zettler and the rest of the crowd formed three sides of a hollow square. The open side of the square contained two posts, each measuring about two feet above the ground, placed approximately thirty feet apart. The prisoner's hands were tied behind them before being attached to the posts. Finally, each was blindfolded. A detail of twelve men then marched in front of the prisoners. Zettler remembered "that only six of the guns in each platoon had balls in them, the others being loaded with blank cartridges." The officer in charge raised his hand, signaling the detail to lower their weapons "to the position of aim." "The orders were given silently by these movements, so that the prisoners would not know the exact moment when they would be killed." Even after sixty years, the elderly veteran recalled the event as a "very sad sight and one that deeply impressed me."[1]

Zettler refrained from sharing more than a cursory description of what transpired during the execution, but it is likely that what "impressed" him helped draw a clear distinction between his life as a civilian and his new role as a soldier. Even during the rush to enlist in the spring of 1861, and roughly a year before the first conscription act was passed, attention to imposing on new recruits a military ethos built around strict discipline and obedience to authority was paramount. The vast majority of young men, like Zettler, who enlisted may have been confident of victory and determined to prove their manhood on the battlefield, but the military first needed to detach these citizens turned soldiers from old patterns of life and instill or foster an identity that promoted esprit de corps and support for the new Confederate nation. White Southerners, like their Northern counterparts, understood that the civic privileges enjoyed in a democracy, from the Revolution through the antebellum period, entailed having to take up arms on occasion and defend their communities and country against external and domestic threats. Those young men who answered the call of the new Confederacy, however, remained steadfastly protective of their individual rights and weary of authority. "After all," writes Joseph Glatthaar, "to adhere to a code of discipline meant that others imposed their will on an individual, . . . and no self-respecting white Southerner could endure that."[2]

Confederate soldiers were subject to a wide range of punishments, many of which were outlined in the Articles of War enacted by Congress in 1806 and utilized by both sides during the Civil War. Article 45, for example, mandated that a soldier found drunk on duty "shall suffer such corporeal punishment as shall be inflicted by the sentence of a court-martial." The majority of cases for such violations were dealt with at the company or regimental level; officers carried out punishments as dictated by local circumstances, a commander's whim, or the decision of a court-martial. General courts-martial at the brigade level or higher typically dealt with the more serious offenses.[3]

Soldiers who committed the most serious crimes, such as insubordination or desertion, risked facing a firing squad. Roughly five hundred men from both the Union and Confederate armies were executed during the war, the majority for desertion, which represented the clearest demonstration of the military's coercive power over the rank and file.[4] While most forms of punishment, such as bucking and gagging and branding, were carried out within the company or regiment to reinforce more localized authority, military executions were carried out on a much larger stage that often included thousands of onlookers. While these events ended lives that were considered beyond redemption and a threat to the integrity of the army, they also offered attendees the opportunity to reflect on their own sense of duty and place within the army and the nation at war. And reflect they did.

Confederate soldiers reacted to the execution of fellow soldiers in their letters, diaries, and memoirs. For many of these men, witnessing an execution left as indelible an impression as did the sight of comrades torn to pieces on the battlefield. The spectrum of experiences shared tells us much about how soldiers came to terms with a war that was at its core an emotionally wrenching experience. More importantly, it sheds light on the challenges the military faced in turning citizens, who guarded their rights and remained wary of authority, into soldiers. The evidence suggests that, although the sight of the execution of their comrades saddened soldiers, they supported the practice as necessary for the maintenance of the army and ultimately as a means to achieve Confederate independence. Accounts of executions on the home front in newspapers reinforced the perception that such drastic measures were necessary and justified. Editorials tended to support this aspect of military justice as did at least one theater company in Atlanta, Georgia, which included in its wartime production a theme involving a soldier's execution. The playwright, known only as the "Lady of Atlanta," tells the story of a family whose father is justifiably shot after deserting the army out of concern for their welfare.[5]

Berrien Zettler's ability to describe a military execution decades afterward attests to how carefully these events were choreographed to make the greatest impression on those in attendance. Regiments were often organized into three sides of a rectangle in double ranks facing each other, creating a corridor through which the condemned soldier proceeded. The third side of the rectangle remained open, where a grave was dug for its future occupant. The procession began at the mouth of the double ranks, led by the provost marshal, the chief law-enforcement officer of the regiment and commander of the proceedings. Often a regimental band followed him, playing appropriately mournful music. Then came the prisoner, sometimes on foot and sometimes in a horse-drawn ambulance, sitting on his casket. Accompanied by a minister and two guards holding his arms, the condemned was followed by the approximately twelve members of the firing squad.[6] After making his way through the corridor created by the members of his unit, the prisoner sat on his casket beside the waiting grave. After a prayer by the chaplain, the man's eyes were covered, his hands tied behind his back, the order of execution announced, and finally the firing squad carried out the sentence.[7]

Confederates who witnessed the executions of the two Louisiana Tigers from Maj. C. Roberdeau Wheat's battalion in northern Virginia noted both the landscape on which this solemn event took place as well as the large number of onlookers. First Lt. William R. Elam of the 18th Virginia recalled the size of the crowd a few days afterward: "I was one of about fifteen thousand in number to witness a few days ago, the solemn sight of two 'Soldier[s]' being *shot*." Once situated at the site of the execution, Elam noticed the "trees of the adjoining woods were crowded as if by wild Pigeons." A soldier serving in the 19th Virginia recalled watching soldiers "moving on over the hills from sun up to 12 o'clock (the hour of execution)." "Every hill," he recalled, "presented the appearance of a swarm of bees." Close to two decades following the war, Brig. Gen. B. T. Johnson remembered that around the perimeter of the square "had gathered thousands from the neighboring camps."[8]

Holding an execution in an open space helped begin breaking down the barriers between individual soldiers, the regiments in which they served, and the rest of the army. Organizing the men into formations that resembled their linear tactical formations reinforced the sense that the execution of a comrade was a shared experience. With only one major battle fought in Virginia by this point, there were likely few opportunities to impress upon individual soldiers their place within the army as a whole. Most importantly, a clear message was delivered to a large number of men simultaneously that acts of insubordination would be dealt with swiftly and harshly.

The approach of the condemned and his entourage also captured the attention and curiosity of onlookers. Stationed at Fort Sumter in the summer of 1863, William Grimball devoted most of a letter to his sister on the preparation and carrying out of an execution for a soldier accused of attempting to desert to the Union naval force stationed offshore:

> The prisoner was brought in a procession, consisting of 1st the provost Marshall, Col. Peter Gailland, then the band playing a dead March, next the prisoner and Bishop Lynch, then the coffin, borne by four men, then the file of men to shoot him, one half with their muskets loaded with ball, the other half with blank cartridges so that no one might know who shot him[.] When the procession arrived at the Square, we commenced on the right and marched along the sides round the Square to the left. The band of the procession playing the

dead march until it reached the left of the 1st regiment when it stopped and the band of that regiment took up the dirge and so it continued of each regiment playing and the prisoner arrived in front of them.[9]

Witnesses paid close attention to the final stages of preparation, aware that the death of a comrade was imminent. The final moments of the condemned were spent fastened to a post, close to his coffin, and usually in counsel with a priest. Grimball recalled that once the procession at Fort Sumter halted, "the prisoner was carried to the post and some minutes were spent in religious exercise" before a "cartridge bag was drawn over his head." William Pence of the 33rd Virginia approached his death "leaning on the arms of two chaplains." Also in attendance that day was Mager Steele of the 48th Virginia: "When we got to the place the men that were carrying the coffin put it down by the side of the stake and the condemned man sat upon it leaning against the stake."[10] The amount of detail provided by onlookers, who stood with shoulder touching shoulder, in their written accounts points to an unfolding drama that increased in intensity as the procession approached its final destination.

Soldiers such as Steele and Grimball framed their accounts from the perspective of an observer, but a closer look reveals that they were as much a part of this event as the condemned , duty officer, priest, and firing squad. Few spectators appreciated their central role or the extent to which this particular event was held for their benefit. Everyone involved, including the condemned, played a specific role and helped give meaning to the rare ritual.

Those who violated military rules typically faced a punishment and level of humiliation that remained contained within the company or regiment. Junior-grade officers from captain to colonel worked to strike a balance between maintaining discipline and respect for superiors and recognizing individual rights among a rank and file that, according to historian Andrew S. Bledsoe, often viewed their officers' elections as "messy affairs, riddled with intrigue and destructive to morale."[11] In addition, these same men remained protective of their personal rights and resisted being treated in a way that threatened the crucial distinction between free men and slaves. Other than cases that warranted a dishonorable discharge, soldiers were thought to be capable of redemption when determining punishment. The death penalty differed in a crucial respect. In contrast with sentences carried out on the company or regimental level in which there was a clear connection between the officers imposing punishment and the offender from their unit's ranks, an execution highlighted the coercive power of the military high command and the army generally. Condemned soldiers were deemed to be beyond rehabilitation and a threat to the cohesiveness and fighting effectiveness of the army. The absolute power of the military was on full display in these instances. Enlisted soldiers could and would be executed as a means to compel obedience from those remaining.

Witnesses took a heightened interest in the conduct of the condemned during their final moments. This allowed the offender one last opportunity to balance out recent transgressions with forbearance and the hope of eternal peace. One Confederate "jerked open his shirt and bared his breast to the bullets," recalled Arthur Ford as the final commands were issued during an execution. "They met their fate without a sigh, without a murmur," asserted another onlooker. "They neither feared God, Man nor the Devil." Writing at the turn of the century about three men executed in Charleston, Col. William Lamb recalled, "They all died fearlessly." Such descriptions tell us as much about the author as it does about the condemned. Unlike the battlefield, which often presented a confusing if not chaotic arena and in which men functioned on adrenalin, witnessing an execution allowed soldiers to reflect, in the presence of comrades from throughout the Confederacy, on how they might conduct themselves in the same situation.[12]

Executions were not designed merely to carry out punishments. These carefully choreographed events provided an opportunity for onlookers to think about the kind of death they wanted for themselves; in short, soldiers were forced to consider the real possibility that their lives might end as a result of the war, and the only remaining question was whether to die well or in shame and ignominy. Though battlefield deaths could be glorified and placed in a moral context, there was no way to understand death by execution in a positive light. In such circumstances witnesses were able to see a clear and direct connection between the disobeying of military rules and its fatal consequences.

As witnesses to these final moments, onlookers played the role of the family in characterizing the condemned's moral conduct, which indicated worthiness of salvation. Indeed, as Drew G. Faust argues, these last seconds on Earth offered a "glimpse of an unvarying perpetuity." Religious tracts distributed throughout Confederate armies warned of the necessity of preparing the soul for the next world: "What you are when you die," asserted one pamphlet, "the same will reappear in the great day of eternity. The features of character with which you leave the world will be seen in you when you rise from the dead."[13] One condemned man received permission to have friends sing a hymn throughout the ceremony, a staff officer recounting that the man "prayed aloud that he might be received into that better land." Appreciating the importance of these final moments for the condemned may have made it that much more difficult for Capt. Jedediah Hotchkiss—who served as "Stonewall" Jackson's cartographer—to relate to his wife the story of a soldier executed in March 1863, noting that the man "wept bitterly, wishing to see his family." A few months later Marion Fitzpatrick took time to evaluate the moments leading to the execution of one man from the 14th Georgia and another from North Carolina. He was pleased to learn after the execution that the Georgian had "expressed a willingness to die and said he had a hope in Christ." As for the North Carolinian, "he was a sorry looking man, and from what I can learn would talk to no one after he was condemned."[14] Fitzpatrick may have felt frustration at this soldier's failure to make public any last thoughts that might bring to a close his life's narrative.

Last words provided the clearest evidence that the condemned had repented and was ready for eternity. Final thoughts could be counted on for their veracity since one assumed that the victim no longer had a reason to lie and was aware of the consequences of such mendacity beyond the material world. The desire to hear the right words was made all the more desirable in light of the sharp transition that was about to take place: "In a few seconds more the souls of these unfortunate men are launched, from healthy friends, a smiling earth, on which they might otherwise [have] spent profitable lives, to an unknown territory, & into the presence of their maker!" For Charles Quintard, who served as a chaplain for the 1st Tennessee Regiment, preparing a soldier for death and urging the condemned to repent and offer final words was of extreme importance. One "poor fellow" under Quintard's guidance urged him to "cut off a lock of his hair and preserve it for his wife." Shortly thereafter he stood up and addressed his comrades: "I am about to die. I hope I am going to a better world." He also urged everyone looking on to "take warning by my fate." Luckily, this soldier's life was spared at the very last moment. James Parrott of the 28th Tennessee was also in attendance and noted that the man was "prepared to meet his God in peace." Not every soldier took advantage of the chance to offer a final statement. One Virginian from Page County responded simply, "No, nothing," to the question of whether he had anything to say. After the order to fire was given, the dying man gasped for breath, fell back, and then cried out, "O what will my poor wife do."[15]

The last words of Capt. Jazeb R. Rhodes occupy a unique position in this survey since they come from the only Confederate officer executed by Southern forces.[16] Rhodes, who commanded Company C, 1st Georgia Infantry, was shot in 1863 for encouraging "men of his own command to desert" and enlisting substitutes who already belonged to the service "and then discharging them for a bonus." According to one observer, the captain made every attempt to remain composed in order to set an example for those present. Though Rhodes "trembled violently" on first entering the grounds, he "quickly recovered himself and entered the wagon and took his seat upon the coffin so soon to enclose his lifeless form, and during the march to the spot selected for execution appeared as calm and collected as though it were all a mockery." His last words are lost to the historical record, however, it is known that he "addressed his late comrades for fifteen minutes, telling them to beware of his untimely fate, and averring the justice of the sentence." Rhodes may have chosen his words not only in preparation for the afterlife but also to salvage what was left of his reputation as an officer within his former command. He may also have hoped that his final words might be shared with loved ones and others back home as a means to salvage what was left of his family's reputation.[17]

To varying degrees, soldiers attempted to communicate the emotions felt as the final orders were carried out. Martin Coiner of the 52nd Virginia described the moment of execution as "one of the greatest sights that I ever want to behold again." For James Pickens of the 5th Alabama Infantry, the moment after the order to fire brought about "an indescribable & mixed sensation of sickness & horror at the sight." Also from Alabama, and in the hours following an early October 1864 execution, Capt. John Hall could only "pray I may never again be called upon to see" another, while Fitzpatrick asserted, "I shall never forget the impression it made on me." In his memoir Lt. Col. William Blackford recounted one execution, "and it shocked me a great deal." He mused, "How strange that the death of men under such circumstances should produce such an effect on one who had witnessed so many deaths in battle."[18]

The physical impact of the bullets on the condemned's body also attracted the attention of onlookers. Roughly sixty years after the event, William N. Wood recalled the execution of a Confederate as the Army of Northern Virginia made its way into Maryland and Pennsylvania in June 1863. He paid particular attention to the pattern of bullets—"four of them could have been covered with a half sheet of note paper, and the other two not far off." Some soldiers did not shy away from sharing the more disturbing details with loved ones back home. Fitzpatrick explained to his wife the final movements of two condemned soldiers following the orders to fire: "He raised himself perpendicular fell forward and turned over on his back and died instantly. He was pierced through with six balls. The other was struck with only one ball. He turned to one side and was some time dying."[19] One wonders whether Mrs. Fitzpatrick appreciated or needed to read the stark detail. Back in North Carolina, William Grimball's sister learned that one condemned soldier offered "two or three convulsive twitches" after having "five balls [pass] through him." Writing at the turn of the century, a veteran of the 1st Florida Reserve Regiment was still able to vividly recall the impacts on two men executed: "The bullets cut the rope that held one of them, and he fell and rolled over on his back. The other man, I think, stood perfectly ridged for five or six seconds before he moved. Finally, continued S. M. Haskins, "his head dropped over and he hung in a lifeless heap until cut loose from the stake."[20] The shift from civilian to soldier encouraged a strong sense of togetherness, but the loss of comrades under such circumstances threatened to undercut morale and lead to depression and guilt among the men's friends and comrades. On the other hand, witnessing an execution in military formation likely helped offset such feelings with a renewed commitment to prevent others from facing a similar fate.

At least one Confederate father hoped the gruesome details of an execution might reinforce his role as disciplinarian while away from his family. This Mississippi soldier used the December 1861 execution of the two Louisiana Tigers as examples of soldiers who "would not behave themselves." He described each step of the ceremony but emphasized that after the final order was given, "these bad men that would not obey orders fell over dead." The soldier closed the letter by urging his children to "be good little boys. Do not quarrel, kiss little Anna four times apiece for me."[21]

Descriptions of executions where it took more than one round to finish off the victim were particularly grim and difficult to describe. Sam Watkins recalled a particularly disturbing example of a botched execution: "It was the sergeant's duty to give the *coup d'etat* [sic], should not the prisoner be slain. The sergeant ran up and placed the muzzle of his gun at the head of the poor, pleading, and entreating wretch, his gun was discharged, and the wretched man only powder-burned, the gun being one that had been loaded with powder only. The whole affair had to be gone over again. The soldiers had to reload and form and fire. The culprit was killed stone dead this time." Watkins was troubled by the fact that within minutes of the execution, soldiers "were throwing snow balls as hard as ever, as if nothing had happened." Serving in the 21st Virginia, John Worsham witnessed only one execution during the war, which involved three men, and it was particularly gruesome. One of the three was not killed outright, and it fell to one of the firing detail to "place another gun against the man's breast and fire; this killed him instantly." Seeing a person killed at point-blank range was enough for Worsham to conclude, "if I live a thousand years, I will never be willing to see another." In the execution witnessed by Captain Hall, "several balls to[ok] effect but a few moments later after life not being extinct entirely, he was again shot, the last trial finishing life." He concluded, "Twas a sad sight." The February 1864 execution of two men witnessed by Benjamin Freeman may have been particularly painful to write home about since one of the condemned was known by name and may have even been recognized by the letter's recipients: "Limuel Smith was not killed on the first fire then Mr. Stark[e] had to step out and kill him he hated to do it but had to do it the blood would rush from the holes where the bullets entered them."[22]

Soldiers acknowledged a qualitative difference between witnessing death on a battlefield and in an execution. The distinction is drawn clearly by a North Carolinian who suggested that witnessing an execution "is a much more shocking scene than a battle for in Battle the blood is up & men excited and as no one expects to be hit positively He feels a hope. But in these military executions the blood is cool & the doom of the victim certain & it freezes the blood to witness it."[23] For men who did what they could to avoid being shot by the enemy on the battlefield, this must have been a particularly difficult moment. Not only could they not prevent the outcome, but they also were forced to consider the experience along with members of their company, regiment, brigade, and even division.

As the war continued, soldiers who struggled with having to participate in public executions went out of their way to avoid the unpleasant sights. Sgt. Maj. William Rouzie of the 55th Virginia requested permission from the acting adjutant to be excused from having to attend a January 1863 execution, "for which I was very much obliged." Another soldier from Alabama admitted that he had "witnessed this unpleasant scene several times" and, rather than go through it again, decided to go off with a friend to "grind some axes (& Spud) in order to avoid it."[24]

Written accounts from later in the war suggest that soldiers by that time treated executions as more of a commonplace event. Brief references point to an emotional numbing or perhaps a psychological distancing on the part of witnesses. In the wake of the bloodshed at Gettysburg in July 1863, attending two executions in the span of eleven days may not have stood out for Samuel Pickens of the 5th Alabama Infantry. At the beginning of September, he noted in passing that ten deserters were shot—"some had to be shot several times." In the last few weeks leading to the opening of the 1864 Overland Campaign, Adam Kersh, who served with the 52nd Virginia, quickly referred to one man from the 58th Virginia shot for desertion and another scheduled to be executed in a few days. The latter, according to Kersh, "was trying to get a reprieve," but "it is thought he will not succeed."[25]

The level of violence and bloodshed witnessed during the Overland and Petersburg Campaigns may have minimized the power of executions even further. Sgt. George Clark of the 7th Virginia Infantry witnessed three executions between the end of July and the middle of October 1864. Diary entries for all three dates total no more than five sentences. The final entry in the series mentions simply that the brigade turned out for the execution of a man serving in the regiment. Clark noted that "the execution was conducted splendidly," then provided a weather report indicating that the day was "warm for the season of the year." Serving in the 17th Mississippi Infantry, John Watson recorded in his diary on February 5, 1864, that he "witnessed the execution of a man for desertion." He noted that the condemned individual "bore it like a man," which he followed by citing the reading of "two chapters in the Bible." Watson made no mention as to whether these two events conflicted in any way. Though William Casey, who served in a Virginia artillery unit, may not have witnessed an execution by the beginning of 1864, he surely would have been aware of the consequences for being caught and convicted of desertion. Still, this did not stop him from requesting that his brother "try to catch a deserter and send me a certificate from the enrolling officers and I can get a fifteen days furlough on it." Clearly Casey valued a few weeks home with his family, but he appeared to be unconcerned that his ticket would be paid for by a man facing a firing squad.[26]

Despite the emotional toll of having to witness the executions of their comrades, evidence suggests that Confederates supported the practice as a necessary deterrent to future desertions. While Arthur Ford acknowledged that "it seemed a sad thing that a really brave man should be sacrificed," he was quick to point out that "it is necessary to deter others from playing the role of traitor." Casting deserters as traitors allowed Ford to more easily balance his emotions with a justification that included the moral goal of Confederate independence. Captain Hotchkiss yearned for the day when "wars will cease and the necessity no longer exist for such brutal punishments." In the meantime, he understood that "in no other way can the discipline of the army be maintained." Serving as captain with the 12th Alabama Infantry, Robert E. Park balanced his feeling that the latest execution was a "sad sight" with a commitment that the man's "death was necessary as a warning and lesson to his comrades." Spencer Welch found it "unfortunate that this thing of shooting men for desertion was not begun sooner." That executions had not become standard earlier, according to Welch, meant that "many men will now have to be shot before the trouble [desertion] can be stopped." After observing an execution outside of Orange Court House, Virginia, in October 1863, a North Carolina lieutenant surmised, "It looks very barbarous to see men shot in that way but it is necessary to maintain the discipline of an army." At the turn of the century, Mercer Otey, who served in the Rockbridge Artillery, recalled that although the execution "looked so cold, so deliberate, almost murder, . . . the discipline of the army must be maintained."[27]

The use of massed tactical formations on Civil War battlefields likely strengthened the resolve of the individual soldier and his sense of responsibility to the man standing next to him amid the chaos and destruction. Witnessing the execution of comrades for desertion, however, reminded these very same men of the fragility of these very same bonds and helps explain their support for such sentences, despite the emotional pain involved.

Amid a religious revival that swept Confederate armies through the winter of 1863–64, the men of the various regiments recommitted themselves to the cause by passing a series of resolutions. Though these revivals were stronger in the two principal armies compared with the home front, they served to bind both military and civilian needs around the goal of Confederate independence. In February 1864 an estimated five hundred members of the 37th Virginia attended a meeting in which a resolution was passed supporting the use of firing squads for those "worthless" men convicted of desertion.[28]

The Rev. John Paris delivered a sermon following what was perhaps the largest mass execution of Confederate soldiers during the war. In the early hours of February 2, 1864, fifty-three North Carolinians were captured by men from the brigade of Brig. Gen. Robert F. Hoke, under the personal direction of Maj. Gen. George E. Pickett. The deserters were captured wearing Union uniforms, and most were natives either of the county in which they were taken prisoner or of bordering counties.[29] Twenty-two were publicly hanged in Kinston, North Carolina, shortly afterward. Generals Pickett and Hoke hoped the harshness of the mass executions would slow the tide of defections from Confederate forces. In addition to the executions, a sermon was read in front of the entire brigade to drive home the importance of maintaining strict discipline and devotion to the cause of Southern independence.[30]

Reverend Paris passionately defended the virtues of patriotism and alluded to the memories of Judas Iscariot and Benedict Arnold as relevant comparisons with the actions of Confederate deserters. Discontent within the army was caused by meetings composed of men "who talk more about their 'rights' than their duty and loyalty to their country" and by those who claimed that "we are whipt!"; "it is useless to fight any longer!"; and "this is the rich man's war and the poor man's fight!" He also cited other clergymen within the army and on the home front as preaching defeatist messages. Finally, newspapers and letters from home, according to Paris, pushed some soldiers over the edge, and "the young man of promise and of hope once, now becomes a deserter."[31] The spiritual glue with which chaplains offered as an incentive to soldiers to stay in the ranks competed with the emotional tugs from home. Those appeals from loved ones only grew louder as the war dragged on with no end in sight. For Reverend Paris, executions allowed the army to rid it of those who had become corrupted by others and had lost sight of the goal of independence.

Soldier support for military executions as a disciplinary necessity, however, was not unconditional. A commander's reputation could be dealt irreparable harm if his men perceived that he unjustly expended the lives of the enlisted. Gen. Braxton Bragg learned this lesson well when he ordered a soldier to be executed for discharging his weapon against strict orders during the retreat from Corinth, Mississippi, in May 1862. The accused argued that his unit had only recently joined the Army of Tennessee and was unaware of the order. Cooler heads prevailed, and the conviction was reversed, but according to historian Earl Hess, "Bragg was hounded by the accusation that he wantonly killed his own men for trivial reasons for the rest of his life."[32]

Accusations of recklessness against Bragg surfaced often during the war, especially following the execution of Asa Lewis of the 6th Kentucky Infantry in December 1862. The general refused to grant Lewis clemency even after it was learned that he had applied for a furlough to assist his family, which was desperately trying to make ends meet following the death of his father. A third execution involving two young and one middle-aged man at Shelbyville did little to repair Bragg's reputation. But despite rumors swirling in camp and on the home front, evidence suggests that the rank and file continued to support the necessity of executions as a deterrent to desertion. Even after Bragg was replaced by Gen. Joseph E. Johnston in 1864, executions occurred in the Army of Tennessee in January, February, March, and finally twelve men at once at the beginning of May.[33] As for Bragg's record, a close examination of court-martial records suggests that he overturned death sentences at a higher rate compared to other generals, and the overall number of executions was likely lower in the Army of Tennessee compared to the Army of Northern Virginia.[34]

While it is clear that some enlisted men believed that executions were necessary to deter future deserters, the way in which those executions in fact discouraged this phenomenon—if at all—is impossible to determine. Regimental officers completed muster rolls on a regular basis, but only those men not present at the times the lists were completed were cited for absences. It can be safely assumed that many others escaped through this loophole. Muster rolls are also silent on the reasons for a soldier's absence without leave. Military records on desertion are also incomplete, especially for the last two years of the war.[35] Most importantly, over the past few years, historians have uncovered a complex web of causes for desertion, taking into account the first conscription act in the spring of 1862, logistical problems in the armies, and varying local conditions on the home front.[36]

Though it is almost impossible to gauge the reaction of civilians to the army's use of capital punishment, many clearly knew of the practice since numerous newspapers included accounts of executions, some of them quite graphically. Both the *Richmond Examiner* and the *Augusta Daily Chronicle & Sentinel* from Georgia covered Captain Rhodes's execution in September 1863. Editors' primary goal for including such accounts was to deter civilians from tempting soldiers from the ranks with the threat of death if their family member was caught. "What a sad warning to the living! Will any profit by it?" The *Chronicle* answered its own question by noting simply that, "Some may; others will not." The *Examiner* took a different approach to sharing the dangers of desertion with its readers by including a more graphic account of Rhodes's execution: "*Attention!* The command startles every one. The doomed man sinks down upon his coffin and fixes his eyes upon the twelve bright tubes that are leveled at his breast, but drops his head the next moment. *Fire!*—a dash, a report—and as the white smoke is slowly lifted by the breeze a mangled, lifeless form is seen lying beside the coffin, and the long lines of soldiers shrink back from the sight."[37]

The *Richmond Daily Dispatch* offered its readers a detailed account of a mass execution that took place on September 5, 1863. The condemned were ten men from the 3rd North Carolina Infantry of Brig. Gen. George H. Steuart's brigade accused of desertion and murder. The account took readers from the placement of the stakes in the ground, the arrival of the condemned, and their final moments. Though the witnesses were veterans of the "blood and carnage of twenty battlefields, . . . they beheld with uncontrollable emotion the solemn preparation for the execution of the condemned, and seemed to be penetrated with the solemnity of the religious services which were being carried on." The final moments of the guilty were particularly poignant. As the firing party was being deployed, "the prisoners broke out into loud and frequent appeals to the Almighty to have mercy on their souls and pardon their sins." The account ends with the "corpses of ten men hung in the horrible relaxation of death to the stakes where they were pinioned." The *Lynchburg Virginian* also offered to its readers a detailed account of the March 1864 execution of Pvts. G. W. Burnside, G. Whitt, and Jacob Winnery—all served in the 36th Virginia. Perhaps out of consideration for the families of the three condemned men, the writer made it a point to note their conduct during their final moments. According to the observer, "Throughout the whole affair the three bore themselves very bravely; few men have ever met death with more calmness and resignation."[38] Highlighting their stoic resolve also suggested to readers that these men acknowledged that the execution was to some extent justified.

Accounts that provided such detail sent a clear message to a number of parties involved, including soldiers in the ranks, loved ones back home, and those enlisted men who had already deserted. Some newspapers chose to forgo lengthy accounts and instead simply provided readers with lists of those sen-

tenced to death. On May 5, 1864, the *Augusta Daily Constitutionalist* published
a list of twenty men from all over the Confederacy who were to be executed
"within the next ten days." For those already shot, the newspaper included
basic information, as in the case of Henry Jerome, who had served in the 17th
South Carolina and was found to be "twice guilty [of] deserting his colors."
The article described him as a "man of mature years, short in stature, [and of
a] quiet demeanor" who was survived by a wife and three children. In addition
to firsthand accounts of executions, most newspapers included notices from
individual units for those absent without leave; monetary rewards were often
given for a successful capture or information leading to the return of a soldier.
The *Richmond Daily Dispatch* for August 22, 1862, listed notices from the 1st
Maryland Regiment, W. Gordon McCabe's battery, the 34th North Carolina
Regiment, the Thomas Artillery, and the 48th and 58th Virginia Regiments.[39]

Newspaper accounts tended to portray executed soldiers not as cowards
or as having lost faith in the Confederacy, but as victims of reports from home
from family members growing ever more desperate. Wives were singled out
specifically in many such notices. One account told the story of a soldier "who
had fought many battles and endured every kind of hardship" but succumbed
to his wife's "exaggerated representations of her trials and sufferings." The
man was caught and executed for desertion. The author encouraged wives
throughout the South to "speak words of encouragement; cheer their hearts;
fire their souls, and arouse their patriotism" if they did not want to end up
responsible for their husband's unnecessary death.[40]

Editorials also provide insight into popular perceptions of the necessity
and justification for executions. The *Richmond Daily Dispatch* contained one
such article in the wake of an execution that took place in August 1862. The
newspaper urged its readers to see desertion as a "crime" and executions as the
only remedy, "unless we have determined to abandon the cause altogether."
It goes on to criticize the "clemency" of the government and its "disastrous
effect" on unit cohesion. What is most telling about this particular analysis is
that the paper asks its readers to identify with the broader cause of Confederate independence and the virtues of sacrifice. Many surely sympathized with
individual stories of soldiers deserting for the sake of family, however, the
author reminded readers that "all have been called to the service of the country at enormous sacrifice." According to the logic of the editor, "What would
be an excuse for one man would be an excuse for all." The lengthy discourse

closed with an appeal to Pres. Jefferson Davis to issue a proclamation offering a pardon to those who would voluntarily return but not to interfere with the death penalty once that time had passed.[41]

A military execution was also the subject of a play that ran in Atlanta in 1862. The playwright, known only as "The Lady of Atlanta," used an execution to appeal to her fellow citizens not to take economic advantage of families with loved ones in the army. The three-act play, *The Soldier's Wife*, tells the story of the Lee family. Act one opens with Mr. Lee about to leave for the army with the encouragement of his wife, who urges him to do his duty to his country and assures him that the family will manage while he is away. Following his departure, Mrs. Lee finds it difficult to secure work due to illness and lack of available jobs. The local official in charge of financial relief, Mr. Thompson, gives her no assistance and instead pockets the money for himself. Meanwhile, on guard duty at the front, Mr. Lee expresses concern about his family, having not received a letter from his wife for months, and fears that she is either dead or too impoverished to afford the price of postage. He therefore resolves to desert and return home. Before he arrives home, however, his family is evicted for nonpayment of rent and end up wandering through the snow-covered woods, where they all die of exposure. Mr. Lee soon discovers their bodies and expresses his grief. He is then arrested for desertion.

The final act begins with Mr. Lee in prison waiting to be hanged for desertion. Before he is, however, he learns that the community has heard of his plight and vows that never again will a family be neglected. Even Mr. Thompson has a change of heart and swears never to betray members of his own community in times of trouble. Mr. Lee waits for the moment of his execution while all his thoughts are of his lost family. He prays that God will forgive him as the officer arrives with two of Lee's friends, Mr. Reid and the family's good neighbor, Pat. The play ends with an epilogue, in the form of a poem, that begs the audience to remember and be generous to the families of those who are off fighting for their country.[42]

The overall message of *The Soldier's Wife* is remarkable not simply for its explicit meaning, but for what it does not address. Not once does a character question whether Mr. Lee should be executed for deserting the army out of concern for his family. Instead, he emerges as a tragic figure whose death was unnecessary but for the selfish behavior of others. The play presents its audience with a moral outlook that places the individual within a broader context of responsibility for families who struggle due to the absence of loved ones in the military. Desertions and executions could be prevented through the aid of others, it proclaims, but the punishment remained a necessity and morally justified nonetheless.

An analysis of Confederate soldiers who witnessed military executions sheds light on just how much soldiers were willing to endure to achieve military victory and independence. Their presence at these solemn occasions, standing shoulder-to-shoulder with their comrades and other members of their regiment and larger organizations, encouraged the transition from civilian to soldier and helped strengthen unit cohesion. The way in which Confederates justified military executions suggests that they acknowledged the importance of sacrifice—not simply for the sake of maintaining organizational effectiveness, but as a means of achieving the ultimate goal of Southern independence. Even as late as 1864, when the course of the war had taken a tremendous toll on morale, Confederates struggled to balance the pain of witnessing comrades shot by firing squads with the belief that such actions were necessary.

Regardless of the emotional difficulty involved in watching these executions, Confederates tended to support capital punishment as a deterrent for deserters. This is all the more interesting considering that many witnesses found it easy to sympathize with deserters—especially those who were motivated by concern for loved ones at home. The evidence suggests that identification with and sacrifice on behalf of the military and by extension the nation as a whole was paramount.

NOTES

1. Berrien M. Zettler, *War Stories and School-Day Incidents for the Children* (New York: Neale, 1912), 79–80.

2. Joseph Glatthaar, *General Lee's Army: From Victory to Collapse* (New York: Free Press, 2008), 176.

3. Jack A. Bunch, *Military Justice in the Confederate State Armies* (Shippensburg, PA: White Mane, 2000).

4. Desertion was not the only justification for execution. Confederates were executed for threatening officers and there was even a report that Gen. Braxton Bragg had a soldier executed

for stealing a chicken. P. D. Stephenson, "Missionary Ridge," *Southern Society Historical Papers* 39 (1914): 19. For a survey of punishments in the Army of Tennessee, see Larry J. Daniel, *Soldiering in the Army of Tennessee: A Portrait of Life in the Confederate Army* (Chapel Hill: University of North Carolina Press, 1991), 101–14. At least one soldier from the 44th North Carolina was executed for "mutinous language" in February 1863. See Earl J. Hess, *Lee's Tar Heels: The Pettigrew-Kirkland-MacRae Brigade* (Chapel Hill: University of North Carolina Press, 2002), 340.

5. Historians who have discussed executions include Ella Lonn, *Desertion during the Civil War*, (1928; repr., Lincoln: University of Nebraska Press), 58–61; Bell I. Wiley, *The Life of Johnny Reb: The Common Soldier of the Confederacy* (Baton Rouge: Louisiana State University Press, 1970), 226–28; James I. Robertson Jr., *Soldiers Blue and Gray* (Columbia: University of South Carolina Press, 1988), 135–38; William Blair, *Virginia's Private War: Feeding Body and Soul in the Confederacy, 1861–1865* (New York: Oxford University Press, 1998), 65, 67, 91–92; Peter S. Carmichael, "So Far from God and So Close to Stonewall Jackson: The Executions of Three Shenandoah Valley Soldiers," *Virginia Magazine of History and Biography* 111, no. 1 (2003): 33–66.

6. The number in the firing party depended on the number to be executed. Thomas Smiley reported to have witnessed a firing party of 120 men in a September 1863 execution of 10 Confederates. Thomas M. Smiley to William Smiley, Sept. 9, 1863, "Valley Personal Papers," *Valley of the Shadow,* http://valley.lib.virginia.edu/papers/A6077.

7. For an overview of various disciplinary measures, including execution, see Charles W. Reed, *Hardtack and Coffee or the Unwritten Story of Army Life* (1887; reprint, Lincoln: University of Nebraska Press), 156–63. It should be noted that Reed was a Union soldier, though his account reflects Civil War executions generally. In addition, see Richard Bardolph, "North Carolina Troops and the Desertion Problem," *North Carolina Historical Review* 66, no. 2 (Apr. 1989): 193–205.

8. Letter of William R. Elam, Dec. 14, 1861, MSS 10662-a, Alderman Library, University of Virginia, Charlottesville; Z. Lee Diary, William Yancey Papers, University of Virginia; Gen. B. T. Johnston, "Memoir of First Maryland Regiment," *Southern Historical Society Papers* 9 (1881): 486. Background to this case is provided in Terry L. Jones, *Lee's Tigers: The Louisiana Infantry in the Army of Northern Virginia* (Baton Rouge: Louisiana State University Press, 1987), 40–42.

9. William H. Grimball to his sister, Aug. 29, 1862, Grimball Family Papers, no. 980, Southern Historical Collection, University of North Carolina at Chapel Hill.

10. Ibid.; Robert Moore, "An Execution . . . a Ghost's Last Hymn . . . and a Curse Fulfilled(?)," *Cenantua's Blog,* Oct. 31, 2010, https://cenantua.wordpress.com/2010/10/31/an-execution-a-ghosts-last-hymn-and-a-curse-fulfilled/, accessed Feb. 20, 2018.

11. Andrew S. Bledsoe, *Citizen-Officers: The Union and Confederate Volunteer Junior Officer Corps in the American Civil War* (Baton Rouge: Louisiana State University Press, 2015), 37.

12. Arthur R. Ford, *Life in the Confederate Army, Being Personal Experiences of a Private Soldier in the Confederate Army* (New York: Neale, 1905), 13; William Lamb, "Fort Fisher: The Battles Fought There in 1864 and '65," *Southern Historical Society Papers* 21 (1893): 265–66.

13. Quoted in Drew Gilpin Faust, "The Civil War Soldier and the Art of Dying," *Journal of Southern History* 67, no. 1 (Feb. 2001): 10–11.

14. McHenry Howard, *Recollections of a Maryland Confederate Soldier and Staff Officer* (1914; repr., Baltimore, MD: Morningside Bookshop, 1975; Jedediah Hotchkiss to Sara A. Hotchkiss,

Mar. 1, 1863, "Valley Personal Papers," *Valley of the Shadow,* http://valley.lib.virginia.edu/papers/ A4025; Jeffrey C. Lowe and Sam Hodges, *Letters to Amanda: The Civil War Letters of Marion Hill Fitzpatrick, Army of Northern Virginia* (Macon, GA: Mercer University Press, 1998), 90.

15. On last words, see Faust, "Civil War Soldier and the Art of Dying," 13; Samuel Pickens Diary, Apr. 28, 1864, in Hubbs, *Voices from Company D,* 254; Sam D. Elliott, ed., *Doctor Quintard, Chaplain C.S.A. and Second Bishop of Tennessee* (Baton Rouge: Louisiana State University Press, 2003), 73–75; James Parrott to his wife, June 15, 1863, last edited Nov. 20, 2003, www.rootsweb. com/~tnoverto/docs/CivilWarLettersParrott.html; "Heritage and Heraldry," *Page News and Courier* (Luray, VA), May 20, 1999.

16. Second Lt. James C. Otey Jr., a member of the Otey, Ronggold, and Davidson Virginia Artillery, was court-martialed for cowardice after the Battle of the Crater in July 1864. Although convicted, his sentence was eventually dropped, and Otey was dismissed from the service. Michael A. Cavanaugh, *Otey, Ringgold, and Davidson Artillery* (Lynchburg, VA: H. E. Howard, 1993), 57–62.

17. Terry Foenander, "The Execution of Captain Jazeb R. Rhodes, C.S.A.," Sept. 7, 2003 http://hub.dateline.net.au/~tfoen/rhodes.html (site discontinued).

18. Martin Diller Coiner to his sister, Aug. 21, 1862, Coiner Family Papers, Mss2C6663b, Virginia Historical Society, Richmond; Henry Beck Diary, Apr. 28, 1864, in Hubbs, *Voices from Company D,* 254; John Hall to his father, Oct. 6, 1864, quoted in J. Tracy Power, *Lee's Miserables* (Chapel Hill: University of North Carolina Press, 1998), 214–15; Lowe and Hodges, *Letters to Amanda,* 90; William W. Blackford, *War Years with Jeb Stuart* (New York: Charles Scribner's Sons, 1945), 280.

19. Lowe and Hodges, *Letters to Amanda,* 90.

20. William N. Wood, *Reminiscences of Big I,* ed. Bell Irvin Wiley (Jackson, TN: McCowat-Mercer, 1956), 58; Lowe and Hodges, *Letters to Amanda,* 90; William H. Grimball to his sister, Aug. 29, 1862, Grimball Family Papers; S. M. Haskins, "My Recollections of the Confederate War," no. 1725, Florida State Archives, Tallahassee.

21. Mills Lane, ed., *Dear Mother: Don't Grieve about Me. If I Get Killed I'll Only Be Dead: Letters from Georgia Soldiers in the Civil War* (Savannah: Beehive, 1990), 90. For a thorough analysis of how fathers used descriptions of battle and camp life to maintain discipline, see James Marten, *The Children's Civil War* (Chapel Hill: University of North Carolina Press, 1998), 81–86.

22. Sam Watkins, *Company Aytch; Or, A Side Show of the Big Show* (1900; repr., New York: Penguin, 1999), 106; John H. Worsham, *One of Jackson's Foot Cavalry: His Experience and What He Saw during the War, 1861–1865* (New York: Neale, 1912), 191–92; John Hall to his father, Oct. 6, 1864, in Power, *Lee's Miserables,* 214–15; Stuart T. Wright, *The Confederate Letters of Benjamin H. Freeman* (Hicksville, NY: Exposition, 1974), 34.

23. Samuel H. Walkup to Minnie Walkup, Jan. 28, 1864, quoted in Carmichael, "So Far from God," 37.

24. William Waller Rouzie to Susan M. Rouzie, n.d., Folder 4, Rouzie Family Papers, Manuscripts and Rare Books Department, Earl Gregg Swem Library, College of William and Mary, Williamsburg, VA; Samuel Pickens Diary, Dec. 13, 1864, in Hubbs, *Voices from Company D,* 332.

25. Pickens Diary, Sept. 9, 1863, in Hubbs, *Voices from Company D,* 198; Adam Wise Kersh to George P. Kersh, Apr. 3, 1864, "Valley Personal Papers," *Valley of the Shadow,* http://valley.lib. virginia.edu/papers/A0350.

26. George Philip Clark Diary, 1863–1865, no. 11025, Albert and Shirley Small Special Collections Library, University of Virginia, Charlottesville; John S. Watson Diary, 1864, Mss5:1W3345:1, Virginia Historical Society, Richmond; William T. Casey to his sister, Feb. 10, 1864, Mss1C2686a, ibid.

27. Ford, *Life in the Confederate Army*, 13; Jedediah Hotchkiss to Sara A. Hotchkiss, Mar. 1, 1863, *Valley of the Shadow;* A. Brock, ed., "War Diary of Captain R. E. Parks," *Southern Historical Society Papers,* 26 (1898), 18; Spencer G. Welch, *A Confederate Surgeon's Letters to His Wife* (New York: Neale, 1911), 79; Wiley Sword, *Southern Invincibility: A History of the Confederate Heart* (New York: St. Martin's, 1999), 231 (North Carolina lieutenant quotation); Mercer Otey, "Story of Our Great War," *Confederate Veteran* 7, no. 6 (June 1899): 262–63.

28. Martin Crawford, *Ashe County's Civil War: Community and Society in the Appalachian South* (Charlottesville: University Press of Virginia, 2001), 136. On the importance of religious revivals in the two principal Confederate armies, see Power, *Lee's Miserables*, 125–27, 193–94, 259–60; Gary W. Gallagher, *The Confederate War* (Cambridge, MA: Harvard University Press, 1997), 49–51, 51–52, 66–67, 86–87; and Daniel, *Soldiering in the Army of Tennessee*, 119–25.

29. The men executed were likely Unionists and not deserters from the army, but Confederate officers and others treated them as such.

30. On the Kinston executions, see Lesley J. Gordon, *General George E. Pickett in Life and Legend* (Chapel Hill: University of North Carolina Press, 1998), 130–35, 157–59, 160–61; Edward G. Longacre, *Leader of the Charge: A Biography of General George E. Pickett* (Shippensburg, PA: White Mane, 1995), 140–41, 173–74; Walter Harrison, *Pickett's Men: A Fragment of War History* (New York: D. Van Nostrand, 1870); and Bardolph, "North Carolina Troops and the Deserter Problem," 204–10.

31. John Paris, *A Sermon: Preached before Brig. Gen. Hoke's Brigade at Kinston, N.C., on the 28th of February, 1864* (Greensboro, NC: A. W. Ingold, 1864), 4–15.

32. Earl J. Hess, *Braxton Bragg: The Most Hated Man in the Confederacy* (Chapel Hill: University of North Carolina Press, 2016), 46.

33. Daniel, *Soldiering in the Army of Tennessee*, 112–13.

34. Hess, *Braxton Bragg*, 268–69.

35. Carmichael, "So Far from God," 36.

36. On the connection between logistics and desertion, see Keith S. Bohannon, "Dirty, Ragged, and Ill-Provided For: Confederate Logistical Problems in the 1862 Maryland Campaign and Their Solutions," in *The Antietam Campaign*, ed. Gary W. Gallagher (Chapel Hill: University of North Carolina Press, 1999), 101–42. Recent local studies of the causes of desertion include Crawford, *Ashe County's Civil War*, 125–48; Kevin C. Ruffner, "Civil War Desertion from a Black Belt Regiment: An Examination of the 44th Virginia Infantry," in *The Edge of the South: Life in Nineteenth-Century Virginia*, ed. Edward L. Ayers and John C. Willis (Charlottesville: University Press of Virginia, 1991), 79–109; Rand Dotson, "'The Grave and Scandalous Evil Infected to Your People': The Erosion of Confederate Loyalty in Floyd County Virginia," *Virginia Magazine of History and Biography* 108 (2000): 393–434; and Mark A. Weitz, *A Higher Duty: Desertion among Georgia Troops during the Civil War* (Lincoln: University of Nebraska Press, 2000).

37. *Richmond Examiner,* Sept. 22, 1863; *Augusta (GA) Daily Chronicle & Sentinel,* Sept. 9, 1863.

38. *Richmond Daily Dispatch*, Sept. 10, 1863; "Execution of Deserters in McCausland's Brigade," *Lynchburg Virginian*, Mar. 22, 1864.

39. *Augusta (GA) Daily Constitutionalist*, May 5, 1864; *Richmond Daily Dispatch*, Aug. 22, 1862.

40. "A Solemn Warning to Wives," *Richmond Daily Dispatch*, Jan. 27, 1863.

41. "The Late Military Execution," ibid., Aug. 27, 1862.

42. "A Lady of Atlanta," *The Soldier's Wife: A Drama in Three Acts* (Atlanta: Franklin Printing House, 1862).

MCCLELLAN'S MEN

Union Army Democrats in 1864

Keith Altavilla

T HE 1864 PRESIDENTIAL CAMPAIGN was as contentious as any other. Motivated partisans on both sides turned out their voters with visions of party government both uplifting and desolate. Even with the Civil War raging around them, voter participation was comparable to other elections during the mid-nineteenth century. While the ongoing war to reunite the nation remained the one significant factor that colored every other issue in the campaign, partisans out of power attacked the present administration on a variety of ethical, racial, and competency grounds. Though events conspired to give the Republican, Abraham Lincoln, a resounding victory over his Democratic opponent, George B. McClellan, the months leading up to the election would look quite familiar to observers of any other presidential campaign in the nineteenth century. Even with the possibility of treason tainting their opposition to the administration, Democratic campaigners sought to win back the White House and regain control over the executive branch, which they had lost four years earlier.[1]

The Democrats waged their campaign on several fronts, but their most prominent public argument was to target the Lincoln administration and the Republican Party as having failed in the war effort. Failure could take many forms, and given the divisions raging in the party's ranks, this was a vague-enough position that would mollify a number of factions and keep Democrats focused on defeating Lincoln rather than fighting each other. Through almost four years of war, Democrats could argue convincingly, the government had been unable to crush the rebellion. The administration had then compounded this failure by attacking the rights and liberties of loyal American citizens.

With the war as pretext, Republicans had closed newspapers, arrested potential dissenters, and forced men to fight via conscription. To Democrats, these were signs that Republicans were more interested in solidifying their own political authority than in reuniting the nation. For more racially minded Democratic voters, Lincoln and his government also placed too much emphasis on destroying slavery. Republicans refused, it seemed, to consider any kind of victory that did not include at least abolition, if not the social and political equality of black Americans, as many charged. This focus on victory and civil rights gave rise to the famous Democratic slogan that they supported "the Union as it was, and the Constitution as it is." In some respects this focus on issues of government power and the rights of white men was quite normal, very similar to the campaigns waged against the Whigs and their Republican successors since the 1830s. This longer-term similarity is important to understanding the possible hold that supporting their party maintained in the minds of many Democrats, especially soldiers.[2]

One of the most significant things about the 1864 election, arising from the war itself, was that soldiers from several Northern states became the first men serving in a wartime army to vote in a presidential contest. While the numbers trended very heavily toward Lincoln, a substantial number of soldiers cast their votes for McClellan, doing so openly. This support for the rival candidate suggests that there was still room to support reunion and the war while also disagreeing with the Republicans and being willing to cast a vote for their political opponents. Peace Democrats, known to soldiers, Republican politicians, and contemporary historians as "Copperheads," held a great deal of sway in their party. They did not, however, control it. Democrats were divided, and they argued about the extension of government power, the restriction of civil liberties, and the status of race relations in the context of the war. Many of these stances emerged from long-standing Democratic themes. This mixed with the period's strong pattern of party loyalty to create a noteworthy minority within the ranks. For these Democratic voters, winning the war did not mean they should, or needed to, abandon their political home. Union soldiers who supported McClellan did so because they thought his election was the best path to winning the war and because of their long-standing loyalty to the party through traditional ideological and ethnic ties.

Union soldiers in the field overwhelmingly supported Lincoln's reelection, providing a significant if not decisive contribution to his victory over

McClellan. The president's substantial margin was most likely driven by military successes in the late summer, particularly William Tecumseh Sherman's capture of Atlanta and Phil Sheridan's success in the Shenandoah Valley. His even larger margin among Union soldiers, 80 percent of the vote, represented a clear statement of support for the president's actions, particularly his leadership in military affairs. Eighty percent is an astoundingly high number and even more impressive when one remembers that Republicans and Republican principles certainly did not represent 80 percent of the army. A substantial number of Democrats, it would appear, switched their allegiances, at least temporarily, to back Lincoln in support of Union and victory.[3]

But what of those remaining 20 percent? Men who voted for Democrats like McClellan did so under a cloud of scrutiny from their comrades. To be a McClellan supporter, or at the very least opposed to the administration, could make a soldier the target of scorn, derision, and more official forms of persecution. As Jonathan White has ably demonstrated, many Union officers were not above using their positions of authority to support Republican politics and intimidate the army's Democrats into silence, resignation, or desertion. This attrition, as well as the actions of vocal Peace Democrats at home, saw many party members switch their allegiances, at least during the war. The siren song of the Union Party, an attempt to unite Republicans and War Democrats, was also strong. This fusionist organization helped convince some men that it was worthwhile to avoid a Democratic campaign tainted by treasonous elements. Yet many did stay true to their prewar allegiances and remained loyal to their party in the election. To support McClellan, and to do so openly, required a fair bit of personal courage in the face of strong institutional and peer condemnation.[4]

Much of the soldiers' desire for political activism came because of the ongoing war. While large portions of the political campaign touched on issues that would be familiar to past elections, the war brought others to the forefront. Emancipation and conscription were the most prominent and touched most directly on the soldiers' experience. Most importantly, for many, was the presence of an active and dangerous antiwar movement on the home front. What would have been normal political argument prior to the war became dangerous subversion during the 1860s. If such Copperheads as Ohioan Clement Vallandigham saw fit to make the war a political issue, then surely the men fighting for union had the right to participate in the process, including the casting of ballots. Pressure from soldiers and politicians, eager to claim the mantle of "the soldiers' friend," as well as the soldiers' votes themselves, led to several state governments extending suffrage by 1864.

Under this stress, and convinced that their party had been overtaken by antiwar or pro-Confederate forces (if there could be a distinction), a number of Democrats had switched their allegiances throughout the war, at least publicly. Hezekiah Cole Clock, writing to his brother back in Warren, Illinois, scolded those "who are holding secret meetings and adopting resolutions in favor of the Southern Confederacy" as tarnishing "that sacred name, Democrat." Clock was one of many enlisted Democrats who abandoned their party during the war. They justified their apparent betrayal by arguing that they were remaining true to party principle, fighting to maintain the Union and Constitution as called for by "the immortal [Stephen] Douglas." Two Democrats from the 154th New York, Col. Patrick H. Jones and 1st Lt. Commodore Perry Vedder, endorsed a Republican in a local election. The *Cattaraugus Freeman,* the local Republican paper, celebrated Vedder as a convert, calling him "a firm and enthusiastic supporter of 'Old Abe.'" The local Democratic paper, the *Cattaraugus Union,* castigated the men for their defection. Its editor complained of "too much politics and too little military service in the army." Without question, political loyalty could play a role in military promotion, and even if Vedder's conversion were genuine, the *Union's* charge of political interference would not be out of the question.[5]

Early in the war the idea of opposing the Republicans was not unusual. John C. Dinsmore, serving with the 99th Illinois, wrote home to his wife suggesting the presence of a large anti-Lincoln faction in the ranks. Some of this came from homefront misunderstanding of how men in the ranks perceived the war. "As I understand," he wrote, "all those who does not agree with Abe, & his gang are called Copperheads. If that is a Copperhead," he concluded, "3 Fourths of the Men in the Army are Copperheads." Much of this sentiment, he suggested, was driven by disagreements over policy. Dinsmore cited soldier discontent over emancipation and the draft and mocked the idea that conscripting antiwar men would help the army, asking, "What is the use to draft Copperheads to fight Copperheads?" On another occasion, writing to his brother, Dinsmore expressed his belief that supporting emancipation was hurting the Republican cause. He criticized abolitionists for calling "all the Democrats Sesech" and foolishly swearing that there "ain't a Democrat in the army." Much as many soldiers tarred Democrats with the Copperhead brush, men like Dinsmore were sympathetic to accusations that Republicans were led by radical abolitionists with little sense about the army or politics.[6]

The brave souls who did stay with their party certainly took their fair share of abuse. One Ohio soldier, who claimed that he did not particularly care how the election turned out, complained to his wife that he would "vote for Lincoln to keep from being called 'disgruntled.'" Andrew Powell, serving in the 123rd Ohio, identified the loyal Democrats as "most of the new recruits whose term of service is somewhat lengthy yet and the old ones who are sick of the war and that class of democrats who would vote for a hog or anything else on the democratic ticket." Another Ohioan, Owen Hopkins, mocked the assertions of his fellow soldiers who believed that the only men who would "vote for the 'Chickahominy racer' are Hospital shirks, pay-offs, [and] men sick of the service." As a McClellan voter, he saw himself as the level-headed man surrounded by wilder sentiments. Hopkins claimed the political middle ground by saying that he was "not a dangerous Copperhead, or a radical Lincoln man."[7]

A few men fought back publicly against accusations of cowardice and anger. John W. Chase of the 1st Massachusetts Artillery identified himself in one letter home as both "a George B [McClellan] admirer . . . and one who is willing to fight for his country." He had enlisted in August 1861 and would serve for the entire length of the war. To him, there was no distinction between his supporting McClellan and answering the call to save his country. Even this support, though, had its limits. Intimidation through numbers, protocol, and other practices kept Chase from openly campaigning for his chosen candidate. Following McClellan's nomination for the presidency, Chase would write to his brother, "if I was a civilian I would say what I thought about it but at present I think it better to keep silent." Rather than openly avow his position, Chase kept his politics to himself. If another soldier should ask about his politics, though, he was ready, reminding others "that Chase is for the little Hero and always was." His response displayed a certain kind of bravery, to be sure, as he at least had the nerve to respond to his critics, if not challenge them on his own initiative.[8]

In addition to their Copperhead faction, Democratic support also lagged due to the party's refusal to endorse the right of soldiers to vote. Even Democrats in the army found this position difficult to accept. John Culver noted that "the members of the party to which I have so long subscribed were wholly instrumental in withholding from us the right to vote." He added a warning that the troops "will certainly remember their charity should we be permitted to exercise the rights of citizenship again." The idea of politically motivated soldiers was itself a unique aspect to the American political and electoral tradition. The United States had long paid lip service to a tradition of a disinterested military, separate and subservient to civilian-dominated political concerns. Prior to the Civil War, when the army remained small and out on the frontier, this distinction was easy to maintain. As the war's progress necessitated ever-larger volunteer armies, though, these new soldiers were less interested in leaving their politics behind. With their military status tied to being citizens, with all attendant rights, many soldiers chafed at this new separation. One man would remark that, as both a citizen and a soldier in early 1862, he felt he was also "two things at once, . . . a voter and yet *not* a voter."[9]

State legislatures had begun considering the military vote in 1863, and eleven out of twenty-five states allowed their citizen-soldiers to vote while away from home by 1864. Democrats had been the most strenuous objectors to the policy. They feared the influence of administration officials and Republican officers in coercing votes, which differs slightly from the view that they sought to suppress the soldier vote because it leaned Republican. In addition, many launched objections surrounding the constitutionality of these proposals, arguing as much over process as policy. The process debates did earn some modifications to soldier-voting laws, though usually after the ballots had been counted. Furthermore, these changes did not reject the larger principle of allowing the troops to vote. Vallandigham, both then and now the archetype of Copperhead sentiment, worried about the electoral process during his 1863 Ohio gubernatorial campaign. Noting that he would need to win "the *home* vote . . . by a considerable majority" to account for the landslide coming from the army, he saw the difficulty of adding a large voter block already predisposed against him and his campaign. While Vallandigham, as the soldiers' symbol of everything wrong with the Democratic Party, is a more extreme case, his concerns highlight the electoral difficulties his party would face heading into the presidential campaign.[10]

When Democratic leadership gathered in Chicago for their 1864 nominating convention, events neatly outlined the divisions within their ranks. Many of the party's traditional Southern leaders had left to join the Confederacy, while other key unifying figures, such as Stephen Douglas, had exited the scene in other ways. Peace and War factions would bicker among the disorganized Democrats. Complicating matters further, several War Democrats had also left the party to join the fusion Union Party for the 1864 cycle. The most famous of these was former senator Andrew Johnson, who had been selected as Lincoln's vice-presidential candidate at Baltimore a few months earlier. United mainly by their desire to unseat the Republicans, party leadership came to a tenuous compromise whereby the War Democrats would get their choice for the presidential nomination, while the Peace faction drafted the party's platform. In the mid-nineteenth century the platform was still an important part of convention and campaign work, laying out the principles upon which all Democrats would campaign in the coming election. This clear distinction was not assured, certainly not to outside observers. Iowa soldier Joseph Culver noted a concern that "the convention should be divided, in which case candidates that have expressed more ultra views would likely be selected." He added his own expectation that "such a diversion [would be] attempted to favor Vallandigham."[11]

Though no such diversion came about, Vallandigham was heavily involved in writing the platform. Along with New York City Copperhead Fernando Wood, he spearheaded the infamous "peace plank," which declared the war to be "four years of failure" and called for "immediate efforts . . . for a cessation of hostilities." War Democrats responded by nominating George McClellan, who had been favored coming into the convention. As a final concession for the Peace faction, McClellan was joined on the ticket by Ohio congressman George Pendleton. Historian John Waugh gives one picture of Pendleton, citing several leading War Democrats who described the new vice-presidential candidate as "querulous, snarling, and meddling, . . . a disaster who had labored hard and long to obstruct and discourage the Union war effort." His pairing with the gentlemanly and more militant McClellan provided additional representation for the party's wartime divisions. While the party was certainly willing to use the general's celebrity for their cause, it came about mostly in their use of him as a foil for Lincoln, the true subject of the campaign. The party's divisions, and McClellan's own unclear views on policy, made him more effective as a cipher than as a distinct vision for the future.[12]

McClellan appeared to be a strong choice. While the view of his military record in the modern day is generally poor, the general had his defenders in 1864. Democrats played up his military background. At least one evening rally in New York's Union Square used a spotlight to project the shadow of General Washington on horseback to the side of a building, an obvious reminder of McClellan's military stature and pro-war views. One distributed pamphlet saw Robert Winthrop, the former mayor of Boston, praising the candidate's military exploits. He lauded "the hero of Antietam" and cited McClellan's actions in Mexico, the Crimean War, and West Virginia. Winthrop blamed Lincoln for mismanaging the Peninsula Campaign, echoing the general's own complaints as he blamed the president for holding troops back to defend Washington. This reduction of available forces made McClellan's actions during the Seven Days' Battles all the more laudable.[13]

One longtime McClellan admirer in the army compared him to the newest Northern hero. As Lt. Gen. Ulysses S. Grant's army sat outside of Richmond in the summer of 1864, John Chase complained, "I fail to see what damn great things Grant has done more than George B done before him." Four years of war had effectively left the Union armies in Virginia in the same position they were two years earlier. Additionally, McClellan's public disagreements with Lincoln had made him a prominent symbol of anti-administration, though not necessarily antiwar, sentiment. Beyond his pro-war stance, his previous service in the military might be able to draw some soldier votes, especially among easterners who had served under him and theoretically still loved their former commander for all he had done. "There is a great many of us glad that McClellan is nominated as president," wrote one Pennsylvania soldier, "and we hope he will be elected."[14]

The general's stature may have been enough to generate support from outside the party, but other events during convention week limited his ability to unite the party. William Sherman announced the capture of Atlanta as McClellan penned his nomination acceptance while at home in New Jersey. McClellan was already unlikely to support a condemnation of the war, and now following an unambiguous success, it would look foolish. Making sure to emphasize the difference between himself and the Peace faction, he took the unusual step of accepting the nomination while repudiating the platform. The general wrote that he would be unable to "look in the face of my comrades . . . and tell them that their labors and the sacrifice of such numbers of their brothers had been in vain." He would campaign on his own terms—to gain peace through victory. The letter generated additional excitement among the troops. "There was first a general feeling of relief and joy when he was nominated," wrote Harvey Reid, "which the publication of his letter of acceptance has increased almost to enthusiasm. I believe if an election was held tomorrow he would receive at least 1/3 of the soldiers' votes. . . . Even the most ardent Republicans express great admiration [for] McClellan himself."[15]

The candidate's personal support for the war notwithstanding, the Chicago Platform and the presence of Pendleton on the ticket continuously weighed down McClellan's campaign. His unwillingness to take a direct hand in constructing his own political operation would further contribute to a lack of direction for pro-war Democrats. Even Reid, in noting the excitement, added that having Pendleton "is a drag upon [the ticket] here." Furthermore, he noted that many soldiers were "willing to trust McClellan but they fear he would be obligated to select a Cabinet deficient in his high soldierly sense of honor": that is, one composed of Peace men. Iowan Culver would note that "the McClellan men have been very quiet" since news of the platform arrived. He later speculated that "had McClellan accepted the nomination upon a strong war Platform, he would have had some friends and five or six of [my company] would have voted for him." But, he continued, "the Chicago Platform has no friends here that I know of, and McClellan's effort to kick aside the Platform and still accept the nomination by a strong copperhead convention has left him very few friends." One army engineer from Michigan also observed, "There is lots of McClellan men in our company but they won't vote for him because Pendleton is on the ticket." Samuel Wildman of the 55th Ohio referred to the choices as "a hard pill to swallow for some of our men" and referenced a sergeant "who was a war supporter of George before the nomination," but who was now preparing to not vote at all. William Orr was concerned that the candidacy was "clogged by *Pendleton* and by his Platform, which I do not altogether like." Still, Orr firmly stated, "I do like his letter of acceptance, and I am for him."[16]

Even at this distinct disadvantage, Democrats were not going to forgo the soldier vote if they could help it. Politics remained a common topic of discussion in camp. The men regularly debated the issues of the day, including emancipation, conscription, black enlistment, and other aspects of government policy. Even as they maintained support for Lincoln, they took great issue with some of the administration's policies, or they debated with more nuance than a simple binary election would suggest. Considering their receptiveness to anti-administration viewpoints, it should not be surprising that many soldiers were on the receiving end of Democratic letters, pleas, and pamphlets; their general lack of success suggests the limits of the party's appeal among the troops. While some of the more famous materials encouraged desertion, many more attempted to sway the men's political sentiments. One Kentucky soldier received a letter from a neighbor in support of antiwar principles. The attempted correspondence backfired when his comrades denounced the letter as "an exhibition of his [the writer's] utter ignorance or a string of glaring *willful* falsehoods." The soldiers then went a step further by writing individual responses to the neighbor—presumably not the reaction he was expecting. Some soldiers even ran for office as Democrats. Others took an active part in campaigning for either side, debating the war with one another and those at home.[17]

Democratic campaigners at home tried to promote McClellan as a guarantor of peace by characterizing Lincoln and his emancipation scheme as the real obstacle to that goal. Paralleling Republican attacks on their loyalty, Democratic campaigners charged that reelecting Lincoln would thus only further embolden the Confederacy. His radical policies, they claimed, entrenched Confederate support in the South, especially his tyrannical use of the military and his odious emancipation policy. To support Lincoln, they argued, would lengthen the war far more than necessary, pointing to Southerners' own words in support of this argument. For instance, a Richmond editorial referred to Lincoln as "the South's best ally," acting as a unifying force to all sections of Southern society. In addition, an anonymous writer from Georgia concurred and promised "a cessation of hostilities" should McClellan win. While the actual likelihood of the Confederacy returning to the United States voluntarily was minimal at best, it remained a persistent belief of Peace Democrats. Many antiwar figures had convinced themselves throughout the war that the South had left because of Lincoln and would not return for him.[18]

Some soldiers echoed these campaign themes, hoping to end the war by removing Lincoln from office. The most common rationale given for supporting McClellan and the Democratic Party in 1864 was the belief that the general was the man to achieve a desired peace. Like many of their party's politicians, including Vallandigham, Democratic soldiers did not necessarily distinguish between a negotiated peace and reunion. Very few Democrats accepted the Confederacy's existence, even as a precondition to negotiating a peace, as their desire for reunion remained strong. "I am in favor of the effort to Stop this

Bloodshed," wrote Orr, who also attacked those "who hold up their hands in holy horror and cry treason if one but say 'peace.'" Being careful, he noted that his desired peace would be an "Honorable" one "on the basis of the *union*" and that "Gen McClellan will do well to bring about such a peace." The pamphlet *General McClellan and the Presidency,* authored by an anonymous "Veteran Soldier," attacked Lincoln and offered the general as the best possible candidate. Its author described McClellan as the conservative choice. The general, he declared, "would conduct the war upon more humane principles, . . . would repeal the Emancipation Proclamation, and probably make overtures to the South to return to the Union."[19]

For many soldiers, peace was equated to the prospect of finally going home. Wilbur Fisk recorded a debate among the men in his camp and noted that "two of the loudest talking McClellanites there would vote for him because they were for peace." One man he recorded as having said "I have been out here long enough and now I want to go home." For others, the peace promised by a McClellan presidency meant an end to the exhausting war. They surrounded their pro-McClellan sentiments with high casualty figures and a desire to return home. A German soldier, while recounting the losses to his corps at Chattanooga, lamented, "Maybe . . . the American people will elect McClellan president and that then there will be peace." One soldier in the 9th New Jersey, writing to his home newspaper, echoed these themes while congratulating his compatriots on backing McClellan. "We look forward to the day with longing hearts," he wrote, "when misrule and corruption will have to give way to 'Little Mac,' Liberty, Union and Justice." Even Andrew Powell, in criticizing the Democrats in his regiment, noted that these men "seem to harbor the idea that Mac. will settle the war sooner than Abe," and more importantly they "don't care on what terms the war settles." Even with their desire for peace, many soldiers kept that beside their support for reunion. Instead of looking at McClellan's ability to negotiate a peace, which could end in separation, they focused on his ability to manage the war to victory.[20]

Much like their civilian counterparts, McClellan voters in the Union armies focused on doing what was necessary to win the war. Convinced that Lincoln's radicalism and mismanagement of affairs would make that impossible, they backed his opponent. Lincoln's antislavery principles played a role in these justifications, primarily providing them evidence of the president's radicalism and serving as further proof that he would be unable to reunite the nation effectively. Historian Chandra Manning concludes that by 1864 many Union soldiers no longer cared about abolitionism or supported emancipation as a wartime policy designed to hurt Confederate logistics. Delavan Bates, commander of the 30th U.S. Colored Troops, described this distinction between the way soldiers and civilians looked at race. Bates saw a colorblind army, interested only in the question of union or disunion. He contrasted that with civilians choosing between "union and peace with slavery or an abolition war ending—no one knew when—without slavery." Where racist sentiment did exist in camp, Bates dismissed it as coming from new recruits and blamed the home front for poisoning their minds before they joined the army.[21]

Much of this belief comes from the idea that those who opposed emancipation and other racial equality measures had already left the army. These men had resigned or deserted in the aftermath of the Emancipation Proclamation or were forced out by a strongly proadministration officer corps. As one example, Illinois soldier Lewis Hanback referenced a Major Cummings, whom he described as "a renegade soldier who says he left the army because he couldn't fight for [abolition]." Yet this is an incomplete picture. Democratic soldiers, though united in their unionism, did not ignore or dismiss racial questions. Furthermore, many opinions had not changed as a result of the fighting or exposure to slaves while in the South. One soldier in a Michigan regiment complained that Lincoln wanted "us all to go down South and fight for the nigger." Hoping for Lincoln's defeat as early as December 1863, he instead sought a president who "don't like nigger blood better than white blood." Arnold Shankman's history of the Pennsylvania antiwar movement quotes several soldiers concerned about the administration's "nigger-fugger" tendencies, men who complained that there was "too much nigger" in Republican policies. A Democratic paper in upstate New York identified one captain in the 154th New York as "a conservative, square-toed Democrat" due to his opposition to the government's "policy of 'nigger-ism' and radicalism."[22]

Racialist thinking certainly played an important role in Democratic campaigning. It was the 1864 campaign that saw the introduction of the term "miscegenation," referring to the mixing of blood that Republicans' racial egalitarianism would encourage. This sort of racial antagonism fit into the long history of mid-nineteenth-century Democratic thinking. Historian Jean Baker refers to the "Negro Speech," described as a "jeremiad" regularly employed alongside speeches other popular issues such as tariffs and monetary policy.

These speeches used popular representations of blacks to express Democrats' concern over their potential political equality that they viewed as impossible given their social inequality. Even if few soldiers were made aware of miscegenation as a substantive issue in the campaign, the specter of racial equality, and the subsequent threat of white subjugation, was easily recognizable.[23]

One area where Democratic racial commentary had little effect among the troops was over the enlistment of black soldiers. Throughout the war, Democratic politicians condemned the notion of black troops, which they viewed as unnecessarily inflammatory toward the South and, in the words of historian Jennifer Weber, "a Trojan horse for racial equality." When black units were involved in military disaster, such as the infamous Battle of the Crater at Petersburg in 1864, their presence was a sign of Republican racial obsession, forcing such men into places they did not belong. Copperhead newspapers throughout the North did their part to rail against arming blacks and regularly accused them of "barbarities," including the burning of Darien, Georgia. For many Union soldiers, though, the issue of black enlistment did not arise when discussing the election. Those who led black troops concluded that they were capable additions to the war effort, even if, in the words of one observer, such officers had "no 'abolition' or 'nigger loving' proclivities." This appears to have been one area of significant change in soldier opinion during the war. By 1864 most of the men who did object to black soldiers seem to have left the army over other racial issues like emancipation. Pro-McClellan and anti-Lincoln voices were not afraid to draw on racial reasoning for their position, but none made reference to black soldiers.[24]

One particularly prolific McClellan supporter, who combined these twin concerns of racial superiority and the chance for peace, was actually a sailor. Henry Coffinberry, who served aboard the river gunboat *Louisville*, was an ardent McClellan man and regularly asked for his parents' thoughts on the general's election prospects throughout the summer of 1864. By October Coffinberry began suggesting that he would resign should Lincoln win reelection. His father, James, was sympathetic but offered that Henry should only do so if he could avoid the draft. For Coffinberry, beyond his belief that Lincoln was a dangerously radical abolitionist, McClellan's election presented the best chance for ending the war in a rapid and positive way. Relating tales of locals met while cruising the Mississippi River, Coffinberry suggested that Southerners would more than willingly come back under a McClellan administration, a government presumably prepared to protect their property rights. "The rebels," he wrote in late August, "are very much afraid McClellan will be elected," for such an event "would unite the north and divide the south." In September he added, "Evry body south but the *rouse* rebels" hoped for McClellan and the war's end. Coffinberry was also opposed to black enlistment, and while he did not express any particular sentiments in 1864, the previous year he had complained, "I didn't come into this service to drill [blacks] and I don't want to." He further ranted about Lincoln and the Republicans overextending the war's aims, attacking Lincoln supporters for enriching themselves by prolonging the conflict.[25]

An Illinois soldier named J. Porter, serving in the Acting Assistant Provost Marshal General's Office, wrote a similarly stirring defense of McClellan to his brother. While he stated that he would not "cast a vote in Support of Any Abolition Candidate," Porter would still consider supporting Lincoln should he be convinced that reelection would end the war, suggesting his tenuous opposition to abolitionism. For Porter, his greatest concern was the dastardly statements made against McClellan and his candidacy. His brother had claimed that the general would call for an armistice without victory. Porter responded that "nowhere in the McClellan platform, can it be found that any such thing should ever take place. . . . [I]t is only a *surmise* of his political opponents." Instead, he pointed out, "*one* thing [McClellan] did publicly declare, . . . *that the Union should be preserved at all hazards*," a statement he described as "all that Mr. Lincoln proposes & more than he has yet done." Even further, addressing concerns of McClellan's earlier mismanagement of the war, Porter was able to turn those problems against the president. First commenting that he "regard[ed] [the charges of incompetence] as being very much magnified," he noted that Lincoln had allowed McClellan to remain in command during the Peninsular Campaign, so that "if disaster happened, *none* but Mr. Lincoln was to blame." Porter did not cast a vote, though his able defense of McClellan against Republican charges suggests the intelligence and fortitude necessary to argue for the Democrat.[26]

Ethnic politics also played a role in determining voter behavior. Long an ardently pro-Democratic group, many Irish voters in the Union army stayed with their roots. Like other War Democrats, they sought to restore the Union as it had existed antebellum and worried about the potential effects of an unfettered Republican administration. Susannah Ural has noted that civilian Irish

Americans, especially in ethnic enclaves like New York City, were some of the strongest supporters of "Little Mac." Like pro-McClellan soldiers, the Irish saw a Democratic victory as a way to take the war's focus away from emancipation and its prosecution away from the anti-immigrant Republicans, who, in the words of one newspaper, saw the Irish only as "food for gunpowder." Whatever the presence of such sentiments among Irish soldiers, Republicans and other Lincoln supporters certainly took notice. Taylor Pierce of the 22nd Iowa wrote, "All the Mc-men are the Irish." Col. Alvin Voris thought little of such Irish loyalty, though, snorting in one letter, "If I had taken a big jug of whiskey, I think I could have controlled the votes of the Irish company." Perhaps most interesting in the context of race and ethnicity, he added, "the intelligent colored man is much more respectable and safe as a voter than the Irish."[27]

Where the Irish were reliably Democratic, the other significant ethnic group in the army's ranks, Germans, were much more politically diverse. Earlier generations of Germans had been staunch Democrats, and many remained skeptical of a Republican Party that continued to have ties to the nation's nativist elements. This began to change following the arrival of the "48ers," political refugees of the failed 1848 Revolutions in Europe. These groups used the language of liberty to justify their political actions and found themselves more closely aligned to the Republican radical wing. There was anti-Lincoln sentiment among German soldiers, including some discontent with the course of the war. Significant opposition, though, attacked the administration for not being radical enough, and Germans formed an important support group for the failed insurgent campaign of John C. Frémont for the Republican nomination. But this resistance fell away in the spring and summer once it became clear that Lincoln had consolidated control of the party. Like other soldiers, the war appears to have strengthened previously held positions among the Germans rather than change any particular minds. While McClellan had German supporters, they never constituted a solid bloc in the same manner as the Irish.[28]

McClellan had been a popular commander of the Army of the Potomac, and many Republicans feared that his reputation among all Union troops would be beneficial. One soldier noted, "Many of the old Potomac boys vote for McClellan because they still remain loyal to him." At the same time, opinions about the general had changed as the war continued. "McClellan has no popularity in the Army except among a few officers in his old Army and these are now growing surprisingly few," remarked Charles Francis Adams Jr. "In the West," he continued, "he [McClellan] has no friends." Jeffry Wert's history of the Army of the Potomac confirms this transformation, even if he suggests that McClellan's personal popularity remained, citing George Meade's figures that Lincoln outpolled McClellan by 8,000 votes out of 19,000 cast in the army. One count of the overall soldier vote from the field seems to confirm this broad lack of support for the challenger. The highest percentage of soldier votes McClellan received from an eastern state was around 30 percent (Pennsylvania). Other eastern states, including Maine, Maryland, New Hampshire, and Vermont, provided anywhere from 10 percent to 25 percent. The only state in which McClellan actually won the vote in the field was Kentucky, whose soldiers served almost exclusively in the West.[29]

One area not mentioned much by soldiers was the draft. Democratic campaigners had regularly invoked conscription as a tyrannical scheme. In their worst rhetoric the draft was meant to force whites to fight in order to free slaves. Rounds of drafting had touched off violence across the North, most famously in New York City during the summer of 1863. Further enlistment calls in March and July 1864 led to greater discontent on the home front. In general, though, soldiers rarely invoked the draft when considering their electoral choices. If anything, their service in the military may have made them more receptive to the idea of conscription. They accepted the idea of bringing in more men to fight, a few concerned only that the drafts would be put off. General Sherman worried about this possibility and suggested to Army Chief of Staff Henry Halleck that "if Mr. Lincoln modifies it to the extent of one man, or wavers in its execution he [Lincoln] is gone. Even the army would vote against him."[30]

The other possible split came from the divide between officers and enlisted men. Most of the army's upper echelon were conspicuous by their absence in the presidential campaign, refusing to give a position or confining their beliefs to private correspondence. Many officers preferred to remain quiet, maintaining the belief that soldiers should stay out of politics, at least when defined as partisan behavior. General Grant was a known Lincoln supporter and allowed political newspapers and pamphlets to circulate in camp even as he discouraged campaigning by outsiders. Some, like Maj. Gen. Winfield Scott Hancock, did as much as they could to discourage political discussion of any kind in the ranks. Hancock in particular remained diplomatically silent when argument raged around him. One biographer suggests that he was personally conflicted between supporting Lincoln's policies and backing a close friend and fellow Democrat in McClellan, a concern likely shared by many other officers. Many higher-ranking generals, like Sherman and Meade, did not even vote and tried to remain outside the process whenever possible.[31]

A few of the infamous "political generals," who held their position at least in part for their electoral usefulness, were less circumspect. Dan Sickles, after some public deliberation and good words for McClellan's pro-war stance, attacked the Chicago Platform and rallied Democrats to Lincoln. Benjamin Butler, John Logan, and others publicly campaigned on Lincoln's behalf. It is noteworthy that all three generals had been prominent Democratic politicians before the war and partially owed their positions to a concern for partisan balance in the officer corps. The war's changing politics had shifted their own positions, making their support for Lincoln necessary to win the conflict and maintain their appointments. Even Thomas Meagher, the famous Irish general, strongly supported Lincoln's reelection, though at great cost personally and professionally. His wife's father and brother-in-law were both strong McClellan supporters, while backing Lincoln undermined his support within the Irish community, which would subsequently make Meagher less valuable to the president. All of this support for Lincoln, though, took place away from the army. It is difficult to determine what influence high-ranking-officer support had on voter behavior among the soldiers, though a few men did make mention of their officers' position when explaining their own.[32]

The actual voting process went off relatively smoothly, though not without some difficulties. Soldiers reported quiet and orderly procedures for casting ballots, with little of the argument and debate that characterized the campaign. To actually cast a ballot involved a cumbersome nineteen-step process, and individual state commissioners had various degrees of power surrounding their ability to catch and discard fraudulent votes. Political figures from both parties worried and complained about the possibilities of fraud. Still, where the will to vote existed, a way could be found. One particularly enterprising Wisconsin soldier described lacking election tickets, "but we managed to get hold of some which were intended for another district & altered them so that we made them answer our purpose." Nothing so simple as not having a ballot would stop men who wanted to vote from doing so. Voting fever swept through the ranks, and even men not able to vote officially, such as Union soldiers held in Confederate prison camps, made sure to tally their support.[33]

Some McClellan supporters voiced concerns before the election. Demo-crats in Wilbur Fisk's brigade "could get no printed McClellan votes," though Fisk chastised them for believing that unionist and Republican soldiers would not be partial and suggested that they needed to find "some way to furnish their own." One Pennsylvania soldier reported how several men in his regiment (in-cluding probably himself) chased away two Democrats with McClellan tickets. After letting them make their pitch for the general, the soldiers "burnt the tickets and told them if they did not get out of there in less than 5 minutes we would ride them out on a rail." Jonathan White has detailed other instances of suspected intimidation, including demotions for Democratic noncommis-sioned officers, and several instances of courts-martial for distributing Demo-cratic literature and of driving Democratic politicians out of military camps.[34]

Some of these failed ballot arrivals, though, were not the result of under-handed Republican dealing, just Democratic incompetence. The process for distributing ballots and tickets was not the government's job. State and local officials were only to supply the log books necessary for reporting votes. Par-ties were responsible for distributing ballots for their candidates, as they were back at home, and potential voters were subject to their varying degrees of competence. While some representatives were indeed chased away by soldiers, others did travel south to pass out ballots. Trouble for Democratic voters was more likely to arrive when these representatives did not. Robert Grandchamp's history of a Rhode Island light artillery battery notes that the state Democratic Party failed to send any ballots to Rhode Islanders in the Shenandoah Valley. Around the 121st New York, Democratic ballots came from agents closely tied to Democratic governor Horatio Seymour, while the Republicans shipped theirs through the mail. The governor's personal involvement earned a nega-tive reaction from both soldiers and civilians, who saw it as a direct attempt to influence the result by an elected official, one that could lead to him being able to change their votes.[35]

Though the larger number of ballots went substantially to Lincoln, "Little Mac" had a few redoubts of strength. John Mattoon's regiment and division in the Army of the Shenandoah gave a majority to McClellan, which he cele-brated by cheering "Bully for Little Mac and Bully for all good Democrats in Canaan [New York] or any where else." One soldier, otherwise celebrating Lincoln's overwhelming victory, noted that if not for the men who used to serve in another, more Democratic regiment, "we would hardly have heard from 'Little Mac' at all." In other cases, though, whether through suppression or a general malaise, Democratic soldiers simply did not cast ballots. Snidely referring to them as "the weak kneed kind," John Chase noted that "a great many of the McClellan men did not vote" in his regiment. Harvey Reid, who had noted great excitement in the army for the general's nomination, noted the change by election day. "The feeling in favor of McClellan that was very prevalent in the army when he was nominated," the soldier wrote to his parents, "has nearly died out."[36]

By any calculation, Lincoln's victory over McClellan was a landslide. He received the highest popular-vote percentage of any candidate since Andrew Jackson, the first candidate since Old Hickory in 1832 to win reelection, and his electoral-college margin of victory remains one of the highest in American history. All of this came despite Lincoln's own concerns as late as August that his administration faced the distinct possibility of defeat. By Arthur Schlesinger Jr.'s counting, Union soldier votes from the field were not decisive but did contribute to the president's margin of victory. This strong support for Lincoln came after four years of war and protest had conflated the Democratic Party with Copperheadism. Soldiers who supported McClellan had to make sure they divorced their candidate from the image of subversion. Instead, they tried to characterize Lincoln as the radical, billing McClellan as a competent, conciliatory choice who would not falter in the pursuit of victory. They remained loyal to their party, and many of its traditional themes, claiming that the general could restore the Union and prevent radical changes to the country's racial and social structure. The resistance from their comrades in arms, fully expressed in Lincoln's resounding electoral victory, did not diminish their desire to see McClellan triumph. Instead, it reinforced notions of party loyalty that remained strong during the tumult of civil war and cast doubt on the notion that a McClellan victory would have meant defeat or disunion.[37]

There are, of course, limits to this analysis. Soldiers who voted for McClellan represented roughly 20 percent of the total number of men who cast ballots. Other informal surveys mentioned in letters and diaries do not suggest a large missing McClellan vote suppressed by certain states not allowing their citizen-soldiers to vote. Furthermore, these numbers only account for men voting in the field. Many more were furloughed to go and vote at home, though several soldiers suspected that these furloughs were politically motivated. Partisan politicians, such as Indiana governor Oliver Morton, certainly made sure to provide as many furloughs as possible during the election. This likelihood suggests that soldiers voting at home did not substantially contribute to any of McClellan's totals, which would artificially deflate the count of Democratic votes. Furthermore, while 20 percent is not insignificant, it is not particularly substantial either. It clearly took some amount of personal and professional courage to support McClellan while serving in the Union army. This courage does not seem to have inspired other men to vote for McClellan, especially in the face of peer pressure and outside evidence that the Democratic Party was the party of antiwar Copperheads rather than unionists committed to victory.[38]

When examining electoral positioning, it is worth considering whether the Democrats' arguments could have succeeded. The timetable for the election and subsequent inauguration in March 1865 suggest that McClellan's influence on the war's progress would have been limited. The most substantial change a McClellan administration might have been able to make to government policy would have been the repeal of the Emancipation Proclamation and a refusal to support what would become the 13th Amendment. This of course does not take into account the physical and social devastation of the Southern states, which had already done substantial damage to the slave-based system. This new reality combined with the unsettled question of what to do with contrabands and other escaped slaves would have threatened to drag the question of slavery well into the future, hardly the "Union as it was" promised by Democratic campaigners. Beyond this, Democratic unionists remained convinced during the election that Lincoln was the main obstacle to reunification. While this view was encouraged and spread by plenty in the South, it is unclear that this kind of reunification was really possible. Jefferson Davis predicated any peace conference on the basis of Confederate independence, which many soldiers did not support. Further projections about the composition of a McClellan administration, particularly the influence of Copperhead politicians, remains speculative at best.[39]

All soldiers sought not only an end to the war but also an end that satisfied their own sense of purpose. Many voters, Republican and Democrat, voted for victory, though there were quite a few ways that victory could be defined. These differing conceptions reflected disagreements over the war's purpose and what soldiers hoped to accomplish through reunion. Did it mean the simple destruction of an internal rebellion and the reestablishment of the country as it otherwise used to be, or was it something more, the radical remaking of Southern (and perhaps even American) society? Between these extremes were numerous shades, all reflected in the way soldiers approached the questions of whether they should vote, and if so, how they would vote.

Union soldiers had a variety of ideas about what the war's end would look like. Many had given too much in terms of their own lives, and the lives of their comrades, to accept anything less than the rebels' surrender and the end of secession. Even considering these similarities, many Democrats were just as concerned with process as with results. Like their nominee, they sought a conservative vision of social change, particularly as it related to slavery. They saw Lincoln and the Republicans as blinded by a love of abolition and radical politics. McClellan, with his record of military success, offered the prospect of a war waged competently and that did not insist on ending slavery and creating racial equality. Writing to his family after the election, German immigrant soldier Christian Bönsel included a verse that encapsulated the variety of complaints against Lincoln and in favor of McClellan:

> A time of great trouble and chill,
> Hangs over this mighty land,
> Their own blood they do spill,
> The citizens upon their hand,
> To raise the Negro up on high,
> They plunge us into slavery,
> High taxes, costly times,
> Eat away at people's lives,
> And instead of making peace,
> To end this horrible fight,
> Their own lives they will cease,
> Finding even suicide right,
> Peace will come to this nation,
> Only through Mck Clellan [sic] and Pendleton.

Touching on several major themes of race and slavery, administrative competency, and the specter of unending war, Bönsel neatly describes the major issues galvanizing Democratic voters in the ranks during one of 1864's most important campaigns.[40]

NOTES

1. Joel H. Silbey, *The American Political Nation, 1838–1893* (Stanford, CA: Stanford University Press, 1991), 145.

2. For Democratic campaign themes in the mid-nineteenth century, and 1864 in particular, see Jean H. Baker, *Affairs of Party: The Political Culture of Northern Democrats in the Mid-Nineteenth Century* (Ithaca, NY: Cornell University Press, 1983), 143–211; and John C. Waugh, *Reelecting Lincoln: The Battle for the 1864 Presidency* (New York: Crown, 1997), 314–15.

3. States that permitted soldier voting include California, Iowa, Kentucky, Maine, Maryland, Michigan, New Hampshire, Ohio, Pennsylvania, Vermont, and Wisconsin. Arthur M. Schlesinger Jr., ed., *History of American Presidential Elections, Volume II: 1848–1896* (New York: Chelsea House, 1971), 1245.

4. Jonathan W. White, *Emancipation, the Union Army, and the Reelection of Abraham Lincoln* (Baton Rouge: Louisiana State University Press, 2014), 38–97.

5. To Brother, Feb. 15, 1863, Hezekiah Cole Clock Papers, Abraham Lincoln Presidential Library and Museum, Springfield, IL (hereafter cited as ALPLM); Mark H. Dunkelman, *Brothers One and All: Esprit de Corps in a Civil War Regiment* (Baton Rouge: Louisiana State University Press, 2006), 62, 65.

6. J. C. Dinsmore to Jane, June 8, 1863, John C. Dinsmore Papers, ALPLM; J. C. Dinsmore to brother, Nov. 4, 1862, ibid.

7. John to My Own Dear Wife, Nov. 7, 1864, John B. Rice Papers, Rutherford B. Hayes Presidential Center, Spiegel Grove, Fremont, OH (hereafter cited as RBH); A. Powell to My Dear Brother, Nov. 11, 1864, Andrew Powell Letters, ibid.; Johns. to Friend, Sept. 11, 1864, in Owen Johnston Hopkins, *Under the Flag of the Nation: Diaries and Letters of Owen Johnston Hopkins, a Yankee Volunteer in the Civil War*, ed. Otto F. Bond (Columbus: Ohio State University Press, 1998), 159. The reference to McClellan as the "Chickahominy racer" refers to his retreat during the Peninsula Campaign, having run from his position astride the Chickahominy River near Richmond.

8. Jack to Brother, July 12, Sept. 15, Oct. 16, 1864, in *Yours for the Union: The Civil War Letters of John W. Chase, First Massachusetts Light Artillery*, ed. John S. Collier and Bonnie B. Collier (New York: Fordham University Press, 2010), 354–55, 363, 368.

9. Culver, No. 155, *"Your Affectionate Husband, J. F. Culver": Letters Written during the Civil War*, ed. Leslie W. Dunlap (Iowa City: Friends of the University of Iowa Libraries, 1978), 298; Edward Coffman, *The Old Army: A Portrait of the American Army in Peacetime, 1784–1898* (New York: Oxford University Press, 1986); William B. Skelton, *An American Profession of Arms: The Army Officer Corps, 1784–1861* (Lawrence: University Press of Kansas, 1992); Samuel J. Watson, *Peacekeepers and Conquerors: The Army Officer Corps on the American Frontier, 1821–1846* (Lawrence: University Press of Kansas, 2013); Robert to Father, Oct. 14, 1862, Caldwell Family Papers, RBH.

10. Josiah Henry Benton, *Voting in the Field: A Forgotten Chapter of the Civil War* (Boston, 1915), 73–74; Arnold M. Shankman, *The Pennsylvania Antiwar Movement, 1861–1865* (Rutherford, NJ: Fairleigh Dickinson University Press, 1980), 171–73; CLV to M. Marble, Esq., Oct. 4, 1863, Clement L. Vallandigham Papers, Ohio Historical Society, Columbus (hereafter cited as OHS).

11. Harold M. Hyman, "Election of 1864," in Schlesinger, *American Presidential Elections,*

1174; Waugh, *Reelecting Lincoln*, 276–94; Jennifer L. Weber, *Copperheads: The Rise and Fall of Lincoln's Opponents in the North* (New York: Oxford University Press, 2006), 166–74; Culver, No. 179, "Your Affectionate Husband," 349.

12. Waugh, *Reelecting Lincoln*, 292; Hyman, "Election of 1864," 1172.

13. Baker, *Affairs of Party*, 295; "Great Speech of Hon. Robert C. Winthrop," *Union Pamphlets of the Civil War, 1861–1865: Volume II*, ed. Frank Freidel (Cambridge, MA: Belknap Press of Harvard University Press, 1967), 1076–1118.

14. Jack to Brother, July 12, 1864, in Collier and Collier, *Yours for the Union*, 354–55; William Gearhart to Brother Ellis, Sept. 6, 1864, in John P. Irwin, *A Quaker Soldier in the Civil War: Letters from the Front* (Xlibris, 2008), 143.

15. Harvey Reid to Father and Mother, Sept. 18, 1864, in Harvey Reid, *The View from Headquarters: Civil War Letters of Harvey Reid* (Madison: Wisconsin Historical Society, 1965), 186–87.

16. Ibid.; Culver, Nos. 187, 189, "Your Affectionate Husband," 362, 366; Mark Hoffman, *"My Brave Mechanics": The First Michigan Engineers and Their Civil War* (Detroit: Wayne State University Press, 2007), 221–22; Sam to Father, Sept. 15, 1864, Wildman Family Papers, OHS; William to Father, Sept. 16, 1864, Orr Family Collection, Lilly Library, Indiana University, Bloomington.

17. George A Remley to Brother Howard, Sept. 15, 1864, *Southern Sons, Northern Soldiers: The Civil War Letters of the Remley Brothers, 22nd Iowa Infantry*, ed. Julie Holcomb (DeKalb: Northern Illinois University Press, 2004), 160; John W. Vaught to Mr. William C. Magill, Jan. 27, 1864, William Magill Papers, Indiana Historical Society, Indianapolis; Thomas T. Maholm to Brother John, Aug. 16, 1863, Dow Family Papers, Filson Historical Society, Louisville, KY; Lewis Hanback to Hattie, October 8, 1864, Lewis Hanback Letters, ibid.

18. "Hear Hon. Geo. H. Pendleton," in Freidel, *Union Pamphlets*, 1126–27; Anonymous, "The Presidential Canvass in the United States," *Chronicle & Sentinel* (Augusta, GA), in *The Civil War: Primary Documents on Events from 1860 to 1865*, ed. Ford Risley (Westport, CT: Greenwood, 2004), 258.

19. Baker, *Affairs of Party*, 175; Will to Maggie, Sept. 11, 1864, Orr Family Collection; "General McClellan and the Presidency: Letter from a Veteran Soldier on the Subject. His Opinion of McClellan" (N.p., 1864), 5, Western Reserve Historical Society, Cleveland.

20. Emil Rosenblatt and Ruth Rosenblatt, eds., *Hard Marching Every Day: The Civil War Letters of Private Wilbur Fisk, 1861–1865* (Lawrence: University Press of Kansas, 1991), 264–65 (Oct. 12, 1864); Carl Uterhard to My dear Mama, Sept. 5, 1864, in *Germans in the Civil War: The Letters They Wrote Home*, ed. Walter D. Kamphoefner and Wolfgang Helbich, trans., Susan Carter Vogel (Chapel Hill: University of North Carolina Press, 2006), 172. Alan A. Siegel, *Beneath the Starry Flag: New Jersey's Civil War Experience* (New Brunswick, NJ: Rutgers University Press, 2001), 139; A. Powell to My Dear Brother, Nov. 11, 1864, Andrew Powell Letters, RBH.

21. Chandra Manning, *What This Cruel War Was Over: Soldiers, Slavery and the Civil War* (New York: Alfred A. Knopf, 2007). See also Baker, *Affairs of Party*, 249–258, Sidney Kaplan, "The Miscegenation Issue in the Election of 1864," *Journal of Negro History* 34, no. 3 (July 1949): 274–343; Michael Vorenberg, "'The Deformed Child': Slavery and the Election of 1864," *Civil War History* 47, no. 3 (2001): 240–57; and Salvatore G. Cilella Jr., *Upton's Regulars: The 121st New York Infantry in the Civil War* (Lawrence: University Press of Kansas, 2009), 255.

22. White, *Emancipation, the Union Army, and the Reelection of Abraham Lincoln*, 69–97; Lewis Hanback to Hattie, Oct. 8, 1864, Hanback Letters; Hoffman, *"My Brave Mechanics,"* 221–22; Shankman, *Pennsylvania Antiwar Movement*, 196; Dunkelman, *Brothers One and All*, 63.

23. Baker, *Affairs of Party*, 252–56.

24. Weber, *Copperheads*, 86–87, 143–45; W. H. Hutter and Ray H. Abrams, "Copperhead Newspapers and the Negro," *Journal of Negro History* 20, no. 2 (Apr. 1935): 137–42; Samuel A. Wildman to Father, May 8, 1864, Wildman Family Papers, OHS.

25. Quotes from Henry to Parents, Aug. 4, 1863, Aug. 24, Sept. 8, 1864; requests for information on McClellan in Henry D. Coffinberry to Parents, Mar. 21, Aug. 11, 1864; discussion on Henry's resignation in Henry to Parents, Aug. 24, Oct. 8, 23, 1864; and J. M. Coffinberry to Son, Oct. 28, 1864; suggestions of Southern support for McClellan in Henry to Parents, Aug. 11, Sept. 8, Nov. 20, 1864; other Lincoln attacks in H. Coffinberry to Parents, Oct. 8, Nov. 20, 1864. All letters in Maria D. Coffinberry Papers, Western Reserve Historical Society, Cleveland.

26. J. Porter Jr. to Brother, Nov. 14, 1864, ALPLM.

27. Christian G. Samito, *Becoming American under Fire: Irish Americans, African Americans, and the Politics of Citizenship during the Civil War Era* (Ithaca, NY: Cornell University Press, 2009), 129–32; Susannah J. Ural, "'Ye Sons of Green Erin Assemble': Northern Irish American Catholics and the Union War Effort, 1861–1865," in *Civil War Citizens: Race Ethnicity, and Identity in America's Bloodiest Conflict*, ed. Susannah J. Ural (New York: New York University Press, 2010), 126–27; Dear Sister, Sept. 19, 1864, *Dear Catherine, Dear Taylor: The Civil War Letters of a Union Soldier and His Wife*, ed. Richard L. Kiper (Lawrence: University Press of Kansas, 2002), 263–64; Alvin C. Voris, *A Citizen-Soldier's Civil War: The Letters of Brevet Major General Alvin C. Voris*, ed. Jerome Mushkat (DeKalb: Northern Illinois University Press, 2002), 141.

28. Bruce Levine, *The Spirit of 1848: German Immigrants, Labor Conflict, and the Coming of the Civil War* (Urbana: University of Illinois Press, 1992), 257–71.

29. George A. Hitchcock, *"Death does seem to have all he can attend to": The Civil War Diary of an Andersonville Survivor*, ed. Ronald G. Watson (Jefferson, NC: McFarland, 2014), 210–11 (Nov. 8, 1864); Charles Francis Adams Jr. to his Father, Oct. 15, 1864, *A Cycle of Adams Letters, 1864–1865*, ed. Worthington Chauncey Ford, vol. 2 (Boston: Houghton Mifflin , 1920), 203–4; Jeffry D. Wert, *The Sword of Lincoln: The Army of the Potomac* (New York: Simon and Schuster), 390–91; Schlesinger, *American Presidential Elections*, 1245.

30. James W. Geary, *We Need More Men: The Union Draft in the Civil War* (DeKalb: Northern Illinois University Press, 1991), 157–58; Sherman quoted in Kirk C. Jenkins, *The Battle Rages Higher: The Union's Fifteenth Kentucky Infantry* (Lexington: University Press of Kentucky, 2003), 245.

31. Skelton, *American Profession of Arms*, 282–97; Brooks D. Simpson, *Ulysses S. Grant: Triumph over Adversity, 1822–1865* (Minneapolis: Zenith , 2000), 288–89; David M. Jordan, *Winfield Scott Hancock: A Soldier's Life* (Bloomington: Indiana University Press, 1995), 165.

32. W. A. Swanberg, *Sickles the Incredible: A Biography of Daniel Edgar Sickles* (New York: Scribner's Sons, 1956), 263–37; Paul R. Wylie, *The Irish General: Thomas Francis Meagher* (Norman: University of Oklahoma Press, 2011), 201, 208–9; David Work, *Lincoln's Political Generals* (Urbana: University of Illinois Press, 2009), 215–18, 223; Waugh, *Reelecting Lincoln*, 304–5.

33. Shankman, *Pennsylvania Antiwar Movement*, 197–98; J. K. Newton to My Dear Mother,

Nov. 9, 1864, in *A Wisconsin Boy in Dixie: Civil War Letters of James K. Newton*, ed. Stephen E. Ambrose (Madison: University of Wisconsin Press, 1995), 127; Davis, *Lincoln's Men*, 220.

34. Rosenblatt and Rosenblatt, *Hard Marching Every Day*, 276 (Nov. 8, 1864); Smith to Aunt Ellen Lee, Nov. 7, 1864, *Aunt and the Soldier Boys: From Cross Creek Village Pennsylvania 1856–1866*, ed. William H Bartlett (New York: McFadden, 1965), 152; White, *Emancipation, the Union Army, and the Reelection of Abraham Lincoln*, 114–20.

35. Robert Grandchamp, *The Boys of Adams' Battery G: The Civil War through the Eyes of a Union Light Artillery Unit* (New York: McFarland, 2009), 263; Cilella, *Upton's Regulars*, 253–54.

36. John to Sister, Oct. 18, 1864, in *Manhood and Patriotic Awakening in the American Civil War: The John E. Mattoon Letters, 1859–1866*, ed. Robert Bruce Donald (Lanham, MD: Hamilton, 2008), 45; J. K. Newton to My Dear Mother, Nov. 9, 1864, in *Wisconsin Boy in Dixie*, 127; Jack to Brother, Nov. 12, 14, 1864, in Collier and Collier, *Yours for the Union*, 375–76; Harvey Reid to Father, Nov. 8, 1864, in Reid, *View from Headquarters*, 198.

37. Schlesinger, *American Presidential Elections*, 1245.

38. Emma Lou Thornbrough, *Indiana in the Civil War Era, 1850–1880* (Indianapolis: Indiana Historical Society, 1965), 220–22.

39. Stephen W. Sears, "A Confederate Cannae and Other Scenarios: How the Civil War Might Have Turned Out Differently," in *The Collected What If?: Eminent Historians Imagine What Might Have Been*, ed. Robert Cowley (New York: G. P. Putnam's Sons, 1999), 255–58; Bruce Levine, *The Fall of the House of Dixie: The Civil War and the Social Revolution That Transformed the South* (New York: Random House, 2013).

40. Christian Bönsel to Brother, Jan. 19, 1865, in Kamphoefner and Helbich, *Germans in the Civil War*, 329–30.

THE HOUR THAT LASTED FIFTY YEARS

The 107th Ohio and the Human Longitude of Gettysburg

Brian Matthew Jordan

A ROUND SIX O'CLOCK ON THE morning of July 1, 1863, the battle-tested veterans of the 107th Ohio Volunteer Infantry, bivouacking near Emmitsburg, Maryland, received orders to trudge north into Pennsylvania. This would be no ordinary Wednesday. Scarcely five miles into the march, a breathless staff officer bolted on horseback toward the regiment, conveying urgent "instructions to hurry forward to General Howard," the one-armed commander of the XI Corps. The distant "noise of firing and cannonading" confirmed that a battle had been joined on the ridges that rippled to the west of a steepled college town called Gettysburg.[1]

The Buckeyes, packed into the XI Corps brigade commanded by Brig. Gen. Adelbert Ames, rushed to the front. They were positioned on the campus of the Adams County almshouse, assigned to hold the right flank of a ribbon of blue-coated troops that now coiled around the Pennsylvania town. The vast expanse of ground between the Carlisle and Harrisburg Roads was especially difficult to defend. In a move that has invited ongoing debate among the battle's devoted students, Ames's division commander, twenty-eight-year-old Harvard valedictorian Brig. Gen. Francis Channing Barlow, summoned his troops to a perch atop a prominence known as Blocher's Knoll. There the Ohioans formed the head of a sharp salient and endured a lethal crossfire from the four Georgia regiments of Brig. Gen. George Doles's brigade, which tore into their left front, and from the men of Brig. Gen. John Gordon's command, who scrambled over the banks of Rock Creek. This blaze was punctuated by the efforts of Lt. Col. Hilary Pollard Jones's Southern artillerists, who pulled their lanyards from positions farther up Harrisburg Road.

The blue-coated soldiers "frantically . . . gnawed paper from cartridges," but in a short interval the rebels overran the Union position, prompting the Federals to scamper through the borough's knotted streets in a harried retreat. They would regroup behind a low stone fence atop Cemetery Hill. Three days later, in an especially stark official report, Capt. John M. Lutz related only that the 107th "suffered heavily in killed and wounded." Decades later the butcher's bill would be chiseled into the blue Westerly granite of the regiment's Gettysburg monument: of 400 personnel engaged, 23 were killed, 111 wounded, and 77 missing, a total loss of 211 men, or nearly 53 percent of the unit's effective strength.[2] The regiment had been shredded.

Rehearsed on battlefield tours, appended to orders of battle, upwardly revised and then endlessly debated, regimental losses have been a currency of Civil War historians since the conflict itself.[3] Beginning with the inventories of the wounded and slain dutifully compiled by William Freeman Fox, Thomas L. Livermore, and Frederick Phisterer in the late nineteenth century, historians have almost mechanically cited the numbers of killed, wounded, missing, and captured to brace their arguments about the heroism of individual units or the size, intensity, and significance of particular engagements.[4] Drew Gilpin Faust's brilliant book *This Republic of Suffering*, together with historical demographer J. David Hacker's "census-based" count of the Civil War dead, invited modern scholars to "stop and reconsider the war's meaning for period Americans." Nevertheless, apart from Lesley J. Gordon's superb history of a hard-luck Connecticut regiment and Susannah J. Ural's work on Hood's Texas Brigade, remarkably few historians have sought to understand the actual meaning of losses—or the lived consequences of battle in the Civil War—for individual units on the ground.[5] Relying on the experiences of a single regiment in a single segment of a single battle, this chapter seeks to recover something of the enduring meaning of losses for the men who fought the Civil War and their loved ones at home; in other words, it aims to measure the human longitude of a fixed moment in this war.[6]

To be certain, this examination makes no pretense to representativeness; as an ethnically German regiment teeming with Democrats, the 107th Ohio Volunteer Infantry was hardly a "typical" unit. At the same time, however, the search for a typical regiment is futile, for each unit experienced the war and its consequences in specific ways. In no small part, then, this study draws much of its interpretive power from its randomness; by inviting us to consider casualties from the bottom up, it forces us to reckon with the reality that the Civil War was composed of thousands of similar hours and actions that, no matter how inconsequentially they may figure into our narratives, rent the fabric of lives, families, and communities. Thus, this look at the 107th Ohio contributes to a much larger and ongoing effort to "rethink" the Civil War regimental history.[7] Furthermore, by getting onto the ground, it invites us to reconsider the "dark turn" in Civil War–era studies. This flood of recent scholarship on the war's violence and its physical, psychological, and environmental consequences has short-circuited our once-congratulatory narratives, inviting both controversy and tart allegations of presentism.[8] Answering these critics, for these veterans and the men and women who cared for them, great physical and emotional suffering was integral to the military narrative of the war and whatever meaning they drew from it. Within the intimate space of the regimental family, the war's devastating realities could never be effaced.

"No Ohio regiment," one local historian insisted of the 107th several decades after the war, "furnishes a more terrible record of its slaughter, or one of more distinguished gallantry."[9] In the late summer of 1862, farmers and shoemakers, carpenters and saddlers gathered in Navarre and Canton, Cleveland and New Philadelphia to enlist in a new unit. Nearly 70 percent of the recruits were foreign born; most were recent German immigrants. Gov. David Tod tapped Seraphim Meyer, a shrewd Canton lawyer, local officeholder, and obedient Democrat, to command the regiment. As with most officers who owed their shoulder straps to patronage, the fact that Meyer had never cracked the spine of a tactical manual was merely a minor detail.[10] Like many new volunteers, these Ohioans anxiously awaited their baptism of fire. "We are for a fight, and if they want to try Gen. Sigel's 'Bully Dutch,' let 'em pitch in," Pvt. Jacob Lichty taunted.[11] After wearisome months of drilling, training, and swinging spades—to say nothing of the numbing winter they weathered in a cheerless, disease-choked camp near Belle Plain, Virginia—the 107th Ohio at last prepared for battle in late April 1863. Maj. Gen. Joseph Hooker had reorganized and rejuvenated the Army of the Potomac, and the men were "in the best of spirits," anticipating victory. "Drawn up in a single line of battle" along an old plank road that led (through a "second-growth Virginia forest") to a crossroads known as Chancellorsville, the regiment assumed a position "on the extreme right" of the Union line and braced themselves for a frontal assault.[12]

That attack never came. Instead, as the sun set on May 2, a "tremendous fire opened upon the flank and rear" of the 107th. After pressing through the scrub on a march around the Union flank, Lt. Gen. Thomas J. "Stonewall" Jackson's troops shattered the XI Corps "with the crushing power of an avalanche." It seemed as though "the population of the lower regions were turned loose to devour [us] upon the spot," Hamilton Starkweather of Company D recalled, yet shuddering at the "wild shrieks and demonic yells" of the rebels. "I never believed that men would fight as well for a miserable cause as the rebels did there for theirs," marveled Adj. Peter F. Young. The Ohioans hastily broke for the rear. "If we had remained five minutes longer," an enlisted man from a neighboring regiment contended, "we [all] should have been killed or taken prisoners."[13] It seemed as though the world had ended; at least 220 officers and men were killed, wounded, or bagged as prisoners that evening. Among the wounded were at least eight beloved officers, including Colonel Meyer and his son, Edward, the captain of Company C. "The battle assumed the character and appearance of a massacre," Jacob Smith declared. Recounting how the "bullets just whistled by my head like a real hailstorm," the 107th's Christian Rieker deemed it nothing short of "a miracle" that he was "still alive."[14]

Beyond the devastating physical losses, the battle produced significant psychological damage. Rieker later reported that since Chancellorsville, Pvt. Godfrey Kappel of Company I had become "very sick," addled by "nervous fever." "He is unaware of what is happening," Rieker explained. "Often he wants to leave, and when one asks him to where, he says to [his home in] Zoar." "In general," he added, "many are dying from the same illness in our regiment."[15] Referring to his "feeble health" as well as the "recent trials and hardships to which the regiment was subjected in the late battles of Chancellorsville," Starkweather "resigned his commission."[16] Sgt. Charles Wimar of Company G was "incapacitated by Insanity."[17] When prompted by a friend to furnish details of the fighting at Chancellorsville, Col. Andrew L. Harris of the 75th Ohio, a regiment brigaded with the 107th, responded that he did "not like to think of the matter long enough to write out the facts." He admitted, "It is rather a hard question for me to answer." A man who served as a captain in the neighboring 55th Ohio later revealed, "I can still see, despite the lapse of more than a third of a century, our regiment falling back from the worse than useless position it was occupying."[18]

Two months later the men again found themselves holding the extreme right of an overextended line, fighting yet another battle under a new army commander. At Gettysburg parallels with Chancellorsville were not lost on the men.[19] The regiment's naïve optimism, on the other hand, *was* lost. John Roedel swiftly and caustically dismissed all pronouncements that Chancellorsville "was the greatest" battle "fought in this war." "If we are asked what was gained by our brave loss of men," he insisted, "the answer is no gain at all." On the eve of the unit's march up to Gettysburg, the men deduced that there would be another battle in the coming days. Regimental historian Jacob Smith noted that it was "with sad and heavily burdened hearts" that the troops "contemplated the picture that presented itself to them now that the issue was near at hand." One veteran recalled of that night, "I stood leaning against a camp stake, gazing dreamily across the hill, with mind reverting to Chancellorsville." Nor did the newspaper editorials—pieces that bristled with nativism as they effortlessly assigned responsibility for Hooker's defeat to the German units of the XI Corps—do much to improve morale.[20]

Gettysburg so convincingly reenacted the horrors of Chancellorsville that Colonel Meyer, having returned to the regiment following his unhappy spell in Libby Prison, emotionally collapsed on the afternoon of July 1. Experience shaped the way that he and his men would respond to the battle. "He appeared fearful of the bullets," recalled one of Howard's staff officers. "I noticed that at the whistling of shells and bullets he would crouch down upon his horse," General Ames observed, "his breast nearly touching the neck of the horse, and at the same time great fear [and] consternation was depicted in his countenance."[21] Patrick Wade of the 17th Connecticut noted years later, "How well I remember the cowardly action of that officer."[22] Leaving his desperate men behind, Meyer bolted from the battlefield and would "not turn up until late the next day."[23]

But by then, all hell had broken loose. In soldiers' postbattle accounts of July 1, it was here that narrative momentum stalled; otherwise detailed letters and diaries devolved into an arduous catalogue of grisly human destruction. What emerges most plainly from the documents is the inability of the men to assemble a coherent chronicle of events. Consider, for example, Capt. Barnet Steiner's July 8 letter to his brother, William: "Our right was compelled for a short time to fall back," he began.

> This was in the early part of the engagement. I was shot in the left shoulder blade, the ball lodging in my breast where it still is and will likely remain. H. Flora was shot through the left breast where the ball lodged. We are both in the hospital together. Among the others in the Company wounded are Hoagland, the little finger; Burnheimer, thigh, ball extracted; Tinkler, in head, pretty bad; L. McKinney, on cheek; Keiffer, same; Dine, forearm; Finkenbiner, shell struck on hip; Keedy and Exline, I think killed; also Palmer, and Lohm and Sinclare taken prisoners; several not heard from.

Fritz Nussbaum's reminiscences make for similarly grim reading: "Soon they succeeded in getting their Batteries to the rear of us and we were compelled to retreat towards the town. The shell that took Major Vignos' arm off, striking the ground bounced up again and killed some officer's horse. Lieutenant Fisher was also badly wounded, having his leg nearly shot off, and was left on the field for dead; also many others." Pvt. John Flory dispatched the battle in his wartime diary, perhaps concluding that the afternoon's events were ineffable, by making no real attempt to translate them into paragraphs or prose.[24]

Devastated for the second time in as many battles, their wounded heaping from ambulance wagons and their dead littering the field, life would never again be the same for the 107th Ohio or their loved ones back home in northeastern Ohio. "We learn that the 107th O.V.I. suffered severely in the late battles at Gettysburg," Canton's *Stark County Democrat* reported on July 15, though it quickly qualified, "we have heard but few particulars."[25] For men and women like Catherine and John Heiss, anxious for a report from their eldest child, William, a private in Company B, it seemed as though those "particulars" would never arrive. Making their residence in a tiny dwelling on Cleveland's Parkman Street (according to Catherine's brother, "the house was little better than a shanty"), the couple, their "industrious" habits notwithstanding, could scarcely support their seven children. Indeed, prior to his enlistment, William worked in a spice mill to supplement his father's earnings as a planer at Sheppherd's Lumber. "They had [a] hard enough time getting along as it was," observed John Grimm, a family acquaintance.[26]

The news arrived that autumn. After receiving a spiteful gunshot wound at Blocher's Knoll, typhoid fever set in, and the nineteen-year-old volunteer died in an army hospital in York, Pennsylvania, about thirty miles east of Gettysburg. John Heiss was inconsolable. "He seemed to break down right after the boy died and was never afterward the man he had been," Grimm noted. "He was sick all over," Catherine attested, and "barely able to work." John "was never much sick till [our] soldier died." Without a steady income, the grieving mother was "compelled to take in washing" as she waited on the federal government to approve her application for William's pension. All the while this "strong woman" who spoke "but little English" tended to the needs of her heartbroken husband. Despite the efforts of his doctors and months of medicine, Heiss "worried himself to death," expiring on September 22, 1864, exactly one year and one month after William's passing.[27] Because Catherine's husband was living at the time of their son's death, the Pension Bureau determined that she was "not dependent on [the] soldier" and rejected her application for relief in April 1867. Not until Pres. Benjamin Harrison signed the Dependent Pension Act of 1890, which gave all honorably discharged Union soldiers access to federal pension dollars, would a full pension certificate be issued to her. But by that time she was in the last decade of her life, living for a while with each of her adult sons and obliged to rent out the old family home for income.[28]

In her penury Catherine Heiss was hardly unique among the survivors and families of the 107th Ohio. Nor was the maddening back and forth with the Pension Bureau—her litany of earnest claims—very exceptional. Because time very often amplified soldiers' wartime injuries, sometimes incapacitating them for trades or manual labor, many veterans became dependent on pensions to support their families.[29] Securing a claim, however, demanded an intimate, working knowledge of the thicket of pension rules, statutes, and legislation (so bewildering that many, of necessity, relied upon the services of pension attorneys such as Milo B. Stevens & Company, James Schoonover, W. W. Clark, or Stoddart & Company). Securing a claim likewise required that veterans supply reams of notarized documents testifying to the wartime origins of their injuries and the soundness of their character. John Becker supplied typical testimony on behalf of Charles Wahler's claim—"I saw him when he held a cloth or something over his head and saw the Blood running down his face," he averred— as did Capt. George Billow of Akron, who described "from personal observation" Theobold Hasman's many physical and psychological struggles. Finally, securing a pension claim condemned the maimed and wounded to a battery of invasive medical examinations.[30] During annual or biennial visits, examining surgeons (not infrequently the very surgeons who assessed their fitness for the army upon their enlistments) evaluated the "degree of disability" so as to determine the appropriate grade of compensation, sometimes making asides about the veterans' "moral habits." These visits likewise sought to combat potential pension fraud.

Not surprisingly, veterans resented these exams; they could become dyspeptic after receiving the examiner's reports. John Leffler, who endured recurring spells of numbness in his right leg, where rebel lead had lodged on July 1, insisted candidly in the fall of 1883 that he was "entitled to a higher rate," his pension being "graded too low for degree of disability."[31] Frank Rothermel sought an increase in his four-dollar monthly pension certificate for nearly three decades before he was successful. Atop Blocher's Knoll, a ball had ripped through his head, entering below his left ear and ejecting three teeth before exiting under the right. "Sleepless in the night," he found it difficult to eat, unable to "move his jaw so as to open his teeth more than 1/3 inch."[32] Daniel Whitmer demanded an increase in the pension he received for the loss of his left leg, amputated in a Gettysburg field hospital after the struggle with the Georgians. Disposed to falls and irritated by his government-issued artificial limb, which chafed his stump, the septuagenarian appealed for a higher rating in March 1905. This prompted the Pension Bureau to dispatch a medical investigator to his Canton home with painstaking instructions to measure and trace the stump, "to determine definitely the point of amputation of claimant's left leg," and to "describe the condition of the knee joint, stump, and cicatrix."[33]

Much like Whitmer (and as the historian Megan Kate Nelson has pointed out), amputees brimmed with almost unanimous frustration about the quality of their prostheses. Soon after his discharge twenty-two-year-old Daniel Biddle of Company A, whose left leg was amputated six weeks after the battle, journeyed more than two hundred miles to Cincinnati, Ohio, to be fitted with a wooden leg. "He would put it on," a friend recalled, "and after wearing it a short time the stump would get sore, and he would have to lay it aside. When the sores were healed he would try it again with the same results. . . .[I]t often made him sick." Moored in bed for at least two weeks on one such occasion, Biddle called upon his cousin to tend the "little grocery" he operated in Navarre. He quickly learned that he "would get around better on his crutches," John Biddle observed.[34] In the late 1860s Frederick Tonsing tried two prosthetic appliances manufactured by Benjamin Palmer, the New Hampshire doctor who landed the patent for an artificial leg more than a decade before the war; however, because surgeons amputated Tonsing's right leg "very close up to his body," the luckless soldier spent the rest of his life on Cleveland's West Side dependent on crutches, nursing a "tender stump." His sworn testimony notwithstanding, examining surgeons from the Pension Bureau refused to believe that he required the "constant aid and attendance of another person."[35]

Considering the profound skepticism with which pension examiners greeted veterans tending perceptible wounds, one can only imagine the obstacles—to say nothing of the struggles—faced by the scores of men who battled the effects of injuries, chronic diseases, and ailments that, while no less painful, were nonetheless inconspicuous. Tom Hoagland, whose painful wound was among those recorded in Captain Steiner's letter, returned from the war "a broken down man." Neighbors attested that "he suffered from general ill health and a broken constitution," describing his jaundiced complexion and recurring bouts of "constipation" and "indigestion."[36] The "shooting pains" that emanated from Jacob Thumm's "shattered" shoulder seemed not to trouble him nearly as much as his piles, chronic diarrhea, and "general debility."[37] Aaron Burnheimer complained about his "dim" eyesight, the result of "a shell bursted over our heads."[38] Nor was there a government form that could rate "the burning sensation" in Samuel Schwab's fractured tibia or adequately compensate him for the sleep he lost while feverishly itching the "painful" scab that would develop "around" his wound. It was little wonder that he felt his pension "unjustly and unreasonably low." And how was one to evaluate the ugly shell wound that not only deafened but also badly disfigured East Sparta, Ohio, native Lanson McKinney's face?[39]

Men who were "broken down" depended on spouses, children, and former comrades for aid and assistance. Harrison Flora would lose the "entire use" of his right arm and hand "for days." The musket ball that struck his shoulder atop Blocher's Knoll "remained lodged" beneath the skin for a year and half afterward as an unwelcome souvenir of Gettysburg. "Confined" to his home nearly "three fourths of the time," he had "to be waited on as a child."[40] Often restricted to his bed, Arnold Streum probably spent many nights lying in urine, his July 1 injury having rendered him not only "utterly unfit to perform any physical labor" but also incontinent.[41] Nicholas Lopendahl's wound, first treated in Gettysburg and then again at the U.S. Military Hospital in Philadelphia, rendered his right arm "totally useless." "I often saw [his] wife . . . bring in cold water to bathe [his] right hand and arm . . . so as to take the fever out," alleged one of his neighbors, who claimed to have assisted the veteran "in washing and dressing himself."[42]

Perhaps most dependent on assistance was Henry Feldkamp, the Cleveland carpenter who, at the age of thirty-four, enlisted as a sergeant in Company E. At the knoll Confederate lead slammed into his left thigh "just above the knee," placing pressure on the sciatic nerve. After several failed attempts to extract the musket ball, it festered there for more than a decade, sending stubborn currents of pain rushing up his sore-pocked limb. His knee, which routinely wept fluid and fragments of bone, swelled to more than twice its natural circumference. "Quite stiff," he could not stand, could not sleep, and could "scarcely get about." Unable to work, Feldkamp moved into a boarding-house on Oregon Street, where a matron had to "daily wait upon him, clothe him, . . . bathe him," drain and elevate his leg, and "bring his food to him." "He is about as helpless as a child," she wailed in lament.[43]

Survivors lacking a caretaker—or who lost one either to death or divorce— sometimes sought "sanctuary" in a local, state, or federal soldiers' home. When John Hemmerling's devoted wife passed away in 1885, the rheumatic veteran still nursing the effects of a gunshot wound moved from Cleveland to the Milwaukee campus of the National Home for Disabled Volunteer Soldiers. The "last reveille" sounded for Frederick Jungling, still suffering from the injury to his left shoulder, at the Ohio State Soldiers' and Sailors' Home in Sandusky. In seeking admission to a soldiers' home, others desired a "reprieve" from unhappy stations in life. "Very eas[ily] excited," Henry Klingaman from Company H "thought he would be better contented at the Soldiers' Home, . . . where he could have the companionship of other soldiers." Klingaman seemed to enjoy his life at the home, but as the historian James Marten and others have pointed out, many of his fellow inmates could not brook life there and griped about their "wretched" conditions.[44]

Mental- and emotional-health issues delivered quite a few veterans to these facilities. Emlen Landon, who suffered a severe gunshot wound to his head on that fated July afternoon, entered the Sandusky home in March 1894, "subject to sudden attacks of violent pain in [his] head" and "spells of dizziness," during which he became "almost completely blind." The twenty-year-old brick maker from Stark County never got over his injury. "His friends claim there has been an entire change in his disposition since receiving his wound," one pension affidavit declared. "[He] complains of being very nervous at times." After three years at the Ohio Home, Landon was discharged for "violating the rules," more than likely the result of an alcohol addiction. He entered the Danville, Illinois, branch of the National Home in January 1899, but from it, too, he would be "dishonorably" discharged only five years later. Fortunately the administrators of the Ohio Home overlooked Landon's previous debauchery and readmitted the homeless old veteran; while absent without leave on the fourteenth anniversary of his first admission to a soldiers' home, Landon was discovered dead of "acute alcoholism."[45]

The musket ball that tore through Pvt. Frederick Bross's body on the retreat from the knoll not only forced the former blacksmith to "quit his business" but also "eventually [a]ffected his mind to such an extent" that he was deposited in Columbus's Central Ohio Insane Asylum. The loss of his trade, unyielding pain, and the "large" exit wound that disfigured his body were simply too much for him.[46] Charles Cordier continued to work in his butcher's shop after he returned home from the war, but the shell that struck his head at Gettysburg continued to vex him. The veteran suffered from "fits every two or three weeks," during which he would "lose control of his mind" and experience lapses in memory. Perhaps trusting that a more salubrious climate might aid his condition, Cordier moved to Jacksonville, Florida, not terribly far from where the regiment toiled on entrenchments following its post-Gettysburg transfer to the war's periphery, the Department of the South. But his health continued to wane. On the morning of August 10, 1889, Cordier's wife awoke to an empty house. Hours later a local police captain discovered her husband's body bobbing "in the St. John's River at the foot of Liberty street." Considering that "for the past two weeks" he had "suffered much from an abscess on his cheek, and from wounds in the head received in the late war," the jury of inquest deemed him on "the verge of insanity" and his death a suicide. For this veteran of the 107th Ohio, twenty-six years later and eight hundred miles away, the battle for Blocher's Knoll—and all of the pain it prompted—was finally over.[47]

On the morning of Wednesday, September 14, 1887, the survivors of the 107th Ohio gathered at Christ Lutheran Church on Chambersburg Street, just off the town "diamond" in Gettysburg. From the church they marched to the storied slopes of Blocher's Knoll. It was "Ohio Day," and along with many other Buckeye State veterans, they had returned to dedicate a regimental monument on the bloodiest battlefield of the war. As the bended and furrowed soldiers huddled around "Ohio's Token of Gratitude," a tiny knot of civilian onlookers gathered behind. On an earlier trip to that field (now embellished with marble and bronze, represented as the "high water mark of the rebellion"), the regiment's historian noted how Gettysburg's scenes "presented themselves again in almost actual, living reality." On this day those scenes must have played themselves over yet again in the minds of many.[48]

Earlier that morning, Ohio's walrus-mustached governor, Joseph Benson Foraker, delivered an address in the National Cemetery that alternated between appeals for sectional reconciliation and "bloody shirt" waving. "Gettysburg," he professed, "was more than a mere battle. It was more than the turning point of a great war. It was an epoch in the history of the world—a crowning triumph for the human race." He continued: "Almost a quarter of a century has passed. The moving columns, glittering bayonets, flashing sabers and charging squadrons of that fearful time are gone forever. The rattling musketry and roaring cannon of the mighty struggle are hushed. Where [there] was the carnage of war is now only peace."[49]

Or that is how it seemed. To be sure, more than a few soldiers returned from the Civil War unscathed; without generating much in the way of a documentary record, they "returned home to become vital members" of "families, communities, and states," making "individual transitions with a surprising degree of success." Maj. Augustus Vignos, for example, who lost his right arm in the battle and delivered "patriotic" remarks at the dedication ceremony, operated a cutlery company until his death in 1925. Active in his local Grand Army of the Republic (GAR) post, he also took a turn as Canton's postmaster. Colonel Meyer mended his reputation after being charged with cowardice; he sat on the Stark County Court of Common Pleas following the war. And there were enlisted men like Theobold Hasman who, though frequently unable to raise his arms, returned home and endured his battle injuries "with patience";

"though a constant sufferer," according to his former comrade and Akron neighbor Capt. George Billow, he "seldom complained."[50]

As the new century dawned, even some of the most cynical old soldiers muffled their misgivings about the war and peddled a new, nostalgic narrative—one that did not pose a threat to the nation's sterilized memory of the conflict. Nonetheless, even these veterans could never truly escape war's legacy of physical and emotional pain. Historian Susannah J. Ural has pointed out that Civil War outfits, most of which were harvested from adjoining counties and geographic regions, did not easily—if ever—disintegrate after the war. Living together as veterans in the same villages and towns that they had left behind in the fall of 1862, attending GAR meetings with former comrades, and supplying much of the supporting testimony for each other's pension cases, the men of the 107th Ohio lived with urgent, intimate, and recurring reminders of the war's human costs; it was difficult for these old soldiers to "move on" when they were confronted so regularly with raw evidence of the war's devastating effects. "We have met each other quite frequently ever since the war of the Rebellion," Isaac Shell explained candidly. The old veterans attended GAR post meetings together (the muster rolls of the William McKinley Post No. 25 in Canton, for example, list no fewer than thirty-five men who had served in the 107th Ohio), looked in on each other, supported disability pension claims, and appeared jointly before local notaries to ink supporting affidavits. As the unit's regimental history (like many contributions to the genre, a work of collaboration among the survivors) explained in verse:

> The sounds of war are silent now;
> We call no man our foe,
> But soldier hearts cannot forget
> The scenes of long ago.[51]

A number of recent scholars have sought to describe those "soldier hearts" and the postwar world. Understanding that words have often imposed "on war . . . [a] . . . coherence it does not possess," these historians have asked some tough questions about the Civil War's consequences, increasingly approaching the conflict from the perspective of individuals. Critics maintain that this fragmentation will erode our comprehension of the war's significance and the heft of its accomplishments. In an important essay the historians Gary W. Gallagher and Kathryn Shively Meier lament the "preoccupation with the war's 'dark side'" and a growing library of books on "atrocities, cowardice, needless bloodshed, physical maiming, or mental breakdowns among soldiers and veterans"; they insist that this trend will lead readers to "infer that atypical experiences were in fact normative ones." Likewise, Peter Carmichael supposes that "largely responsible for the distorted portrait of Civil War veterans as a lost generation" is an "antiwar" presentism. "Our desire to encourage empathy for soldiers in the past and in the present can easily lead to sloppy thinking," he writes. "If we insist on portraying Civil War soldiers as either depressed or deranged, we then risk losing the crucial realities of the Civil War, and quite likely much of our popular audiences who want to find strength in their histories, rather than history lessons used to point out the moral failings of the United States as a world power today."

One wonders how the men of the 107th Ohio would respond to these suggestions. For them—as for many veterans—the pain of the war became a profound source of their pride. As Civil War historians, we need to do a better job of explaining how actual people on the ground intuited, experienced, and rummaged through the meaning of their participation in the conflict. To restore to view the war's human consequences is not to embrace the barren notion that these veterans were "victims" and their suffering "needless"; to the contrary, it is to acknowledge "crucial realities" that traditional narratives have noiselessly effaced. For those who lived it, the conflict was not a coherent narrative, but rather a parade of "episodes" that could beguile or exhilarate, anguish or inspire. Only in retrospect did the war read like an epic, and only with the passage of time did individual battles assume their logic, rationality, or sense of significance. For the men and women discussed above, Gettysburg was an event with multiple meanings, not all of which were reassuring or decisive. For these men and women, Gettysburg meant a shattered limb, a disfigured face, or a kaleidoscope of images unmoored from any context. Until we measure the human longitude of Civil War battles and the shadows that those events cast over regimental families and ordinary towns—until we consider much more than the tactical consequences of those arrows, squiggles, and lines on our battlefield maps—our military historical narratives will remain inadequate. An hour in the Civil War could indeed last fifty years.[52]

Brian Matthew Jordan

NOTES

1. Jacob Smith, *Camps and Campaigns of the 107th Ohio Volunteer Infantry, 1862–1865* (1910; repr., Navarre, OH: Indian River Graphics, 2000), 86; U.S. War Department, *The War of the Rebellion: A Compilation of the Official Records of the Union and Confederate Armies,* 70 vols. in 128 pts. (Washington, D.C.: Government Printing Office, 1880–1901), ser. 1, 27(1):720; Silas Shuler to Asa Shuler, July 16, 1863, *Pennsylvania Folklife* 29, no. 3 (Spring 1980), copy in 107th Ohio Regimental File, Gettysburg National Military Park Library, Gettysburg, PA (hereafter cited as GNMPL); B. T. Steiner to W. H. Steiner, July 8, 1863, in Smith, *Camps and Campaigns,* 235. See also Harry W. Pfanz, *Gettysburg: The First Day* (Chapel Hill: University of North Carolina Press, 2001), 138.

2. Smith, *Camps and Campaigns,* 86–87; War Department, *War of the Rebellion,* ser. 1, 27(1):720, 721, 712–13; *Summit County Beacon* (Akron, OH), Sept. 21, 1887; William B. Southerton Memoir, William B. Southerton Papers, Ohio Historical Society, Columbus (hereafter cited as OHS). See also *Report of the Gettysburg Memorial Commission* (1877; repr., Baltimore: Butternut and Blue, 1998), 41; and *Canton (OH) Repository and Republican,* Sept. 22, 1871.

3. See J. David Hacker, "A Census-Based Count of the Civil War Dead," *Civil War History* 57, no. 4 (Dec. 2011): 307–48; Mark Neely, *The Civil War and the Limits of Destruction* (Cambridge, MA: Harvard University Press, 2007); Nicholas Marshall, "The Great Exaggeration: Death and the Civil War," *Journal of the Civil War Era* 4, no. 1 (Mar. 2014): 3–27; J. David Hacker, "Has the Demographic Impact of Civil War Deaths Been Exaggerated?" *Civil War History* 60, no. 4 (Dec. 2014): 453–58.

4. William Fox, *Regimental Losses in the American Civil War* (Albany: Albany Publishing, 1889); Thomas L. Livermore, *Numbers and Losses in the Civil War in America, 1861–1865* (Boston: Houghton, Mifflin, 1900); Frederick Phisterer, *Statistical Record of the Armies of the United States* (New York: Charles Scribner's Sons, 1883). For a recent effort that testifies to an enduring fascination with counting the Civil War dead, see Darrell L. Collins, *The Army of the Potomac: Order of Battle, 1861–1865, with Commanders, Strengths, Losses, and More* (Jefferson, NC: McFarland, 2013).

5. Drew Gilpin Faust, *This Republic of Suffering: Death and the Civil War* (New York: Alfred A. Knopf, 2008); Lesley J. Gordon, introduction to Hacker, "Census-Based Count of the Civil War Dead," 308 (quote); Gordon, *A Broken Regiment: The Sixteenth Connecticut's Civil War* (Baton Rouge: Louisiana State University Press, 2014); Susannah J. Ural, "'In Good Shape, Relative to the Rest of the South'? Confederate Veterans and Their Communities in Post–Civil War Texas," paper delivered at Society for Military History Annual Meeting, Apr. 16, 2016, Ottawa, Ontario, copy in author's possession. This chapter confirms and builds on Ural's important insights. For important exceptions that predate both the "memory boom" and the "dark turn," see Kenneth W. Noe, *Perryville: This Grand Havoc of Battle* (Lexington: University Press of Kentucky, 2001); and Megan McClintock, "Civil War Pensions and the Reconstruction of Union Families," *Journal of American History* 83, no. 2 (1996): 456–80. Lastly, Carol Reardon and Tom Vossler spice their Gettysburg battlefield guide with vignettes drawn from pension files. See *A Field Guide to Gettysburg: Experiencing the Battlefield through Its History, Places, and People* (Chapel Hill: University of North Carolina Press, 2013).

6. Relying on the annotated regimental roster appended to the unit's official 1910 regimental history, I compiled a list of men killed, wounded, or captured at Gettysburg on the afternoon of July 1. Using these names, I searched the federal pension index for applications made by or certificates awarded to these men and/or their families. I then reviewed the extant applicants and certificates—as well as relevant material from postwar newspapers, census records, and genealogical data—to assemble a picture of how survivors lived on. Despite an early appeal from Maris Vinovskis, Civil War scholars, much unlike historians of colonial or early America, have not been quick to embrace either the community study or genealogical methods. My thanks to David Blight for making this point. For an exceptional case study of an Indiana county, see Nicole Etcheson, *A Generation at War: The Civil War Era in a Northern Community* (Lawrence: University Press of Kansas, 2011).

7. On regimental histories, see Peter Luebke, introduction to Albion Tourgee, *The Story of a Thousand* (Kent, OH: Kent State University Press, 2011); and Gordon, *Broken Regiment*, 3, 237n9. A roundtable discussion, "New Approaches to Old Questions," held at the Society of Civil War Historians biennial meeting in Chattanooga, Tennessee, in 2016 featured Susannah J. Ural's paper, "Why Unit Histories Still Matter."

8. On the "dark turn," see Yael Sternhell, "Revisionism Reinvented? The Antiwar Turn in Civil War Scholarship," *Journal of the Civil War Era* 3, no. 2 (June 2013): 239–56. For important contributions that fall under this heading, see, for example, Stephen Berry, ed., *Weirding the War: Stories from the Civil War's Ragged Edges* (Athens: University of Georgia Press, 2011); Michael C. C. Adams, *Living Hell: The Dark Side of the Civil War* (Baltimore: Johns Hopkins University Press, 2014); Brian Matthew Jordan, *Marching Home: Union Veterans and Their Unending Civil War* (New York: Liveright/W. W. Norton, 2014); and Matthew Stith, *Extreme Civil War: Guerrilla Warfare, Environment, and Race on the Trans-Mississippi Frontier* (Baton Rouge: Louisiana State University Press, 2016).

9. William Henry Perrin, ed., *History of Stark County: With an Outline Sketch of Ohio* (Chicago: Baskin and Battey, 1881), 264.

10. Smith, *Camps and Campaigns*, 9–10, 13; 107th Ohio Regimental Descriptive Books, RG 94, National Archives Building, Washington, D.C. (hereafter cited as NA); "From the 107th Ohio, on [Folly] Island, South Carolina," *The Crisis* (Columbus, OH), Oct. 28, 1863; "From the 107th Regiment—The Democratic Soldiers Not Permitted to Vote," *Crawford County Forum* (Bucyrus, OH), Nov. 20, 1863.

11. Jacob Lichty to Daniel Lichty, Dec. 28, 1862, Folder 3, Box 2, Thomas J. Edwards Papers, Center for Archival Collections, Jerome Library, Bowling Green State University, Bowling Green, OH.

12. Smith, *Camps and Campaigns*, 67, 73; Capt. E. R. Monfort, "The First Division, Eleventh Corps, at Chancellorsville," in *Papers Read before Fred C. Jones Post, No. 401, Department of Ohio, Grand Army of the Republic*, vol. 1 (Cincinnati: Fred C. Jones Post, 1891), 61.

13. Smith, *Camps and Campaigns*, 67, 73; "From the 107th Ohio," *Daily Cleveland Herald*, May 25, 1863; "Army Correspondence," ibid., May 14, 1863; James Middlebrook to his wife, May 10, 1863, Middlebrook Family Papers, 1782–1929, Connecticut Historical Society, Hartford. See also "Letter from the 107th Regiment," *Defiance (OH) Democrat*, May 23, 1863.

14. Whitelaw Reid, *Ohio in the War: Her Statesman, Her Generals, and Soldiers*, vol. 2 (Cincin-

nati: Moore, Wilstach, and Baldwin, 1868), 577; *Elyria (OH) Independent Democrat*, July 29, 1863; Smith, *Camps and Campaigns*, 74; Christian Rieker to his sister, May 11, 1863, Folder 1, Box 96, Society of Separatists of Zoar Records, OHS. See also "From the 107th Regiment," *Stark County Republican* (Canton, OH) July 1, 1863.

15. Christian Rieker to Mari Rouf, May 30, 1863, Folder 1, Box 96, Society of Separatists of Zoar Records.

16. "From the 107th Ohio," *Daily Cleveland Herald*, May 25, 1863.

17. "Special Orders No. 22," 107th Ohio Volunteers Descriptive Books, vol. 4, RG 94, NA.

18. Andrew Harris to "Friend Lough," June 7, 1863, Folder 1, Box 1, Andrew L. Harris Papers, OHS; "Letter from the 107th Regiment," *Defiance (OH) Democrat*, May 23, 1863; Capt. W. S. Wickham, "Recollections of Chancellorsville," in *Trials and Triumphs: The Record of the Fifty-Fifth Ohio Volunteers*, ed. Hartwell Osborn (Chicago: A. C. McClurg, 1904), 77.

19. An unidentified soldier from the 17th Connecticut Volunteers, a unit brigaded with the 107th Ohio, noted of July 1, "the experience of Chancellorsville was here repeated." See "17th Connecticut Infantry," memoir, 17th Connecticut Regimental File, GNMPL, typescript; and James Bailey [alias Manton], "Under Guard or Sunny South in Slices," *Danbury (CT) Times*, Sept. 17, 1863.

20. "Letter from the 107th Regiment," *Defiance (OH) Democrat*, May 23, 1863; Smith, *Camps and Campaigns*, 86; "Manton's Gettysburg," 17th Connecticut Regimental File, GNMPL, typescript; "The 11th Corps," *Sandusky (OH) Register*, May 30, 1863; "The Eleventh Corps at Chancellorsville," *National Tribune*, Oct. 22, 1885; "From the 107th Regiment," *Stark County Republican* (Canton, OH), July 1, 1863.

21. Seraphim Meyer Court-Martial Transcript, RG 153, NA.

22. Patrick Wade to M. H. Daniels, Mar. [?], 1886, 17th Connecticut Regimental File, GNMPL, typescript.

23. "From the 25th Ohio—A Correction as to Gettysburg, and a Sketch of the Closing Days of the War," *National Tribune*, June 4, 1885. Temporarily relieved of command, Meyer was court-martialed for cowardice at Gettysburg. An error in the conduct of the ensuing trial resulted in a dismissal of the charges despite persuasive evidence of his guilt. Still, Meyer would not escape scrutiny; in 1864, after failing a test of tactical knowledge, he was relieved of command.

24. B. T. Steiner to W. H. Steiner, July 8, 1863, in Smith, *Camps and Campaigns*, 235–36; Fritz Nussbaum Reminiscences, ibid., 225 (quoted); John Flory Diary, 107th Ohio Regimental File, GNMPL, copy.

25. "The 107th," *Stark County Democrat* (Canton, OH), July 15, 1863. See also "Gettysburg," *Canton (OH) Repository*, July 22, 1863.

26. William H. Heiss Pension File, application 131,306, certificate 281,913, RG 15, NA.

27. Ibid.

28. Ibid. On the Dependent Pension Act of 1890, see also Jordan, *Marching Home*.

29. Joseph Romig Pension File, application 193,514, certificate 130,870, RG 15, NA; Joseph Weis Pension File, application 558,604, certificate 349,368, ibid.

30. George Zuern Pension File, application 199,307, certificate 138,981; Joseph Kieffer Pension File, application 85,881, certificate 107,288; Philip May Pension File, application 596,485,

certificate 365,482; Charles Mueller Pension File, application 36,223, certificate 21,388; and Theobald Hasman Pension File, application 78,049, certificate 51,003, ibid.

31. John Leffler Pension File, application 114,733, certificate 156,058, ibid.

32. Frank Rothermel Pension File, application 99, 713, certificate 57,730, ibid.

33. Daniel Whitmer Pension File, application 42,007, certificate 28,466, ibid.

34. Daniel Biddle Pension File, application 49,149, certificate 45,074, ibid.

35. Frederick Tonsing Pension File, application 50,849, certificate 33,198, ibid.

36. Thomas Hoagland Pension File, application 475,343, certificate 517,409, ibid.

37. Jacob Thumm Pension File, application 359,132, certificate 214,806, ibid. Scholars have not paid enough attention to the legacy of chronic ailments and diseases among Civil War veterans. James Marten also notes the need for additional work on this topic in *Sing Not War: The Lives of Union and Confederate Veterans in Gilded Age America* (Chapel Hill: University of North Carolina Press, 2011).

38. Aaron Burnheimer Pension File, application 531,181, certificate 315,044, RG 15, NA; "The Deaf Soldier—Why He Is Entitled to a Larger Pension Than He Now Receives," *Wilmot (OH) Review*, Mar. 21, 1889.

39. Samuel Schwab Pension File, application 41,243, certificate 27,897; and Lanson McKinney Pension File, application 558,708, certificate 396,638, RG 15, NA.

40. Harrison Flora Pension File, application 104,423, certificate 63,484, ibid.

41. Arnold Streum Pension File, application 73,937, certificate 50,375, ibid.

42. Nicholas Lopendahl Pension File, application 108,683, certificate 85,101, ibid.

43. Henry Feldkamp Pension File, application 101,337, certificate 58,251, ibid.

44. Henry Klingaman Pension File, application 226,324, certificate 151,844, ibid.

45. John Hemmerling Pension File, application 145,879, certificate 99,665; and Emlen Morgan Landon Pension File, application 338,343, certificate 222,446, RG 15, NA; Admission Records for Emlen Landon, Ohio State Soldiers' and Sailors' Home, Microfilm 3399, OHS; Historical Register of National Homes for Disabled Volunteer Soldiers, 1866–1938, Microfilm M1749, 282 rolls, RG 15; NA. On life in soldiers' homes, see Jordan, *Marching Home;* Marten, *Sing Not War;* and Patrick J. Kelly, *Creating a National Home: Building the Veterans' Welfare State, 1860–1900* (Cambridge, MA: Harvard University Press, 1997).

46. Frederick Bross Pension File, application 134,062, certificate 93,743, RG 15, NA.

47. Charles T. Cordier Pension File, application 415,799, certificate 460,095, ibid.

48. "The 107th Dedication at Gettysburg," *Canton (OH) Weekly Repository,* Sept. 29, 1887; "Ohio at Gettysburg," *Cleveland Plain Dealer,* Sept. 14, 1887; "Memorial Address," *Gettysburg Star and Sentinel,* Nov. 1, 1887; Smith, *Camps and Campaigns,* 126–27, 133.

49. "107th Dedication at Gettysburg"; "Ohio at Gettysburg"; "Memorial Address"; Smith, *Camps and Campaigns,* 126–27, 133.

50. Paul Cimbala, *Veterans North and South: The Transition from Soldier to Civilian after the American Civil War* (Santa Barbara, CA: Praeger, 2015), xv; *Journal of the Executive Proceedings of the Senate of the United States of America, from March 4, 1885 to March 4, 1887, Inclusive* (Washington, D.C.: Government Printing Office, 1901), 259. On Augustus Vignos, see "Real Knife Lore: Augustus Vignos" thread, Specialty Forums, Knife Forum, All about Pocket Knives list, June 30,

2009, http://www.allaboutpocketknives.com/knife_forum/viewtopic.php?t=13701; Headquarters Book, William McKinley Post No. 25, Grand Army of the Republic, William McKinley Presidential Library, Canton, OH; and *Honor Roll and History, William McKinley Post No. 25, Canton, Ohio* (Canton: S. T. May, 1932).

51. Philip Seltzer Pension File, application 149,360, certificate 101,745, RG 15, NA; Smith, *Camps and Campaigns*, 217; Headquarters Book, William McKinley Post No. 25; *Honor Roll and History, William McKinley Post No. 25*. Here and throughout, my ideas about the significance of veterans' geographic proximity to one another (and their continued interactions with one another) are indebted to Susannah Ural.

52. Wayne Hsieh, review of *The Battle of Ezra Church and the Struggle for Atlanta*, by Earl J. Hess, in *Civil War Monitor*, Nov. 18, 2015, www.civilwarmonitor.com/blogs/hess-the-battle-of-ezra-church-and-the-struggle-for-atlanta-2015; Gary W. Gallagher and Kathryn Shively Meier, "Coming to Terms with Civil War Military History," *Journal of the Civil War Era* 4, no. 4 (Dec. 2014): 492; Peter S. Carmichael, "Relevance, Resonance, and Historiography: Interpreting the Lives and Experiences of Civil War Soldiers," *Civil War History* 62, no. 2 (June 2016): 184, 173. At the Society of Civil War Historians biennial meeting in 2016, Lesley J. Gordon made similar points in remarks aimed at the critics of the "dark turn." I am indebted to John J. Hennessy, who over the years has helped me think about the war as a sequence of "episodes." Also useful here is Michael E. Woods's thoughtful essay, "Interdisciplinary Studies of the Civil War Era: Recent Trends and Future Prospects," *Journal of American Studies* 51, no. 2 (2017): 349–83.

"HIS DEATH MAY HAVE
LOST THE SOUTH HER INDEPENDENCE"

Albert Sidney Johnston and Civil War Memory

Robert L. Glaze

O N APRIL 6, 1862, Confederate general Albert Sidney Johnston, commanding the soon-to-be-christened Army of Tennessee, was seemingly
on the cusp of a great victory over Union general Ulysses S. Grant. Despite
recent defeats that had tarnished his once-sterling reputation, Johnston had
managed to surprise Grant with an attack at Shiloh Church in southwestern
Tennessee. Union forces soon recovered from their initial shock, however, and
began offering stiffer resistance. Johnston, hoping to maintain the initiative,
inspire his men, and no doubt restore his reputation and honor, led from the
front all day. Around two o'clock in the afternoon, he took charge of a battered
and demoralized regiment. After riding along its line, tapping the tips of the
men's bayonets with a tin cup, he called out, "I will lead you!" With their
commanding general guiding them, the reenergized troops surged forward,
driving back the Union forces in their front. Despite this localized success the
battle continued, Johnston in the thick of it. But suddenly he reeled in the
saddle, having been struck in the right calf by a spent round. Quickly losing
consciousness, the general was helped off his horse by a staff member. Having
sent his personal surgeon to tend to Union wounded, Johnston was without
medical aid and at two thirty died of blood loss. The tide soon turned, and the
following day Shiloh became one of the most significant Union victories of the
war, an indispensable step in the ascendance of U. S. Grant.[1]

Twenty-one years later, aging Confederate veterans gathered in Metairie
Cemetery in New Orleans to decorate the graves of fallen comrades and
observe the laying of the cornerstone of an equestrian statue of Johnston.
Charles E. Hooker, a Mississippi congressman and former rebel officer, gave

the oration. "The records of the war show no more knightlier warrior" than the general, Hooker declared. He went on to name the "triumvirate" of great Southerners who he believed ranked above all others: Robert E. Lee, John C. Calhoun, and Albert Sidney Johnston. On the platform with Hooker was former Confederate president Jefferson Davis, who in response to the crowd's demands rose to further eulogize Johnston. Davis had been friends with the general in the antebellum years, and his sentiments were well known. Like many others, he believed that Johnston's death at Shiloh was an irreparable loss to the South—one that led to ultimate defeat in the Civil War. Voicing a belief common in the postwar South, the old commander in chief assured the crowd that "had [Johnston] lived but half an hour longer, Grant would have been a prisoner."[2]

Albert Sidney Johnston occupies an anomalous position as a Lost Cause icon. Several prominent historians have noted that his untimely death at Shiloh, one of the war's great contingencies, made him a Confederate idol. Thomas L. Connelly argues that, for postwar white Southerners, "Johnston would epitomize the might-have-been situation," while T. Harry Williams likens him to "the promising artist who dies young." Yet assertions such as these, usually appended as a coda or mentioned in passing, are where historians' analyses stop. Moreover, foundational studies of Civil War memory and the Lost Cause have altogether ignored Johnston's place in the ideology of the former Confederacy, insisting on the primacy of a trinity of supreme Confederate heroes: Robert E. Lee, Thomas J. "Stonewall" Jackson, and Jefferson Davis.[3]

Johnston's image occupied a prominent place in late-nineteenth- and early twentieth-century Confederate memory that historians have overlooked. While its "might-have-been" aspect undoubtedly explains its postwar allure, historians have yet to place that posthumous image under the scholarly microscope. The sole scholarly biography of Johnston is half a century old, and serious discussion of his life has been largely devoted to his and Gen. P. G. T. Beauregard's respective culpability for rebel defeat at Shiloh. Regardless of who was responsible, for many ex-Confederates there was a direct link between Johnston's death and Confederate defeat, both in that battle and in the war. Southern whites constructed an image of Johnston that not only helped explain their defeat in the Civil War but also helped assuage the shame that accompanied it.[4]

In addition to being useful to the Lost Cause, Johnston's image fits comfortably within nineteenth-century white Southern culture. Few qualities were more valued by white Southerners than masculinity and honor. Johnston's posthumous advocates relied heavily on the tropes of masculinity when crafting his mythology, and his noble death in battle made easier his incorporation into the ranks of Confederate idols. As one historian notes: "Death in combat assured an eternal life on earth. A man's death and subsequent rebirth in the masculine community of fellow fallen soldiers manifested itself in the community's collective memory, where he achieved immortal manhood." If, as some scholars have argued, the outcome of the Civil War provoked a crisis of manhood in the former Confederacy, Johnston served as welcome evidence that the South could produce masculine heroes.[5]

The prominence and power of Johnston's image also demonstrates the inextricable links between Civil War memory studies and the conflict's military history. Focusing on historical memory is to examine the creation and manipulation of historical narratives. This is a prerequisite to identifying the uses of constructed memories. To divorce Civil War memory studies from military history is to lose the ability to identify this manipulation and thus jeopardize the scholar's ability to decipher the process of memory construction. Military historians strive to understand war and its participants. Memory studies provide an ideal avenue through which to pursue this goal. The general's contemporaries were invested in the war's military narrative and, as the Johnston myth shows, specific military contingencies. A public memory that aided a society both in processing the trauma of defeat and in justifying valued cultural convictions began on the Shiloh battlefield in 1862.

While the myth of Albert Sidney Johnston reached its full flowering only in the late nineteenth century, its foundations predated the Civil War. Thanks to a prestigious antebellum army career, Johnston by 1861 was a soldier of considerable reputation. Although born in Kentucky, he considered himself a Texan, and when his adopted home state seceded, he resigned from the army, offered his services to the Confederacy, and reported to his old friend Davis in Richmond. Johnston's star was on the rise even before he arrived at the capital. The *Richmond Enquirer,* on learning of his resignation, reported that he was "one of the most skillful and accomplished officers in the U.S. Army." A rebel officer in Texas at the time later recalled, "for days I had been looking to the West as for a Military Messiah in the person of Albert Sidney Johnston."[6]

Convinced that Johnston was the South's best soldier, Davis commissioned him a full general and placed him in command of Department No. 2, a vast area stretching from the Appalachians to the Mississippi River. News of this appointment was greeted with universal approval. "It is useless to reiterate what we have repeated over and over again—that this appointment will give the most universal satisfaction throughout the Southwest as one most eminently fit to be made," declared the *Memphis Appeal*. A Georgia newspaper wrote that the people of the South were confident in Johnston's abilities and looked to his department, "feeling assured that there no disaster will be encountered which energy of character, military skill or superior generalship can in any manner avert." A year after the war, Richmond journalist Edward Pollard recalled that Johnston "was popularly expected . . . to take Cincinnati and march to the Northern Lakes." Many Southerners, especially those threatened with Union invasion, were coming to see him not just as a good soldier, but as a deliverer.[7]

As departmental commander Johnston was responsible for defending the heartland of the nascent Confederacy along a line of roughly four hundred miles. Despite his impressive record, the Texan had never exercised such responsibility. As one historian of the western theater has noted, Johnston "faced a situation unprecedented in his experience or in that of any other living American." The Confederacy's fortunes in the West, unpromising to begin with, quickly waned. Following the fall of Forts Henry and Donelson, Johnston was forced to abandon Nashville, the first rebel state capital to fall in the war.[8]

The press, the politicians, and the people, who just weeks before had sung the general's praises, now called for his removal. Citizens stormed Johnston's headquarters demanding action, concerned commentators insisted that President Davis take personal command of the western army, and others argued that Johnston should be replaced by another general. "The people, the army under General Johnston's command, and the people of Tennessee had lost confidence in the military capacity of General Johnston," insisted members of the Confederate Congress. A former rebel officer reflecting on this deterioration of Johnston's image stated later that he went from being "Alexander, Hannibal, Caesar, Napoleon" to "a miserable dastard and traitor, unfit to command a corporal's guard." Davis was one of the few dissenting voices; he responded to one demand for Johnston's removal, "gentlemen, I know Sidney Johnston well. If he is not a General, we had better give up the war, for we have no general."[9]

Aware of his reputation's downward spiral, Johnston also knew that further disaster loomed on the horizon. Federal armies under Grant and Maj. Gen. Don Carlos Buell were in the process of uniting. Combined, they would make a force of seventy-five thousand men. Johnston's only hope of regaining the initiative was to attack each force before they united. He ordered his forty thousand spread-out troops to concentrate at Corinth, Mississippi, thirty miles southwest of Grant's camp at Pittsburg Landing, in preparation for a counterstrike—one that would culminate in the surprise attack against Grant at Shiloh and Johnston's death.[10]

With Johnston dead, General Beauregard took command at Shiloh and soon afterward ordered rebel forces to halt their attacks. The next day a reinforced Grant turned the tide. For the next three years, the South suffered defeat after defeat in the West. Success had not come under Albert Sidney Johnston. Nor, however, did it come under his successors. The South possibly lost a major battle because the general fell, but it certainly gained a martyr. Johnston's significance in Confederate history rests more on how others shaped his image after his death than on anything he did in life. Military historians disagree about the role of his death in Shiloh's outcome, but there was no debate among former rebels in the postwar period. The myth of Johnston, like many others, did not distinguish between correlation and causation: the Confederacy lost Shiloh, and the war, when the general breathed his last on the battlefield.

While Johnston's prewar reputation allowed his legend to take root, his death allowed it to flower. His prestige, destroyed by his brief wartime career, was resurrected quickly in the wake of his demise. Journalists, who just weeks had ridiculed Johnston and called for his resignation, now grieved him. "The hero of the battle of Shiloh is fallen!" lamented a North Carolina paper. "The Confederacy contained few such men as Albert Sidney Johnston." Reporting on his death, the *Charleston Courier* praised his manliness and generalship and blamed the "cloud . . . lately cast over his fame" on the "the ignorant licentiousness of demagogues and . . . critics." In a matter of months, Johnston had made the transition from deliverer to pariah to martyr.[11]

Over the next several decades, former Confederates elaborated and expounded the Johnston myth, which came to present the general as a potential savior. In death he became a Confederate Atlas, a deity who had carried the weight of Southern independence on his capable shoulders. This image was especially suited for the Lost Cause. While it had several central tenets, such as insisting on the legality of secession, the benevolence of Southern slavery, and the numerical superiority of the Union as the sole cause of Confederate defeat, the Lost Cause was not a monolithic and unchanging ideology. For example, another central element historians identify is that white Southern memory was dominated by Lee, Jackson, and the Army of Northern Virginia. It is understandable that scholars came to this conclusion. The Lost Cause's three primary architects—J. William Jones, John Brown Gordon, and Jubal Early—served under Lee. These men, especially Early, were powerful personalities and prolific writers who made great efforts to see that Virginia dominated Confederate military history. But the majority of Southern veterans did not serve in Lee's army, and these men and their families would have heroes that were not dictated by Early and company, as the ubiquity of Johnston's image demonstrates.[12]

In addition to serving immediate political and social purposes, the Lost Cause explained Confederate defeat and helped whites cope with it. The postwar Johnston myth argued that the South lost the war because the general was killed before he could destroy Grant and his army. For the war's survivors, ultimate defeat was easier to accept knowing it was the result of fate and not their own actions. As the general's son and biographer, William Preston Johnston, stated, victory was all but assured before Johnston fell "by the chance of war."[13]

But Jefferson Davis did more than any other person to foster the legend. Less than two weeks before Shiloh, the commander in chief told his beleaguered general that "my confidence in you has never wavered, and I hope the public will soon give me credit for my judgment rather than arraign me for obstinacy." Johnston's passing did nothing to change the president's opinion. "Without doing injustice to the living," he remarked on learning of his friend's death, "it may be safely asserted that our loss is irreparable." Nearly twenty years later Davis wrote in his memoirs: "In his fall the great pillar of the Southern Confederacy was crushed, and beneath its fragments the best hope of the Southwest lay buried."[14]

Davis expressed these opinions for three reasons. First, he was genuinely convinced of Johnston's abilities. Second, the two men had been friends for decades. Third, the Johnston myth was inextricably linked to Davis's own image. Davis was a divisive figure during and after the war. Two of Johnston's successors, Beauregard and Gen. Joseph E. Johnston, were the president's harshest critics, yet neither of them, nor Gens. Braxton Bragg or John Bell Hood, were able to turn the tide in the West. Quite the contrary, these men led the Army of Tennessee from one disaster to the next. Davis has been censured by contemporaries and historians for appointing these commanders and for his conduct of the war in the West. But as he saw it, none of them would have ever commanded the Army of Tennessee had Johnston lived. Praising the general was a subtle way for Davis to rebuke his critics and defend his record as commander in chief. He had trumpeted Johnston's abilities from the war's beginning, thus the ubiquity of the Johnston myth could be the difference between Davis being a false prophet or a soothsayer.

Other members of the Confederate high command likewise fostered the Johnston myth in their postwar writings. "With him at the helm," declared Richard Taylor, "there would have been no Vicksburg, no Missionary Ridge, no Atlanta." Despite having served under both Lee and Jackson, Taylor insisted that Johnston was "the foremost man of all the South; and had it been possible for one heart, one mind, and one arm to save her cause, she lost them when Albert Sidney Johnston fell on the field of Shiloh." Similarly, Basil Duke stated that "it would be difficult to induce the people of the South to admit that any other man . . . is worthy to be ranked on the same level with General Lee. But if any of the great men of the Confederacy shall, in the estimation of his countrymen or by the verdict of history, be accorded that extraordinary eminence, it will be, I believe, Albert Sidney Johnston." Even officers of the Army of Northern Virginia echoed these pronouncements. William C. Oates of Little Round Top fame thought Johnston "perhaps the greatest general the war would have developed." John Brown Gordon compared him to Lee and George Washington and lamented that "a great light had gone out when Albert Sidney Johnston fell. . . . [I]n him more than in any other man at that period were centered the hopes of the Southern people."[15]

Lesser officers joined the chorus. Scarcely a year after the war's end, Edward Fontaine, Patrick Henry's grandson and an ex-captain of a Mississippi regiment, wrote an impassioned letter to the *Natchez Daily Courier*. With the wounds of defeat still fresh, Fontaine proclaimed that "if [Johnston] were living, and in arms with Stonewall Jackson; and Robert E. Lee, Joseph E. Johnston and Beauregard ready to take the field again, and I had to appoint one of these illustrious heroes the generalissimo of our army, I would not hesitate to give him command of the whole." In a postwar interview F. A. Shoup, Lt. Gen.

William J. Hardee's chief of artillery, was asked if Shiloh would have ended differently had Johnston lived. "It would indeed," he answered. "In my opinion Johnston was a new man from the moment he sent his Generals whirling to their posts with orders to advance at dawn. . . . That battle won, he would have shown himself the great man he was." Fifty years after the war, a former Confederate captain visiting Shiloh was reminded that "Napoleon, standing by the grave of Frederick the Great, said: 'If you were living, I would not be here.' I imagined General Grant at Johnston's monument . . . saying 'If you had not fallen, I would not have been President of the United States.'"[16]

While Davis and former officers had a hand in creating the Johnston myth, rank-and-file veterans also proved indispensable in this deification. The most physically prominent display of veterans' adoration of Johnston is the general's bronze equestrian statue in Metairie Cemetery. The Association of the Army of Tennessee raised twelve thousand dollars to construct the monument. Unveiled in 1887 on the twenty-fifth anniversary of Johnston's death, the statue sits atop a tumulus containing the remains of over two hundred veterans. As W. Fitzhugh Brundage points out, historians should pay special heed to how groups take ownership of public space: "By insinuating their memory into public space, groups exert the cultural authority, express the collective solidarity, and achieve a measure of the permanence that they often crave. To infuse objects and places with commemorative significance is to combat the transitory nature of memories and underscore the connectedness of the past and present."[17]

For the crowd gathered in New Orleans, there was to be nothing transitory about Johnston's image. Senator and former Confederate general Randall Lee Gibson gave the oration. The veterans in the crowd, insisted Gibson, knew that Johnston's generalship and character would be recorded "on the brightest pages of our country's history." He also seemed to be aware of the "what if?" appeal of the general's image, asking, "who can look upon this bronze image without recalling the early days of the war[?]" Of his leadership at Shiloh, Gibson argued that "in any war," you could count "on the fingers of your left hand" the number of commanders with comparable abilities. Gibson evoked Johnston's masculinity as well, lauding him as "the perfect type of manly grace and power. . . . [A] man who is a man . . . is the lordliest thing in the universe." Like many other Johnston storytellers, Gibson concluded his speech proclaiming that it was "in the full tide of victory, that Albert Sidney Johnston received his death wound, and fell like Wolfe on the heights of Abraham—as a true soldier would love to die—on the edge of battle, in the moment of triumph."[18]

The equestrian statue was not the only way veterans commemorated their former commander. Two simple acts by a former private and unnamed mourner were especially enduring. While Johnston was temporarily buried in New Orleans, John Dimitry, a Shiloh survivor, penned an epitaph on a plank and placed it at the grave. Johnston, it said, was "a man tried in many high offices and critical enterprises, and found faithful in all. His life was one long sacrifice of interest to conscience. . . . Not wholly understood was he while he lived; but, in his death, his greatness stands confessed in a people's tears. . . . In his honor—impregnable; in his simplicity—sublime. No country e'er had a truer son—no cause a nobler champion, no people a bolder defender—no principle a purer victim than the dead soldier who sleeps here." When a later graveside visitor discovered the fading paean, she transcribed it and submitted it to local newspapers. This brought it to the attention of the memorial committee in charge of the general's grave, which subsequently designated it the official epitaph engraved at the base of the statue at Metairie.[19]

While prevalent in stone, the Johnston myth was ubiquitous in print. The story of the paean on the plank was the first tribute to a rebel officer published in the *Confederate Veteran*. Founded in 1893, this magazine had a circulation of over twenty thousand by the turn of the century. Its editor in chief, S. A. Cunningham, a veteran of the Army of Tennessee, accepted contributions from other veterans, their wives, their widows, and their progeny. Even a cursory examination of the magazine reveals that Johnston's memory had a prevalence historians have failed to appreciate. At the dawn of the twentieth century, Cunningham proclaimed that "if Gen. Johnston had lived but three hours longer, the result of this battle would have been differently written, and the eagles of victory would have perched upon the banner of the Confederacy."[20]

Former soldiers were eager to assume the panegyrist's role in the *Veteran*. Tennessean George E. Purvis recounted the military trials of the Confederacy. "The student," he stated, "in reviewing some of the great battles of our civil war . . . can scarcely resist becoming a fatalist. He will be impelled to the conviction that the dismemberment of the American Union was *just not to be*." Illustrating yet again the centrality of contingency to the Johnston myth, Purvis affirmed that "Southern soldiers . . . won great victories on many fields. But there was always that 'something' which prevented the reaping of the fruits of their victories." Conspicuously absent is any mention of often-cited "somethings" such as Stonewall Jackson's death or Pickett's Charge. Purvis's first "something" was "Gen Johnston's death at Shiloh, just when the field was won." Quoting Oliver Wendell Holmes Jr., he concluded that "there are battles with Fate that can never be won."[21]

Other aging soldiers expressed similar sentiments. In 1894 A. S. Horsley, a veteran of the 1st Tennessee Infantry, told of Johnston spurring the morale of troops at Shiloh: "The spectacle was an imposing one," and "the soldiers were deeply impressed by the majestic presence, the noble and kindly face, and impressive words of the commanding general. I would give much, hard as times are, for a picture of that scene." Had he lived, "all the histories of America today would have to be rewritten." Five years later another Shiloh veteran came to a similar conclusion. Had Johnston survived the battle, insisted James A. Jones, the rebels would have captured Grant's army, "chased Buell back into Kentucky and retaken Nashville and the State of Tennessee. Let the result . . . be imagined." In a memorial address the next year, a former regimental surgeon declared that "had Albert Sidney Johnston lived, . . . Grant would have been annihilated, . . . and history might have told a different story."[22]

Lowly privates who never more than glimpsed their commander along with the staff officers who served by Johnston's side alike expressed such convictions. Thirty-five years after Shiloh, George Withe Baylor of Johnston's staff reflected on the general's final hours: "I thought of the dauntless warrior, . . . the personification of Southern chivalry. . . . He died as a soldier must like to die: at the moment of victory." Pondering the contingencies of the battle, Baylor concluded that "if Gen. Johnston had not been killed, . . . why there would have been no 'ifs' about it; but the chances are that Gen. Grant would have shared the fate of our own gallant leader and the horrors of the war would probably have been prolonged for several years." Similarly J. B. Ulmer, an enlisted man at Shiloh, insisted that had Johnston lived, "General Grant would not have been at Appomattox to receive General Lee's surrender." By referring to Grant as the "vanquisher of Lee," Ulmer subtly argued that Johnston was Lee's superior as a general—had fate not interceded, Grant would never have been the vanquisher of Johnston.[23] R. R. Hutchinson, another staff officer, also believed that Johnston's passing "was one of those fateful incidents which seem to change the whole course of contemporary events. In all human probability it alone saved one great army . . . and doomed another."[24]

Civilians were also active in constructing the Johnston myth. Few individuals of the wartime generation were more influential in shaping the public's perceptions and memories of the Civil War than Mary Boykin Chesnut. Initially serialized in the *Saturday Evening Post,* her *A Diary from Dixie* was published in book form in 1905. (Despite its title, the book was largely written in the 1880s with the aid of her wartime journals.) Chesnut was one of the most prominent consumers and distributors of the Johnston myth. On learning of the general's death, she recorded, "my heart stands still. I feel no more. I am, for so many seconds, so many minutes, I know not how long, utterly without sensation of any kind—dead." Reflecting on Confederate fortunes following his death, Chesnut observed, "there is grief enough for Albert Sidney Johnston now; we begin to see what we have lost. . . . Without him there is no head to our Western army."[25]

She claimed that Johnston's image loomed large in her mind for the remainder of the war. Cautiously optimistic about Lee's success in the Seven Days' Battles, Chesnut admitted, "we do hope there will be no 'ifs.' 'Ifs' have ruined us. Shiloh was a victory if Albert Sidney Johnston had not been killed. . . . The 'ifs' bristle like porcupines." Following the Army of Tennessee's defeat at Chattanooga and subsequent retreat into Georgia, she exclaimed, "oh, for a day of Albert Sidney Johnston out West!" As victory seemed less and less likely, Chesnut reflected on the character of Confederate generals, asserting that in contrast to the uncivilized Lincoln and Grant, "General Lee and Albert Sidney Johnston show blood and breeding." According to Chesnut, had Johnston lived, the Deep South would have been spared the onslaught of William T. Sherman; as the Yankee general prepared to embark on his March to the Sea, she lamented, "if Albert Sidney Johnston had lived! Poor old General Lee has no backing."[26]

The ubiquity of the Johnston myth, for a time at least, spanned generations. Born in Kentucky in 1862, Joseph A. Altsheler, author of the popular Young Trailers Series of juvenile historical fiction, espoused the legend in another series that dramatized the Civil War. In *The Guns of Shiloh: A Story of the Great Western Campaign,* readers are thrust into the war's early months through the eyes of Dick Mason, a young Union soldier fighting with Grant's army. The narrator praises Johnston, whom he portrays as a tragic hero and potential rebel messiah, "the most formidable foe of all," and "a general upon whom the South, with justice, rested great hopes." Mason's sergeant, cautioning his men against overconfidence on the eve of Shiloh, says: "An' I tell you that General Johnston, with whom we've got to deal, is a great man. I wasn't with him when he made that great march through the blizzards an' across the plains . . . to make the Mormons behave, but I've served with them that was. An' I never yet found one of them who didn't say General Johnston was a mighty big man. Soldiers know when the right kind of a man is holdin' the reins an' drivin' 'em." In the novel's final chapters, the narrator, resuming the omniscient perspective, remarks that "it seemed that nothing could deprive the Southern army of victory, absolute and complete." Nevertheless, "fate in the very moment of triumph that seemed overwhelming and sure was preparing a terrible blow for the South," which resulted in "the most costly death, with the exception of Stonewall Jackson's, sustained by the Confederacy in the whole war."[27]

Although most famous for his novel *The Clansman* (1905) and its film adaptation *The Birth of a Nation* (1915), Thomas Dixon echoed the Johnston myth in his later book *The Victim: A Romance of the Real Jefferson Davis* (1914). In it Dixon asserts that Davis, through his unyielding support of Johnston, "inspired him to begin the most brilliant campaign on which the South had yet entered." His portrayal of Shiloh has Grant's army retreating in panic in the face of Johnston's onslaught. "The first great battle of the war had been fought and won by the genius of the South's commander," and Johnston's critics "stood dumb before the story of his genius." While fighting Johnston, Dixon claims, Grant and the rest of the Union army realized what the rebels were capable of. Shiloh was the bloodiest battle in U.S. history at the time, and both sides suffered tremendous casualties. But "great as the losses were to the North they were as nothing to the disaster which this bloody field brought the Confederacy. Albert Sidney Johnston alive was equal to an army of a hundred thousand men—dead; his loss was irreparable."[28]

The Johnston myth spanned generations in more than just fiction. Those who had lived through the war were eager to pass their version of it down to their progeny. In the decades after Appomattox, Confederate heritage organizations such as the United Daughters of the Confederacy (UDC) and the United Confederate Veterans (UCV) exercised remarkable control over the selection of textbooks used in Southern schools. In striving to ensure that white children were taught a Lost Cause narrative, one rebel hero they exalted was Johnston. In 1898 the UCV Committee on History declared that "to brand such men as Albert Sidney Johnston, Stonewall Jackson, Robert E. Lee, or Jefferson Davis as traitors is not to stain the whiteness of their lives, but rather to spoil the world for any useful purpose, to make of traitor a title which [John] Hampden and Washington might have born as well had the fortunes of war gone against them."[29]

Heritage organizations not only condemned texts hostile to the Confederacy but also officially sanctioned schoolbooks that espoused the Lost Cause. For example, Susan Pendleton Lee, daughter of Robert E. Lee's chief of artillery, authored *A Brief History of the United States*, an apologia for secession, slavery, and the Confederacy that offered a streamlined version of the Johnston myth to Southern youth. The general is presented as a martyr whose death at Shiloh when Confederate victory seemed certain "was an irretrievable loss to the Southern army and cause."[30]

Like most Civil War generals, Johnston was especially popular in his home state. *Footprints in Texas History*, a widely used textbook for second graders first published in 1901, insisted that "every child should read History Stories at an early age, because they have great value in forming the character of the young." The author, schoolteacher Minnie G. Dill, chose Johnston as the final biographical subject to include in her book. Chronicling his death, she granted him final words in verse that he was denied in life:

> "Now, away," he cried, "your aid is vain.
> My soul will not brook recalling;
> I have seen the tyrant enemy slain.
> And like autumn vine leaves falling.
> I have seen our glorious banner wave
> O'er the tents of the enemy vanquished;
> I have drawn a sword for my country brave.
> And in her cause now perish.
> Leave me to die with the free and brave,
> On the banks of my noble river,
> Ye can give me naught but a soldier's grave,
> And a place in your hearts forever."[31]

In another state history for grade-schoolers, Katie Daffan, president of the Texas Division of the UDC, ranked Johnston alongside Stephen Austin, David Crockett, and Sam Houston as exemplars of "heroic achievement, adventure, . . .

sacrifice and martyrdom." Johnston's generalship, she avowed, was matched only by "his loving, tender heart, unaffected modesty and purity of character." At Shiloh he was struck down "when it seemed that Grant's army would certainly be annihilated, . . . and victory was crowning every attempt made by the Confederates." Daffan concluded her biographical sketch with the assurance that "men like Albert Sidney Johnston make us proud of our kind."[32]

Students outside of Texas were also instructed in the Johnston myth. Berrien McPherson Zettler, in his book *War Stories and School-Day Incidents for the Children* (1912), informed readers of the value of hard work, education, and states' rights while assuring them that, had abolitionists not started the Civil War, Southern slavery would have faded away. Moreover, Zettler, a veteran of Lee's army and superintendent of schools in Macon, Georgia, wanted children to know of two fateful moments in Confederate history. One was Stonewall Jackson's death after Chancellorsville in May 1863. The second was Johnston's death: "*if* Albert Sidney Johnston had not received a mortal wound at a critical moment in the Battle of Shiloh, . . . General Grant would never have been heard of after that battle."[33]

John Lesslie Hall, an English professor at the College of William and Mary, embraced and propagated the Johnston myth in his book *Half-Hours in Southern History* (1907). Taking readers from the colonization of Roanoke Island to Reconstruction, Hall intended to highlight "the salient features of Southern heroism and achievement." To him, Johnston was the paragon of Southern manhood. Aside from Lee and Jackson, the Texan was the only Confederate commander to whom a whole chapter was devoted. Hall insisted that "every Southern boy and girl should know about General Albert Sidney Johnston. His death may have lost the South her independence." Like many other Johnston storytellers, Hall linked him with the Confederacy's supreme hero, Robert E. Lee: Johnston "was the brother of Jackson. The latter was 'Lee's right arm'; the former, the greatest soldier of the Southwest." Johnston was the man capable of defeating Grant before he became the North's greatest hero and ultimate victor over Lee: "if Johnston had lived to follow up his victory, there would have been no Vicksburg, no siege of Petersburg, no capture of Richmond, no Appomattox."[34]

Eccentric Kentucky-born columnist and essayist Eugene W. Newman saw in Johnston not only a peer of Lee but also a useful role model of Southern manhood. An unreconstructed rebel, Newman's goal was to write for the "benefit of intelligent boys," for "youths of today must come to be the future public servants of our great country." He claimed that "if Robert E. Lee, the man, was as noble as Sidney, and if Robert E. Lee, the soldier, was as brilliant as Montrose, Albert Sidney Johnston, the man, was as heroic as Bayard and Albert Sidney Johnston, the soldier, was as formidable as Conde." Johnston was "the ideal cavalier of the South" and "a king of men. Perhaps not even in the history of that war did any other commander accomplish so much with means so inadequate." Finally, "his career culminated and closed at Shiloh. It was a brilliant victory. No Southern man can read the story of that first day without closing the volume with the thought: 'It might have been.'"[35]

Although her brand of Civil War memory was not as fixated on martial themes as those of other Johnston storytellers, journalist Edith D. Pope also propagated the legend. In 1913 S. A. Cunningham died and Pope, his longtime secretary and the daughter of a rebel soldier, became editor in chief of the *Confederate Veteran*. She subsequently feminized the magazine by increasing coverage of UDC events and the number of profiles of prominent Southern women; narratives of the "moonlight and magnolias" Old South abounded at the expense of tales of battlefield heroics and great generals. Nevertheless, Johnston did not vanish from the pages of the magazine. UDC member F. A. Inge of Corinth, Mississippi, provided a piece in 1915 asserting that when the general died, "many seemed to think it but the beginning of the end." In 1928 A. M. Herald of the Tampa UDC submitted a short history of Shiloh in which she claims that "the death of General Johnston changed the result . . . and prevented the capture of Grant's army." Quoting an unnamed officer, she continues: "Sometimes the hopes of millions of people depend upon one head and one arm. The West perished with Albert Sidney Johnston and the Southern country followed."[36]

The Lost Cause identified by past scholarship regards Lee, Jackson, and Davis as the holy trinity of Confederate heroes. The Johnston image has been a sort of historiographical apocrypha—acknowledged but marginalized. Yet former Confederates themselves idolized the fallen general and summoned his memory as they tried to come to terms with defeat. In the decades following the Civil War, when those who identified with the Confederacy, whether Jefferson Davis, a veteran, or a member of the UDC, struggled to explain the failure of their cause, they often pointed to the death of Albert Sidney Johnston. The appeal of his postwar memory is anchored in contingency. While it

Robert L. Glaze

is uncertain whether the Confederacy's fortunes would have improved had he lived, it is certain that Johnston meant more to the people of the Confederacy in death than he ever did in life.

Ever cognizant of the Civil War's hold on the white Southern mind, William Faulkner evoked, in *Intruder in the Dust* (1948), the most famous contingency of the Lost Cause narrative, taking his readers back to the third day at Gettysburg in the moments before Pickett's Charge. Lee's army had "all this much to lose and all this much to gain: Pennsylvania, Maryland, the world, the golden dome of Washington itself to crown with desperate and unbelievable victory." Unbelievable victory would not be achieved, but as Faulkner knew, that would not prevent white Southerners in succeeding years from revisiting that moment in time when it was still possible. In an oft-quoted passage, Faulkner wrote that "for every Southern boy fourteen years old, not once but whenever he wants it, there is that instant when it's still not yet two o'clock on that July afternoon in 1863." Likewise, for many white Southerners of the postwar decades, it was still not yet two thirty on that April afternoon in 1862, and Albert Sidney Johnston had not yet fallen.[37]

NOTES

1. Charles P. Roland, *Albert Sidney Johnston: Soldier of Three Republics* (Austin: University of Texas Press, 1964), 335–39; Timothy B. Smith, "To Conquer or Perish: The Last Hours of Albert Sidney Johnston," in *Confederate Generals in the Western Theater: Essays on America's Civil War*, ed. Lawrence Lee Hewitt and Arthur W Bergeron Jr., 3 vols. (Knoxville: University of Tennessee Press, 2011), 3:21–35.

2. *Fayetteville (NC) Observer*, Apr. 26, 1883; *St. Louis Globe-Democrat*, Apr. 8, 1883.

3. Thomas L. Connelly, *The Marble Man: Robert E. Lee and His Image in American Society* (Baton Rouge: Louisiana State University Press, 1977), 23; T. Harry Williams, *P. G. T. Beauregard: Napoleon in Gray* (Baton Rouge: Louisiana State University Press, 1955), 116; Stephen D. Engle, "Thank God, He Has Rescued His Character," in *Leaders of the Lost Cause: New Perspectives on the Confederate High Command*, ed. Gary W. Gallagher and Joseph T. Glatthaar (Mechanicsburg, PA: Stackpole, 2004), 153–55; Charles Reagan Wilson, *Baptized in Blood: The Religion of the Lost Cause, 1865–1920* (Athens: University of Georgia Press, 1980), 48–52. Connelly is the historian most aware of the ubiquity of Johnston's image. His discussion of the general's popularity is the most sustained analysis of the Johnston myth to date. See *Marble Man*, 23–25.

4. For an introduction to this decades-old historiographical debate, see Roland, *Albert Sidney Johnston*, 326–51; and Williams, *P. G. T. Beauregard*, 133–49.

5. Harry S. Laver, "Refuge of Manhood: Masculinity and the Militia Experience in Kentucky,"

in *Southern Manhood: Perspectives on Masculinity in the Old South*, ed. Craig Thompson Friend and Lorri Glover (Athens: University of Georgia Press, 2004), 15; Leanne Whites, "The Civil War as a Crisis in Gender," in *Divided Houses: Gender and the Civil War*, ed. Catherine Clinton and Nina Silber (New York: Oxford University Press, 1992), 21; Craig Thompson Friend and Lori Glover, "Rethinking Southern Masculinity: An Introduction," in Friend and Glover, *Southern Manhood*, vii.

6. *Richmond Enquirer*, May 10, 1861; *Confederate Veteran* 2 (1894): 116 (hereafter cited as *CV*); Roland, *Albert Sidney Johnston*, 258–60.

7. *Memphis Appeal*, Sept. 13, 1861; *Macon (GA) Daily Telegraph*, Sept. 14, 1861; Engle, "Thank God, He Has Rescued His Character," 148; Edward A. Pollard, *The Lost Cause: A New Southern History of the War of the Confederates* (New York: E. B. Treat, 1866), 378.

8. Steven E. Woodworth, *Civil War Generals in Defeat* (Lawrence: University Press of Kansas, 1999), 4, 9–10; Thomas L. Connelly, *Army of the Heartland: The Army of Tennessee, 1861–1862* (Baton Rouge: Louisiana State University Press, 1967), xi.

9. Roland, *Albert Sidney Johnston*, 298–99; Engle, "Thank God, He Has Rescued His Character," 147–49; *Richmond Examiner*, Mar. 11, 1862; Richard Taylor, *Destruction and Reconstruction: Personal Experiences of the Late War* (New York: D. Appleton, 1879), 284; *CV* 2 (1894): 82, 137; William Preston Johnston, *The Life of Gen. Albert Sidney Johnston, Embracing His Services in the Armies of the United States, the Republic of Texas, and the Confederate States* (New York: D. Appleton, 1879), 496. For more on Johnston's reputation at this juncture, see Larry J. Daniel, "'The Assaults of the Demagogues in Congress': Albert Sidney Johnston and the Politics of Command," *Civil War History* 37 (1991): 328–35.

10. Steven E. Woodworth, *Jefferson Davis and His Generals: The Failure of Confederate Command in the West* (Lawrence: University Press of Kansas, 1990), 96.

11. *Weekly Raleigh Register*, Apr. 16, 23, 1862; *Charleston Courier*, Apr 10, 1862.

12. For more on Jubal Early, the Lost Cause, and the longevity of the Virginia-centric conception of the Confederate war effort, see Gary W. Gallagher, *Lee and His Generals in War and Memory* (Baton Rouge: Louisiana State University Press, 1998), 199–226; and Gallagher, *Lee and His Army in Confederate History* (Chapel Hill: University of North Carolina Press, 2001), 255–82.

13. Wilson, *Baptized in Blood*, 13; Gaines M. Foster, *Ghosts of the Confederacy: Defeat, the Lost Cause, and the Emergence of the New South* (Baton Rouge: Louisiana State University Press, 1987), 11–35, 196; Thomas L. Connelly and Barbara L. Bellows, *God and General Longstreet: The Lost Cause and the Southern Mind* (Baton Rouge: Louisiana State University Press, 1982), 10–20, 93–94, 108; David W. Blight, *Race and Reunion: The Civil War in American Memory* (Cambridge, MA: Harvard University Press, 2001), 77, 258, 261; Thomas J. Brown, *The Public Art of Civil War Commemoration: A Brief History with Documents* (Boston: Bedford/St. Martins, 2004), 10–13; James C. Cobb, *Away Down South: A History of Southern Identity* (New York: Oxford University Press, 2005), 62–66; Caroline E. Janney, *Remembering the Civil War: Reunion and the Limits of Reconciliation* (Chapel Hill: University of North Carolina Press, 2013), 134; Alan T. Nolan, "The Anatomy of the Myth," in *The Myth of the Lost Cause and Civil War History*, ed. Gary W. Gallagher and Alan T. Nolan (Bloomington: Indiana University Press, 2000), 11–34; William Preston Johnston, "Albert Sidney Johnston at Shiloh," in *Battles and Leaders of the Civil War*, ed. Robert U. Johnson and Clarence C. Buel, 4 vols. (New York: Century, 1887), 1:564. The most comprehen-

sive study of the political uses of Civil War memory in the former Confederacy is William Blair, *Cities of the Dead: Contesting the Memory of the Civil War in the South* (Chapel Hill: University of North Carolina Press, 2004).

14. U.S. War Department, *War of the Rebellion: A Compilation of the Official Records of the Union and Confederate Armies,* 70 vols. in 128 pts. (Washington D.C.: U.S. Government Printing Office, 1880–1901), ser. 1, 10(2):365; *Macon (GA) Daily Telegraph,* Apr. 12, 1862; Jefferson Davis, *Rise and Fall of the Confederate Government,* 2 vols. (New York: Appleton, 1881), 2:67.

15. Taylor, *Destruction and Reconstruction,* 283–85; Basil Duke, *The Civil War Reminiscences of General Basil W. Duke, C.S.A.* (New York: Doubleday, Page, 1911), 100; William C. Oates, *The War between the Union and the Confederacy: and Its Lost Opportunities* (New York: Neale, 1905), 309; John Brown Gordon, *Reminiscences of the Civil War* (New York: Charles Scribner's Sons, 1904), 125.

16. *Natchez Daily Courier,* June 29, 1866; *CV* 2 (1894): 116, 139; *CV* 23 (1915): 173. Statements akin to these are common in the pages of the *Confederate Veteran.* See, e.g., *CV* 8 (1900): 500, and *CV* 9 (1901): 166–67.

17. W. Fitzhugh Brundage, *The Southern Past: A Clash of Race and Memory* (Cambridge, MA: Harvard University Press, 2005), 6.

18. Randall Lee Gibson, *Shiloh. Equestrian Monument, Erected by the Veterans of the Army of Tennessee: Unveiled April 6th, 1887. Metairie Cemetery, New Orleans, La.* (New Orleans: Picayune Job Print, 1887), 2–9.

19. *CV* 1 (1893): 3; Mary Louise Benton Bankston, *Camp-Fire Stories of the Mississippi Valley Campaign* (New Orleans: L. Graham, 1914), 37. For more on Johnston's burial and reburial, see Jerry Thompson, "When General Albert Sidney Johnston Came Home to Texas: Reconstruction Politics and the Reburial of a Hero," *Southwestern Historical Quarterly* 103 (2000): 452–78.

20. Blight, *Race and Reunion,* 181; Janney, *Remembering the Civil War,* 180–81; *CV* 3 (1895): 208; *CV* 9 (1901): 22. For more on Cunningham and the *Confederate Veteran,* see John A. Simpson, *S. A. Cunningham and the Confederate Heritage* (Athens: University of Georgia Press, 1994).

21. *CV* 5 (1897): 262.

22. *CV* 2 (1894): 234; *CV* 7 (1899): 556; *CV* 8 (1900): 362.

23. *CV* 5 (1897): 610–11; J. B. Ulmer, "A Glimpse of Albert Sidney Johnston through the Smoke of Shiloh," *Quarterly of the Texas Historical Association* 10 (1907): 287–88.

24. *CV* 6 (1898): 311–13.

25. Isabella D. Martin and Myrta Lockett Avary, eds., *A Diary from Dixie, as Written by Mary Boykin Chesnut, Wife of James Chesnut, Jr., United States Senator from South Carolina, 1859–1861, and Afterward Aide to Jefferson Davis and Brigadier General in the Confederate Army* (New York: D. Appleton, 1905), 156, 182. On the authorship and publication history of *A Diary from Dixie,* see C. Van Woodward, ed., *Mary Chesnut's Civil War* (New Haven, CT: Yale University Press, 1981), xv–xxix.

26. Martin and Avary, *Diary from Dixie,* 196, 265, 270, 299, 331.

27. Joseph A. Altshelter, *The Guns of Shiloh: A Story of the Great Western Campaign* (New York: D. Appleton, 1919), 242, 266, 306–7.

28. Thomas W. Dixon, *The Victim: A Romance of the Real Jefferson Davis* (Toronto: Copp Clark, 1914), 305, 313–14.

29. CV 6 (1898): 478; CV 8 (1900): 398.

30. Fred Arthur Bailey, "The Textbooks of the 'Lost Cause': Censorship and the Creation of Southern State Histories," *Georgia Historical Quarterly* 73 (1991): 508; Cobb, *Away Down South*, 101–3; Susan Pendleton Lee, *A Brief History of the United States* (Richmond: B. F. Johnson, 1896), 210, 254.

31. Minnie G. Dill, *Footprints of Texas History* (Austin: Ben C. Jones, 1901), i, 103–5. Dill's text was in its sixth edition by 1916.

32. Katie Daffan, *Texas Hero Stories: An Historical Reader for the Grades* (Boston: Benjamin H. Sanborn, 1908), ix, 111–18. Johnston's presence in state histories was not restricted to those of Texas. Other texts suggest, either explicitly or implicitly, causation between Johnston's death and Confederate defeat. See G. R. McGee, *A History of Tennessee from 1663 to 1900: For Use in Schools* (New York: American Book, 1900), 204; Gustavus W. Dyer, *A School History of Tennessee* (Chattanooga: National Book, 1919), 120; and William Robertson Garrett and Albert Virgil Goodpasture, *History of Tennessee: Its People and Its Institutions* (Nashville: Brandon Printing, 1900), 211–12.

33. Berrien McPherson Zettler, *War Stories and School-Day Incidents for the Children* (New York: Neale, 1912), 88.

34. John Lesslie Hall, *Half-Hours in Southern History* (Richmond: B. F. Johnson, 1907), 5, 262–64.

35. CV 9 (1901): 72; "Interesting People: Savoyard," *American Magazine* 61 (1911): 735–37; Savoyard, *Essays on Men, Things and Events: Historical, Personal and Political* (New York: Neale, 1904), 202–3.

36. John A. Simpson, *Edith D. Pope and Her Nashville Friends: Guardians of the Lost Cause in the Confederate Veteran* (Knoxville: University of Tennessee Press, 2003), 43–44, 62–63; CV 23 (1915): 413, 534; CV 26 (1918): 335–36; CV 25 (1917): 474; CV 36 (1928), 335–36.

37. William Faulkner, *Intruder in the Dust* (New York: Random House, 1948), 190.

CONTRIBUTORS

Keith Altavilla is assistant professor of history at Lone Star College–CyFair. He previously served as an associate editor for *The West Point History of Warfare* and *The West Point History of the Civil War* projects.

Andrew S. Bledsoe is assistant professor of history at Lee University. He is the author of *Citizen-Officers: The Union and Confederate Volunteer Junior Officer Corps in the American Civil War* (2015). His current research explores command and leadership in American Civil War armies.

Gary W. Gallagher is John L. Nau III Professor of History Emeritus at the University of Virginia. His recent books include *The Union War* (2011), *Becoming Confederates: Paths to a New National Loyalty* (2013), and *The American War: A History of the Civil War Era* (with Joan Waugh, 2015).

Robert L. Glaze is postdoctoral lecturer at the University of Tennessee, Knoxville. He is the author of numerous published articles and essays.

John J. Hennessy is the author of three books, including *Return to Bull Run: The Campaign and Battle of Second Manassas* (1993), as well as dozens of articles and essays—many of them focused on the Army of the Potomac. He is presently the chief historian at Fredericksburg and Spotsylvania National Military Park.

Earl J. Hess, Stewart W. McClelland Chair at Lincoln Memorial University, is the author of twenty-five books. His *Civil War Infantry Tactics: Training, Combat, and Small-Unit Effectiveness* (2015) won the Tom Watson Brown Book Award of the Society of Civil War Historians in 2016.

Brian Matthew Jordan is assistant professor of history at Sam Houston State University. He earned a doctorate at Yale and is the author of *Marching Home: Union Veterans and Their Unending Civil War* (2014), which was a finalist for the 2016 Pulitzer Prize in History.

Andrew F. Lang is assistant professor of history at Mississippi State University. He is the author of *In the Wake of War: Military Occupation, Emancipation, and Civil War America* (2017), which won the 2018 Tom Watson Brown Book Award.

Kevin M. Levin is an independent historian based in Boston. He is the author of *Remembering the Battle of the Crater: War as Murder* (2012), editor of *Interpreting the Civil War at Museum and Historic Sites* (2017), and is currently completing *Searching for Black Confederate Soldiers: The Civil War's Most Persistent Myth*. He operates the website Civil War Memory (http://cwmemory.com).

Brian D. McKnight is professor of history and founding director of the Center for Appalachian Studies at the University of Virginia's College at Wise. He specializes in conflicted and coerced loyalties and has produced several books on the subject, including, with Barton A. Myers, *The Guerrilla Hunters: Irregular Conflicts during the Civil War* (2017).

Jennifer M. Murray, a military historian at Oklahoma State University, is the author of *On a Great Battlefield: The Making, Management, and Memory of Gettysburg National Military Park, 1933–2013* (2014). Murray is currently working on a biography of Maj. Gen. George Gordon Meade.

Kenneth W. Noe is the Draughon Professor of Southern History at Auburn University. He is the author or editor of several books, including *Reluctant Rebels: The Confederates Who Joined the Army after 1861* (2010). His current research concerns the role of climate and weather in the American Civil War.

INDEX

Baton Rouge, LA, 191, 192
battle and campaign studies, 20, 30, 33, 35–36, 40n17
Bayou Boeuf, LA, 186
Beale, Jane, 127, 128, 133
Beatty, Taylor, 118
Beatty, "Tinker Dave," 175
Beaty, James, 151
Beaufort, NC, 187
Beaufort, SC, 196
Beauregard, P. G. T., 272, 275, 276, 277
Becker, John, 258–59
Belle Plain, VA, 254–55
Bennett, Jake, 170–71
Biddle, Daniel, 259–60
Billow, George, 259, 264
Bishop, William, 176
Blackford, Lewis, 151
Blackford, William, 212
Bledsoe, Andrew S., 209
Boggs, Patsy Keel, 174
Booneville, KY, 169
borderlands, 165–69, 172
Boughton, Clement Abner, 196
Bowman, Harrison, 174
Boyd, Cleve, 170
Bragg, Braxton, 11, 63, 94–95, 217–18, 222n4, 277; generalship, 95, 99, 100, 101, 112–13, 114, 115–16, 119–20; relationship with subordinates, 99–100, 101–2, 103–5, 106, 108, 111, 117–18; strategy for McLemore's Cove operation, 101–3, 105, 108, 110
Brainerd, Wesley, 59, 137
Bramlette, Thomas, 172, 175, 176–77
Brashear City, LA, 188
Brasher, Glenn David, 45
Brewster, Charles Harvey, 49–50, 56, 61, 197, 198
bridges, 46, 48, 58–59, 60–61, 62, 140–41, 142; pontoon, 78, 80, 89n35, 134, 137–38
Bross, Frederick, 262
Brown, Edwin Y., 54

Brown, Jacob, x
Buckner, Simon Bolivar, 99–100, 104, 109–10, 111, 114–15; relationship with Bragg, 108, 111, 112; relationship with Hill, 111–12; relationship with Hindman, 109–10, 116, 117, 118–19
Bull Run, Battle of, 125, 150
Bunker Hill, Battle of, 26
Bureau of Military Intelligence, 91n68
Burnside, Ambrose, 88n14, 133–39, 141–42, 146, 148, 150, 152
Burnside, G. W., 219
Butler, Benjamin, 130, 243

Cades Cove, TN, 173–74
Caldwell, Mary, 151
Calvin, Charles Enslow, 190–92
Carmichael, Peter, 265
Casey, William, 215
Cassady, J. B., 177
Castle's Woods, VA, 170
casualties. See wounded
Catlett's Gap (GA), 101, 105, 106, 110, 116, 117
Cemetery Ridge (Gettysburg, PA), 76, 77
Central Ohio Insane Asylum, 262
Centreville, VA, 48, 50
Chancellorsville, Battle of, 255–56, 284
Chatham (Lacy House), 126–27, 159n41
Chattanooga, TN, 94, 99, 100, 110, 113
Cheatham, Benjamin F., 101, 103–4, 112, 121n26
Chesnut, Mary Boykin, 281
Chickahominy River, 57, 58, 59, 60–62
Chickamauga Campaign, 11, 94, 120
children, 124, 128, 135, 136, 140, 151, 164n85, 213, 220, 257, 260, 282, 284; African Americans compared to, 187; and irregular war, 169, 173
citizen-soldier, concept of, ix, 12–14, 37, 75, 195, 232, 245
Civil War centennial, 31, 32
Civil War History, 22